Classifier Structures in Mandarin Chinese

Trends in Linguistics
Studies and Monographs 263

Editor
Volker Gast

Founding Editor
Werner Winter

Editorial Board
Walter Bisang
Hans Henrich Hock
Natalia Levshina
Heiko Narrog
Matthias Schlesewsky
Niina Ning Zhang

Editors responsible for this volume
Walter Bisang and Volker Gast

De Gruyter Mouton

Classifier Structures in Mandarin Chinese

by
Niina Ning Zhang

De Gruyter Mouton

ISBN 978-3-11-048805-0
e-ISBN 978-3-11-030499-2
ISSN 1861-4302

Library of Congress Cataloging-in-Publication Data
A CIP catalog record for this book has been applied for at the Library of Congress.

Bibliographic information published by the Deutsche Nationalbibliothek
The Deutsche Nationalbibliothek lists this publication in the Deutsche Nationalbibliografie;
detailed bibliographic data are available in the Internet at http://dnb.dnb.de.

© 2013 Walter de Gruyter GmbH, Berlin/Boston
Printing: Hubert & Co. GmbH & Co. KG, Göttingen
♾ Printed on acid-free paper
Printed in Germany
www.degruyter.com

For James Tomlinson Myers

Contents

Acknowledgments

My gratitude goes to all those who gave me comments and support on different stages of the writing of this book, including: Paolo Acquaviva, Junghsiung Chang, Yungli Chang, Guglielmo Cinque, Elizabeth Cowper, Jenny Doetjes, Jonathan Evans, Susan Fischer, Lewis Gebhardt, David Gil, Giuliana Giusti, One-Soon Her, Daniel Hole, Su-ying Hsiao, Miao-ling Hsieh, Hanchun Huang, Hui-hua Huang, James Huang, Shizhe Huang, Linxin Jin, Young-Wha Kim, Chin-Man Kuo, Jenny Kuo, Yukari Kurita, Chia-Ying Lee, Chungmin Lee, Audrey Li, XuPing Li, Jo-wang Lin, Johna Lin, Chen-sheng Liu, Diane Massam, James Myers, Victoria Rau, Susan Rothstein, Tim Dingxu Shi, Thomas Stolz, Jim Tai, Jane Tang, Sze-Wing Tang, Jen Ting, Dylan Tsai, Jane Tsay, Chiu-yu Tseng, Akira Watanabe, Ting-Chi Wei, Hunter Wu, Iris Wu, Dong-Whee Yang, Byeong Yi, and my students Ann Chang, Edgar Chang, Michael Chang, Li-ting Chien, Diego Chung, Minty Chung, Siyu Guo, Jan Huang, Yu Hung, Alice Kao, Ansel Liu, Yu-leng Lin, Chia-wen Lo, Julia Su, Derrick Wang, Hank Yen, Adam Zheng, especially Chentsung Chen, Yuanlu Chen, and Guy Emerson.

Early versions of various parts of the book were presented at many conferences, workshops, and invited talks in Bochum, Brussels, Budapest, Cambridge of Massachusetts, Chiayi, Chung-Li, Hsinchu, Kaohsiung, Poznań, Seoul, Stockholm, Taipei, and Toronto. I am grateful to all of the audiences for their fruitful discussion, challenges, and encouragements. I also got help from many anonymous reviewers and editors of journals and books with early versions of some parts of the book. I want to thank them. The contents of my following papers are related to four chapters of the book. Chapter 2 is based on 'Countability and numeral classifiers in Mandarin Chinese', in Diane Massam (ed.), *Count and mass across languages*, 220–237, Oxford University Press (2012). Chapter 4 is based on 'Expressing number productively in Mandarin Chinese', *Linguistics* (Under review). Chapter 5 is based on 'The constituency of classifier constructions in Mandarin Chinese', *Taiwan Journal of Linguistics* 9: 1–50 (2011). Chapter 7 is based on 'Noun-classifier compounds in Mandarin Chinese', in Young-Wha Kim (ed.), *Plurality in classifier languages: Plurality, mass/kind, classifiers and the DPs*, 195–244, Hankukmunhwasa (2011).

At the final stage, I received further comments from the anonymous reviewers and Volker Gast, copy-editing help from Franzi Kurtz, and technical help from Birgit Sievert, Hannes Kaden, and Julie Miess. The research has received financial support from the grants of the National Science Council of Taiwan. I am grateful to them all.

Abbreviations

1	first person
2	second person
3	third person
ADESS	adessive case
BA	causative marker
CL	classifier
DE	associative particle
DelP	Delimit Phrase
DEM	demonstrative
DIM	diminutive
DUR	durative aspect
EXP	experiential aspect
E-YI	the existential quantifier *yi*
FEM	feminine
FUT	future tense
G-YI	the generic quantifier *yi*
INT	interjection
M-YI	the maximal quantifier *yi*
MASC	masculine
MonP	Monotocity Phrase
NumP	Number Phrase
ORD	ordinal
PART	partitive case
PASS	passive
PL	plural
PRF	perfect aspect
PRT	sentence-final aspect particle
PST	past
Q	question
QuantP	Quantifier Phrase
RED	reduplicant
RUW	reduplicated unit word
SG	singular
SUW	simple (not reduplicated) unit word
UW	unit word
TOP	topic
UnitP	Unit Phrase

Chapter 1
Introduction

Three kinds of innovations are offered in this book: new observations, new generalizations, and new analyses, with respect to a kind of linguistic formatives, namely, *classifiers* (or CL for short), in Mandarin Chinese. The word *zhi* in example (1a) (unless specified otherwise, all examples in this book are from this language) is a CL. The CL occurs between the numeral *san* 'three' and the noun *bi* 'pen'. In (1b), *di* is also a CL.

(1) a. *Yaoyao kanjian-le san   zhi bi.*
      Yaoyao see-PRF   three CL   pen
      'Yaoyao saw three pens.'
   b. *Yaoyao kanjian-le san   di   you.*
      Yaoyao see-PRF   three CL   oil
      'Yaoyao saw three drops of oil.'

Some languages have CLs and some do not. Some languages have the counterpart of the CL in (1b), but not that in (1a). From the English translations of the two examples we can see that English has a correlate for the CL *di* in (1b) (*drop*), but does not have a counterpart to the CL *zhi* in (1a). In this book, CLs like *zhi* are called *individual CLs* (they are called individual measures in Chao 1968: 585), and CLs like *di* are called *individuating CLs* (they are grouped into partitive measures in Chao 1968). Languages that have both types of CLs, such as Mandarin Chinese, Japanese, and Mayan languages, are called numeral CL languages.

Mandarin Chinese is a typical CL language. This is because, first, in a numeral expression (or 'numeral-plus-noun construction', as in Gil 2008), the occurrence of a CL is obligatory in the language (except in idiomatic expressions, compounds, or certain list contexts), whereas it can be optional in some other CL languages such as Indonesian. Second, the word order of a numeral expression is fixed in this language: the CL follows the numeral and precedes the noun. There is no variance in word order for the three elements in a nominal.[1] This is different from Japanese and Korean. Third,

---

1. Following the convention of generative grammar, I use the term *nominal* to cover all levels of elements that are [+V, -N]: word, phrase, and word-internal element.

the three elements are next to each other, and thus no other functional elements such as case markers intervene in the elements of a numeral expression. This is again different from languages such as Japanese and Korean. These characteristics of Mandarin Chinese represent a simple pattern of numeral expressions. This book gives a thorough syntactic analysis of CL constructions of this simple pattern.

One hypothesis about the contrast between CL languages and other languages is that nouns like *bi* 'pen' are mass nouns in Chinese, and therefore, like the word *oil* in English, such nouns require CLs. Accordingly the function of individual CLs like *zhi* in (1a) is to individuate mass. Such a hypothesis is falsified in this book. In addition to falsifying problematic hypotheses like this, we have developed a new understanding of the relation between mass nouns and other types of nouns. Our new analysis of the issue shows that the traditional binary count-mass division is not fine-grained enough to reach an acceptable level of descriptive adequacy. Instead, we identify two new properties (called features, in a technical way) to capture the contrasts of four basic types of nominals, represented by the English words *pen, oil, belief,* and *furniture,* respectively. We argue that Chinese *bi* 'pen' correlates with the *furniture*-type only, not with the *oil*-type. There are also languages in which neither the *zhi*-type of CLs in (1a) nor the *di*-type of CLs in (1b) occurs in numeral expressions, in contrast to both English and Chinese. For instance, it is perfectly fine to say *txabïa apeta* 'three blood' in Yudja (an indigenous language spoken in Brazil; Lima 2010; 2012). This type of languages has been generally ignored in the literature, although their existence has been noted since the early 1940s (Whorf 1941). Comparing Chinese with these under-studied languages enlightens our understanding of the functions and structural properties of CLs in the language system.

Another influential hypothesis regarding the contrast between CL languages and other languages is that the CL *zhi* in (1a) is required to correlate with a plural marker, such as *s* in the English word *pens*. In Mandarin Chinese, a bare noun may encode either singular or plural entities, as shown by the two translations of *shuye* 'leaf' in (2).

(2)   *He-li   piao-zhe   shuye.*
      river-in   float-DUR   leaf
      'There are leaves floating on the river.'
      'There is a leaf floating on the river.'

It has been declared that CL languages have no systematic way to encode the contrast between singularity and plurality. We however observe that Mandarin Chinese does have a systematic and productive way to encode the contrast. In (3a), the reduplicative CL *pian-pian* introduces a plural reading; and in (3b), the simple form of the CL *pian*, in the absence of a numeral, introduces a singular reading.

(3) a. *He-li   piao-zhe   (yi)   pian-pian   shuye.*
      river-in float-DUR   one   CL-RED   leaf
      'There are many leaves floating on the river.'
      Not: 'There is a leaf floating on the river.'
  b. *He-li   piao-zhe   pian   shuye.*
      river-in float-DUR   CL   leaf
      'There is a leaf floating on the river.'
      Not 'There are leaves floating on the river.'

We show that all CLs can be reduplicated to encode unit-plurality in the language. The semantic type of the encoded plural is abundant plural, which has been attested in many languages. We also provide a series of arguments to falsify the traditional assumption that constructions like (3b) are derived by a numeral-deletion operation. In neither examples like (3a), nor examples like (3b), is there a syntactic position for a numeral. We thus investigate the interactions between plural markers and certain kinds of quantifiers, and the correlation between semantic and morphological markedness of plural markings, from a cross-linguistic perspective.

It has been recognized in the literature that CLs in CL languages may play multiple roles, beyond that in a numeral expression (Bisang 1993, 1999). In (1a) and (1b), the CLs function as counting units. In (3a) and (3b), the CLs function as number markers. What is the function of a CL in other constructions, such as *ke* in (4a) and *pian* in (4b)? In such constructions, *yi* 'one' does not contrast with any other numeral, and thus is not a numeral. Importantly, as in (1a) and (1b), the CL is obligatory in such constructions, and exhibits similar selectional restrictions on the nouns. It seems that when Mandarin Chinese is labeled as a numeral CL language, what we really see is that CLs occur in various kinds of nominal expressions, not restricted to numeral expressions at all.

(4) a. *Yi   ke shu   zong   you   shu-gen.*
      one   CL tree   always   have   tree-root
      'A tree always has roots.'

b. *Jie-shang   yi   pian   hunluan.*
   street-on   one   CL   choas
   'There is choas in the street.'

In addition to identifying the distributions and functions of CLs in various kinds of nominals, we also examine their positions in syntactic structures. As we have seen, numeral expressions, such as (1a) and (1b), are composed of three basic elements: a numeral, a CL, and an NP. It has long been unclear how these three elements are organized in the syntactic structure: which two of them are combined first before the third element is integrated? Or, talking in a technical way, does the CL c-command the NP? Some propose the structure in (5a), and others propose the structure in (5b), for the expression in (1a), for example.

(5) a.

                     NP
    san   zhi   *bi*
    three   CL   pen

  b.

    san
    three   *zhi*   NP
             CL   *bi*
                     pen

Not many arguments can be found in support of either proposal, although this is a basic issue of the syntax of numeral expressions. In this book, all arguments that we can find are shown to be problematic. New arguments that are directly relevant to constituency are looked for. Considering the interactions of the elements of a numeral expression, and the way these elements interact with modifiers, we find new generalizations that show two constituency patterns: although CLs like those in (1) exhibit the right-branching structure, as in (5b), some other types of CLs exhibit the left-branching structure, as in (5a).

One more fresh set of facts explored in this book is a special type of compound, which has not been paid enough attention in the literature: the one that is composed of a noun and a CL, such as *hua-duo* 'flower' in (6).

(6) *Yaoyao na-le   san   ge hua-duo.*
   Yaoyao take-PRF three CL flower-CL
   'Yaoyao took three flowers.'

In (6), the CL *ge* must still necessarily occur between the numeral and the compound, although the latter already contains the CL *duo*. The syntax and semantics of this kind of compound confirm that the occurrence of individual CLs with numerals in CL languages is a syntactic requirement, and that the position of such CLs is a functional head position, which may be taken by a place-holder, i.e., a semantically vacuous element.

Although we are still not confident about many details of various CL structures in Mandarin Chinese, we are confident in the progress of our understanding of the empirical issues, and to some extend, the understanding of the general natural laws beneath the facts.

The theoretical framework of this book is generative grammar. We focus on the uses of CLs in nominals such as (1), (3), (4), and (6), rather than other constructions such as verbal constructions. The acceptability judgment of the examples is based on the northern dialect of Mandarin Chinese, my mother tongue.

In Chapter 2, the issue of countability is investigated. In Chapter 3, we discuss the relationship between CLs and quantifiers in Mandarin Chinese. Next, in Chapter 4, we probe the number markers of the language. Then in Chapter 5, we study the constituency of numeral constructions in the language. The constituency patterns reached are then spelled out into enriched syntactic structures in Chapter 6. In this chapter, relevant functional projections are also established with empirical considerations. Meanwhile, typological patterns of the properties of the functional categories are discussed. In Chapter 7, noun-CL compounds are analyzed, and thus one more new dimension of knowledge is added. Chapter 8 concludes the book.

Chapter 2
Classifiers and countability

2.1. Introduction

Why does a numeral expression need a CL in CL languages such as Mandarin Chinese?[2] It has been widely assumed that the obligatory occurrence of a CL with a numeral and a noun in CL languages is related to the count-mass contrast in nominals. The goal of this chapter is to show that this traditional assumption is not fine-grained enough to cover the systematic contrasts of various types of nominals in either Mandarin Chinese or other languages. Instead, I argue that two syntagmatic properties of nominals are syntactically significant: the ability of a noun to combine with a numeral directly, and the ability of a noun to be modified by a delimitive (size, shape, or boundary) modifier. The two newly recognized properties or features can be attested in the co-occurrence restrictions of articles, quantifiers, adverbs, and CLs, in pronominalization, and in certain context-triggered shifts. It is the combination of the different values of the two features, rather than the alleged binary count-mass contrast, that explains various syntactic contrasts of different types of nominals, cross-linguistically. I argue that although the positive value of the first feature alone is enough to define the count status of a nominal, it is the combination of the negative values of both features that defines the mass status of a nominal. This chapter shows that the popular assertion that all nouns in Chinese are mass nouns is not accurate. Instead, all nouns in Chinese are non-count nouns, but they are further divided into mass and non-mass ones.

The chapter also falsifies the generally believed entailment relation between plurality and the count status. Furthermore, it also identifies the distinctive function of CLs of CL languages, which separates the languages from non-CL languages such as English.

The two features argued for in this chapter, Numerability and Delimitability, also set the scene for the analysis of other syntactic issues to be dis-

---

2. CLs in general are called *liang-ci* 'quantity-word' in Li (1924), *danwei-ci* 'unit-word' in Lü (1942: Ch. 11.72), and *measures* in Chao (1968). See Section 6.2.1 for more names for CLs in various theories.

cussed in this book. They are encoded in functional categories, to be shown in later chapters.

In order to introduce the empirical range of the discussion, I use the traditional term *countability* as a convenient cover term. Readers will eventually see that facts are analyzed based on the two features mentioned above, without any implementation of the term.

In addition to this introductory section and the last, the summarizing one, this chapter is composed of five substantial parts. Section 2.2 introduces the two features and proposes my new theory of the count-mass contrast, based on the features. Section 2.3 and Section 2.4 are investigations of the features in Chinese nouns and unit words, respectively. Section 2.5 compares this new analysis of the count-mass contrast with other approaches in the literature. Section 2.6 further argues that the count and non-count contrast is syntactic, and shows the problems of certain current syntactic analyses of CLs in numeral expressions.

2.2. Decomposing countability

2.2.1. Identifying two new features syntagmatically

It is well-recognized that there are two kinds of relationship between linguistic elements: paradigmatic and syntagmatic. A paradigmatic relationship is established by a substitution test. For instance, the three words *of, by,* and *for* establish a paradigmatic relation in forming the string *government {of/by/for} the people*, since one of them can substitute another, i.e., each of them may occur in the same syntactic position. A syntagmatic relationship, however, is defined by the compatibility of co-occurring elements in the same construction, e.g., the relationship between *the* and *people* in the string *the people*. Paradigmatic and syntagmatic relationships have been metaphorically viewed as vertical and horizontal ones, respectively.

Many formal features such as tense and aspect of verbal expressions, gender and person of nominal expressions are defined paradigmatically. Selection features are typical syntagmatic features. For instance, the transitive verb *drink* c-selects a nominal, because it needs to occur with a nominal; and it s-selects a liquid-denoting nominal, because it needs to combine with this type of nominal.

Different kinds of syntagmatic relations exhibit different properties. In selection, the occurrence of the selected element is obligatory. But there are other syntagmatic relations that do not exhibit this kind of strict relation. For instance, gradability of adjectival expressions is defined by the possibility to occur with a relative degree word such as *quite, terribly*, and *fairly* (e.g., Sapir 1944; Bolinger 1972). In (7a), the adjective *nice* is gradable since it may occur with the degree word *quite*. In contrast, the adjective *next* is not gradable, since it may not occur with any degree word, such as *quite*, as shown in (7b).[3]

(7) a. *the quite nice book*   b. *the (*quite) next book*

Another example of non-obligatory co-occurrence relation is seen in the feature of agentivity. Agentivity of a verbal expression is defined by the possibility to be modified by an agent-oriented adverb. For instance, the VP *shouted* in (8a) is agentive since it may occur with the agent-oriented adverb *deliberately*, and the VP *arrived* in (8b) is not agentive, since it may not occur with *deliberately*.

(8) a. *Kim shouted deliberately.*   b. *Kim arrived (*deliberately).*

In defining gradability and agentivity, a feature is identified simply in the way that it allows X. Allowing does not mean requiring. Therefore the presence of X is not obligatory.

With this background in mind, I now introduce two features which are also defined syntagmatically, in order to analyze the count-mass contrast.

Some nouns may combine with a cardinal numeral directly, and some may not. In (9a), for instance, the noun *unicorn* combines with the numeral *one* directly. In (10a), however, the noun *oil* may not do so.[4]

(9)   a. *one unicorn*   b. *five unicorns*   c. *zero unicorns*
       d. *0.5 unicorns*   e. *1.0 unicorns*   f. *five beliefs*

(10) a. *(*one) oil*   b. *(*one) furniture*

---

3.   The word *very* may occur with non-gradable adjectives such as *next*. However, in addition to being a degree word, *very* also means actual or precise, used to emphasize the exact identity of a particular person or thing, according to *The New Oxford American Dictionary* (Second Edition 2005, Oxford University Press).

4.   In this book, I do not discuss the construction in which a numeral is semantically related to a noun phrase but occurs external to the noun phrase, e.g., as an adverbial. See Rijkhoff (2002: 33) for such constructions.

The contrast can also be seen in predication (the examples in (11) are adapted from Chierchia 2010: 104):

(11)   a.   *The boys are at least thirty.*   b.   **The gold is at least thirty.*
       c.   *The gold is at least thirty pounds.*

The numeral *thirty* is the predicate of the nominal *the boys* in (11a), whereas it may not be a predicate of the nominal *the gold* in (11b). Comparing (11b) and (11c), we see that the numeral needs the support of the measure word *pounds* to function as the predicate of the string *the gold*. Following the assumption that the copula in a nominal predicate construction in English is a tense-bearer or a raising verb (Stowell 1981, 1983, among others) and therefore the surface order of the subject-copula string is derived by the raising of the subject from its base-position, I assume that the combination of the subjects with the numeral predicates in their base-positions is possible in (11a), but not in (11b). The contrast is related to the type of nominal instantiated by *boy* and that by *gold*.

A similar contrast is also seen between Argument Structure Nominals and their correlated simple nominals. According to Grimshaw (1990) and Alexiadou (2011: 34), in English and Greek, Argument Structure Nominals, such as *jumping of the cow* in (12a), may not occur with a numeral, whereas the correlated simple nominals may, as shown by *jump* in (12b, c):

(12)   a.   **One jumping of the cow was interrupted by the fireworks.*
       b.   *One jump was disqualified.*
       c.   *two jumps*

I use the feature *Numerability* to represent the contrast between nominals that may combine with a numeral directly and nominals that may not do so. Accordingly, [+Numerable] means allowing a numeral, and [–Numerable] means disallowing a numeral. Therefore, the nominals in (9), (11a), and (12b/c) are [+Numerable] and those in (10), (11b/c), and (12a) are [–Numerable].[5]

The numerals in the nominals in (9) are different. In this analysis, Numerability cares about the ability to occur with a numeral only; no special status is given to the contrast among *one*, *zero*, integers, and other numerals.

The feature Numerability is attested in the fact that certain elements intrinsically bring about a relevant effect. For instance, the occurrence of

---

5.   I use bivalent, rather than privative, feature analysis in classification of nominals (see Harbour 2011).

English suffixes such as *-er, -ee, -ant/-ent,* and *-ist* makes a noun able to occur with a numeral. In (13a), the noun *advice* has [−Numerable], since it may not occur with the numeral *one.* In (13b), however, the suffix *-er* occurs with the noun, and the numeral may occur. The acceptability contrast in (13) indicates that it is the suffix that brings about the feature [+Numerable] to the nominal.

(13)   a. *one advice   b. *one adviser*

On the other hand, in Dutch, the presence of a collective affix such as -*werk* makes the noun unable to occur with any numeral (de Belder 2010; 2011a: 218) and thus the affix is a marker of [−Numerable] in my analysis. In (14a), the nominal *suiker* 'sugar' has [+Numerable], since it occurs with the numeral *drie* 'three'. In both (14b) and (14c), -*werk* occurs. In the presence of the numeral *drie* 'three', (14b) is not acceptable. The acceptability contrast between (14b) and (14c) indicates that it is the suffix that brings about the feature [−Numerable] to the nominal (COL = COLLECTIVE).

(14)   a. *drie suiker*-en   b. **drie   suiker-werk*-en   [Dutch]
           three sugar-PL   three sugar-COL-PL
           'three sugars'
       c. *suiker-werk*
           sugar-COL
           'confectionery'

In addition to Numerability, we also identify the feature Delimitability. Some words may be modified by a size-denoting expression (e.g., *big, small*), shape-denoting expression (e.g., *long, round, square, thin*), or boundary expression (e.g., *whole*), and some may not. I use the general term *delimitive modifier* to cover size-, shape-, and boundary-denoting modifiers. In (15a), (15b), and (15c), the delimitive adjectives *big, large,* and *square* modify the concrete nouns *unicorn, furniture,* and *watermelon,* respectively. In (15d), (15e), (15f), and (15g), however, the adjectives may not modify *oil, music, belief,* and *wine* (see Jespersen 1924: 198, Quine 1960: 104, McCawley 1979 [1975]: 170, Bunt 1985: 199). In (16a), the abstract noun *story* may be modified by *whole,* but in (16b), the abstract noun *leisure* may not.[6]

---

6. Dixon (1982) calls shape and size modifiers *dimension modifiers.* In Tang (2005: 456), "m-feature" refers to [+/−bound].

(15) a. *a big unicorn*   b. *large furniture*   c. *square watermelon*
      d. **large oil*   e. **large music*   f. **huge belief*
      g. **square wine*

(16) a. *whole story*   b. **whole leisure*

The contrast is also found in predication, as seen in (17) (Chierchia 2010: 110; Vázquez Rojas 2012: 66):

(17) a. *The violets are small.*   b. *The furniture is small.*
      c. **The snow is small.*

(18) a. *The luggage is round.*   b. **The blood is round.*

In (17a), the delimitive adjective *small* is the predicate of *the violets*, and in (17b), the adjective is predicated of *the furniture*. In (17c), however, the adjective may not be the predicate of *the snow*.[7]

I use the feature Delimitability to represent the contrast between nominals that may be modified by a delimitive modifier and nominals that may not. Thus, [+Delimitable] means allowing a delimitive modifier, and [–Delimitable] means disallowing a delimitive modifier. The nominals in (15a), (15b), (15c), (16a), (17a), and (17b) are [+Delimitable] and other nominals in (15) through (17) are [–Delimitable].

Although Delimitability is defined syntagmatically, it has a semantic correlation. When a nominal has [+Delimitable], its denotation must have "a certain shape or precise limits" (Jespersen 1924: 198). The shape or limits are delimitable in certain dimensions (e.g., length, size, volume, shape, and time), and therefore, atomicity is exhibited. In contrast, a nominal with [–Delimitable] denotes either material, which is in itself independent of shape or size, such as *silver, water, butter, gas, air*, or immaterial notions that have no intrinsic boundaries, such as *leisure, music, traffic, success, tact, commonsense* (cf. Jespersen 1924: 198).[8] In my understanding, the

---

7. The example in (i) is from Bunt (1985: 213). According to Schwarzschild (2011), although the word *sugar* is normally used as a mass noun, similar to *snow*, in (i), however, it has the same use as words such as *furniture*.

    (i) *The sugar in these boxes is cubic.*

8. Note that dimensional abstract nouns such as *tiji* 'volume' and *chicun* 'size' may be modified by a size adjective (e.g., *da chicun* 'big size'). Such relational nouns must be saturated by a delimitable noun (e.g., *qunzi de chicun* 'the size of the skirt' vs. **lilun de chicun* '*the size of the theory'), unlike other types of

former group of nouns can occur with a standard or container measure, as seen in (19a) and (20a), whereas the latter group cannot, as seen in the rest of the examples in (19) and (20).[9]

(19)   a. *a kilo of butter*   b. **a kilo of leisure*   c. **a kilo of beliefs*

(20)   a. *a bowl of butter*   b. **a bowl of leisure*   c. **a bowl of beliefs*

Note that immaterial nouns such as *belief* can be [+Numerable], as seen in (9f), although they are [–Delimitable], as seen in (15f).

Similar to Numerability, Delimitability is also attested in the fact that certain elements intrinsically bring about a relevant effect. For instance, *shui* 'water' alone may not be modified by *xiao* 'small', as seen in (21a); but if it is followed by a CL such as *di*, the whole compound *shui-di* can be modified by *xiao*, as seen in (21b). Similarly, *ni* 'mud' alone may not be modified by *xiao*, as seen in (22a); but if it is followed by a CL such as *kuai*, the whole compound *ni-kuai* can be modified by *xiao*, as seen in (22b). The examples in (23a) and (23b) show the same point (This issue is further discussed in Section 7.3.1).

(21)   a. **xiao shui*
           small water

       b. *xiao shui-di*
           small water-CL
           'small drop(s) of water'

(22)   a. **xiao ni*
           small mud

       b. *xiao ni-kuai*
           small mud-CL
           'small chunk(s) of mud'

(23)   a. **da yun*
           big cloud

       b. *da yun-duo*
           big cloud-CL
           'big piece(s) of cloud'

On the other hand, English words such as *woman, brother*, and *child* may be modified by a delimitive adjective such as *tall*, but if the suffix *-hood*

---

abstract relational nouns (e.g., *xingzhi* 'nature'), which can be saturated by a non-delimitable noun (e.g., *gai lilun de xingzhi* 'the nature of the theory').

9.   In idiomatic expressions, *ton* can occur with any noun. But *ton* in expressions such as *tons of leisure* may not be replaced by, or in contrast with, other standard measures such as *pound* and *kilo*. I thank Audrey Li for pushing me to clarify this.

or *-ship* occurs with a noun, no delimitive adjective may occur, as seen in (24). Therefore, the suffixes *-hood* and *-ship* are markers of [–Delimitable].

(24)   a.   *tall {woman/brother/child}*
       b.   **tall {womanhood/brotherhood/childhood}*
       c.   *tall {lady/friend/priest}*
       d.   **tall {ladyship/friendship/priestship}*

Delimitive adjectives are different from but not contrastive to gradable adjectives. The latter has an argument of type <d>, which is bound by a degree operator. The binding is seen if a degree word occurs or the adjective is in a comparative construction (Higginbotham 1985; Kennedy 1997, among others). Words like *big* are both gradable and delimitive, but words like *absolute* are neither. In addition, words like *square* and *whole* are delimitive but not gradable, whereas words like *heavy* and *cheap* are gradable but not delimitive.

Unlike other adjectives, delimitive adjectives reject collective readings. Moltmann (2004: 766; 2012: 24) notes that size and shape adjectives may not have collective readings. In (25a), *heavy* has both reading A, a distributive reading, and reading B, a colletive reading. In (25b), however, *round* does not have a collective reading.

(25)   a.   *The boxes are heavy.*
         A. Each one of the boxes is heavy.
         B. The total sum of boxes is heavy, each individual box is not necessarily heavy.
       b.   *The boxes are round.*
         A. Each one of the boxes is round.
         B. #The total sum of boxes is round, each individual box is not necessarily round.

Schwarzchild (2011) calls size and shape adjectives stubbornly distributive predicates. He claims that such a predicate applies to singularities only. In our viewpoint, such a predicate is delimitive, and its argument is [+Delimitable]. The contrast between stubbornly distributive and other predicates instantiates the contrastive values of delimitability in a plural context.

The fact that delimitive adjectives are different from gradable adjectives and reject collective readings indicates that they form a natural class semantically. Our feature Delimitability seems to get support from this semantic perspective.

I now clarify two further issues with respect to the feature Delimitability. First, words such as *big, small, enormous, huge,* and their Chinese counterparts have an intensifier usage. As stated in Morzyski (2009: 176), "an adjective that normally expresses size characterizes the degree to which the gradable predicate holds", as shown in (26) (also see Constantinescu 2011: 35). In adjectives used in this way, *big* can be replaced by *real*, *da* 'big' can be replaced by *zhenzhengde* 'real' or *qiang* 'strong', and *xiao* 'small' can be replaced by *shaowei* 'moderately' in certain contexts.

(26)　a.　*big idiot*　　　　b.　*big smoker*　　　　　c.　*big idea*

　　　d.　*da bendan*　　　e.　*da hao xingshi*
　　　　　big fool　　　　　big good situation
　　　　　'big fool'　　　　　'very good situation'

　　　f.　*xiao xian shenshou*　　　g.　*da huo*　　h.　*da feng*
　　　　　small show skill　　　　　big fire　　　big wind
　　　　　'show the skill a little bit'　　'strong fire'　'strong wind'

The intensifying readings are not size readings, and thus the adjectives in such a use are not delimitive adjectives. Similar intensifying readings are also found in other adjectives such as *good*, as in (27) (Levinson 2010: 150; Kayne 2005a: 195):[10]

(27)　a.　*He braided her hair <u>good</u> and tight.*
　　　b.　*A <u>good</u> many linguists went to the conference.*

Second, the adjectives *deep* and *shallow* in expressions such as *deep water* and *shallow water* do not semantically modify *water*. Instead, the delimitive adjectives may modify the source location of water, and the type of the location is used for the type of water.

---

10. The retroflection suffix *-r* in Mandarin Chinese encodes endearment, as well as diminutiveness. In the former reading, no size meaning is expressed, as seen in (i).

　(i) a.　*da-men-r*　　　　　　b.　*qi-shui-r*
　　　　　big-door-ENDEARMENT　　air-water-ENDEARMENT
　　　　　'big door'　　　　　　　'soda water'

　In Cinque (2011: 6), the functional projection to host an endearment element is ranked lower than the one for a diminutive element. Also see Fortin (2011: 3) for the distinctions between the two readings of diminutives.

2.2.2. Defining count and mass by the two features

Traditionally, the notion of count is in direct contrast to the notion of mass. Different from this binary analysis, I use the two values of the two features, Numerability and Delimitability, to make a more fine-grained classification. The four possible combinations of the two values of the features are summarized in (28). Among the four possibilities, (28a) and (28b) are both count, (28d) is mass, and (28c) is non-count and non-mass.

(28)

	[Numerable]	[Delimitable]	example	countability status
a.	+	+	*unicorn* in (9a), (15a)	count with a delimitable feature
b.	+	–	*belief* in (9f), (15f)	count without a delimitable feature
c.	–	+	*furniture* in (10b), (15b)	non-count, non-mass
d.	–	–	*oil* in (10a), (15d)	mass

In this analysis, the feature Numerability alone may distinguish a count noun from a non-count noun. If a nominal may combine with a numeral directly in the context, it has [+Numerable] and thus is a count nominal in that context. Otherwise, it is a non-count one. According to Chierchia (1998: 353; 2010: 104), the ability to combine with a numeral is the signature property of a count nominal.

But Numerability alone is not enough to decide whether a noun is a mass noun. A non-count noun is not necessarily a mass noun. Well-recognized mass nouns, such as the word *oil*, may be neither combined with a numeral directly, nor modified by a delimitive adjective. In my analysis, it is the combination of [–Numerable] and [–Delimitable] that defines the mass status of a nominal.

The independent status of (28c) shows that non-count nominals do not have to be mass ones. Words like *furniture* may be modified by a delimitive modifier, although they may not be combined with a numeral directly.

Thus, [+Delimitable] is not part of the defining property of a count element (contra Wiltschko 2005, among others). On the one hand, *duckling* and the German word *Eichhörnchen* 'squirrel' can be modified by delimitive modifiers (e.g., *small duckling*), but they can occur as non-count nouns, in addition to count nouns (see de Belder 2011b: 181, fn. 12). On the other hand, words such as *belief* may combine with a numeral, and thus are count nouns, but they may not be modified by a delimitive adjective.

In my approach, like the feature of gradability for APs and the feature agentivity for VPs, the features related to the count-mass contrast for NPs can also be defined syntagmatically. I claim that the two features, Numerability and Delimitability, are available in identifying the countability status of nouns in all languages that have adnominal numerals and delimitive modifiers. Also, the two features are the only criteria to be considered in analyzing the count-mass contrast. The relationship between plural markers and the count-mass contrast will be discussed in Sections 2.2.6 and 2.5.3.

2.2.3. Attesting the two features in co-occurrence restrictions

The linguistic reality of Numerability and Delimitability is independently attested in co-occurrence restrictions of articles, quantifiers, adverbs, and CLs.

It is well-known that indefinite articles and some quantifiers occur with count nouns in English. For instance, *every, many, a few, several,* and *another* occur with nouns that have [+Numerable] (e.g., {*many/*much*} *unicorns*), and *much, little,* and *a little* occur with nouns that have [−Numerable] (e.g., {**many/much*} *oil*; {**many/much*} *furniture*). A clearer contrast is seen in the Turkish examples in (29) and (30). The nouns in these examples have neither a plural marker nor a CL. The words *kitap* 'book' and *şehir* 'city' may combine with a numeral, and they are compatible with the quantifiers *kaç (tane)* 'how many', *birkaç* 'a few', or *birçok* 'many', but not the quantifier *ne kadar* 'how much'. The last quantifier is for words such as *para* 'money' and *su* 'water', which may not combine with a numeral (Göksel & Kerslake 2005: 163–164; Görgülü 2010).

(29) a. *Kaç   (tane) kitap oku-du-n?*
          how   item book   read-PST-2SG
          'How many books did you read?'

      b. *Kaç   (tane) şehir gez-di-n?*
          how   item city   travel-PST-2SG
          'How many cities did you travel?'

(30) a. *Ne   kadar   para   harca-di-n?*
          what amount   money   spend-PST-2SG
          'How much money did you spend?'

      b. *Ne   kadar   su   iç-ti-n?*
          what amount   water drink-PST-2SG
          'How much water did you drink?'

The feature Delimitability is also attested in a parallel way. In Japanese, no noun may combine with a numeral directly, therefore, I do not use nouns of this language to show the different values of Numerability. Nevertheless, it is easy to see the contrastive values of Delimitabilty in the language. The quantifiers *tasuu* 'many' and *shoosuu* 'a few' may occur with words such as *isha* 'doctor' or *hon* 'book', but not with words like *inku* 'ink' or *gyunyu* 'milk'. This contrast is shown in (31a) and (31b). The word *isha* or *hon*, but not *inku* or *gyunyu,* can be modified by a delimitive adjective. Therefore, the quantifiers occur with [+Delimitable] nominals. However, the opposite pattern is seen with the quantifiers *taryoo* 'much' and *shooryoo* 'a little'. They may occur with words such as *inku* or *gyunyu*, but not words like *isha* or *hon*, as shown in (32a) and (32b), and therefore, they occur with [–Delimitable] nominals (Kobuchi-Philip 2011: 307; similar examples have also been provided to me by Yukari Kurita, p.c., Sept. 23, 2010).

(31) a. {*tasuu/shoosuu*}-*no isha*   b. *{*tasuu/shoosuu*}-*no inku*
        many/a few-GEN   doctor   many/a few-GEN   ink

(32) a. *{*taryoo/shoorryoo*}-*no isha*   b. {*taryoo/shooryoo*}-*no inku*
        much/a little-GEN   doctor   much/a little-GEN   ink

The Korean counterparts of the examples show the same contrast (Yi 2010: Sec. 4.4.1).

Adverbs such as *each* may not be in construal with nouns that have [–Delimitable], as shown by the contrast between (33a) and (33b). The Mandarin Chinese adverb *zuge* 'each' is subject to the same constraint, as seen in the contrast in (34).

(33) a. *The balls each fell down off the table.*
      b. **The oil each fell down off the table.*

(34) a. *Qiqiu*   *zuge xiaoshi-le.*
        balloon   each   disappear-PRF
        'The balloons disappeared one by one.'
      b. **Zhima-you zuge xiaoshi-le.*
        sesame-oil   each   disappear-PRF

In Chinese, some CLs are sensitive to the delimitable feature of the noun. For instance, no liquid-denoting noun may be modified by a delimitive adjective, as seen in (35a). Such a noun is [–Delimitable]. It can occur with the CL *di*, as seen in (35b). *Di* takes nouns with [–Delimitable] only.

(35) a. **chang {you/shui/xue/niao/yanlei/mo-shui}*
          long   oil/water/blood/urine/tear/ink-water
      b. *san   di {you/shui/xue/niao/yanlei/mo-shui/*putao}*
          three CL oil/water/blood/urine/tear/ink-water/grape
          'three drops of {oil/water/blood/urine/tear/ink/*grape}'

In contrast, *putao* 'grape' can be modified by a delimitive adjective, as seen in (36a) below. This noun is thus [+Delimitable]. It may not occur with *di*, as seen in (35b) above. Other CLs that reject nominals with [+Delimitable] include *ji* (for liquid medicine), *pao* (for urine), *tan* (for any liquid). I call such CLs (part of Chao's 1968 partitive measures) individuating CLs, which select [–Delimitable].

(36) a. *da putao*
          big grape
          'big grape'
      b. *san   ke putao/*you/*zhi/*zheng-qi/*xue/*rou/*bu/*qian/*yanlei*
          three CL grape/oil/paper/steam-air/blood/meat/cloth/money/tear

Words like *putao*, which are [+Delimitable], can be selected by another kind of CLs, individual CLs (called individual measures in Chao 1968: 585). The CL *ke* in (36b) is such a CL. CLs such as *ben* (for books), *tou* (for animals such as cows), and *zhi* (for animals such as chickens) are also individual CLs. Moreover, collective CLs, such as *zu* 'group', *qun* 'crowd', *da* 'dozen', *shuang* 'pair', *dui* 'pair', and partitive CLs, such as *ye* 'page', *duan* 'paragraph', and *zhang* 'chapter' (they all belong to Chao's 1968 partitive measures), also occur with nouns with [+Delimitable] only.

2.2.4. Attesting the two features in pronominalization

The English proform *one* can only take a count noun as its antecedent (Schütze 2001; Barbiers 2005; Ojeda 2005: 404). The same constraint is seen in the Afrikaans proform *een* 'one' (Corver & van Koppen 2011: 376). This constraint indicates that such pronominalization is sensitive to the feature Numerability.

(37) a. *Would you like a red bike or a white one?*
      b. **Would you like red wine or white one?*

In Mandarin Chinese, the word *liaoliaowuji* 'few' can be used as a pronoun. Like other pronouns, it can function as an argument independently,
taking another nominal in the context as its antecedent. The antecedent of
the pronoun *liaoliaowuji* must be a noun that is able to be modified by a
delimitive adjective. In (38a), the antecedent of *liaoliaowuji* is *mao-bi*
'brush-pen', which can be modified by a delimitive adjective such as *chang*
'long'. In contrast, in (38b), the antecedent of *liaoliaowuji* is *mo-shui* 'ink-
water', which, as shown in (35a) above, cannot be modified by a delimitive
adjective. The pronominalization in (38b) fails. The acceptability contrast
in (39) exhibits the same pronominalization constraint.

(38) a. *Wo yiqian mai-guo henduo mao-pi,*
     1SG before buy-EXP many   brush-pen
     xianzai shengxia liaoliaowuji.
     now   remain   few
     'I bought many brush-pens before, but few of them remain now.'
  b. *Wo yiqian mai-guo hendu mo-shui,*
     1SG before buy-EXP many ink-water
     *xianzai sheng-xia liaoliaowuji.
     now   remain   few
     'I bought much ink before, *but few of them remain now.'

(39) a. *Women guji   daliang youke hui lai   zheli,*
     1PL   estimate a.lot   tourist will come here
     keshi zhi jin zhi lai-le   liaoliaowuji.
     but   up.to today only come-PRF few
     'We estimated that a lot of tourists would come here, but up to
     today only a few have came.'
  b. *Women guji   daliang zheng-qi hui cong zhe ge kong*
     1PL   estimate a.lot   steam-air will from DEM CL hole
     mao-chulai, *keshi zhi   mao-chulai-le liaoliaowuji.
     rise-outbut but   only rise-out-PRF few
     Intended: 'We estimated that a lot of steam would come out of
     this hole, but only little came out.'

The contrast between (38a) and (38b) and the one between (39a) and
(39b) indicate that pronominalization of *liaoliaowuji* is sensitive to the
feature Delimitability.

2.2.5. Attesting the two features in shifts

In this subsection, I argue that the two features are also attested in the input and output of three shifts: Universal Grinder, Universal Packager, and Universal Sorter.

Universal Grinder

Imagine we have a big grinder. We can put things in and what we get is a massive object, which does not have a shape intrinsic to the property of the input. This is the so-called effect of Universal Grinder (Pelletier 1979 [1975]: 6). Compared with the word *apple* in (40a), the word *apple* in (40b) denotes a massive object.

(40) a. *There is an apple on the table.* b. *There is apple in the salad.*

Universal Grinder has been viewed as an effect of changing a "count" noun into a "mass" noun. I claim that it is an effect of blocking the projection of the feature [+Delimitable], in a specific context. In other words, the output of the shift must be [−Delimitable]. For instance, the word *apple* in (40b) may not be modified by the delimitive adjective *small*, as shown in (41a) (Bunt 1985: 207). (41b) shows the same point.

(41) a. *There is (*small) apple in the salad.*
      b. *There wasn't much (*long) cucumber in the salad.*

The effect of the Universal Grinder is also seen in Chinese:

(42) a. *Wo   yu   bu   chi-le.*
         1SG   fish   not   eat-PRF
         A: 'I will not eat the whole fish anymore.'
         B: 'I will not eat the fish meat anymore.'
      b. *Wo da de yu   bu   chi-le.*
         1SG big DE fish not eat-PRF
         ✓A: 'I will not eat the whole big fish anymore.'
         ✗B: 'I will not eat the (big) fish meat anymore.'

The word *yu* 'fish' in (42a) is ambiguous. Reading A is attested when the speaker has a plate of whole fish in front of him, and Reading B is attested when the speaker is in front of a plate of processed fish meat (e.g., fish slices or chunks). The meat reading is an effect of Universal Grinder. However, in (42b), the adjective *da* 'big' occurs, and then *yu* must have the whole fish reading. Note that only delimitive modifiers can bring about the blocking effect. In (43), the modifier is not a delimitive one and thus the ambiguity remains (in this case, the Universal Grinder effect is observed even in a complex nominal. Cf. Acquaviva 2010: 9).

(43) *Zuotian   mai   de   yu   wo   bu   chi-le.*
      yesterday   buy   DE   fish 1SG not   eat-PRF
      A: 'I will not eat the whole fish that {was/were} bought yesterday.'
      B: 'I will not eat the fish meat that was bought yesterday.'

We can see that the presence of the delimitive adjective correlates with the atomicity reading. The fact that the output of the Universal Grinder may not allow a delimitive adjective means that the output of the shift is not only [–Numerable], but also [–Delimitable].

Examples of the effect of the Universal Grinder in Chinese, such as (42), are easy to find (contra Cheng et al. 2008; and Cheng 2012; See de Belder 2011a: 91, or 2011b: 198, for a discussion of the markedness of examples like *There is dog all over the wall*, and her pragmatic account). The experimental studies in A. Huang (2009) and A. Huang & Lee (2009) also show that Chinese has Universal Grinder effects. (44) gives us another pair of such examples (if we change *jidan* 'egg' in (44) into *pingguo* 'apple', we get a parallel effect).

(44) a. *Panzi-li you   jidan.*
         plate-in   have egg
         A: 'There are whole eggs in the plate.'
         B: 'There is scrambled egg in the plate.'
      b. *Panzi-li you   da   jidan.*
         plate-in   have big egg
         ✓A: 'There are big whole eggs in the plate.'
         ✗B: 'There is big scrambled egg in the plate.'

Now let us turn to the input of the shift. The word *furniture* is [–Numerable] (see (10b)). After an earthquake, for example, when items of furniture pieces such as legs of chairs and tops of tables are all over a place, one can say (45), and thus the Universal Grinder effect is also available.

(45) *There is furniture all over the place.*

In Chinese, no noun may combine with a numeral directly and thus all nouns are [–Numerable] (Section 2.3.1), but the Universal Grinder effect is still available. Considering both the Chinese examples in (42a), (43), (44a), and the English example in (45), we can see that the input of the shift is not restricted to [+Numerable]. So the shift is not a shift from a count noun to something else, since the input can be a non-count noun.

The above discussion shows that the input of Universal Grinder is specified with [+Delimitable] only, but the output is the negative values of both features.

(46)   Universal Grinder:
       [α Numerable, +Delimitable] → [–Numerable, -Delimitable]

The two features are thus attested in a more precise description of the shift.

Universal Packager

In a perspective different from the Universal Grinder, all kinds of the material type of massive objects can be put in containers or be apportioned in a certain way, and after doing so, the massive objects become discrete portions and thus can be counted. For instance, the word *water* and *beer* in (47a) each occur with a numeral and are thus [+Numerable], i.e., countable.

(47)   a. *Give me two waters and one beer.*
       b. *I'll have another {beer/wine/whiskey}.*
       c. *I had too many {beers/wines/whiskeys} already.*

This is the so-called effect of Universal Packager (Pelletier 1979; Bach 1986: 10; Jackendoff 1991; 1997: 53). It has been viewed as an effect of changing a "mass" noun into a "count" noun, since the massive objects become "the individuations based on the glasses or servings thereof" (Ojeda 2005: 405). This conventional unit or portion reading is commonly found (Corbett 2000: 37). In fact, it is a contextually induced Numerability effect. The denoted entity must be quantized in a certain way in the context. The discourse context specifies the exact unit of counting. The feature [+Numerable] emerges in the context where the noun occurs with a numeral, as in (47a), or with a determiner or quantifier that occurs with a noun that exhibits [+Numerable], such as *another* and *many* (see Section 2.2.3), as in (47b) and (47c) (cited from Ojeda 2005: 404).

Examples like (48) further show that the output of Universal Packager also includes [+Delimitable].

(48)   *Give me one big water and two small beers.*

Universal Packager applies to nouns with [–Delimitable] only, but not to [+Delimitable] words such as *furniture* and *cutlery*. (49) does not mean three packages of cutleries (Borer 2005: 103, fn. 14; Acquaviva 2010: 3).

(49)   **three cutleries*

If the shift is understood as a simple switch from "mass" to "count" nouns, one cannot explain why certain "mass" nouns reject the shift consistently. The two features proposed in this book can give a more precise description of the input of the shift. The packager effect applies to [–Numerable, -Delimitable] nouns only, but not [–Numerable, +Delimitable] nouns.[11]

(50)   Universal Packager:
       [–Numerable, -Delimitable] → [+Numerable, +Delimitable]

No noun in Chinese can be preceded by a numeral directly (Section 2.3.1). So no result of the shift is observed in the language, although the language has [–Delimitable, –Numerable] (i.e., mass) nouns. Nevertheless, the shift seems to be attested in an indirect way, and it is subject to the same input condition. In (51a) (Yu Hong, p.c., Dec. 3, 2010; Jane Tang, p.c., Jan. 17, 2011) and (51b) (Doetjes 1997: 33), the noun *pijiu* 'beer' is interpreted as packages of beer. But importantly, first, the package interpretation emerges only when such a noun follows a unit word, such as the

---

11. Comparative constructions have a similar effect as Universal Packager (Bale & Barner 2009; 2012: 241, 246). In (ia) the noun *water* is used as a mass noun, but in (ib) *waters* denotes portions of water. The decision of "who has more" is based on volume for the mass usage in (ia), but on number (e.g., number of portions) for the non-mass usage in (ib). In (iia), the decision of "who has more" is based on number (e.g, number of the furniture pieces), as in (ib). (iib) is not acceptable.
   (i) a. *Mary has more water than Jane does.*
        b. *Mary has more waters than Jane does.*
   (ii) a. *Mary has more furniture than Jane does*
        b. *??Mary has more furnitures than Jane does.*

collective CL *da* 'dozen' in (51a) and the individual CL *ge* in (51b) (Persian examples similar to (51b) are seen in Ghomeshi 2003: 55 (25c) and Cowper & Hall 2012: (48b); see (139c, d) later). This is different from examples such as (47). Second, the package interpretation is not observed if the noun following a CL has [+Delimitable]. In (51c), *pingguo* 'apple', which can be modified by a delimitive adjective such as *xiao* 'small' and thus has [+Delimitable], does not have a package reading. Thus we see the same constraint on the same type of nouns, (49) in English and (51c) in Chinese.

(51) a. *yi   da   pijiu*   b. *Gei   wo   liang ge pijiu.*[12]
         one dozen beer   give 1SG two CL beer
         'a dozen packages of beer'   'Give me two units of beer.'
      c. *yi   da   pingguo*
         one dozen apple
         'a dozen (*packages of) apples'

Universal Sorter

Counting kinds is to count abstract units. Examples like (52a) (Chierchia 2010: 106) are discussed in Lyons (1977: 463), Allan (1977: 294), and Bunt (1985: 11). The word *wines* in (52a) follows a numeral and thus behaves like a count noun. Allan calls nouns used in this way pseudo-uncountable nouns, and Bunt calls this phenomenon the effect of Universal Sorter.

(52) a. *I like only three wines: chardonnay, pinot, and chianti.*
      b. **I like only three small wines: chardonnay, pinot, and chianti.*

---

12. In Mandarin Chinese (but not in some dialects of Chinese), *liang* 'two' is restricted to adnominal use (i.e., preceding a unit word), whereas *er* 'two' may also be used in arithmetics and ordinals. The numeral *er* 'two' occurs with standard measures only, but not other unit words.

    (i) *er   {jin/*bao/*ge/*pian/*dui/*zhong}   juzi*
        two catty/bag/CL/ slice/ pile/ kind   orange

    Liang can also be used as an existential quantifier, alternating with *ji* 'a few, several', as seen in (ii).

    (ii) *Guo {liang/ji}   tian zai   shuo.*
         pass two/several day   again   talk
         'Let's talk about it a few days later.'

As in the case of the Universal Packager, the denoted entity in the output of Universal Sorter is also quantized. But the quantization is accomplished in an abstract sense. In both cases, a noun combines with a numeral, and it thus exhibits a [+Numerable] feature. Therefore, like the words *water* and *beer* in (47), the word *wine* in (52a) also behaves like a count noun.

(52b) is different from (52a) only in the occurrence of the delimitive adjective *small*. Its unacceptability indicates that the shift does not change the value of the feature Delimitable.

As pointed out by Cowper & Hall (2012: 29), the Universal Sorter effect is not seen in words such as *furniture*. We have seen above that the Universal Packager effect is also absent from *furniture*-type words. In my feature analysis, we can make a precise description, namely, like the shift of Universal Packager, the shift of Universal Sorter applies to [–Numerable, –Delimitable] nouns only, but not to [–Numerable, +Delimitable] nouns. So we find the following description for the shift:

(53)   Universal Sorter:
       [–Numerable, –Delimitable] → [+Numerable, –Delimitable]

The input condition in (53) is the same as that of the Universal Packager, but the output is different. The negative value of Delimitability remains in the output. The differences of the two shifts are precisely represented by the two features.

Like Universal Packager, no direct effect of Universal Sorter is seen in Chinese.

The three shifts, Universal Grinder, Universal Packager, and Universal Sorter, have been found in various languages, and their existence is independent of morphological number marking (Wiese 2012: 70; see Wyngaerd 2009 for a semantic analysis of the shifts). In all of the shifts, Delimitability and Numerability are attested in either the input or output.

2.2.6. Numerability and number

Numerability is different from the notion of number. The former is concerned with the possibility to combine with a numeral, but does not have to be sensitive to the contrast between singular and plural markers. However, the latter is concerned with the contrast between singular and plural in morphology, but does not have to be sensitive to the occurrence of a numeral. When we consider the two values of Numerability and the two values of number, we see four possible patterns. All of them are attested.

First, a nominal can be both [+Numerable] and [+Plural], as seen in (54) and (55) (Saka 1991: 279) (I thank James Myers for giving me Saka's work).

(54) a. *two unicorns*   b. *0.5 unicorns*
      c. *1.0 unicorns*   d. *zero unicorns*

(55) a. *The temperature is <u>negative-one degrees</u>.*
      b. *The angle is <u>point-four degrees</u>.*
      c. *At the end of its first semester the college awarded <u>zero degrees</u>.*

The denoted referents of the nominals in (54b) through (54d) and those of the underlined nominals in (55) are not plural objects, but the plural markers are required. Moreover, words such as *scissors, trousers,* or *glasses* (in the sense of "binoculars") appear only in their plural form, even though they might refer to single objects (they are called defectives in Corbett 2000: 174).

Second, a nominal can be [+Numerable] but [–Plural], as seen in (56).

(56) *one unicorn*

In languages such as Yudja (Lima 2010; 2012), there are neither CLs nor obligatory plural markers, but all nouns can combine with a numeral directly. (57) is an example (Lima 2010: 7).

(57) *txabïa apeta*   [Yudja]
      three blood
      'three units of blood'
      (the unit is identified in the context: drops, puddles, or containers)

In Yudja, when a numeral and a noun are combined, the exact unit of counting depends on the discourse context (Lima 2010: 13). Lima reports the naturalness of data like (57) in the absence of either Universal Sorter or Universal Packager effects.

Third, a nominal can be [–Numerable] but [+Plural]. McClawley (1979 [1975]: 172) shows that the word *clothes* is plural, since it takes plural agreement in (58a), but it may not combine with a numeral, as seen in (58b). Words such as *guts, intestines, outskirts, oats, grits,* and *masses* behave the same. Jespersen (1961 [1909]) gives dozens of such words in English (also see Huddleston & Pullum 2002: 342; Acquaviva 2010: 2). Such nouns are called *pluralia tantum* ('plural only') in traditional grammar. Gillon (2012:

Sec. 3.1) claims that the plural feature of such words should be assigned in their lexical entry.

(58) a. *My clothes {are/*is} in this locker.*
      b. **I've just bought five clothes.*

Similarly, although mass nouns such as *water* have been found in a plural form to denote many instances of x, as in (59a) (Krifka 2008: Sec. 7.1), they may not occur with a numeral, as shown by (59b). This is different from the effects of Universal Packager and Universal Sorter (Section 2.2.5). When mass nouns are pluralized in such a case, there is no conventionalized counting unit in the context (see Mathieu 2012a: 185). We will say more about this kind of plural in Section 4.1.3.[13]

(59) a. *the waters of the Nile*   b. **the three waters of the Nile*

In the above two cases, the values of Numerability and plurality are different. The contrastive values of the two features are also seen in the fact that some nouns may occur with a numeral, and thus have [+Numerable], but they reject a plural marker when they do so. For some languages, this is a consistent pattern. In the Hungarian examples in (60), the plural marker *-k* may not occur with the numeral *három* 'three' (Csirmaz & Dekany 2010: (88); see our Section 4.2.5 for further discussion of the interaction).

(60) a. *három takaró-(*k)*   b. *három kutyá-(*k)*   [Hungarian]
          three   blanket-PL   three   dog-PL
          'three blankets'   'three dogs'

Fourth, a nominal can be both [−Numerable] and [−Plural]. English words such as *luggage* and *furniture* have this property. We thus see that nouns with [−Numerable, +Delimitable] can be either [+Plural], such as *clothes*, or [−Plural], such as *furniture*. Moreover, some nouns are found in singular, since they are preceded by the indefinite singular article *a*, but they never occur with a numeral, including *one*. The nominal *shortage of engineers* in (61a) and the nominal *good knowledge of Greek* in (61b) may

---

13. The term mass plural is used to refer to examples like (59a) in Tsoulas (2006), but it also refers to examples like (58a) in Ojeda (2005). I follow the former convention (also see Section 4.1.3).

not be preceded by the numeral *one*. In my analysis, the nominals here do not have [+Numerable] and thus they are not count ones.

(61)   a.   *{a/*one} shortage of engineers*
       b.   *Jill has {a/*one} good knowledge of Greek.*

The combination of [–Numerable] and [–Plural] is also attested in nouns of certain constructions. In the English NPN construction, as in (62a), the reduplicated noun may neither follow a numeral nor have a plural form (Travis 2001; Jackendoff 2008). This construction expresses many objects in succession, a plural reading (see Section 4.1.3), but no plural marker is allowed (cf. *trousers*).

(62)   a.   *day after day*   b.   **one day after one day*   c.   **days after days*

Another construction where nouns have both [–Numerable] and [–Plural] is represented by the examples in (63). The nouns after the prepositions in these examples occur with neither a plural marker nor a numeral (see Kiss 2010; de Swart et al. 2010). Such bare singular nouns also occur in other syntactic positions, as seen in (64) (Stvan 2009: 319; Espinal 2010: 985).

(63)   a.   *at school*   b.   *in prison*
       c.   *Van anar a escola.*   [Catalan]
            PST   go   to   school
            'They went to school.' (It could be one, or more than one)
       d.   *Estuvieron en prisión.*   [Spanish]
            were   in   prison
            'They spent time in prison.' (It could be more than one prison)

(64)   a.   *I've left town and I want to keep it that way.*
       b.   *Has portat samarreta.*   [Catalan]
            have   worn   T-shirt
            'You have worn a T-shirt.' (It could be one, or more than one)
       c.   *Comprará cochel.*   [Spanish]
            buy-FUT   car
            '(S)he will buy a car.' (It could be one, or more than one)

Examples like those in (63) and (64) have been labeled as number neutrality in languages that usually express number in noun morphology (Espinal 2010: 985), and analyzed as the result of pseudo-incorporation in the sense of Massam (2001) (see Stvan 2009; Farkas & de Swart 2003; Espinal & McNally 2011, among others).

All of the cross-linguistic facts discussed in this section indicate that Numerability and number are two different grammatical notions, although they may interact in a certain language-specific way. This is similar to the situation that modality and tense may interact closely, but they are recognized as two different notions. The possible interactions also do not mean that one is a sub-type of the other. Unfortunately, it is still widely believed that plurality is an issue of the count-mass contrast, assuming only count nouns may be plural.

Syntactic features are distributed in different types of elements cross-linguistically and within the same language. In the following two sections, we discuss the two features with respect to nouns and unit words in Chinese, a CL language, compared with non-CL languages, such as English.

2.3. The two features in nouns

2.3.1. Numerability of nouns

If we put unit words (e.g., *dui* 'pile') aside, it is undeniable that no noun in Chinese may combine with a numeral directly in a numeral expression, regardless of whether the nominal is an argument or predicate, and whether it is concrete or abstract (cf. Muromatsu 2003: 79, 85), as shown in (65). Therefore, all nouns in the language have the feature [–Numerable]. This means that no noun in the language is a count noun.[14]

(65) a. *Nali   you   san   *(tiao) xianglian.*
       there have three CL   necklace
       'There are three necklaces.'

---

14. A numeral can combine with a month-denoting noun or kinship term directly, as in (ia) and (ib), but in this case, the numeral is not used for counting. Instead, it is used as an ordinal number (Ōta 2003: 151). This fact shows that if the combination of a numeral and a noun is not used for counting, no CL occurs. But when a CL follows a numeral, it represents a counting unit.

(i) a. *{er/san} yue*   b. *{er/san} ge*
       two/three month   two/three elder.brother
       'February/March'   'the {second/third} elder brother'

b. *Nali   you   san   *(di)   you.*
there   have   three   CL   oil
'There are three drops of oil.'

c. *Baoyu   gen   Daiyu   shi   liang   *(ge)   gudian.*
Baoyu   and   Daiyu   be   two   CL   classic
xiaoshuo-zhong   de renwu.
novel-in   DE character
'Baoyu and Daiyu are two characters in a classic novel.'

d. *You   liang   *(zhong) feipang: jiankang de   gen   bingtai de.*
have   two   CL   fat   health   DE and sick   DE
'There are two kinds of fatness: the healthy one and the sick one.'

The occurrence of a unit word such as a CL is obligatory between a numeral and a noun in Chinese. It has been noted that a CL can be optional after the numeral *yi* 'one' in colloquial Beijing dialect of Mandarin Chinese, in examples such as (66a), (66b) (H. Huang 1981), (66c), and (66d) (Lü et al. [1980] 1999: 599; Yucheng Chung, p.c.).

(66)   a. *chi   yi   mantou*
eat   one   steamed.bread
'eat one steamed-bread'

b. *bei   yi   shu-bao   shangxue   qu*
carry   one   book-bag   go-school   go
'carry one school bag and go to school'

c. *ban   yi   shouxu*
do   one   procudure
'go through a procedure'

d. *zhe   yi   qingkuang/shigu/banfa/jiazhi/xinnian/chengjiu/*
DEM   one   situation/accident/method/value/belief/achievement/
benzhi/rongyu
nature/honor
'this situation/accident/method/value/belief/achievement/nature/
honor'

However, Du (1993) and Jing (1995) find that the omission of a CL in such data must satisfy two conditions. First, the noun must be a "count noun". More precisely speaking, the noun must be the one that may occur with the CL *ge*. This can be seen in (67a). Some other nouns may not occur with *ge*, as seen in (67b). (68) shows that those nouns in (67b) may not follow *yi* directly (see Section 2.4.5 for more discussion of *ge*).

(67) a. *yi*   *ge*   {*mantou/shu-bao/qingkuang/shigu/banfa*}
        one   CL   steamed.bread/book-bag/situation/accident/method
      b. *yi   *ge*   {*you/zhi/zheng-qi/xie/rou/bu/qian/yanlei*}
        one   CL   oil/paper/steam-air/blood/meat/cloth/money/tear

(68) *yi {*you/zhi/zheng-qi/xie/rou/bu/qian/yanlei*}
      one oil/paper/steam-air/blood/meat/cloth/money/tear

Second, the tone of the numeral *yi* 'one' consistently undergoes the tone sandhi as if it is followed by a fourth tone syllable (Jin 1979), i.e., the tone is changed from the first tone to the second tone. Importantly, the CL *ge* has the fourth tone. In all of the examples in (66), the CL *ge* may show up. The syllable *man* in (66a), which follows *yi* immediately, has the second tone. The syllable *shu* in (66b) and *shou* in (66c) also follow *yi* immediately. The former has the first tone, and the latter has the third tone. None of these post-*yi* syllables is able to trigger the tone sandhi of *yi*. Jing (1995: 14) thus points out that in data like those in (66), an implicit version of the CL *ge* occurs between *yi* and the noun, and that is why *yi* undergoes the tone sandhi. The tone sandhi fact clearly shows that the CL *ge* occurs in the syntax and even the phonological structure of the apparent CL-less examples like those in (66). Thus, there is always a unit word between a numeral and a noun in Mandarin Chinese. Since it is the unit word that is next to a numeral, it is the unit word, rather than the associated noun, that exhibits [+Numerable].

In contrast to Chinese, "there are a considerable number of Amerind languages as well as some elsewhere, for example, in New Guinea which do not have measure constructions. Numerals occur directly both with nouns designating mass as well as countable objects." (Greenberg 1972:16) In Hopi (Whorf [1941] 1956: 141; Greenberg 1972: 16), Karitiana (Müller et al. 2006), Halkomelem Salish (Wilhelm 2008: 64), and Yudja (Lima 2010, 2012), all nouns can combine with a numeral unconditionally (also, the same quantifier may occur with any noun in Yudja). The Yudja example in (57) is repeated here as (69). We can see that all nouns in such languages may have the feature [+Numerable].

(69) *txabïa apeta*   [Yudja]
      three   blood
      'three units of blood'
      (the unit is identified in the context: drops, puddles, or containers)

Between the two extreme patterns of Modern Mandarin Chinese and Yudja discussed above, in languages such as English and Dëne, Karitiana (Müller et al. 2006), and Haitian Creole (Deprez 2005: 861), some nouns may combine with numerals directly and some may not. We have seen the contrast between *unicorn* in (9) and *oil* and *furniture* in (10). The following Dëne examples are from Wilhelm (2008).

(70)   a.   *solághe   dzól*   b.   **solághe   bër*   [Dëne]
           five   ball   five   meat
           'five balls'

In some languages, such as Jingpo (Dai 1991) and Indonesian, there is optionality with respect to the occurrence of a CL between a numeral and a non-mass NP. The Indonesian examples in (71) (Sato 2009: 15; Dalrymple & Mofu 2012: 230) show this optionality.

(71)   a.   *tiga   (orang)   siswa*   b.   *lima   (orang)   guru*
           three   CL   student   five   CL   teacher
           'three students'   'five teachers'

As in Yudja, in Indonesian, a numeral may also be directly followed by a liquid or material-denoting noun, as seen in (72) (Dalrymple & Mofu 2012: 239). In these examples, as in Yudja, "the mass noun does not have conventional portions", (72a) refers to geographical areas of sea water and (72b) refers to pieces of wood (Dalrymple & Mofu 2012: 238).

(72)   a.   *duo   air   laut*   b.   *sepuluh   kayu*   [Indonesian]
           two   water sea   ten   wood
           'two (areas of) sea water'   'ten (pieces of) wood'

The optionality of the occurrence of CLs in numeral expressions is also seen in certain semantic types of nominals in other languages (see Tang 2004 for a discussion). Tang calls languages that require a CL or measure word to occur with a numeral "rich" CL languages, and CL languages that do not have this requirement "poor" CL languages.

The apparent cross-linguistic variation is also found within the same language. In Mandarin Chinese, in a normal phrasal nominal, a unit word is obligatory between a numeral and a noun; but in idiomatic expressions, compounds, or some list contexts, the language may pattern with Yudja: no unit word appears in this position. In the idiom and compound examples in

(73), a kind CL is implied in (73a, b, c), and an individual CL is implied in (73d, e, f). In each example in (74), multiple numeral expressions co-occur, denoting a list. An individual CL is implied for each numeral in (74a) and a container measure is implied for each numeral in (74b). Note that there is no fourth-tone-triggered tone sandhi of *yi* in (73e), so such examples are different from those in (66).

(73) a. *wu-xiang-fen*
      five-spice-powder
      'five-spice-power'

    b. *wu-du-ju-quan*
      five-poison-all-complete
      'all five kinds of sins'

    c. *wu-jin   shangdian*
      five-medal shop
      'hardware store'

    d. *san-jiao-guanxi*
      three-angle-relation
      'love triangle'

    e. *Yi   xin   bu   neng er   yong!*
      one heart not able two use
      'Don't be absent-minded!'

    f. *San   ren   xing bi   you wo   shi.*
      three person walk must have 1SG teacher
      'One can always find a teacher around.'

(74) a. *san   fang liang ting*
      three room two   sitting.room
      'three bedrooms and two sitting rooms'

    b. *si   cai   yi   tang*
      four vegetable one soup
      'four units of vegetable and one unit of soup'

The frequent occurrence of such expressions does not mean they are productive. One cannot replace a component of such an expression with another element of the same type freely. For instance, compared with (73a), neither of the two examples in (75) is acceptable. So we need to distinguish the productivity of types of construal from frequency of tokens (similar idiomatic expressions or compounds in which no CL occurs with a numeral and a noun are also found in other CL languages such as Thai; see Hundius & Kölver 1983: 209, fn. 5).

(75) a. **liu-xiang-fen*   b. **wu-chou-fen*   (cf. (73a))
      six-spice-powder   five-stink-powder

Similarly, in English compounds, not only count nouns, but also mass nouns, can be next to a numeral, as seen in (76a) and (76b) (Wiltschko 2012: 157), respectively.

(76)   a. *three card trick*   b. *five spice powder*

Moreover, if a numeral denotes a high round number, a CL can be op-tional for a non-mass noun, as seen in (77a) and (77b) (cited from Xing 1997: 191).

(77)   a. <u>*Liu-yi*</u>   *(ge)*   *funü*   *cheng*   *ban-bian tian.*
          six-billion   CL   woman   support   half-part heaven
          'Six billion women take half of the responsibilities of the world.'
       b. <u>*Wu-qian-wan*</u>   *(ge)*   <u>*jiaoshou*</u>   *touzi*   *gupiao.*
          5-1000-10000   CL   professor invest stock
          'Fifty million professors invest in stocks.'
       c. *liu-yi*   *ling san*   **(ge)*   *funü*
          six-billion zero three   CL   woman
          'six billion and three women'

In a round number such as the ones in (77a, b), the last morpheme is called *wei-shu* 'position-number' in Chinese grammar (Zhu 1982: 45), i.e., *yi* 'billion' in (77a), or *wan* 'ten thousand' in (77b). When no CL shows up between a complex numeral and a noun in data like (77a, b), the *wei-shu* functions as a collective CL, like *shuang* 'pair' or *da* 'dozen' (the noun can also be *ren* 'person', but not the inanimate *shu* 'book' or *deng* 'lamp'; see Watanabe 2013: Sec. 1 for a discussion of the relevant issue in Japanese). In (77c), the morpheme left-adjacent to the CL is *san* 'three', which is not a *wei-shu* and thus may not function as a collective CL, and therefore, the CL *ge* is obligatory. Like other unit words, a *wei-shu* can follow *haoji* 'several' (e.g., *haoji shi* 'dozens') and be followed by *duo* 'more', as seen in (78) (1 *catty* = 500 grams) (see Section 5.3.4.1).

(78)   a. *liu-shi* <u>*duo*</u>   *ge   pinguo*   b. *liu-shi jin* <u>*duo*</u>   *pigguo*
          six-ten   more CL   apple   six-ten catty more apple
          '60 some apples'   '60 catties and more apples'
       c. **liu* <u>*duo*</u>   *ge   pingguo*
          six   more CL   apple

The pattern of the CL optionality in (77a) and (77b) is also seen in other languages. Aikhenvald (2003: 100) observes that for numeral CLs, "[I]n many languages, they are obligatory with smaller numbers, and optional with larger ones." In Gilyak, individual CLs are used only with the first five numerals (Comrie 1981: 269).

2.3.2. Delimitability of nouns

Although all nouns in Chinese are non-count nouns, they are not the same, with respect to Delimitability. In Section 2.2.3, we saw that nouns with [+Delimitable] are selected by individual CLs, and nouns with [−Delimitable] are selected by individuating CLs. As shown in (79), nouns like *he* 'river' may be modified by a delimitive adjective such as *changchang* 'long'. In contrast, material nouns such as *you* 'oil' in (80a) may not (ignore the occurrence of *de*).

(79) a. *changchang de he*
      long   DE river
      'long river'

    c. *fang (de) xigua*
       square DE   watermelon
       'square watermelon'

    b. *da (de) qi-qiu*
       big DE air-ball
       'big balloon'

(80) a. **changchang (de) you*
       long   DE   oil

    c. **fang (de) mianfen*
       square DE flour

    b. **da (de) zheng-qi*
       big DE   steam-air

The contrast is shown not only in modification, but also in predication. The string *hen chang* 'very long' may not be the predicate of the mass noun *you* 'oil' in (81a), but it can be the predicate of the non-mass noun *he* 'river' in (82a). The string *hen da* 'very big' may not be the predicate of the mass noun *zheng-qi* 'steam-air' in (81b), but it can be the predicate of the non-mass noun *qi-qiu* 'balloon' in (82b).[15]

---

15. Audrey Li has mentioned to me an asymmetry in the word *tiankong* 'sky': it may not be modified by *da* 'big', but can take *hen da* 'very big' as its predicate.

  (i) a. **da tiankong*
       big sky

     b. *Tiankong hen da.*
       sky   very big
       'The sky is very big.'

The acceptability of (ib) can be accounted for by the traditional understanding that the sky has a certain shape (as in the expression *tian fang di yuan* 'the sky is square and the earth is round', and the question *Tiankong da-bu-da* 'Is the sky big?'). The unacceptability of (ia) shows the idiosyncratic property of certain nouns, which reject modifiers that denote the (assumed) intrinsic properties of their denotation, according to Paul (2010) (e.g., **tian fengmi* 'sweet honey').

(81) a. **You   hen   chang.*   b. **Zheng-qi   hen   da.*
          oil   very   long   steam-air   very   big

(82) a. *He   hen   chang.*   b. *Qi-qiu   hen   da.*
          river very   long   air-ball   very   big
          'The river is very long.'   'The balloon is very big.'

Abstract or immaterial nouns are generally not modified by shape or size modifiers (but see footnote 8). Nevertheless, some abstract nouns may, and some may not, be modified by boundary modifiers such as *wanzheng* 'complete', which are also delimitive modifiers. Nouns such as *xiaohua* 'joke' can be modified by *wanzheng,* as in (16a), whereas nouns such as *chouhen* 'hatred' reject the modifier, as seen in (16b).

(83) a. *wanzheng   de   {xiaohua/jianyi/gushi/jihua}*
          complete   DE   joke/suggestion/story/plan
          'a complete {joke/suggestion/story/plan}'
      b. **wanzheng   de   {chouhen/kongju/heping/youxian/fuyu/*
          complete   DE   hatred/fear/peace/leisure/poverty/richness}

This contrast shows that the feature Delimitability can divide Chinese nouns, which are all non-count ones, into the mass-type, which has [–Delimitable], and the non-mass-type, which has [+Delimitable].

Greenberg (1972: 26) claims that nouns in CL languages have the characteristics of a mass noun. The idea is also seen in Hansen (1972), Graham (1989), Krifka (1995), Doetjes (1996, 1997), Chierchia (1998), among many others. If mass nouns have [–Delimitable], not all nouns in Chinese are mass nouns.

2.4.   The two features in unit words

2.4.1. CLs and measure words

Following Li (1924 [1992: 81]), we assume that in a numeral expression, a CL expresses the unit for counting. The CLs in (84) (= (1)) can be compared with other types of unit words. According to Croft (1994: 151–152),

---

Note that such a rejection is not a general property of nouns, since expressions like *ku kafei*, 'bitter coffee', *re huoguo* 'hot hotpot', *xiao mayi* 'small ant' are perfectly fine.

standard measures such as *liter* in (85a), container measures such as *bottle* in (85b), kind CLs such as *kind* in (85c), partitive CLs such as *section* in (85d), and collective CLs such as *group* in (85e) are universally available.

(84) a. *Yaoyao kanjian-le san   <u>zhi</u> bi.*   [Individual CL]
          Yaoyao see-PRF   three CL   pen
          'Yaoyao saw three pens.
     b. *Yaoyao kanjian-le san   <u>di</u> you.*   [Individuating CL]
          Yaoyao see-PRF   three CL   oil
          'Yaoyao saw three drops of oil'.

(85) a. *Kim bought three <u>liters</u> of milk.*   [Standard Measure]
     b. *Kim bought three <u>bottles</u> of milk.*   [Container Measure]
     c. *three <u>kinds</u> of chocolate*   [Kind CL]
     d. *three <u>sections</u> of orange*   [Partitive CL]
     e. *three <u>groups</u> of students*   [Collective CL]

Greenberg (1972: 10) points out that "all the classifiers are from the referential point of view merely so many ways of saying … 'times one'." This is also true of all measure words. All types of CLs and measure words are used in counting, telling us the unit of counting in the context (see Croft 1994: 152 and Allan 1977: 293). When one wonders about the price of carrots in a market, the answer in (86) tells us that both the individual CL *gen* and the standard measure *gongjin* 'kilogram' can be used as counting units, and thus the two units can be in contrast.

(86) *Zhe shi mei yi   <u>gen</u>   hulubo de jiaqian, bu shi*
      DEM be every one CL   arrot   DE price,   not be
      mei yi <u>gongjin</u> huluobo de jiaqian.
      every one kilogram carrot   DE price
      'This is the price of each carrot, not that of each kilogram of carrots.'

Both CLs and measure words have the so-called additive measure function, or have a monotonic interpretation (Schwarzschild 2006), which means that if we add m units of x and n units of x together, we get the sum (superset) of the two quantities; and if we divide m units, we get the subpart of the m units. In Haas (1942), all unit words in Thai are given the label "classifier"; in Chao (1968), all unit words in Mandarin Chinese are given the label "measure". In this book, I treat all types of CLs and measure words as unit words.

Semantically, counting with either a CL or a measure word is a process of cardinal number assignment (Wiese 2003: 18). But the two kinds of cardinal number assignments are different. Cardinal number assignments with CLs, exclude properties like weight or volume, whereas those with measure words do not (see Wiese 2003: 21). In my opinion, this difference correlates with the fact that abstract notions are never counted by measure words (see (19) and (20)).

There is no stable "transformation" between a measure word and a CL. *2 kilos of beef* means the same as *2000 grams of beef*; a bottle of wine generally contains 0.75 liters, and two cups make a pint (Guy Emerson, p.c.; also Partee and Borschev 2012: 469). We thus see the transformation either between standard measrues or between a standard and a container measure. Within CLs, *san shuang kuaizi* 'three pair chopstick' gives the same counting result as *liu gen kuizi* 'six CL chopstick', and *san da jidan* 'three dozen egg' gives the same counting result as *36 ge jiadan* '36 CL egg' (I thank James Myers for discussing this issue with me; cf. Wiese 2003: 21). Between a CL and a measure word, we may establish an ad hoc transformation in a specific discourse context, e.g., *liu ge pingguo* 'six CL apple' has the same quantity as *yi he pingguo* 'one box apple' in a certain shop, but there is no context-free transformation relation between the two types of unit words.

In counting, there is no restriction to numerals. If a numeral-like element in a construction is not in paradigmatic relation with any other numeral, the construction is not a numeral construction (see Section 3.5 for various uses of *yi* 'one').

In the following subsections, we will see the differences among different types of unit words with respect to the feature [Delimitable] of nouns.

2.4.2. Unit words that occur with [–Delimitable]

Unit words that exclusively select [–Delimitable] nouns are individuating CLs (Section 2.2.3), as shown in (87).

(87) a. *shi   dui   tu*   b. *wu   gu   zheng-qi*
         ten   CL   earth   five   CL   steam-air
         'ten heaps of earth'   'five puffs of steam'
      c. *wu   di   you*   d. *liang gu   sichao*
         five   CL   oil   two   CL   thought
         'five drops of oil'   'two schools of thought'

Recall that all nouns in Mandarin Chinese are [–Numerable]. Therefore, such CLs occur with [–Delimitable, –Numerable] nouns, which are mass nouns. Such CLs are called "Partitive Measures" in Chao (1968), and "Classifiers for massive objects" in Gerner & Bisang (2010: 606) (also see, e.g., Croft 1994: 162). Semantically, individuating CLs are associated with the idea that "the noun refers to some kind of mass and the classifier gives a unit of this mass" (Denny 1986: 298, cited in Aikhenvald 2003: 318).

Individuating CLs divide massive objects into units, but not necessarily the minimal units (contra Wilhelm 2008: 49). Both *di* in (88a) and *tan* in (88b) are individuating CLs. The unit encoded by the latter is bigger than that encoded by the former. Moreover, a chunk of mud or meat can be big or small, and such chunks are not the minimal units of mud or meat.

(88) a. *san   di shui*   b. *san   tan shui*
         three CL water   three CL water
         'three drops of water'   'three puddles of water'

Not all languages have individuating CLs. As seen in (57), in Yudja, a numeral and a mass noun combine directly, without any CL, e.g., *txabïa apeta* 'three blood'. In Purépecha (a language of Central Western Mexico), a CL can occur only in the presence of a numeral or an interrogative quantifier meaning 'how many'. But when a numeral occurs with a mass noun, only a measure word such as *tsuntsu* 'cup' may link them together; no CL may occur in the construction (Vázquez Rojas 2012: 87; 60; 89).

2.4.3. Unit words that occur with [+Delimitable]

A noun with [+Delimitable] is a non-mass noun. Since such a noun can be modified by a delimitive modifier, it refers to an entity that has its natural unit. Unit words that occur with [+Delimitable] nouns are divided into three types.

A. What counts as one unit is bigger than the natural unit of the element denoted by a non-mass noun. In this case, a collective CL occurs, as in (89). A collective CL expresses a unit for counting sets of elements that are encoded by a non-mass noun. In (89a), *dui* expresses a unit that covers a group of entities that are called *luobo* 'carrot', and the noun *luobo* can be modified by a delimitive adjective such as *da* 'big'. In (89b), *zu* also expresses a unit that covers a group of concepts encoded by *xiaohua* 'joke', and the noun can be modified by a delimitive adjective such as *wanzheng* 'complete'. Both nouns are thus non-mass nouns.

(89)   a. *shi   dui   luobo*   b. *san   zu   xiaohua*   [Collective CL]
      ten   CL   carrot   three   CL   joke
      'ten piles of carrots'   'three groups of jokes'

Collective CLs (called Group Measures in Chao 1968: 595, and Aggregate Measure in Li & Thompson 1981: 107) include the so-called multiply-
ing or number set type, such as *shuang* 'pair', *dui* 'pair', and *da* 'dozen' (cf.
Bender & Beller 2006: 397), and the so-called blurring type, which includes *qun* 'crowd', *zu* 'set, group', and arrangement CLs, such as *pai*
'row' and *luo* 'stack'.[16]

   B. What counts as one unit is smaller than the natural unit of the element denoted by a non-mass noun. In this case, a partitive CL occurs, as in
(90). In (90), *pian* expresses a unit that represents a part of an entity encoded by *luobo* 'carrot', which is [+Delimitable].[17]

---

16. In Gebhardt (2011: 127), the collective CL *luo* 'pile' is labeled as a "mensural
    classifier", and at the same time, it is claimed that "mensural classifiers can be
    used with both count nouns and mass nouns". But it is clear that *luo*, as well as
    any other collective CL, may not occur with a mass noun.
17. Partitive CLs represent one of the various types of unit words for pseudo-
    partitive constructions. Such constructions denote the quantity of entities (e.g.,
    three slices of watermelon), whereas partitive constructions (e.g., Fodor & Sag
    1982, Jackendoff 1977) denote a part-whole relation within a definite domain
    (e.g., *three slices of the watermelon*). Crosslinguistically, the two constructions
    can be morphologically and syntactically different (Koptjevskaja-Tamm
    2009). The numeral expressions discussed here, including those containing a
    partitive CL, are all pseudo-partitive constructions. The fractional unit word
    cheng 'one tenth' in Chinese is used in partitive constructions only. I do not
    discuss this unit word in this book.
    (i) *Ba   cheng xuesheng yijing   kao-le   Tuofu.*
        eight   1/10   student   already test-PRF TOEFL
        '80% of the students have taken the TOEFL test.'
    Liao and Wang (2011: 150) claim that in a partitive construction, an individual
    CL or measure word precedes a kind CL, as in (iia). Their discussion does not
    cover partitive CLs. In data like (iib), a partitive CL precedes an individual CL
    (also see Hsieh 2008: 181 (45b)).
    (ii) a. *liu zhi zhe liang zhong gou* b. *liu pian zhe liang ge gua*
           six CL DEM two kind dog   six CL   DEM two   CL melon
           'six of these two kinds of dog'   'six slices of these two melons'

(90) *shi   pian   luobo*   [Partitive CL]
     ten   CL   carrot
     'ten slices of carrot'

C. What counts as one unit matches the natural unit of the element denoted by a non-mass noun. In this case, an individual CL is used, as in
(91a) and (91b). In other words, an individual CL expresses the natural unit
of an element that is encoded by a noun with the feature of [+Delimitable].

(91) a. *shi gen luobo*   b. *shi ze xiaohua*   [Individual CL]
         ten CL   carrot   ten CL joke
         'ten carrots'   'ten jokes'

Individual CLs encode intrinsic units of atomic elements, whereas other
types of unit words encode provided units of various kinds of elements (cf.
Hundius & Kölver 1983: 169). The three types of CLs introduced in this
subsection can be distinguished from each other by the following tests.
    The semantic differences between individual CLs and the other two
types of CLs can be seen in (92), where each CL is modified by the adjective *da* 'big'. In the unavailable reading for (92a) and (92b), i.e., Reading
A, the meaning of the adjective *da* 'big' is associated with the noun *luobo*
'carrot'; but in the available reading, i.e., Reading B, *da* 'big' is associated
with the unit. Only the individual CL construction in (92c) expresses the
meaning that the carrot is big, parallel to Reading A. The other two constructions in (92a) and (92b) do not express such an assertion. The reading
contrasts tell us that when an adjective precedes a CL, the association between the adjective and the noun is possible for individual CLs, but not for
collective and partitive CLs.

(92) a. *liang da dui luobo*   [Collective CL]
         two   big CL carrot
         ✗A: 'two piles of big carrots'
         ✓B: 'two big piles of carrots'
      b. *liang da pian luobo*   [Partitive CL]
         two   big CL   carrot
         ✗A: 'two slices of big carrots'
         ✓B: 'two big slices of carrots'
      c. *liang da gen luobo*   [Individual CL]
         two   big CL carrot
         'two big carrots'

We now see that the individual CL *gen* may occur with *luobo* 'carrot' and function as a unit to count the natural unit of carrots. We make use of this knowledge to further distinguish collective CLs and partitive CLs. Conceptually, we know that a group of x is bigger than an individual x, and a part of x is smaller than an individual x. If a CL X occurs in the position marked as X in the formula in (93a) and the sentence is acceptable and semantically reasonable, X is a collective CL. In contrast, if a CL Y occurs in the position marked as Y in the formula in (93b) and the sentence is acceptable and semantically reasonable, Y is a partitive CL. The result of (94a) tells us that *dui* is a collective CL; and the result of (94b) tells us that *pian* is a partitive CL, in the context.

(93) a. *Mei   yi   X   luobo da-yu   yi   gen   luobo.*
       each one CL carrot big-than one CL   carrot
       'Every X of carrots is bigger than one carrot.'

    b. *Mei   yi   Y   luobo xiao-yu   yi   gen   luobo.*
       each one CL carrot small-than one CL   carrot
       'Every X of carrots is smaller than one carrot.'

(94) a. *Mei   yi   {dui/*pian} luobo da-yu   yi   gen* carrot.
       each one CL/CL   carrot big-than one CL   luobo
       'Every pile of carrots is bigger than one carrot.'

    b. *Mei   yi   {*dui/pian} luobo xiao-yu   yi   gen   luobo.*
       each one CL/CL   carrot small-than one CL   carrot
       'Every slice of carrots is smaller than one carrot.'

So far, we have discussed four types of CLs: individuating, individual, collective, and partitive CLs. Generally speaking, the same form of a unit word can belong to different types, depending on the type of the associated noun, and the function of the unit in the context. In (87a), the CL *dui* occurs with the mass noun *tu* 'earth', and it is thus an individuating CL. However, in (89a), *dui* occurs with the non-mass noun *luobo* 'carrot', and it is a collective CL. Similarly, when the CL *pian* occurs with different kinds of non-mass nouns, it may play different roles. When it occurs with *luobo* 'carrot' in (90), it denotes a part of a carrot and thus it is a partitive CL. When it occurs with *qiche* 'car', as in (95a) below, it is a collective CL. When it occurs with *shuye* 'leaf', as in (95b), it represents the natural unit of a leaf, and therefore it is an individual CL. Moreover, if the CL *pian* occurs with the mass noun *mutou* 'wood', as in (95c), it is an individuating CL. The two examples of the CL *duo* in (78) and the two examples of the CL *ceng* in (97) also show the ambiguity of the CLs.

(95) a. *Shan-jiao-xia ting-zhe yi pian qiche.* [Collective CL]
          hill-foot-below park-DUR one CL   car
          'At the foot of the hill was a group of cars.'
      b. *san   pian shuye*   [Individual CL]
          three CL   leaf
          'three leaves'
      c. *san   pian mutou*   [Individuating CL]
          three CL   wood
          'three pieces of wood'

(96) a. *san   duo   hua*   [Individual CL]
          three CL   flower
          'three flowers'
      b. *san   duo   yun*   [Individuating CL]
          three CL   cloud
          'three pieces of cloud'

(97) a. *Na   san   ceng lou, deng dou huai-le.* [Partitive CL]
          DEM three CL   floor light all broken-PRF
          'Those three floors of the building, their lights are all broken.'
      b. *Di-shang   xia-le   yi   ceng xue.*   [Individuating]
          ground-on fall-PRF one CL   snow
          'There is a layer of snow on the ground.'

In English, unit words may also be ambiguous. The unit word *piece* is an individuating CL in (98a), but a partitive CL in (98b) (see Lehrer 1986: 115). Moreover, the unit word *heap* is an individuating CL in (99a), but a collective CL in (99b).

(98) a. *two pieces of paper*   b. *two pieces of celery*

(99) a. *three heaps of sand*   b. *three heaps of books*

2.4.4. Unit words that occur with [±Delimitable]

Kind CLs occur with either [+Delimitable] or [−Delimitable] nouns. Standard and container measures occur with either [+Delimitable] nouns or material type [−Delimitable] nouns, but reject nouns denoting immaterial

notions (see (19) and (20)).[18] So in general, these three types of unit words
are not sensitive to the contrast between [+Delimitable] and [−Delimitable].
In the following data, the nouns in the a-examples are [+Delimitable] and
those in the b-examples are [−Delimitable].

(100) a. *shi zhong luobo*
     ten kind carrot
     'ten types of carrots'

    b. *shi zhong mianfen* [Kind CL]
     ten kind flour
     'ten types of flour'

(101) a. *shi jin luobo*
     ten catty carrot
     'ten catties of carrots'

    b. *shi jin mianfen* [Standard M.]
     ten catty flour
     'ten catties of flour'

(102) a. *shi bao luobo*
     ten bag carrot
     'ten bags of carrots'

    b. *shi bao mianfen* [Container M.]
     ten bag flour
     'ten bags of flour'

When standard and container measures occur with [+Delimitable]
nouns, they do not have to represent the natural units of the elements encoded by the nouns. For instance, *shi gongjin luobo* 'ten kilos of carrots'
can be more or less than ten carrots, and it can also be the weight of ten
carrots coincidentally. If each carrot is exactly one kilo, ten kilos of carrots
correspond to ten carrots. In this special case, the standard measure *gongjin*
'kilo' happens to denote the natural unit of carrots. Moreover, if each kilo
of carrots consists of multiple carrots in the discourse context, the standard
measure unit happens to get the same interpretation as a collective CL; and

---

18. Standard measures should also include units for measuring time (e.g., *yue*
'month'), money (e.g., *yuan*), and electricity (e.g., *wa* 'watt') (Cheng 1973: 286).

   The words *nian* 'year', *yue* 'month', *ri* 'day', and *xiaoshi* 'hour' may be
ambiguous between unit words and regular nouns (T'sou 1976: 1239; Tang
2005: 457). When they follow a CL, as in (i), they are nouns; but when they
follow a numeral immediately, as in (ii), as pointed out by T'sou (*ibid.*) and Li
& Thompson (1981: 105), they occur in the position of a unit word. In this
case, either the noun *shijian* 'time' is silent (Cinque 2011: 3), or the measure
word moves from N to the position of an individual CL.

(i) *san ge xiaoshi*
   three CL hour
   'three hours'

(ii) *san xiaoshi*
   three hour
   'three hours'

It seems that different words that measure time undergo different stages of
grammaticalization. Their Japanese counterparts also behave differently in this
respect (Watanabe 2012, 2013).

if each kilo corresponds to less than one carrot in the context, the standard unit happens to get the same interpretation as a partitive CL. The same is true of container measures. For instance, *san xiang dian-shan* 'three box electric-fan' may mean either three boxes of fans and each box contains several fans, or three boxes and each contains one fan. In the latter reading, the container measure *xiang* happens to denote the natural unit of fans. So the functions of a container measure may also overlap with those of other unit words. Since measure words do not impose selectional restrictions on the delimitability of nouns, but individual CLs do, it is not surprising that the former may have functional overlap with the latter.

Note that when the kind CL *zhong* occurs with a noun that does not refer to an animal or plant, it denotes a unit of sort, rather than species. *Zhong* may also occur with abstract nouns, as seen (103).

(103) a. *Yani you   san   zhong xin-tai.*
　　　　 Yani have three CL   mind-state
　　　　 'Yani has three kinds of mind.'
　　　b. *Yani you   san   zhong xinnian.*
　　　　 Yani have three CL   belief
　　　　 'Yani has three beliefs.'

In addition to standard and container measures, there are also ad hoc measures, which are defined in the contexts, and are transformable into standard or container measures. One such measure is *pi* 'batch'. For instance, (104a) may refer to 5 tons in one context, but 24 cars in another context. The same is true of (104b). Like other measures, ad hoc measures do not impose occurrence restrictions on the value of Delimitability of the noun. In (104a), *liangshi* 'food' is [–Delimitable], but in (104b), *shu-bao* 'schoolbag' is [+Delimitable]. I will not discuss this kind of unit words any further in this book.

(104) a. *yi   pi   liangshi*　　　　b. *yi   pi   shubao*
　　　　 one batch food　　　　　　　 one batch schoolbag
　　　　 'one batch of food'　　　　　　 'one batch of schoolbags'

The classification of various unit words is summarized in (105):

(105) UNIT WORD　　　　　　　　　　　　　　　N

　　　Individuating CLs　　　　　　　　　　　　 [–Delimitable]
　　　Collective/Partitive/Individual CLs　　　　 [+Delimitable]
　　　Kind CLs/Container measures/Standard measures　 [±Delimitable]

In numeral expressions, different types of unit words are contrastive. In (106) and (107), except (106b), the nouns are the same, *xigua* 'watermelon', and the numerals are also the same, *san* 'three', but the examples do not mean the same. Three units of x can mean different quantities of x, depending on what the unit is.

(106) a. *san   ke   xigua*   [Individual CL]
          three CL watermelon
          'three watermelons'

    b. *san   di   xigua-zhi*   [Individuating CL]
          three CL watermelon-juice
          'three drops of watermelon juice'

    c. *san   dui   xigua*   [Collective CL]
          three CL   watermelon
          'three piles of watermelons'

    d. *san   pian   xigua*   [Partitive CL]
          three CL   watermelon
          'three slices of watermelons'

    e. *san   zhong xigua*   [Kind CL]
          three CL   watermelon
          'three kinds of watermelons'

(107) a. *san   gongjin xigua*   [Standard Measure]
          three kilo   watermelon
          'three kilos of watermelons'

    b. *san   xiang xigua*   [Container Measure]
          three box   watermelon
          'three boxes of watermelons'

2.4.5. The CL *ge*

The CL *ge* in Mandarin Chinese is special. In many situations, when it occurs, it can be replaced with another CL. In the three examples in (108), *ge* and another individual CL are both possible; in (109a) *ge* and the kind CL *zhong* are both possible (the CL *zhong* in the two examples in (103) can also alternate with *ge*), and in (109b) and (109c) *ge* may alternate with the individuating CLs *dian* and *tiao*, respectively.

(108) a. *san   {ge/ke}   xigua*   b. *san   {ge/tiao} jianyi*
       three CL/CL   watermelon   three CL/CL   suggestion
       'three watermelons'   'three suggestions'

   c. *san*   {*ge/chang*} *shigu*
      three   CL/CL   accident
      'three accidents'

(109) a. *Mei ge cunzi   dou faxian-le zhe   liang {ge/zhong} bingdu.*
         every CL village all find-PRF DEM wo   CL/CL   virus
         'These two kinds of virus have been found in every village.'
    b. *Ni   zheyang zuo you   san   {ge/dian} haochu.*
       you so   do have three CL/CL   benefit
       'Your so doing has three benefits.'
    c. *san   {ge/tiao} xinxi*
       three CL/CL   information
       'three pieces of information'

However, the alternation is not always possible. For instance, the individual CLs in (110) and the kind CLs in (111) may not be replaced with *ge*, without changing either the acceptability or the intended meanings (see Loke 1994).

(110) a. *san   zhi bi*   b. *san   tiao daolu*
         three CL pen   three CL road
         'three pens'   'three roads'

(111) a. *san   zhong shu*   b. *san   zhong xiaohua*
         three kind book   three kind joke
         'three kinds of books'   'three kinds of jokes'
    c. *san   kuan maozi*
       three style hat
       'three styles of hats'

Moreover, between *ge* and an individuating CL that occurs with a concrete noun, no alternation in either direction is possible. The individuating CLs in the three examples in (112a, b, c) may not be replaced by *ge*, as shown in (112d). (112d) also shows that other non-abstract mass nouns may not combine with *ge*, either. Thus Chao's (1968: 508–509) generalization that "[M]ass nouns do not take the individual classifier g" (sic) is right for non-abstract mass nouns.[19]

---

(112) a. *san   di   you*　　　　b. *san   zhang zhi*
　　　　three CL oil　　　　　　three CL　 paper
　　　　'three drops of oil'　　　　'three pieces of paper'

　　　c. *san   gu   zheng-qi*
　　　　three CL steam-air
　　　　'three puffs of steam'

　　　d. **san   ge   {you/zhi/zheng-qi/xie/rou/bu/qian/yanlei}*
　　　　　three CL oil/paper/steam-air/blood/meat/cloth/money/tear

The difference in the replacement possibility can be explained by the gradient grammaticalization of CLs. Historically speaking, *ge* emerged quite late (Wang 1989; see our Section 2.6.3.4). If a CL is still in a low stage of grammaticalization, it cannot be replaced by *ge*, as seen in (110), (111), and (112). But when *ge* is found, it is possible that another CL is still in use, and thus the two CLs are both available, as seen in (108) and (109). With the progress of grammaticalization, especially in the northern dialect of Mandarin, *ge* is found to occur with more and more nouns. When *ge* is found in the position of an individual CL, the noun can have various semantics (e.g., *ren* 'person', *guojia* 'country', *xigua* 'watermelon', *taiyang* 'sun'), as pointed out by Myers (2000). Thus, *ge* has no semantic sorting function at all. It has become the most frequently used CL. Many nouns, especially abstract nouns, nouns denoting new concepts, and nouns denoting the results of certain acts, such as those in (113), occur with *ge* only. Myers calls *ge* a default CL.

(i) a. *Akiu   pao-le *(ge) kuai.*　　　b. *Akiu   xiao *(ge) bu-ting.*
　　　Akiu   run-PRF GE fast　　　　　Akiu laugh GE not-stop
　　　'Akiu ran fast.'　　　　　　　　　'Akiu laughed endlessly.'

No other CL occurs in such contexts. Lü (1983: 131) claims that in certain cases, *ge* is used for prosodic reasons (cf. W. Zhang 1991: 266). Liu (2006: 41) assumes that *ge* in data like (i) heads a subordinate clause. Q. Zhang (2009) analyzes such a use of *ge* as a degree word, and Shu (2012) treats it as a mood/ aspect marker. In (ii), *ge* rejects a numeral (Q. Zhang's 2009 event CL). In (iii), *ge* precedes a proper name (Lü [1944] 1990: 159; Cheng & Sybesma 1999: 523; Chen 2003: 1172). *Ge* can also precede pronoun (Cheng & Sybesma 1999: 538).

(ii) *Wo he (*yi) ge shui jiu lai.*　　(iii) *Na *(ge) Hufei zhen bu xianghua.*
　　1SG drink one GE water then come　　DEM CL Hufei truly not decent
　　'I'll come after I drink some water.'　　'That Hufei is really unreasonable.'

However, examples like (iii) may show that the uses of pronouns and proper names have the syntax of common nouns (Ōta 2003: 75; X. Zhang 2008: 413; De Clercq 2008; cf. Geurts 1997).

(113) a. *Ta   da-le   san   ge {ge/penti/haqian}.*
     3SG   do-PRF   three CL hiccup/sneeze/yawn
     'He made three {hiccups/sneezes/yawns}.'
   b. *Ta   fang-le   san   ge pi.*
     3SG   emit-PRF three CL fart
     'He emitted three farts.'

One issue that needs to be clarified is the following. It has been assumed that individual CLs typically mark the first mention of a new item; they occur with indefinite nouns and the CL *ge* may take another CL as an antecedent (Erbaugh 1986: 408; Aikhenvald 2003: 324, 328). The example in (114a) is used to illustrate this. However, if we exchange the positions of the two CLs in the example, as in (114b), the meaning is the same. Our (114c) is another example in which it is the CL *ge* that occurs first, and another CL occurs later in describing the same entity.

(114) a. *Cong   neibian guolai yi   ge xiaohaizi,   uh ... qi,   qi,*
     from   there   come one CL child   uh   ride ride
     qi-zhe   yi   liang jiaotache uh shi yi   ge   hen ke'ai
     ride-DUR one CL   bike   uh be one CL very cute
     de xiao de jiaotache.
     DE little DE bike
   b. *..., qi-zhe yi   ge jiaotache, shi yi   liang hen*
     ride-DUR one CL bike   be   one CL   very
     ke'ai de xiao de jiaotache.
     cute   DE little DE bike
     Both: 'From there comes a child, riding a bike, (it) is a very cute little bike.'
   c. *Yuanyuan de   lai-le   yi   ge ren,   yuanlai shi*
     far   DE   come-PRF one CL person in.fact be
     yi   wei lao jiaoshou.
     one CL old professor
     'A person came from far away. It was in fact an old professor.'

2.4.6. Unit words as unique Numerability bearers in Chinese

All unit words may combine with a numeral directly. Therefore all unit words have the feature [+Numerable], and thus countable. As stated in Grimshaw (2007: 204 fn. 6), unit words in English can never be mass nouns. For instance, Chierchia (2010: 103) claims that in (115), the unit word *quantities* is countable, and thus the whole NP *quantities of water* is countable, although *water* is not countable. In my analysis, *quantities* bears [+Numerable] in the example.

(115) *I am going to spill three quantities of water on your floor.*

Since no noun in Chinese has the feature [+Numerable] and all unit words have the feature, the latter are the unique Numerability bearer in numeral expressions of the language. We can see that Numerability does not have to be anchored to lexical or root elements. The analytical realization of Numerability is parallel to the situation that tense information can be realized by either verbs or auxiliaries in English. Formal features in general can be distributed over various types of elements.

2.4.7. Delimitability of unit words

In the previous subsections, we showed that unit words may have different co-occurrence restrictions with the nouns following them, but they are also different with respect to whether they themselves are able to be modified by a delimitive modifier. Modifiers of unit words vary cross-linguistically. I discuss delimitive modifiers of unit words in Mandarin Chinese only.

Kind CLs may not be modified by any delimitive modifier (the same constraint is seen in other CL languages; see Bisang 1993: 47 fn. 6):

(116) a. *san   zhong qianbi*
          three kind pencil
          'three kinds of pencil'
    b. **san {chang/da/zheng} zhong qianbi*
          three long/big/whole   kind pencil

Standard measures may not be modified by shape and size modifiers (Liu 1980: 10; cf. Lu 1987: fn. 3), but they can be modified by boundary modifiers:[20]

---

20. In expressions such as *yi zheng-nian* 'one whole year', *yi zheng-yue* 'one whole month', the last morpheme can be a unit word, which is followed by a deleted *shijian* 'time' or a null noun meaning time (see footnote 18).

(117) a. *san   sheng you*   b. **san {chang/da} sheng you*
      three liter   oil   three long/big   liter   oil
      'three liters of oil'

   c. *san   zheng dun you*   d. *san   zheng bang   yingtao*
      three whole ton   oil   three whole pound   cherry
      'three whole tons of oil'   'three whole pounds of cherries'

Note that the adjectives *da* 'big' and *xiao* 'small' may mean 'significant' and 'insignificant', respectively (see the discussion of (26) above). Such readings are not delimitive readings, and thus the two adjectives in these readings may modify abstract nouns (cf. English *big idea, big chance*), abstract units, as in (118a, b), and standard measures, as in (118c):

(118) a. *si   da bi jiaoyi*   b. *si   xiao tiao jianyi*
      four big CL transaction   four small CL   suggestion
      'four significant transactions'   'four minor suggestions'

   c. *Ta   zuzu   chi-le   liang da jin   putao!*
      3SG as-much-as eat-PRF   two   big catty   grape
      'He ate as much as two big catties of grapes.'

All other types of unit words may be modified by a shape or size adjective in Chinese (Lu 1987, Luo 1988, among others), and thus have the feature [+Delimitable] (Note that Cheng & Sybesma 1998: 390 claim that individual CLs may not be modified and only the numeral *yi* 'one' may be followed by an adjective; but our data in (119) show that the two restrictions assumed in their theory cannot be maintained).

(119) a. *san   chang tiao xianglian*   [Individual CL]
      three long   CL   necklace
      'three long necklaces'

   b. *san   da   di you*   [Individuating CL]
      three big CL oil
      'three big drops of oil'

   c. *san   da   pian xigua*   [Partitive CL]
      three big   CL   watermelon
      'three big slices of watermelon'

   d. *san   da   qun yang*   [Collective CL]
      three big CL sheep
      'three big flocks of sheep'

    e. *san   da xiang xianglian*   [Container Measure]
       three big box   necklace
       'three big boxes of necklaces'
    f. *san   da   ping   you*
       three big bottle oil
       'three big bottles of oil'

Individual CLs in other languages such as Thai (Hundius & Kölver 1983: 169–171), Kiriwina (Croft 1994: 150), and Hungarian (Csirmaz & Dékány 2010: e.g., (36)) may also be modified by delimitive adjectives. In non-CL languages, individuating CLs are available and they may also be modified by delimitive adjectives. For instance, although *spherical wine* is not acceptable, *a spherical drop of wine* is possible (Schwarzschild 2006: 88). CLs in Korean (Byeong Yi, p.c., Sept. 16, 2010) and Purépecha (Vázquez Rojas 2012: 121), however may not be modified. Since kind CLs may not be modified, the feature is not a defining property of CLs.

I leave to Section 6.4 the discussion of the morphological constraints on such modifications in Chinese and possible derivations of the constructions.

2.5.   Reflections on the studies of countability

2.5.1. What's new

The study of the contrast between count and mass nouns dates back to Aristotle. Developing the insights of many previous studies, I have made the following three main claims with respect to the contrast.

First, a count noun is defined exclusively by [+Numerable], i.e., the possibility to combine with a numeral directly. It has been generally recognized that such a combination possibility is the "signature" grammatical property of count nouns (e.g., Chierchia 2010: 104). I have now further claimed that this is the only defining grammatical property of a count noun. Examining the feature of nouns, we can see that in Chinese, generally speaking, no noun may combine with a numeral directly, and therefore, no noun is a count noun. Numerability is instead represented exclusively by CLs and measure words. In languages such as Yudja (Lima 2010, 2012) and Halkomelem Salish (Wilhelm 2008: 64), no individual or individuating CL exists in the language, and every noun can combine with a numeral directly. Thus every noun is a count noun. Between these two patterns, in languages such as English, Haitian Creole (Deprez 2005: 861), Karitiana

(Müller et al. 2006), and Dëne (Wilhelm 2008), in an unmarked situation (i.e., without a shift), some words are [+Numerable], and others are [–Numerable] (see Section 2.3.1). In this syntagmatic approach, the count/non-count distinction is clearly linguistic, rather than extra-linguistic. It is thus not surprising that the contrast is expressed in various ways, cross-linguistically and within the same language.

Second, the notion of mass is not the direct negation of count. Instead, it is the combination of the two syntagmatic properties: [–Numerable] and [–Delimitable]. Obviously, Numerability alone is not sufficient to distinguish between *oil*-type of nouns and *furniture*-type of nouns in English, and it does not classify nouns in either Chinese or Yudja.

It is not controversial that words such as *oil* in English and their counterparts in Chinese are mass nouns. Quine (1960: 104) notes the unacceptability of **spherical water* and **spherical wine*. Bunt (1985: 199) also points out that mass nouns such as *water* may not be modified by adjectives such as *large*. Krifka (2008: Sec. 1) states that mass nouns such as *water, milk,* and *gold* denote liquids and substances that do not have defined boundaries. Our feature [–Delimitable] captures their insight, showing the similarity between *oil* in English and *you* 'oil' in Chinese. We are then also able to distinguish the *you*-type of nouns from *zhuozi* 'table' type of nouns in Chinese.

On the other hand, it is obvious that count nouns such as *belief* also reject *spherical*. *Water* may not combine with a numeral, but *belief* may. The two types of words are the same with respect to the combination with *spherical,* but different with respect to the combination with a numeral. Our refined feature analysis represents their relations more precisely: *water* is [–Numerable, –Delimitable], but *belief* is [+Numerable, –Delimitable]. The contrast correlates with the contrast that the former can occur with a standard or container measure word, whereas the latter cannot.

Importantly, our refined feature analysis makes it possible to precisely identify the nature of one more type of elements, those that may not combine with a numeral directly but allow a delimitive adjective, e.g., *furniture* or *luggage* in English and *qiqiu* 'balloon' in Chinese.

In English, *luggage*-type words do not denote massive objects, although like *oil*, they may not combine with a numeral directly. As Chierchia (2010: 144) put it, "we know right off the bat that *furniture* cannot be treated on a par with *water*." Such words have been called "count mass nouns" in Doetjes (1996: 44, 2010: 44), "object mass nouns" in Barner & Snedeker (2005), Bale & Barner (2009: 229; 2012), "fake mass nouns" in Chierchia (2010: 110), "naturally atomic mass" elements in Rothstein (2010b: 403), and "collectives" in Wiese (2012). Doetjes (1996: 34) uses the term "count mass nouns" for the words which are semantically count but behave like a mass noun syntactically.

McCawley (1975: 170) finds that words like *furniture* and *footwear*, which have been treated as "mass" nouns, admit size modification "much more readily than hard-core mass nouns such as *rice*". The acceptability of examples such as *'There is small furniture in the doll's house'* is also mentioned in Bunt (1985, 200 & 207ff). In Ojeda (2005: 404), "modification in terms of size and shape" is mentioned as one of the "well-known differences between count and mass nouns". In Svenonius (2008), to capture the incompatibility between delimitive adjectives and mass nouns, such adjectives are assumed to be in the Specifier of SortP, which is the locus of count nominals, rather than mass ones. The generally recognized special properties of the *furniture*-type of nouns are represented by [–Numerable, +Delimitable] in our analysis.

The similarity between such words and the Chinese counterparts of English count nouns has been discussed in Doetjes (1996: 35), Portner (2005: 98), Krifka (2008: Sec. 6.5), Chierchia (2010: 111, fn. 12), Bale & Barner (2012: 245), Cowper & Hall (2012: 34), Wiese (2012), among others. Although it has been widely believed that all nouns are mass nouns in Chinese, the difference between English mass nouns and Chinese non-mass nouns, with respect to Delimitability, has been stated in Gil (2008: 8). He finds that unlike the former, the latter can be modified by "size and shape adjectives". Explicitly, he states:

> … whereas in English, constructions such as *big water* are bizarre, in Mandarin, constructions such as *da pingguo* 'big apple' are syntactically well-formed, and understood in the same way as their English counterparts.

In my analysis, both *furniture* and *pingguo* 'apple' are [–Numerable, +Delimitable]. Therefore, *da pingguo* 'big apple' is as natural as *big furniture*. Consequently, CL languages like Chinese are able to distinguish mass and non-mass nouns. Our identification of the location of [+Numerable] in CLs rather than in nouns for CL languages is more precise than the vague statement that such languages do not have count syntax.

In English, [+Delimitable] nouns are divided into two groups: the [+Numerable] group and the [–Numerable] group (*fly* vs. *furniture*). The latter group has no plural marker and shares quantifiers with mass nouns (*little, much*). In Purépecha (Vázquez Rojas 2012), [+Delimitable] nouns are also divided into two groups (*tíndi* 'fly' vs. *shaníni* 'corncob'). But both groups are [+Numerable], and both groups occur with the same type of quantifiers that are different from those for mass nouns. The two groups are different in that, first, plural markers are obligatory for the fly-group, but optional for the corncob-group (mass nouns of the language may not have plural markers); and second, CLs may not occur in a numeral construction for the fly-group, but optionally appear for the corncob-group (mass nouns of the language may not occur with a CL). We can see that formal properties are grouped differently in different languages. In English, words of the *furniture*-group are typically derived through a small set of affixes, such as -*ware*, -*wear*, -*age*, -*ing*, -*(er)y* (*silverware, kitchenware, footwear, sportswear, baggage, coverage, bedding, lighting, jewellery, stationery*; see Cohen & Zribi-Hertz 2012). The morphological properties are language-specific. There is no universal semantics for how [+Delimitable] nouns are divided into sub-types. But the feature Delimitability is identifiable in all languages.

The close interaction between the traditional notion countability and our notion Delimitability has long been recognized in the literature, but the nature of the relation has not been clarified. Jespersen (1924: 198) makes the following statement:

> There are a great many words which do not call up the idea of some definite thing with a certain shape or precise limits. I call these "mass-words"; they may be either material, in which case they denote some substance in itself independent of form, such as *silver, quicksilver, water, butter, gas, air*, etc., or else immaterial, such as *leisure, music, traffic, success, tact, commonsense*

The most recent and thorough discussion of the relation between the count-mass contrast and size adjectives is de Belder (2011b). Her discussion does not cover other delimitive modifiers such as *thick, thin, round, complete*, though (according to Rijkhoff 1999: 249, shape features seem to be even more reliable than size features for Delimitability; unlike size adjectives, shape adjectives do not have non-delimitive uses, see (26)). Crucially, she claims that "if something acquires the [Size] feature, it automatically becomes countable." (p. 183) So in her analysis, size features entail the count status. This is different from my analysis, which gives an equal status to Numerability and Delimitability: neither entails the other, and thus there are four possibilities. One empirical consequence of her analysis is that it is not able to capture the fact that non-count nouns such as *furniture* may have size features. This kind of noun is predicted to be "illicit" in her theory (de Belder 2011a: 83 (34); 2011b: 180), contrary to the fact. We also see that count nouns such as *belief* reject a size feature.

The proposed two features, Numerability and Delimitability, are both related to the traditional notion of countability. This is parallel to our understanding that tense and aspect features are different, but they are both related to the temporal information encoded by linguistic elements.

Third, Numerability, which is one of the two features for the mass-count contrast, is different from morphological number, as shown in Section 2.2.6. I will say more about this issue in Section 2.5.3.

In Sections 2.5.2 through 2.5.5, I will discuss some alternates to identify the count-mass contrast: the semantic approach, the morphological approach, the multiple-criteria approach, and some other non-binary analyses.

2.5.2. The semantic approach to countability

In a purely semantic approach, only nouns that denote elements that show natural atomicity are analyzed as count nouns. Whorf (1956 [1941]: 140) states that "[I]ndividual nouns denote bodies with definite outlines: 'a tree, a stick, a man, a hill.' Mass nouns denote homogeneous continuance without implied boundaries". Quine (1960), Goodman (1966), Cheng (1973), McCawley (1979 [1975]), Wierzbicka (1985), among others (see Joosten 2003 for a survey) all try to approach the count-mass contrast semantically. For a brief review of the semantic studies on the issue, from the perspectives of cumulativeness, divisiveness, to the homogeneousness of the referent, see Doetjes (2012: Section 2.1). Recently, the atomicity approach is defended in Wilhelm (2008). The semantic criteria are also taken for granted in works such as de Belder (2011a: 73). However, Rothstein's (2010a: 14) following statement clearly tells us why this approach is inadequate:

> inherent, or natural, atomicity is neither a necessary nor a sufficient criterion
> for count noun predicates, and homogeneity v. non-homogeneity cannot be
> at the root of the mass/count distinction. *Furniture* is mass but naturally
> atomic and non-homogeneous since it denotes sets of individual units and
> *fence* is count but homogeneous and not naturally atomic. This means that a
> theory of count nouns cannot rely on presuppositions of atomicity. [sic.]

In addition to *fence*, nouns such as *segment* and *line* are also count but denote homogeneous entities, like mass nouns (Aquaviva 2010: 4). Moreover, the denotation of collective nouns such as *family* is similar to that of mass nouns. "When a family is expanded (as when, for instance children are born into the family) you still have a (one) family, that is, adding members to a family gives you a bigger family but not more families (cf. the example with portions of water above). Similarly, when a family member dies, the others are still family. Thus, both mass nouns and collective nouns define homogeneous entities." (Rijkhoff 1999: 232) But collective nouns are count nouns.

As pointed out by Rothstein (2010a: 19), "the mass/count distinction can only be explained in terms of how the expressions refer, and not in terms of the things they refer to. This means it is a grammatical and not an ontological distinction." Doetjes (2010: 10) also points out that "meaning does not determine whether a noun is mass or count in an unambiguous way" (a similar idea can be seen in Chierchia 2010: 103). The problems of semantic approaches are also discussed in Bale & Barner (2009: 230). As frequently noted in the literature, the same type of notions can be expressed by both count and non-count words in the same language, and by count words in one language but non-count ones in another language. Some well-known examples can be found in McCawley (1975: 165). The first two pairs in (120) are cited from Kiss (2010) and the rest are from Chierchia (2010: 101, 110).

(120)		COUNT	NON-COUNT	
	a.	*vegetable*	*fruit*	
	b.	*Obst*	*Gemüse*	[German]
		fruit	vegetable	
	c.	*mobile/mobili*	*mobilia*	[Italian]
		furniture.SG/furniture.PL	furniture	
	d.	*virtue*	*beauty*	
	e.	*belief*	*knowledge*	
	f.	*jump*	*jumping* (see (12))	

Theoretically, our approach defines grammatical notions in a system syntagmatically. Instead of stipulating various semantic features for nouns directly, such as [+/–Shape] (Rijkhoff 2002: 51), [+/–Concrete] (Muromatsu 2003), [+/–Size] (de Belder 2011b), or [+/–Individuated] (Bobyleva 2011: 58), we examine the compatibility of different types of elements in the same constructions. Linguistic categories are defined by the relations of elements in the language system, rather than by the properties of the denoted referents. The latter approach fails to account for cross-linguistic variations (see Sections 2.5.5.2 and 2.5.5.3 for our further comments on Rijkhoff 2002 and Muromatsu 2003).

In Wilhelm's (2008: 64) semantic approach, examples like *furniture* are treated as semantics-syntax mismatches. Since all non-mass nouns in Chinese behave like *furniture*, as recognized by many scholars, one would claim that Chinese is a typically mismatched language. However, as correctly pointed out by Wiese (2012), nouns like *furniture* are a general, systematic option for nouns, rather than an idiosyncratic phenomenon. Chierchia (2010: 103) points out that "the existence of the mass/count distinction in grammar is neither a logical nor, perhaps, a communicative necessity." "Language, viewed as specifically human aggregate of cognitive capacities, must have developed an autonomous apparatus responsible for the mass/count system." In this book, we have identified two linguistic features of the apparatus, and therefore, the system of the count-mass contrast becomes less vague now (for more arguments against the purely semantic approach and arguments against Chierchia's 2010 vague approach to countability, see Gillon 2012).

2.5.3. The morphological approach to countability

A purely morphological approach to the count-mass contrast would assume that count nouns are identified by their number markers, but mass nouns are signaled by the rejection of a number marker. Such an approach has been found in Link (1983: 306), Doetjet (1996, 1997), Chierchia (1998), among others. However, we have extensively discussed the differences between the count status and number in Section 2.2.6.

There are at least four problems in a number marking approach to the count-mass contrast. First, the expectation of a "count" noun fails when we consider the so-called mass plural, seen in Section 2.2.6. Such plural nouns remain to be mass nouns, since they reject delimitive modifiers (e.g., *the (*big) waters of the Nile*). More examples of mass plurals are listed in (121) (Acquaviva 2010: 3, 8; Acquaviva & Panagiotidis 2012: 12; see Ojeda 2005 for similar examples in Bantu languages), where the occurrence of the plural marker leads to a possible mass reading, instead of the expected count reading.

(121)   COUNT   MASS
    a. *brain*   *brains*
    b. *fund*   *funds*

c. *ksilo*   *ksila*   [Modern Greek]
   wood.SG   wood.PL
   'piece of wood' 'wood'

d.   *nera* (cf. *nero* 'water')   [Cypriot Greek]
                     water.PL
                     'heavy rain'

Huddleston & Pullum (2002: 343) state that *bushes* and *mountains* in *We should plant a few bushes* and *She climbed two mountains in one day* are regular count plurals; but "they have <u>non-count</u> interpretations in examples like [33]:" (their [33] = (122) below)

(122) a. *He threw it in the bushes.*   b. *She lives in the mountains.*

Corbett (2000: 173) reports that "in Manam (Lichtenberk 1983: 269) *all* mass nouns are plural, (as marking on the verb shows). In Turkana, some are singular and some are plural (Dimmendall 1983: 224). In Bantu languages too, mass nouns are frequently split between singular and plural (Guthrie 1948: 851)." Similarly, both mass and non-mass nouns can occur with the plural clitic *mga* in Tagalog (Corbett 2000: 133–134). In languages such as St'át'imcets, all nouns, including those referring to snow, honey, and water, may freely take plural determiners. Davis & Matthewson (1999: 60) report that "nouns whose English counterparts are mass may freely take plural determiners in St'át'imcets."

As clearly stated in Mathieu (2012a: 189), mass plural is "one of several plurals (plural of modesty, exaggerative plural, hyperbolic plural, approximative plural, anti-associative plural, etc.) that has nothing to do with counting individuals." See Harbour (2008) for a formal analysis of mass plurals.

Second, the expectation of a "mass" noun fails, when we consider the bare nouns in certain PPs and VPs, introduced in Section 2.2.6. For instance, the noun *prison* in the PP *in prison* neither has a plural form nor is it preceded by any article. The absence of a number marker does not lead to a mass reading. The nouns in such constructions denote either one or more than one atom.

Third, plurality that is not for counting is seen in Acquaviva's (2010: 2) following examples (I thank Jonathan Evans for providing me with more examples of this kind):

(123) a. *I saw you in my dreams* ≠ *several different dreams*
      b. *a house in the woods* ≠ *in several different woods*
      c. *I have plans for tonight* ≠ *I have a few plans for tonight*

A count noun is always compatible with a counting context. The existence of non-counting plural does not support the correlation between plural-marking and count status.

Considering both the first and the third point above, what we see is that plural marking is not only "not interpreted uniformly across languages" (Bale & Khanjian 2008: 86), but also not interpreted uniformly in the same language such as English.

Fourth, mutual exclusiveness between a numeral and a plural marker is observed in certain constructions and certain languages (see the Hungarian examples in (60) before and more in Section 4.2.5). If the possibility to occur with a numeral is the signature property of a count noun (Chierchia 1998: 353), the conflict indicates that plural markers cannot be a reliable signal for count nouns.

Realizing the complexity of plural markers, scholars have used different terms to cover the patterns unpredicted by the morphological approach. Doetjet (2010: 45) calls the plurals in *oats* and *grits*, which may not occur with a numeral, defective plural, and finds that they often correspond to mass nouns in other languages. Some researchers treat such plurals as idiosyncratic ones and still keep number marking as an effective way to distinguish count from mass nouns (e.g., de Belder 2011a: 72; 205). Some other researchers (e.g., Harbour 2008) distinguish morphological number from semantic number. Krifka (2008) distinguishes semantic plurals and agreement plurals. As stated in Wilhelm (2008: 47, also see 57), "number marking is not a necessary property of count nouns" (also see Wiese 2012: 74 for the same conclusion).

Semantically, singular count nouns such as *scarf* refer to entities taken individually, and plural count nouns such as *scarfs* refer to entities taken in bulk. In addition to these two types of nouns, Ojeda (2005) uses the term *cosingular* to refer to mass plurals such as *clothes* (see Section 2.2.6) and the term *coplural* to refer to mass nouns such as *clothing*. He specifies that "cosingular nouns can refer to entities taken in bulk – but without having to refer, at the same time, to entities taken collectively" (p. 390), whereas "coplural nouns will be able to refer to entities taken in bulk, but without having to refer, at the same time, to entities taken individually" (p. 391). We can see that the new terms are invented to regulate the arbitrariness of the mapping between morphological forms and the encoded meanings. However, arbitrary mapping between form and meaning is seen beyond number morphology. It is well-known that the German noun *Mädchen* 'girl' is neuter instead of feminine, although its referent is female. We might need terms such as "cofeminine" or "comasculine" to cover this mismatch. Adding new terms shows that plural forms may encode different things. Similar "non-count plurals" in Arabic are discussed in Acquaviva (2008: 229). The existence of such "non-count plurals" challenges the claim that plural markers are markers of count nouns.

There are three ways to encode quantity: quantifiers such as *much* and *less*, cardinality, and the singular-plural contrast (Rijkhoff 2012: 5). The contrast between count and non-count (i.e., the contrastive values of Numerability) is related to the way of representing cardinality only. See the next two chapters for a discussion of quantifiers and the singular-plural contrast in Mandarin Chinese. In Chapter 6, I will argue that each of the three ways is represented by a functional projection: QuantP, UnitP, and NumP.

2.5.4. The multi-criteria approach to countability

The multi-criteria approach (Allan 1980) puts various considerations together, including the possibility to occur with a numeral, semantic and morphological factors, and ranks the degree of countability for each noun. This approach is adopted in Joosten (2003) and Kuo & Wu (2010). However, I have shown that semantic and morphological approaches to the count-mass contrast are both problematic. Then, logically, if some of the individual factors are problematic, putting them together does not help.

Moreover, since some linguistic phenomena are not observed in certain languages, in order to measure the countability of words in different languages, different criteria are used in this approach. For instance, in Kuo & Wu (2010), in order to judge the countability of a noun, articles and plural markers are used for English, but individual CLs are used for Chinese. This inconsistency is not desirable, unless the relations among the criteria are clarified.[21]

2.5.5. Other non-binary analyses of countability

The idea that the count-mass contrast is not a dichotomous contrast and that we need more features to represent them is also seen in the literature. As I mentioned above, de Belder (2011a,b) proposes that the feature [Size] should

---

21. Other problems in Kuo & Wu (2010) include the claim that container measures are more countable than standard measures, and the absence of individuating CLs in their analysis of Chinese CLs. Neither is justified.

be considered. I have already compared her analysis with ours in Section 2.5.1. In this section, I briefly address the inadequacies of certain other non-binary analyses of countability.

2.5.5.1. T'sou's (1976) [Entity] and [Exact]

T'sou (1976) uses different values of the feature [Exact] to represent whether a numeral expression denotes an exact quantity, and uses different values of the feature [Entity] to represent whether the nominal denotes discrete physical entities. He claims that "the semantic distinctions of such a system are supported as well by evidence from syntax." His three pieces of syntactic evidence in Mandarin Chinese are the co-occurrence restrictions of a unit word with other three elements: ordinal number, fractional number, and the functional particle *de* (his *de*-adjectival). I have some doubts about this analysis. First, the effect of universal grinder is not distinguished from the unshifted cases. The word *ji* 'chicken' is used as a representative noun to make his analysis, but it refers to either animals or chicken meat in his analysis. One sees both *di san zhi ji* 'the third chicken' and *ban jin ji* 'half catty of chicken' in his examples (p. 1217). As we saw in Section 2.2.5, the two uses of *ji* 'chicken' are different with respect to Delimitability. Second, although a kind CL may not occur with a fractional number (**ban zhong ji* lit. 'half kind chicken'), an individuating CL may not do so, either (**ban tan shui* lit. 'half puddle water'). T'sou does not separate individuating CLs from individual CLs, and therefore the properties of the former is not discussed. Third, the *de* argument is not reliable, since all unit words can be followed by *de* in an appropirate context (see Section 2.6.4).

T'sou also applies his classification of unit words directly to nouns. In his system, mass nouns such as *water* are [αEntity, −αExact], "to capture the fact that the values of its feature specification will be opposite. This will account for *three cans of water* [+Entity, −Exact], *three gallons of water* [−Entity, +Exact] and **three pieces of water* [+Entity, +Exact], as well as *two kinds of water* (soft and hard): [−Entity, −Exact]" (p. 1222). Note that the acceptability of the last example, which has the same value for the two features, is not predicted by his theory for mass nouns. It is thus not clear whether it is the semantics of the noun or the semantics of the whole numeral expression that is under the classification.

Abstract nouns in his system are [−Entity, −Exact], "so that they can only occur with classifiers such as *type* or *kind*". However, "[S]ince all nouns may be classified with *type* or *kind*, it may be stated as a meta rule that all nouns may be optionally specified as [–Entity, –Exact]." (p. 1222) Accordingly, "[A]n example such as *boy* will be marked [+Entity, αExact] to provide for *three boys* [+Entity, +Exact] and *three groups of boys* [+Entity, –Exact] (as well as *two kinds of boys* by the optional meta rule)." (T'sou 1976: 1222) Thus, it is not clear to me how much this feature analysis helps us to analyze the countability of nouns. Moreover, on the same page, T'sou also states that "[P]articular languages will require additional features." Since he does not mention what other features are, it is hard to evaluate his analysis, and therefore, I do not consider his analysis a plausible alternative to the proposal made in this book.

2.5.5.2. *Rijkhoff's (2002) [Shape] and [Homogeneity]*

Rijkhoff (2002) uses the positive, negative, and underspecified values of two features, [Shape] and [Homogeneity], to classify nouns with respect to countability. Although the goal of the classification is to capture syntagmatic patterns, e.g., whether the nouns in a language may combine with a numeral directly without a CL and whether they require a number marker (p. 29), the two features themselves are defined semantically (p. 50): "If the property designated by a noun is coded as having a shape (+Shape), this means that the property (and by extension, the referent of the NP) is characterized as having a definite outline in the spatial dimension"; "If the property designated by a noun is coded as being homogeneous (+Homogeneity), this means that the property (and by extension, the referent of the NP) is characterized as being agglomerative."(p. 53)

The main problems of this approach are the following. First, all nouns in Mandarin Chinese (also in other CL languages) are classified as [–Shape]. Rijkhoff explicitly claims that "as a rule the value –Shape correlates with the use of classifiers (or: individualizers), and, conversely, the value +Shape correlates with the absence of classifiers" (p. 51; also in Rijkhoff 1999: 229, 235). He claims that such an analysis of CL languages does not necessarily mean that the speakers of the languages do not know that a table in the physical world is a discrete object, but rather that this particular piece of knowledge is simply not part of the lexical semantics of the noun, instead it would be part of the encyclopedic knowledge about the referent of the NP (Rijkhoff 2002: 55 fn. 39). Although real mass nouns are classified as [–Shape, +Homogeneity], and non-mass nouns such as *zhuozi* 'table' in Mandarin Chinese are classified as [–Shape, –Homogeneity] in his system, the relation between the label [–Shape] for words like *zhuozi*, and the fact that such nouns can be modified by shape adjectives is not addressed. If the value –Shape simply correlates with the use of CLs, the term itself (= +CL) does not categorize the distinctive nature of CL languages. Second, nouns such as *idea* and *suggestion* in English may directly combine with a numeral, and thus are classified as [+Shape, –Homogeneity], but such nouns may not have a shape modifier. Although Rijkhoff (2002: 28) restricts his classification to spatial objects in the real world, the mismatch between the properties of such abstract nouns and the feature analysis indicates the limitation of the theory.

2.5.5.3. Muromatsu's (2003) 3D analysis

Muromatsu (2003) proposes that abstract, mass, and count nouns are 1-, 2-, and 3-dimensional (-D) expressions, respectively. She correctly points out that abstract nouns may not occur as the predicate of *weighs six pounds* (e.g., {*This honey*/*The peace} *weighs six pounds*) (p. 68). She further claims that either a plural marker or a CL marks a 3D noun. However, the theory is not convincing.

First, it is claimed that only count nouns may occur with plural markers, and thus if an abstract noun such as *idea* occurs with a plural marker, as in *two ideas*, it denotes a 3D notion, similar to that of *two apples* (p. 84). But neither *idea* nor *two ideas* may occur as a predicate of *weighs six pounds*.

Second, it is claimed that "A classifier works on the 2D space, individuating the mass, rendering the space three-dimensional" (p. 72), however, in Mandarin Chinese examples like the following, the CLs do not create concrete notions, and thus do not render the space three-dimensional. Specifically, neither *san ge jianyi* 'three suggestions' nor the bare *jianyi* 'suggestion' may be a predicate of *zhong liu bang* 'weighs six pounds'.

(124) a. *san   ge   jianyi*   b. *san   zhong   taidu*
       three   CL   suggestion   three   CL   attitude
       'three suggestions'   'three kinds of attitude'

Third, it is claimed that "*furniture* is conceptualized as 2D," as massive as *honey* (p. 71), however, the former may be modified by a delimitive adjective, whereas the latter may not, and thus they are different.

2.5.6. Experimental perspective

Our decomposition of the traditional notion countability into the two features, [Delimitable] and [Numerable], is supported by experimental evidence.

The contrastive values of [Delimitable] correlate with the contrast between mass and non-mass entities, a contrast independent of the notion of quantity or counting with numerals. The referents of nouns with [+Delimitable] are discrete individuals, which have non-arbitrary shape, size, or boundaries. Infant research has demonstrated that infants as young as 4 months use spatio-temporal information to identify discrete individuals, and they respond quite differently to discrete individuals and to non-solid substances (e.g., Spelke 1985; Huntley-Fenner, Carey & Solimando 2002). "There is also a developmental progression of the perceptual dimensions that infants use in object individuation: by 4.5 months infants use shape and size as the basis for object individuation; but it is not until 7.5 months that infants use pattern, and 11.5 months that they use color and luminance information to do so" (Xu 2007: 402).

The contrastive values of [Numerable] are related to the knowledge of counting with numerals. Such knowledge develops much later (e.g., Le Corre & Carey 2007). The acquisition studies in A. Huang (2009) and A. Huang & Lee (2009) report that children younger than two years did not understand the meaning of numerals. For instance, when they were asked how many eyes their aunt had, they answered three (Lee 2012: Sec. 3.1).

The identification of the two features is also supported by experimental research of noun classification. In Barner & Snedeker (2005, 2006), based on an experimental study of both children and adults, the so-called mass nouns in English are divided into object-mass nouns (*furniture, jewelry*) and substance-mass nouns (*mustard, toothpaste*). They elicited quantity judgments for different types of nouns. Their subjects were asked to compare scenes and answer "Who has more ... e.g., *silverware* (object-mass noun), *shoes* (count noun), or *toothpaste* (mass noun)?" Each scene showed one large instance of the nominal referents, e.g., a large piece of silverware (e.g., a large fork), a large shoe, or a large glob of toothpaste, and one group of several small instances, that is, several small forks, shoes, or globs of toothpaste. Although the small instances were higher in number, the larger instances made up the bigger overall amount. Regardless of whether the subjects were children or adults, they chose the higher number of objects for both count nouns and object-mass nouns, but the larger overall amount for mass nouns. Thus, object-mass nouns show "number-based judgment," patterning with count nouns, whereas the mass nouns show "quantity-based judgment". Their classification correlates with our feature analysis, as shown in (125) (although their study does not cover nouns such as *belief*, which are [–Delimitable, +Numerable]). Parallel experimental studies of Mandarin Chinese with a similar result are reported in Cheung et al. (2010, 2012) and Liu (2010), and a parallel experimental study of Japanese, also with a similar result, is reported in Inagaki & Barner (2009).

(125)

	shoes, candles	*furniture, jewelry*	*mustard, toothpaste*
Barner & Snedeker (2005, 2006)	Count nouns	object-mass noun	substance-mass noun
	Number-based judgment		Quantity-based judgment
Our analysis	[+Delimitable, +Numerable]	[+Delimitable, –Numerable]	[–Delimitable, –Numerable]

2.6.   Reflections on the studies of CLs in numeral expressions

2.6.1. The syntactic foundations of the presence of CLs

The novel analysis of the count-mass contrast proposed in this book opens a new window to see the syntactic foundations of individual CLs in numeral expressions. Counting is possible in the presence of a unit. The general function of a unit word in a numeral expression is to specify the unit for counting. Such a word is [+Numerable]. In Chinese, when a noun occurs with a CL, it is the CL rather than the noun that is the bearer of [+Numerable].

Individual CLs are syntactically different from nouns. The fact that [+Numerable] is realized on CLs rather than nouns is a syntactic issue. The syntactic nature of the existence of individual CLs can be seen in another fact: the occurrence of such CLs is sensitive to syntactic categories in English. Assuming that the word *times* in verbal numeral expressions such as (126a) is a CL (e.g., Landman 2004), we can see that in English, verbal numeral expressions require the occurrence of CLs (Krifka 2007: 39), but nominal numeral expressions do not. There is no CL in the nominal numeral expression *three trips to Paris* in (126b), but the CL *times* is obligatory in the verbal numeral expression in (126a). Like nominals in Chinese, verbal phrases in English are not [+Numerable] bearers, and thus need CLs in counting. If we consider the representation of Numerability in verbal phrases, English should be treated as a CL language.[22]

(126) a. *Bill traveled to Paris three *(times).*
 b. *Bill made three trips to Paris.*
 c. *Bill danced three *(times).*

It needs to be emphasized that the requirement of the CL *times* in (126a) is independent of the telic status of traveling to Paris. Both the telic event expressed by (126a) and the atelic event expressed by (126c) need the overt CL *times* (Moltmann 2013: 21). Telicity can be represented by the feature [Delimitable], which is independent of the feature [Numerable]. My refined analysis of countability thus shows that the popular belief that CLs in numeral expressions in nominals correlate with telicity aspect in the verbal domain is not adequate.

This Numerability-bearer analysis of CLs calls for a review of our current understanding of CLs in CL languages.

2.6.2. How special are the CLs of CL languages?

It has been widely believed that all nouns in CL languages are mass nouns, and therefore, the basic function of CLs is to divide mass into units (e.g., Thompson 1965; Greenberg 1972: 26; Lyons 1977: 462; Link 1991; Senft 2000: 27; Grinevald 2000: 79; Krifka 2008: Sec. 6.3). For instance, Rijkhoff (2002: 162) claims that CLs exist because the properties that nouns in CL languages designate "are not characterized as having a boundary in the spatial dimension". The word *shu* 'book' in *wu ben shu* 'five CL book' in Mandarin Chinese might be glossed as 'bookness' in pseudo-English, instead of 'book' (Rijkhoff 2002: 147). Similarly, Borer (2005: 101) claims that the main function of CLs "is that of dividing mass". One can see that the real argumentation for this belief is that because CLs are obligatorily used in numeral expressions in CL languages, all nouns of the languages must be mass nouns. Beyond the use of CLs, there is really no independent motivation for the belief. In the previous discussion, I have shown that CL languages can distinguish mass from non-mass nouns. As a consequence, the general function of CLs is not dividing or individuating.

---

22. If we consider classification markers instead of numeral CLs, verbal CLs are indeed not as widespread as nominal ones, as shown in Bisang (2011). Chinese, however, does have several verbal numeral CLs, but not as many as nominal ones (see e.g., Zhang 2002).

In Section 2.4.1, we listed seven types of unit words: standard and container measures, and five types of CLs. They "are closely related in grammar and function" (Croft 1994: 152). Like measure words, CLs are also counting units or "unit counters" (Allan 1977: 293). Let us examine how the dividing assumption misrepresents the basic function of CLs. The five types of CLs listed in Section 2.4.1 are exemplified as follows:

(127) a. *san   zhong yang*   [Kind CL]
         three kind   sheep
         'three kinds of sheep'
      b. *san   di shui*   [Individuating CL]
         three CL water
         'three drops of water'
      c. *san   qun   yang*   [Collective CL]
         three CL   sheep
         'three flocks of sheep'
      d. *san   pian xigua*   [Partitive CL]
         three CL   watermelon
         'three slices of watermelon'
      e. *san   ben   shu*   [Individual CL]
         three CL   book
         'three books'

From the translations of (127a), (127b), (127c) and (127d), we can see that English also has kind CLs such as *kind*, individuating CLs such as *di* 'drop', collective CLs such as *flock* and partitive CLs such as *slice*. Among the five types of CLs, the individuating CL in (127b) indeed divides a massive object into units (also see the examples in (87)). Such CLs are also found in non-CL languages such as English, as seen in the word *drop* in the translation of (127b). Obviously, the availability of individuating CLs cannot distinguish CL languages from other languages.

What English does not have is individual CLs. There is no English counterpart for *ben* in (127e). It is this type of CLs that distinguishes CL languages from non-CL languages.[23] In non-CL languages, it has been as-

---

23. The word *head* in the English example (i), and the word *Stück* in the German example (ii) function as individual CLs. (i) means the same as *four cattle*. But such examples are not systematic in the languages.

    (i) *four head cattle*   (ii) *vier Stück Vieh*
                                    four piece cattle
                                    'four cattle'

sumed (Quine 1969: 36) that the semantics of an individual CL is integrated either in the noun or in the numeral. Krifka (2008: Sec. 6.3) states that "[C]ount nouns in [+Num –Cl] languages have meaning with 'built-in' classifiers" (also Krifka 1995: 406; Chierchia 1998; Rijkhoff 2002: 50; Kratzer 2008: 272). For the idea that the semantics of an individual CL is integrated in numerals, see Wilhelm (2008: 55; see Section 6.7.2 for more discussion).

Crucially, individual CLs do not have the function of dividing or individuating. They do not occur with mass nouns. As pointed out by Bale & Barner (2012: 243), "default classifiers only specify that the noun can be counted, the method of individuation being determined by the content of the noun itself." The same idea is also seen in Wiese (2012: 65–66). Such CLs neither individuate anything nor do they create new units for the individuals any more, unlike collective or partitive CLs. Therefore, the popular belief that it is the individuating (discrete set-creating) function of CLs that is special in CL languages should not go unexamined.

A more accurate generalization is that in addition to the various ways of specifying a unit for counting, CLs in CL languages may also directly represent the natural unit of entities that show atomicity, whereas the CLs of other languages do not have this function. In other words, CL languages have unit words to encode both intrinsic and provided units, whereas non-CL languages have units words for encoding provided units only.

In Liao & Wang (2011), only two types of CLs are considered: individual and kind CLs. They (p. 148) thus claim that "the function of a classifier is to distinguish the ambiguous NP denotations by selecting a corresponding counting level (a KCL [= kind CL – NZ] selects a level which consists of kind terms, and an ICL [= individual CL – NZ] a level that consists of atomic individuals)." Considering the existence of collective, partitive, and individuating CLs, in addition to individual and kind CLs, we think Liao & Wang's claim does not capture the general function of CLs. In numeral expressions, the general function of CLs, like that of measure words, is simply to tell us the unit in counting, beyond distinguishing the denotations of NPs.

The alleged dividing function of CLs in numeral expressions is also challenged in languages such as Purépecha and Niuean. In these languages, first, a CL can only occur in the presence of a numeral or certain quantifiers (Vázquez Rojas 2012: 87; Massam 2009: 682). Second, CLs do not occur with mass nouns (Vázquez Rojas 2012: 90; Diane Massam, p.c.; we ignore the effects of the Universal Packager shift). If the primary function of CLs in numeral expressions is to divide mass, why may the CLs in these languages not occur with mass nouns? What we observe is that languages such as English have individating, but not individual CLs; languages such as Purépecha and Niuean have individual, but not individuating CLs; and languages such as Mandarin Chinese have both. Moreover, in Purépecha, among non-mass nouns, nouns of human reference may not occur with a CL. The two types of elements that reject CLs, mass nouns and human nouns, do not seem to form a natural class semantically. The Purépecha and Niuean facts further show that different languages and different types of nouns in the same language may vary with respect to the use of CLs in numeral expressions, and the occurrence of a CL does not mean that the associated noun must be a mass noun.

2.6.3. The sortal-mensural contrast and CLs that do not classify

Some scholars divide CLs into sortal and mensural ones. Tang (2005: 453) uses s(ortal)-feature to label the former. However, neither are the definitions of the terms clear, nor are the classifications consistent in the literature.

2.6.3.1. The inconsistency in the classification

According to Lyons (1977: 463), "A sortal classifier ... individuates whatever it refers to in terms of the kind of entity it is", whereas "A mensural classifier . . . individuates in terms of quantity." Lyons (1977: 464) also mentions that CLs such as *kuai* 'chunk' in Chinese can be both sortal and mensural. In this definition, both types of CLs individuate, and they are different only in the way of individuating. I have just argued that not all CLs individuate, since not all nouns in Chinese are mass nouns.

There seems to be no general agreement with respect to whether certain types of CLs are sortal or not, although individual CLs are generally treated as sortal ones. For Grinvald (2002: 261), only individual CLs are sortal ones and all other types of CLs are mensural. The same contrast is used in Li et al. (2008: Methods of Experiment 2), although they call sortal CLs count CLs. In Cheng & Sybesma (2012: 637), the individuating CL *tiao* in *san tiao zhi* 'three slips of paper' "can arguably be regarded as a nonsortal" CL. Their classification seems to be similar to Grinvald's. In Rijkhoff (1999: 246; 2002: 48), individual and collective CLs are sortal, but individuating CLs are mensural (he also has a general type, which does not belong to either sortal or mensural CLs). In Gerner & Bisang (2010), sortal CLs include individual and individuating CLs, whereas mensural CLs include collective and partitive CLs. Velupillai's (2012: 172 fn. 109) sortal CLs also include individual and individuating CLs, although she does not discuss other types of CLs. In Li et al. (2010: 209, 217), individual, individuating and partitive CLs are sortal but collective CLs are mensural. The disagreement among the above mentioned publications is summarized in (128) (S = sortal CL; M = mensural CL):[24]

(128)	Individual CL	Individuating CL	Partitive CL	Collective CL	Kind CL
Grinvald (2002: 261), Li et al. (2008)	S	M	M	M	
Rijkhoff (1999: 246; 2002: 48)	S	M		S	
Gerner & Bisang (2010)	S	S	M	M	
Velupillai (2012)	S	S			
Li et al. (2010: 209, 217)	S	S	S	M	

The alleged two types are usually defined by listing the subtypes, which themselves are described by examples, without any further discussion of their contrasts. If the alleged division between sortal and mensural CLs is not formally defined, it is not surprising that the groupings are different for different scholars. Note also that in these works, it is not clear whether kind CLs are sortal or mensural.

It needs to be pointed out that although most scholars treat both collective CLs and measure words as mensural CLs, there is a fundamental difference between the two types of unit words: the former may occur with abstract nouns, whereas the latter may not. Collective CLs such as *zu* 'group' and *xilie* 'series' may occur with abstract nouns such as *jianyi* 'suggestion' and *xiaohua* 'joke', but no standard or container measure word may do so (see (19) and (20); Section 2.4.1).

---

24. Hsieh (2008: 36) states that "If the partitioning involves natural singularities based on the inherent properties of the nouns, what is involved is a sortal classifier. If the divider imposes an arbitrary division, it is a massifier." Her definitions seem to separate individual CLs from other unit words, although she does not specifically discuss various types of other unit words.

2.6.3.2.   The dual-functions of some CLs

In addition to the primary function of CLs, i.e., to tell us the unit of counting, "[I]n some instances the size, shape, or function of the object referred to serves as a partial guide in determining which classifier should be used" (Haas 1942: 202). Thus some CLs may have semantic contents (Allan 1977: 285; Tai & Wang 1990). Consider the examples in (129) through (134). The first three pairs have individuating CLs and the remaining three pairs have individual CLs. All of the CLs both contain the information about how the quantity of the referent is calculated and, to a certain degree, also characterize the referent (the translations of the pairs in (133) and (134) come from Ōta 2003: 151).

(129) a. *yi   dui   {yan/tang}*
   one   CL   salt/sugar
   'one pile of {salt/sugar}'

 b. *yi   kuai   {yan/tang}*
   one   CL   salt/sugar
   'one chunk of {salt/sugar}'

(130) a. *liang zhang zhi*
   two   CL   paper
   'two sheets of paper'

 b. *liang juan   zhi*
   two   CL   paper
   'two rolls of paper'

(131) a. *liang duo   yun*
   two   CL   cloud
   'two 3-D units of cloud'

 b. *liang pian   yun*
   two   CL   cloud
   'two 2-D pieces of cloud'

(132) a. *liang zhi   hua*
   two   CL   flower
   'two flowers on their stalks'

 b. *liang duo   hua*
   two   CL   flower
   'two flowers (not focusing on the stalks)'

(133) a. *san   ben   shu*
   three CL   book
   'three books (in regular shapes)'

 b. *san   juan   shu*
   three CL   book
   'three books (in the ancient roll form)'

(134) a. *san   jia   qiao*
   three CL bridge
   'three frame-like bridges'

 b. *san   zuo   qiao*
   three CL   bridge
   'three hill-like stone bridges'

Moreover, different individual CLs for the same noun may be contrastive in the different foci of the properties or different perspectives of the same entity (Her 2012: 1217), as seen in (135) and (136) below.

(135) a. *liang mian qiang*
      two CL   wall
      'two walls (2-dimension perspective)'
  b. *liang du qiang*
      two CL wall
      'two walls (3-dimension perspective)'

(136) a. *san tiao yu*
      three CL fish
      'three fish (focusing on body shape)'
  b. *san wei yu*
      three CL fish
      'three fish (focusing on the tails)'

Thus, even if an additional sorting function is available to some CLs, it never occurs independently of the basic function, i.e., as a counting unit, in numeral expressions.

2.6.3.3. *The absence of the sorting function in some individual CLs*

Collective, partitive, and kind CLs generally do not classify the semantic types of the associated nouns. It is not surprising that they are not generally treated as sortal ones (see (128)). So in this subsection, we discuss individual CLs only, which have been regarded as sortal CLs, consistently.

In certain cases, the choice of CL for certain nouns is predictable. "[I]n a number of other instances, however, the choice of classifier is entirely arbitrary." (Haas 1942: 203) For instance, the two uses of the individual CL *zhang* in (137a) and (137b) do not exhibit semantic similarity (also see Myers 2000: 193; H. Zhang 2007).

(137) a. *san zhang zui*   b. *san zhang chuang*
    three CL mouth   three CL bed
    'three mouths'   'three beds'

This kind of variation is seen not only in the same language, but also cross-linguistically. The word *head* in (138a) is used as a CL for *cattle* in English, but its counterpart in German, *Kopf*, is not used as a CL for *Vieh* 'cattle'. Instead, it is used for *Salat* 'lettuce', and the CL for *Vieh* is *Stück* 'piece', as seen in (138b) and (138c) (Wiese 2012: 66).

(138) a. *four head of cattle*

    b. *vier   Kopf   Salad*   c. *vier   Stück   Vieh*   [German]
       four   head   lettuce   four   piece   cattle
       'four heads of lettuce'   'four head of cattle'

Second, the same noun may arbitrarily occur with different individual CLs. For example, *mousha-an* 'murder-case' can be counted by the CLs *zong, qi, jian, chu, zhuang*, and *chang*, but *qiangdao-an* 'robbery-case' can be counted by the same set of CLs except the last two (*zhuang* and *chang*) (Ansel Liu p.c., Feb. 24, 2012). More such examples can be found in H. Zhang (2007: 53) (The arbitrariness of the selection of CLs will also be seen in later examples in (336) and (338)).

Third, the most frequently used individual CL is the default CL *ge*, which obviously does not classify the semantic types of nouns (Myers 2000, among others) (see our Sections 2.4.5 and 2.6.5 for further discussion). However, no one treats *ge* as a mensural CL. If CLs are disjunctively specified into either sortal or mensural, the status of *ge* is not clear. If the most frequently used CL has no place in a theory of CLs, the theory does not seem to be convincing.

The existence of general or default CLs is also found in Persian. Like Mandarin Chinese, "numerals must be accompanied by a classifier even if the nominal is a count noun" (Ghomeshi 2003: 55). In this language, the CL *ta* may occur with a noun of any type. Since this CL does not classify semantic types of nouns and may occur with mass nouns, Cowper & Hall (2012: 46) claim that it is not a CL. In our opinion, *ta* simply shows the basic property of CLs; it represents a counting unit. In (139a) and (139b), it occurs with a non-mass noun, and thus functions as an individual CL; and in (139c) and (139d), it occurs with a mass noun, and thus functions as an individuating CL (or introduces the effect of Universal Packager; see Section 2.2.5). The examples in (140) show that in this language, non-general CLs also exist (Cowper & Hall 2012: 50; Ghomeshi 2003).

(139) a. *se-ta   ketab*   b. *do-ta   deræt*   [Persian]
       three-CL book   two-CL   tree
       'three books'   'two trees'

    c. *se-ta   næmæk*   d. *se-ta   čai*
       three-CL salt   three-CL tea
       'three salts'   'three teas'

(140) a. *se   næfær   kargær*   b. *se   jeld   ketab*
 three CL^{person} worker   three CL^{volume} book
 'three workers'   'three books'

2.6.3.4. *The source of the non-systematic sorting functions of some CLs*

Both the construction of numeral CL expressions and the combinability of various individual CLs with nouns are the result of historical changes. There existed two parallel constructions of numeral expressions in early Chinese (before Qin Dynasty, i.e., before 220 BC), according to Wu et al. (2006). As shown in (141a) (UW = unit word), the modern construction of a nominal numeral construction derives from the loss of the modification marker *zhi*. The *zhi*-construction is exemplified in (142a), where the standard measure *mu* occurs. In (142b), *zhi* does not occur with the container measure *hu* 'pot'. Finally, in (142c), the individual CL *pi* occurs without *zhi* (Wu et al. 2006: 396 (23a), (27h), (38d))). The other construction was a nominal predicate construction, illustrated in (141b). The examples in (143) show this clausal construction (Ōta 2003: 149) (the pinyin transcriptions of the examples are based on the modern pronunciations of the characters).

(141)   EARLY CHINESE   MODERN CHINESE
  a. [Numeral UW (*zhi*) N]$_{NP}$ $\Rightarrow$ [Numeral UW N]$_{NP}$
  b. [NP$_{SUBJECT}$[Numeral UW]$_{PREDICATE}$]$_{CLAUSE}$ $\Rightarrow$ marked or disappearing

(142) a. *bai   mu   zhi   tian*
  hundred mu   ZHI   farmland
  'one hundred mus of farmland'   (1 mu = 0.667 hectares)
 b. *er   hu   jiu*
  two   pot   alcohol
  'two pots of alcohol'
 c. *qian   pi   ma*
  thousand CL   horse
  'one thousand horses'

(143) a. *Ren   shi   ren.*
  person   ten   person
  'As for persons, there are ten.'

b. *Luan-chen   shi   ren.*
   choas-official ten   person
   'As for rebellious officials, there are ten.'
c. *Che   shi   liang.*
   carridge   ten   CL
   'As for carridges, there are ten.'

All CLs are the result of the grammaticalization of substantive categories such as nouns or verbs (e.g., Li 1924; Loke 1997). The question when individual CLs started to grow is still under debate (see Huang 1964: 441; Liu 1965: Ch. 1; Loke 1997: 1; Wu 2006). It is generally recognized that they were well-developed after the Tang Dynasty (618–907 AD) (Wu 2006).

As for the combinability of CLs with nouns, Wu (2006: 555) uses the CL *tiao* as an example, to show how it came to occur with more and more different types of nouns. Originally, *tiao* was designated to occur with *shu-zhi* 'tree-branch', as in (144a). Then it started to combine with more concrete nouns such as *huanggua* 'cucumber' and *shengzi* 'rope', as seen in (144b). Later, it came to combine with even abstract nouns such as *xinwen* 'news' and *yijian* 'opinion', as seen in (144c).

(144) a. *yi   tiao   shu-zhi*
         one   CL   tree-branch
         'one tree branch'
      b. *liang tiao   huanggua*   *san   tiao   shengzi*
         two   CL   cucumber   three CL   rope
         'two cucumbers'   'three ropes'
      c. *si   tiao   xinwen*   *wu   tiao   yijian*
         four   CL   news   five   CL   opinion
         'four pieces of news'   'five opinions'

Since the CLs of the pattern represented by (144a) and (144b) shared certain semantic features with the co-occurring nouns (e.g., shape), they seemed to represent the semantic features of the nouns. Consequently, they seemed to sort or classify the semantic types of the nouns. But this function disappears in the pattern represented by (144c).

Wang's (1989) research shows that the general CL *ge* was used for animals, plants, persons, ghosts or spirits, body parts of human or animals in the Weijin-Nanbei Dynasty (220–581 AD), but it was also used for units of time, locations, numerals, characters, words or other language-units, and abstract concepts in the time of Tang Wudai (618–960 AD). It has been generally recognized that the closer the semantic relation is between the CL and the noun, the less likely it is for *ge* to be available as a replacement (Ahrens 1994; Myers 2000). The degree of the abstractness depends on the degree of grammaticalization (see Section 2.4.5).

As pointed out by Greenberg (1972: 15), a study of the semantic classification of a CL on the associate noun "becomes valuable in considering further stages of dynamic development". In modern Mandarin, the semantic correlation of a CL with nouns has no systematic pattern, and is thus subject to co-ocurrence restrictions, which are arbitrary (see Section 5.2.4). The correlation is not amenable to true generalizations but only to descriptive approximations. It is also not surprising that the correlation is not easy to learn for children (Li et al. 2008) (see Section 2.6.5 for a discussion of the issue from the experimental perspective).

We conclude that synchronically, the general and basic function of CLs in modern Mandarin Chinese is not sorting the semantic types of nouns.

2.6.3.5. *CL languages without sortal CLs*

If the basic function of CLs in a numeral expression is not sorting, we expect to see the existence of languages in which CLs do not classify nominals at all. Indeed, Niuean (Massam 2009) and some Oceanic languages (Mathew Dryer, p.c. July 2008) are such languages. In these languages, every non-mass noun is in construction with the same CL when it combines with a numeral or quantifier. In the following Niuean examples (Massam 2009: 679), the CL *e*, which is marked as DIV in (145), occurs with various semantic types of nouns. This CL has no sorting function at all. The CL in the nominal domain parallels to the CL *time* in the verbal domain in English, as in (126a, c), which also does not have any sorting function.

(145) a. *(e)*   *ua*   *e*   *kuli*
      ABS.C two DIV dog
      'two dogs'
   b. *tokolima*   *e*   *tagata loloa*
      PERS-five DIV person tall
      'five tall people'
   c. *(e)*   *loga* *e* *fua* *loku*
      ABS.C many DIV fruit papaya
      'many papayas'

d. *tokologa*   *e*   *Niue*
    PERS-many   DIV   Niue
    'many Niueans'

Thus, on the one hand, CLs in numeral expressions do not always classify nominals. On the other hand, the CLs found in Bantu languages (e.g., Carstens 1991; Aikhenvald 2003), and the CLs that are incorporated into verbal expressions in predicate CL languages (Allan 1977: 287) and sign languages (e.g., Sandler & Lillo-Martin 2006), do classify argument nominals, but they do not have to occur with a numeral or quantifier, and thus are not used as counting units. The latter kind of CLs is similar to gender markers in general. It might be more appropriate to call all CLs in numeral expressions mensural markers and the CLs in verbal expressions, as well as gender markers, sortal ones. The two types of formatives are different. In Purépecha, both types of CLs are used (Vázquez Rojas 2012).

2.6.4. The unreliability of the *de* and pre-CL adjective arguments

In this section, I argue against the assumed correlation between the count-mass contrast and two phenomena in Mandarin Chinese: the occurrence of an adjective to the left of a unit word (UW), as illustrated in (146a), and the occurrence of the functional element *de* to the right of a unit word, as illustrated in (146b) (Cheng & Sybesma 1998, 1999).

(146) a. Numeral <u>Adjective</u> UW Noun   b. Numeral UW <u>DE</u> Noun

I have argued that in Chinese, neither nouns nor CLs make a distinction between count and non-count elements themselves, since all nouns are non-count elements (Section 2.3.1) and all CLs are count elements (Section 2.4.6). But the value of delimitability may determine whether a noun is a mass or non-mass one. Individual, collective, and partitive CLs occur with non-mass nouns and individuating CLs occur with mass nouns (other unit words, i.e., kind CLs, standard and container measures, occur with either mass or non-mass nouns).

Cheng & Sybesma (1998, 1999) try to make a distinction between count CLs and mass CLs (called massifiers) (also see Cheng 2012). The names are used to show that in Chinese, the contrast between count and mass nouns can be distinguished at the level of CLs, if not at the level of nouns. Their count CLs are equivalent to individual CLs and all other kinds of unit words are mass CLs. They formalize the following two criteria.

Criterion A. A pre-CL adjective may occur with a mass noun, as seen in (147a), but not with a "count" noun, as seen in (147b) (Cheng & Sybesma 1998: 390, 1999: 516; Wang 1994: 30). In other words, the construction in (146a) is assumed to hold for mass nominals only.

(147) a. *yi   da   zhang zhi*   b. **yi   da   wei   laoshi*
        one   big   CL   paper   one   big   CL   teacher
        'one big piece of paper'

      c. *yi   da   tiao   hao-han*   d. *san   da   zhi   laohu*
        one   big   CL   good-guy   three big   CL   tiger
        'one big good guy'   'three big tigers'

      e. *san   chang   tiao   xianglian*
        three long   CL   necklace
        'three long necklaces'

Although (147b) is not acceptable, other examples of the same type are acceptable, as seen in (147c, d, e) (see Cheng & Sybesma 1998: 390 fn. 4 for their acknowledgement of counter-examples). Tang (2005), Hsieh (2008), Liu (2010), and X. Li (2011a: 34), among others, all present lots of counter-examples to this claim about pre-CL adjectives. More examples can be found in Zhu (1982: 52), T'ung & Pollard (1982), Lu (1987), Luo (1988), and H. Yang (2005: 33) (Examples of various types of CLs with adjectives are seen in Section 2.4.7 above). Therefore, the adjective criterion is empirically problematic.

Criterion B. *De* may occur between a measure word and a mass noun, but not between a CL and a "count" noun (Chao 1968: 555, 588; T'sou 1976; Paris 1981: 32; Zhu 1982: 51; Cheng & Sybesma 1998: 388, 1999: 515). In other words, the construction in (146b) is assumed to hold for mass nominals only. A typical pair of examples is (148):

(148) a. *san   wan   de   tang*   b. **san   ge   de   laoshi*
        three bowl   DE   soup   three CL   DE   teacher
        'three bowls of soup'

Again, the unacceptability of (148b) is not representative. In fact, all types of CLs can be followed by *de* in an appropriate context, as shown in (149a). (149b) (X. Li 2011a: 40) and (149c) (mentioned by James Huang in his talk at National Tsing Hua University, Hsinchu, on July 9, 2010) further show that *de* may follow the individual CLs *li* and *tiao*, respectively.

(149) a. *Lulu   chi-le   yi-bai   {ge/gongjin/bao/pian/dui/zhong}*
         Lulu   eat-PRF   one-hundred   CL/kilo/bag/slice/pile/kind
         de pingguo.
         DE apple
         'Lulu ate 100 apples or 100 {kilos/bags/slices/piles/kinds} of apples.'
    b. *Lulu   chi-le   san-fen-zhi-yi   li   de   ganmao-yao.*
         Lulu   eat-PRF   one-third   CL   DE   cold-pill
         'Lulu took one third of a cold pill.'
    c. *Yi   liang tiao de   maojin ni   zong   mai-de-qi   ba!*
         one   two   CL   DE   towel   2SG   after.all   buy-can   PRT
         'You should be able to afford to buy one or two towels!'

The context for *de* to show up has nothing to do with the count-mass contrast. In Section 5.5, I will spell out my analysis. Shortly speaking, *de* surfaces at two positions. In one position, it surfaces in a comparative ellipsis construction, but in another position, it introduces a constituent directly. The former situation is seen in constructions of individual, individuating, and kind CLs, whereas the latter situation is seen in constructions of other types of unit words. Note that the division here does not match with Cheng & Sybesma's distinction between count and mass CLs. If one just considers the phonological form of *de* without considering its structural position, then, *de* may occur with all types of unit words, as seen in (149). Therefore, Cheng & Sybesma's (1998, 1999) claim that one type of CLs (the "count" type) may not be modified by an adjective, and may not be followed by *de*, whereas the other type (the "mass" type) can, is descriptively inadequate.

As mentioned above, several works have already presented a lot of counter-examples to falsify the alleged distinction. Wu & Bodomo (2009: 489) point out that the two alleged types of CLs can occur with the same NP (See also Borer 2005: 98), as shown in (150) and (151). *Ben* in (150a) and *li* in (151a) are Cheng & Sybesma's count CLs, and *xiang* in (150b) and *wan* in (151b) are their mass CLs.

(150) a. *san   ben   shu*   b. *san   xiang shu*
        three CL   book   three box   book
        'three books'   'three boxes of books'

(151) b. *san   li   mi*   b. *san   wan   mi*
        three CL rice   three bowl   rice
        'three grains of rice'   'three bowls of rice'

Examples like (152) (see Her & Hsieh 2010: 541) show that the two alleged constraints on the assumed count CLs (i.e., individual CLs) can even be violated at the same time. The CLs *ke* in (152a) and *tiao* in (152b) are typical individual CLs, but they are both preceded by a modifier and followed by *de*.

(152) a. *san   da ke de gaolicai*   b. *san   da tiao de yu*
       three big CL DE cabbage   three big CL   DE fish
       'three big cabbage'   'three big fish'

In conclusion, the alleged two criteria cannot make any distinction in CLs in Chinese, regardless of whether the assumed distinction correlates with the count-mass contrast (see Fassi Fehri 2004: 77–78 for critical comments on the assumed distinction).

2.6.5. Experimental perspective

We have claimed that the special function of CLs in CL languages is not dividing. On the contrary, it is the existence of individual CLs, which do not divide, that separates CL languages from non-CL languages (Section 2.6.2). Thus, the traditional hypothesis that all nouns in CL languages are mass nouns is wrong.

The hypothesis that all nouns in CL languages are mass nouns has even led people to believe that speakers of CL languages think differently about objects and stuff in the world from speakers of non-CL languages (a Whorfian effect), and some experimental studies such as Lucy (1992) have tried to provide evidence for this belief. However, recent studies such as Sandhofer et al. (2000), Colunga & Smith (2005), Barner et al. (2009), Li et al. (2009a, b), and Cheung et al. (2010, 2012) have not only come to a different conclusion than the Lucy-type of experiments, but also shown new experimental results that do not support the idea. The new results from the experimental studies of both children and adults "presented evidence that speakers of Japanese, English, and Mandarin Chinese do not perceive objects differently" (Barner et al. 2009: 331). Saalbach & Imai's (2007) experimental investigation of CL and non-CL languages concludes that "the global structure of everyday object concepts is strikingly similar across different cultures and languages." Cheung et al. (2012) conducted various experiments (A) to test the interpretations of bare nouns, (B) to test the interpretations of the parts of broken objects, (C) to test whether individual

CLs, when they are highlighted and not highlighted, play any special role in quantity judgment tasks for flexible nouns such as *bingguo* 'apple', which is either non-mass or mass in the universal grinder context. Cheung et al. (2012: 215) conclude that "the current studies provide strong evidence that nouns have similar semantic content crosslinguistically, regardless of variation in their syntactic expression. Nouns in classifier languages such as Mandarin and Japanese encode individuation like nouns in English, and can express this content without requiring the overt use of classifiers. Not only are classifiers unnecessary for individuation in Mandarin, but they also appear to be relatively weak cues to meaning."

We have also claimed that the basic function of CLs is to encode units, rather than to classify (Section 2.6.3). The separation of the general function from other functions of CLs is attested in acquisition research, such as Fang (1985), Erbaugh (1986), Miao & Zhu (1992), Hu (1993), Myers & Tsay (2000), Chien et al. (2003), A. Huang (2009), and Li et al. (2010), from both production and comprehension perspectives. Chien et al. (2003: 96) state that "Different studies have shown different results regarding the order of classifier acquisition, but they all pointed to the conclusion that children first acquire the general classifier *ge* and use it as a "syntactic place-holder"; they report (p. 113) that "supporting the well-established finding from earlier production studies that young children predominately use the general classifier *ge* for almost any noun, we found that hearing the general classifier *ge* did not make young children search for a particular referent." Li et al. (2010: 224) report on similar findings. To be a unit for counting is the primary function of CLs, and to sort elements is a secondary function of (only) some CLs. The primary function is acquired earlier than the secondary one. As expected, non-native adult learners of Mandarin also overuse *ge* (Polio 1994). Moreover, aphasia studies indicate that brain damage patients neutralize CLs to *ge* more often than normals do (Tzeng, Chen and Hung 1991). As pointed out by Myers (2000: 204), the finding of the aphasia study "is consistent with our claim that *ge* is chosen by default when memory-access problems prevent accessing the exemplars that guide the selection of specific classifiers." All of the experimental studies show that the primary function of CLs is structural and the choice among different CLs of the same type for a specific position is lexical. The former function is acquired earlier and easier to be maintained than the latter.

2.7. Chapter summary

In this chapter, I have argued for a more refined syntactic analysis of the count-mass contrast. I list my main conclusions as follows:

A. The count-mass contrast of linguistic elements is decomposed into two features: [Numerable] and [Delimitable]. [+Numerable] means a noun can combine with a numeral directly, and thus it is a count noun. [–Numerable] nouns are non-count nouns. No noun in Chinese is a count noun. [+Delimitable] means a noun can combine with a shape, size, or boundary modifier, and thus it is a non-mass noun. A mass noun is defined by both [–Numerable] and [–Delimitable]. Not all nouns in Chinese are mass nouns.

B. Some CLs occur with mass nouns and some with non-mass nouns. In numeral expressions, like measure words, all CLs specify counting units. Individual CLs occur with non-mass nouns, and their semantic function is to represent the natural units of the elements denoted by non-mass nouns. Such CLs have no dividing function at all. It is the existence of this type of CLs that separates CL languages from other languages.

C. The feature [+Numerable] may be distributed in different types of elements cross-linguistically and within the same language. In Mandarin Chinese, except in idiomatic expressions, compounds and list contexts, nouns do not have this feature, whereas unit words do. In some languages, all nouns are [+Numerable].

D. Numerability is different from the notion of number, although they may interact in various ways cross-linguistically.

Chapter 3
Classifiers and quantifiers

3.1. Introduction

Mandarin Chinese is called a numeral CL language, which means that CLs typically occur with numerals. But CLs also occur with elements other than numerals in the language. The general goal of this chapter and another two chapters of the book (Chapter 4 and Chapter 7) is to find out the syntactic status of CLs beyond numeral expressions in the language. I will show that CLs, as a special type of formatives, may exhibit different structural properties in different contexts. In this chapter, we study the occurrence of CLs with quantifiers in nominals.

The general function of CLs in numeral expressions is to express counting units, rather than individuating mass (Section 2.6.2). In this chapter, we will seek answers to two questions: which non-numeral quantifiers (simply called quantifiers henceforth) in nominals require a CL to occur, and if a CL occurs with a quantifier, what its function is.

One difference between quantifiers and numerals is that the former may not be modified by expressions such as *zhengzheng* 'whole', *zonggong* 'total', *dayue* 'about', and *zuzu* 'as many as', where as the latter may. The contrast is shown by (153). In Gebhardt (2009), a numeral has the feature [+Absolute], for a precise quantity, and a quantifier has the feature [−Absolute], for a non-precise quantity.

(153) a. *Yani   mai-le   {zonggong/dayue/zuzu}   shi   ben   shu.*
       Yani buy-PRF total/about/as.many.as ten CL book
       'Yani bought {ten books in total/about ten books/as many as} ten books.'

   b. Yani mai-le   *{zonggong/dayue/zuzu} ruogan ben shu.*
      Yani buy-PRF total/about/as.many.as several CL book
      'Yani bought several books.'

According to Partee (1989), quantifying elements can be modifiers or non-modifiers, cross-linguistically, and they are syntactically different (also see Cardinaletti & Giusti 2006). In Chinese, modifiers can be followed by the functional particle *de*. Quantifying elements such as *daliang* 'a lot', *suoyou* 'all', *quanbu* 'all', *daduoshu* 'most', *dabufen* 'most' can be followed by *de*, and thus they should be modifier-like quantifiers. They may not be followed by a CL, as seen in (154) (see Tang 2007: 984; Hsieh 2008: 61; X. Li 2011a: 6):[25]

(154) a. *suoyou (de)* (**duo*) *hua*   b. *daliang* (*de*) (**ping*) *shui*
        all   DE   CL   flower   a.lot   DE   bottle   water
        'all of the flowers'   'a lot of water'

Excluding such modifiers, I consider only quantifiers that may not be followed by *de*. Note that words such as *renhe* 'any' and *mei* 'each' are D-elements, base-generated higher than a numeral, since they may precede a numeral (e.g., {*renhe/mei*} *san ba san* '{any/every} three umbrella(s)'). We do not discuss them in this book.

In Sections 3.2 and 3.3, we discuss quantifiers that must and must not occur with a CL, respectively. Then in Section 3.4, we point out that the status of some quantifiers is ambiguous. In Section 3.5, we distinguish three non-numeral uses of *yi* 'one', showing that they are different quantifiers and that the element following them is diffent from the CL in a numeral expression. We summarize our discussion in Section 3.6.

3.2. Quantifiers that occur with a unit word

In addition to cardinal numerals, quantifiers such as *ji* 'how many' (Chao 1968: 580; it is called "unknown figure" in Iljic 1994: 107, and "vague number" in Hsieh 2008: 62), *ji* 'a few, several', *haoji* 'several', *ruogan* 'several', and the paucal quantifier *liang-san* 'two-three ⇒ a few' (Ōta 2003: 134) must also be followed by a unit word, as seen in (155). Moreover, the distributive quantifier *ge* 'each' (Kuo & Yu 2012: 666) and the quantifier *ban* 'half' must also be followed by a unit word of an appropriate type, as seen in (156) (*ban* is also used after a unit word, see Section 5.3.4).[26]

---

25. *De* precedes the unit word in (154) and (171). The issue is different from the one in Section 2.6.4, where it was discussed whether *de* may follow a unit word.
26. Numerals with the ordinal marker *di* in Mandarin also require the occurrence of a unit word, as shown in (i).

(i) *di*   *san*   *(*duo*) *hua*
    ORD   three   CL   flower
    'the third flower'

But see footnote 14, where ordinal numbers occur with neither *di* nor a CL. In Thai, ordinal numerals must also be next to a unit word such as a CL (Haas 1942: 204). I do not discuss ordinal numeral construction in this book.

(155) a. *Ni   you   ji   *(duo) hua?*   b. *haoji *(duo) hua*
        2SG   have   how.many CL   flower   several CL   flower
        'How many flowers do you have?'   'several flowers'
     c. *liang-san   *(duo)   hua*
        two-three   CL   flower
        'a few flowers'

(156) a. *Mei *(ben) riji   dou   xie-zhe   liang ge zi: jian   fei.*
        each CL   diary all   write-DUR two   CL word lose   fat
        'Each diary is written with two words: lose weight.'
     b. *Yani mai-le   ban *(ge)   xigua.*
        Yani buy-PRF half   CL   watermelon
        'Yani bought a half watermelon.'

In these quantifier constructions, different types of unit words semantically contrast with each other, as in numeral constructions. For instance, in (155a), the individual CL *duo* occurs, whereas in (157a), the collective CL *dui* 'pile' or the kind CL *zhong* 'kind' occurs. The different CLs are used to ask different questions. (157b) further shows the contrasting meanings of different counting units.

(157) a. *Ni   you   ji   {dui/zhong}   hua?*
        2SG   have   how.many   pile/kind   flower
        'How many {piles/kinds} of flowers do you have?'
     b. *Yani mai-le   ban   ge xigua,   er   bu   shi   ban*
        Yani buy-PRF half   CL watermelon but   not   be   half
        xiang xigua.
        case watermelon
        'Yani bought a half watermelon, but not a half case of watermelons.'

Moreover, if the unit word in the quantifier constructions is an individual CL, it shows selectional restrictions with the noun. For instance, the CL *duo* is for flowers and the CL *zhang* is for tables. As shown in (158), one may not be replaced with the other. This is again similar to the CL in a numeral expression (see Section 5.2.3).

(158) a. *Ni   you   ji   {duo/*zhang} hua?*
        2SG   have   how.many   CL/CL   flower
        'How many flowers do you have?'
     b. *Ni   you   ji   {*duo/zhang} zhuozi?*
        2SG   have   how.many   CL/CL   table
        'How many tables do you have?'

However, like other quantifiers of the language, the quantifiers that must be followed by a unit word do not show any selectional restrictions on other elements. In (157), we see that such quantifiers may be followed by various unit words.

Furthermore, like the CLs in numeral expressions, the CLs with the above quantifiers also license ellipsis of the NP to their right, and may be stranded, as seen in (159a) and (159b), respectively.

(159) a. *Wo   you   liu duo hua.   Ni   you   ji   duo?*
        1SG   have six CL   flower 2SG   have how.many   CL
        'I have six flowers. How many do you have?'
    b. *Hua,   ni   you   ji   duo?*
       flower 2SG   have five   CL
       'As for flowers, how many do you have?'

Summarizing, the CLs following the quantifiers discussed in this section exhibit the same properties as those in numeral expressions. They express counting units in quantification.

In other languages, the same kind of CLs may also occur with both numeral and certain non-numeral quantifiers. For instatnce, the Persian CL *ta* occurs with both a numeal and the quantifier *čænd* 'several, how many' (Cowper & Hall 2012: 45). See Massam (2009) and Vázquez Rojas (2012) for an extensive discussion of such a case in Niuean and Purépecha, respectively.

3.3. Quantifiers that occur without a unit word

Some quantifiers reject CLs or any unit words. If *yi* 'one' to the left of *dian* 'point' is in contrast to another numeral, it is a numeral, and *dian* can always be replaced by the individual CL *ge*. For instance, in (160a), *yi* in the second conjunct contrasts with *san* 'three' in the first conjunct, and *dian* may be replaced by *ge*. In such constructions, *dian* is a counting unit, a regular CL in a numeral expression. However, if *yi* to the left of *dian* is not in contrast to another numeral, as in (160b), it is not a numeral. Instead, the whole cluster (*yi*)-*dian* or (*yi*)-*dianr*, encodes the meaning of 'some, a little', functioning as an existential quantifier.

(160) a. *Wo   you   san   {dian/ge}   {jianyi/yiwen},   bu   shi*
       1SG   have   three   CL/CL   suggestion/doubt   not   be
       yi   {dian/ge}   {jianyi/yiwen}.
       one   CL/CL   suggestion/doubt
       'I have three {suggestions/doubts}, rather than one.'
    b. *Nali   you   (yi)-dianr   niunai   *(bu   shi   san   dian   niunai).*
       there   have   one-DIAN   milk   not   be   three   CL   milk
       'There is a little milk.'

Importantly, the cluster *(yi)-dian* or *(yi)-dianr* may not be followed by any unit word, as shown in (161).

(161) a. *Nali   you   (yi)-dianr   (*ping/*di)   niunai.*
       there   have   one-DIAN   bottle/CL   milk
       'There is a little milk.'
    b. *Duo   xue   (yi)-dianr   (*ge)   Ma-Lie!*
       more   study   one-DIAN   CL   Marx-Lenin
       'Study more of Marxism and Leninism!'
    c. *Nali   you   (yi)-dianr   (*ke)   xiao   xigua.*
       there   have   one-DIAN   CL   small   watermelon
       'There are a few small watermelons.' (e.g., in the context of talking about the quantity of the storage in a certain place)

We have observed two morphological differences between the string *yi dian* in a numeral expression, as in (160a), and the one that is an existential quantifier, as in (161). First, *yi* is not optional in the former case, but it is in the latter case. Second, in the Northern dialect of Mandarin, *dian* may not have a retroflectional ending in the former, but it has in the latter. Thus *(yi)-dian* or *(yi)-dianr* is clearly not a combination of a numeral and a CL.

Lü et al. (1999: 581) and Iljic (1994: 107) claim that *(yi)-dianr* is usually for mass or abstract nouns. Precisely speaking, it is a unit word, rather than a non-mass noun, that may never follow the quantifier. In (161c), *xigua* 'watermelon' is not a mass noun, but it follows *(yi)-dianr*. The following two examples in (162) are like (161c) in this respect.

(162) a. *Jia-li   zhi   sheng   (yi)-dianr   yangcong.*
       home-in   only   remain   one-DIAN   onion
       'Only a few onions remain in the home.'

b. *Shu-jia-shang   mei   shenme   xiangyang   de   shu,   zhi*
   book-shelf-on not.have what   decent   DE   book   only
   you   (yi)-dianr   zazhi.
   have   one-DIAN   magazine
   'In the bookshelf, there is no decent book, only a few magazines.'

Morphologically speaking, (*yi*)-*dianr* is composed of *yi* 'one' and the CL *dian*, which has developed from the noun *dian* 'point'. One may claim that (*yi*)-*dian* or (*yi*)-*dianr* may not precede a CL because it ends with a CL already, and two CLs never occur in a row. But this use of *dian* is different from the CL in a numeral expression, in at least three aspects. First, the CL *dian* encodes a counting unit in a numeral expression. In (163), for example, *dian* or *ge* in the first conjunct contrasts with the collective CL *dui* 'pile' in the second conjunct. But *dian* in (*yi*)-*dian* or (*yi*)-*dianr* does not encode a counting unit, since it does not contrast with any other unit-denoting formative. In (164), *dian* may not contrast with the individuating CL *di* 'drop'.

(163)   *Wo   you   yi   {dian/ge}   {jianyi/yiwen},   bu   shi   yi*
        1SG   have   one CL/CL   suggestion/doubt   not be   one
        dui   {jianyi/yiwen}.
        pile   suggestion/doubt
        'I have one {suggestion/doubt}, rather than a pile of {suggestions /doubts}.'

(164)   **Nali   you   (yi)-dian   niunai, bu   shi   yi   di   niunai.*
        there   have   one-DIAN   milk   not be   one   CL   milk

Second, unlike an individual or individuating CL, and like other quantifiers in the language, *dian* in (*yi*)-*dian* or (*yi*)-*dianr* does not show any selectional restrictions on other elements. In (161) and (162), we see that it may be followed by various nouns. Third, unlike individual or individuating CL, and like other quantifiers in the language, *dian* in (*yi*)-*dian* or (*yi*)-*dianr* may not be modified. In (165a), *da* 'big' modifies the CL *di*, but in (165b), *da* may not modify *dianr*.

(165) a. *yi   da   di   niunai*   b. *(yi) (*da)   dianr   niunai*
         one big CL   milk   one   big   DIAN   milk
         'one big drop of milk'   'a little milk'

If the *dian* in the cluster is semantically different from a counting unit, why does it never occur with a word that functions as a counting unit? Cardinality or counting requires counting units. Since the quantifier (*yi*)-*dianr*, as shown by (161), may not be followed by a unit word, and *dian* itself does not express a counting unit, the quantifier is not used for counting. It is similar to the quantifiers *much* and *less*. For the same reason, the quantifiers in (154), which also reject a counting unit-encoding element, are not used for counting, either.

One important property of (*yi*)-*dianr* is that elements to its right may be elided:

(166) *Ta   chi-le   (yi)-dianr   yu,   wo   ye   chi-le   (yi)-dianr.*
     3SG   eat-PRF   one-DIAN   fish   1SG   also   eat-PRF   one-DIAN
     'He ate a little fish, and so did I.'

It is possible that *dianr* in (*yi*)-*dianr* is at a certain head position, which licenses ellipsis. We will give a formal presentation in Section 6.2.3.

In addition to (*yi*)-*dianr*, another quantifier that rejects unit words is (*yi*)-*xie* 'some' (I thank Ansel Liu for a discussion of the issue with me). The examples in (167) are similar to the (*yi*)-*dianr* examples in (161).

(167) a. *Lulu   mai-le   (yi)-xie   (*ben)   shu.*
       Lulu   buy-PRF   one-XIE   CL   book
       'Lulu bought some books.'
     b. *Lulu   mai-le   (yi)-xie   (*ping)   niunai.*
       Lulu   buy-PRF   one-XIE   bottle   milk
       'Lulu bought some milk.'

Like the *yi* in (*yi*)-*dianr*, the *yi* 'one' in (*yi*)-*xie* does not contrast with any other numeral. Like the word *dianr* in (*yi*)-*dianr*, *xie* in (*yi*)-*xie* is also different from a CL in a numeral expression. The three contrasts between the word *dianr* in (*yi*)-*dianr* and a CL in a numeral expression are also seen between *xie* and a CL in a numeral expression. Also like (*yi*)-*dianr*, (*yi*)-*xie* licenses ellipsis. Thus the acceptability of all of the above (*yi*)-*dianr* examples remains the same if we replace (*yi*)-*dianr* with (*yi*)-*xie*. However, one difference between (*yi*)-*dianr* and (*yi*)-*xie* is that the former denotes a small quantity, whereas the latter is underspecified with the amount of the quantity (Lü et al. 1999: 581). Note that the small quantity reading is also available for (*yi*)-*dian,* which does not have a retroflection ending and is used in southern dialect of Mandarin.

One special property of *xie* is that it can be followed by the CL *ge*, as in (168) (Lü et al. [1978] 2002: 1391):

(168) a. *zhe   xie-ge   rizi*   b. *chi   xie-ge   dongxi*
       DEM XIE-CL day   eat XIE-CL stuff
       'these days'   'eat something'

But the *ge* following *xie* has two restrictions. First, it must be in a neutral tone, i.e., in a reduced phonological form (Lü et al. 2002: 1391). Second, it may not be replaced with any other CL. These two restrictions indicate that the *ge* is not a regular CL. Similarly, the retroflection ending of (*yi*)-*dianr* also has a reduced phonological form and it may not be replaced with any other morpheme. I thus treat both the *ge* following *xie* and the retroflection ending of (*yi*)-*dianr* in the Northern dialect of Mandarin as an empty morph, which does not have a syntactic position.

3.4. The ambiguous cases

In addition to the two types of quantifiers introduced in the above sections, the interrogative quantifier *duoshao* 'how many/much' may optionally be followed by a unit word, as seen in (169) (Note that *ji* in (155a) also mean 'how many', but it must be followed by a unit word). I claim that the quantifier is ambiguous in its status: when it is followed by a unit word, it belongs to the type of quantifiers discussed in Section 3.2; but when it is not followed by a unit word, it belongs to the type of quantifiers discussed in Section 3.3.

(169) a. *Nali   you   duoshao   (zhang)   zhuozi?*
         there have how.many CL   table
         'How many tables are there?'
     b. *Ni   mai-le   duoshao   (kuai)   doufu?*
         2SG buy-PRF how.many CL   tofu
         '{How much/How many pieces of} tofu did you buy?'

Quantifiers such as *henduo, haoduo,* or *haoxie,* which all mean 'many, much', may occur with any type of nouns or unit words (Tang 2007: 984, Hsieh 2008: 61) (the same is true of *takusan* 'many, much' in Japanese, another CL language; see Iida 1998: 4; Kobuchi-Philip 2011: 307).[27]

---

27. The example in (i) seems to show that the expression *hen-shao* 'very few' may not be followed by a unit word. However, unlike other quantifiers, *hen-shao* may always be followed by *you* 'have'. (i) and (ii) mean the same. Lü et al.

(170) a. *henduo (ben) shu*   b. *henduo (di)   shui*
        many   CL   book   many   CL   water
        'many books'   'a lot of {water/drops of water}'

However, when *henduo* occurs with a unit word, e.g., a CL, it may not be followed by *de*, as in (171a). This restriction makes this use of *henduo* pattern with a quantifier that occurs with a unit word, such as *ji* 'how many', as seen in (171b). In contrast, when *henduo* occurs without a unit word, it may be followed by *de*, as in (172a). This makes the use of *henduo* pattern with a quantifying modifier such as *suoyou*, as seen in (172b) (see (154a)) (Hsieh 2008: 61).

(171) a. *henduo (*de) ben shu*   b. *ji   (*de) ben shu*
        many   DE   CL book   how.many   DE   CL   book
        'many books'   'how many books'

(172) a. *henduo (de) shu*   b. *suoyou   (de) shu*
        many   DE   book   all   DE   book
        'many books'   'all items of the books'

Such quantifiers are thus ambiguous between quantificational modifiers and non-modifying quantifiers. If we consider the non-modifying use, their co-occurring CLs are similar to those in Section 3.2. Specifically, different types of unit words contrast semantically. In (173), the individual CL *ke* in the first conjunct is in contrast to the kind CL *zhong* in the second conjunct. Therefore, the CLs encode counting units.

(173) *Nali you   henduo ke shu, bu shi henduo zhong shu.*
       there have many   CL tree not be   many   kind   tree
       'There are many trees, but not many kinds of trees.'

(1999: 480) claim that *hen-shao* functions as a predicate or a modifier of a verb. If their claim is true, the expression is not a nominal-internal element.

(i) *Henshao (*ge) xuesheng neng zai 20 fenzhong-nei gei-chu huida.*
    few   CL   student   can at 20 minute-in   give-out answer

(ii) *Henshao you   xuesheng neng zai 20 fenzhong-nei gei-chu huida.*
    few   have   student   can at 20 minute-in   give-out answer

    Both: 'Very few students can give an answer in 20 minutes.'

3.5. Non-numeral uses of *yi* 'one' in nominals

In addition to the cardinal numeral use of *yi* 'one', called C-YI (for Cardinal Numeral *Yi*) henceforth, there are also three non-numeral uses of *yi* in nominals.

3.5.1. G-YI: *Yi* as a generic quantifier

The word *yi* 'one' can be used as a generic quantifier, as in (174) (Wu & Bodomo 2009: 492; Cheng & Sybesma 2012: 640). *Yi* in this use may not be replaced with any other numeral such as *san* 'three'. I call *yi* in this use G-YI (for Generic *Yi*).

(174) a. *Yi *(ge) ren   yao   you   liangxin.*
      one CL person   should have morality
      'A person should have moralities.'
   b. *Yi *(jia) feiji   de sudu bi   yi *(sou) lunchuan de*
      one CL   airplane DE speed than one CL   ship   DE
      sudu   kuai.
      speed fast
      'An airplane's speed is faster than a ship's.'
   c. *Yi *(zhong) zongjiao zong   you   qi wenhua genyuan.*
      one CL   religion always have its culture   origin
      'A religion always has its cultural origin.'

As seen in (174), the occurrence of the CL following G-YI is obligatory. The generic reading of G-YI nominals, which require the occurrence of a CL, falsifies the claim that generic nominals must be bare nouns in the language (Li & Thompson 1981: 129–130; Kuo & Yu 2012: 675).

Not only must both C-YI and G-YI be followed by a CL, but the CL may in both cases also show selectional restrictions on the noun (see Section 5.2.3). In the numeral expressions in (175a) and (175b), we see that the CL *jia*, but not *sou*, goes with *feiji* 'airplane'; but for *lunchuan* 'ship', the opposite restriction applies. The same restrictions are observed in the G-YI construction in (175c).

(175) a. *san   {jia/*sou} feiji*   b. *san   {sou/*jia} lunchuan*
      three CL/CL   airplane   three CL/CL   ship
      'three airplanes'   'three ships'

    c. *Yi* {*jia*/*sou} *feiji*   *de sudu bi yi* {*sou*/*jia}
      one CL/CL   airplane DE speed than one CL/CL
      lunchuan de sudu   kuai.   (G-YI)
      ship   DE speed fast
      'An airplane's speed is faster than a ship's.'

However, G-YI is different from C-YI in at least four aspects. First, G-YI does not contrast with any real numeral. In (174), if *yi* is replaced with a numeral such as *san* 'three', the generic reading disappears. Note that *yi* in examples like (176) below does contrast with other numerals and thus is C-YI. Accordingly, the *yi*-initial nominals are numeral expressions.

(176) a. *Yi di you jiu zuyi   rang men de zaoyin xiaoshi.*
       one CL oil   just enough let   door DE noise   disappear
       'One drop of oil is enough to get rid of the noise of the door.'
    b. *Yi he jidan you 12 ge, yi xiang jidan ze   you 60 ge.*
       one box egg have 12 CL one case egg   however have 60 CL
       'There are 12 eggs in one box, but 60 ones in one case.'

Second, unlike C-YI, G-YI does not license a numeral-oriented modifier such as *zonggong* 'total', *zhengzheng* 'whole', *dayue* 'about', and *zuzu* 'as many as'.

(177) a. *Naxie shipin wei-le   zonggong yi   ge yinger.*   (C-YI)
       DEM food feed-PRF total   one CL baby
       'That amount of food was used to feed one baby in total.'
    b. (*Zonggong) *Yi ge yinger zong   yao   ku.*   (G-YI)
       total   one CL baby usual will cry
       'A baby usual cries.'

    Third, the CL following G-YI does not contrast with a CL of another counting-unit type (Section 2.4), unlike that following C-YI. A generic property of x is a general property of x, and thus it has nothing to do with counting. Therefore, there is no contrast in counting units. Accordingly, in (178a), the CL *ge* does not contrast with the collective CL *qun* 'group'; similarly, in (178b), the CL *ke* does not contrast with the collective CL *pai* 'row'. In (178c) (= (174c)), the CL *zhong* may not be replaced with the kind CL *lei*, although two CLs may be exchangable in numeral expressions.

(178) a. *Yi   *ge* xuezhe, er   bu shi yi   *qun*   xuezhe,   yao
      one   CL scholar but   not be   one   group scholar   should
      zunzhong shishi.
      respect   fact

    b. *Yi *ke* shu,   er bu   shi yi   *pai*   shu,   zong   you
      one CL   tree   but not   be one   row   tree   always   have
      shugen.
      root

    c. *Yi* {*zhong*/**lei*} *zongjiao zong*   *you*   *qi wenhua*
      one   CL/CL   religion   always   have   its   culture
      genyuan.   (G-YI)
      origin
      'A religion always has its cultural origin.'

Fourth, G-YI constructions may not contain any expression that signals an episodic eventuality, such as *zuotian* 'yesterday' or *turan* 'suddenly'. C-YI constructions are not subject to this constraint.

(179) a. *Yi*   *jia feiji*   *de*   *sudu (*zuotian)*   *bi*   *yi*   *sou*
      one   CL airplane DE speed   yesterday   than   one   CL
      lunchuan de sudu   *kuai.*   (G-YI)
      ship   DE speed   fast
      'An airplane's speed is faster than a ship's (*yesterday).'

    b. *Yani zuotian*   *mai-le*   *yi*   *jia feiji.*   (C-YI)
      Yani yesterday buy-PRF one CL   airplane
      'Yani bought one airplane yesterday.'

I thus claim that although for both C-YI and G-YI, the occurrence of a CL to their right is obligatory, and the CL may impose selectional restrictions on the noun, the CL denotes a counting unit in the former case, but not in the latter.

3.5.2. E-YI: *Yi* as an existential quantifier[28]

The word *yi* 'one' can also occur in constructions such as (180). But *yi* in this use does not introduce a generic reading, unlike the *yi* in (174). Instead, it behaves like an existential quantifier. I thus call *yi* in this use E-YI (for Existential *Yi*).

---

28. I am grateful to Liu Chensheng for a discussion that inspired me to think about the two more uses of *yi*, to be addressed in this subsection and the next subsection.

(180) a. *Baoyu   zhongyu kandao-le {yi/*san}   xian   xiwang.*
       Baoyu   finally   see-PRF   one/three   CL   hope
       'Baoyu finally saw a hope.'
   b. *Shichang-shang chuxian-le {yi/*san}   pai   fanrong*
       market-on   appear-PRF one/three   CL   prosperity
       jingxiang.
       scene
       'Prosperity appears in the market.'

E-YI constructions are similar to C-YI and G-YI constructions in that, first, the occurrence of a CL is obligatory.

(181) a. *Baoyu   zhongyu kandao-le   yi   *(xian) xiwang.*
       Baoyu   finally   see-PRF   one   CL   hope
       'Baoyu finally saw a hope.'
   b. *Shichang-shang chuxian-le yi   *(pai)   fanrong   jingxiang.*
       market-on   appear-PRF one   CL   prosperity scene
       'Prosperity appears in the market.'

Second, the CL following E-YI may impose selectional restrictions on the noun. The example in (182a), for instance, shows that *mangran* 'confusion' goes with the CL *pian*, but not the CL *xian*.

(182) a. *yi   {pian/*xian}   mangran*   b. *yi   {tuan/*pai} zao*
       one   CL/CL   confusion   one   CL/CL   mess

(183) a. *yi   gu   {kongju/*heping}*   b. *yi   pai {*kongju/heping}*
       one   CL   fear/peace   one   CL   fear/peace

(184) *yi   duan {youyi/jiaoqing/*chouhen}*
     one   CL   friendship/friendship/hatred

E-YI also shares certain properties with G-YI that distinguish them from C-YI. First, E-YI does not contrast with any other numerals. The examples in (180) already show that E-YI may not be replaced by *san* 'three'. Second, unlike C-YI, E-YI does not license a numeral-oriented modifier such as *zonggong* 'total', *zhengzheng* 'whole', *dayue* 'about', and *zuzu* 'as many as'.

(185) *Yani gandao (*zonggong) yi   si   beishang.*   (E-YI)
     Yani feel   totoal   one   CL   sad
     'Yani felt sad.'

Third, the CL following E-YI does not contrast with a CL of another counting-unit type, unlike that following C-YI. In (186a), for instance, the CL *si*, which can be an individuating CL in a numeral expression (e.g., *liang si zhouwen* 'two CL wrinkle'), can be replaced with the CL *zhong*. In (186b), when the two CLs occur in a contrasting construction, the sentence makes no sense.

(186) a. *Yani gandao yi {si/zhong} beishang.*   (E-YI)
        Yani feel one CL/CL sad
        'Yani felt sad.'

     b. **Yani gandao yi si beishang, er bu shi yi*
        Yani feel one CL sad but not be one
        zhong beishang.
        CL sad

When the CL *zhong* 'kind, type' follows E-YI, it does not encode a kind unit at all. We have already seen this in the translation of (186a) above. This is also shown by the fact that *zhong* in this use may not be replaced with another kind CL *lei* 'kind, type', although the two CLs are generally exchangeable in numeral expressions. The examples in (187) are parallel to the G-YI example in (178c).

(187) a. *Yani gandao yi {zhong/*lei} beishang.*   (E-YI)
        Yani feel one CL/CL sadness
        'Yani feels sad.'

     b. *Wo hun-shen like chong-man yi {zhong/*lei}*
        1SG whole-body immediately fill-full one CL/CL
        kewang.[29]   (E-YI)
        desire
        'My whole body is filled with a desire suddenly.'

However, E-YI is different from G-YI in the following aspects. First, E-YI is compatible with an element that signals an episodic eventuality, whereas G-YI is not (see (179a) above). The adverb *turan* 'suddenly' in (188a) signals that the eventuality denoted by the clause is episodic. In (188b), E-YI occurs in the resultative expression *yi tuan zao* 'a mess'. All resultative constructions encode episodic eventualities.

---

29. It has been mentioned to me that E-YI encodes a small quantity or minimality, but the E-YI in (187b) occurs with *chong-man* 'fill-full', which seems to express maximality rather than minimality.

(188) a. *Yani   turan   gandao   yi   si   beishang.*   (E-YI)
Yani suddenly feel   one   CL   sad
'Yani felt sad suddenly.'

b. *Yani   ba   shiqing   gao-de   yi   tuan   zao.*   (E-YI)
Yani BA matter   make-DE one   CL   mess
'Yani made the matter into a mess.'

Second, E-YI can be replaced by *ji* 'a bit, several' in certain contexts, without a change of the meaning, as seen in (189a). As seen in (189b), if G-YI is changed into *ji*, the sentence is not acceptable. (189c) shows that if C-YI is changed into *ji*, the meaning is changed from 'one' to 'several'.

(189) a. *Baoyu   gandao {yi/ji}   si   beishang.*   (E-YI)
Baoyu feel   one/a.bit CL sadness
'Baoyu feels a bit sad.'

b. *{Yi/*Ji} ge   yuyanxue-yanjiuzhe   yao   zunzhong*
one/a.bit CL language-researcher should respect
yuyan   shishi.   (G-YI)
language fact
'A linguist should respect language facts.'

c. *Baoyi   mai-le   {yi/ji}   zhi   ji.*   (C-YI)
Baoyu buy-PRF one/several CL   chicken
'Baoyu bought {one chicken/several chickens}.'

In my analysis, E-YI is an existential quantifier, and it does not assert any exact quantity. Therefore, the vague quantity-denoting *ji* 'a bit, several' may play the same role as E-YI. On the other hand, C-YI is a numeral, and thus it has a different meaning from *ji*. Moreover, a G-YI construction characterizes a certain general property, and thus is semantically incompatible with any vague quantity.

Third, E-YI is compatible with a demonstrative. An existential quantifier introduces an indefinite reading by default. If E-YI is preceded by a demonstrative, as in (190), the whole nominal is definite, as expected. A demonstrative or article is base-generated at DP-level, but a quantifier can be base-generated below DP, in QuantP (In this case, E-YI might be similar to *many* and *little* in *those many students* and *the little water*, although the English quantifiers could also be quantificational modifiers).

(190) *Baoyu zong   xiang-zhe   na   yi   xian   xiwang.*
Baoyu always think-DUR DEM one   CL   hope
'Baoyu always thinks about that hope.'

G-YI, on the other hand, by definition, may not occur with a demonstrative, to encode any definite reading.

Fourth, the CL following E-YI can also be replaced by *dian* in certain cases, but the similar replacement is not possible for a G-YI construction. The contrast is seen in (191).

(191) a. *Baoyu   gandao   yi   {si/dian}   {beishang/mangran}.* (E-YI)
       Baoyu   feel   one   CL/CL   sadness/confusion
       'Baoyu feels a bit {sad/confused}.'
   b. *Yi   {ke/*dian}   shu   zong   you   shugen.*   (G-YI)
       one CL/CL   tree always have root
       'A tree always has roots.'

Note that if the *yi* to the left of *dian* is optional, the surface form of the cluster is identical to the one discussed in Section 3.2. The difference between the E-YI construction and (*yi*) *dianr* construction can be explained by the degree of grammaticalization. The more general the string *yi*-CL is, i.e., the further the string goes down the continuum of grammaticalization, the greater its phonological reduction will be (see Chen 2003: 1171). If the string E-YI-CL undergoes further grammaticalization, *yi* will become optional, and the CL will lose its selectional restriction. This is exactly the case of (*yi*)-*dianr*.

One might wonder why in the E-YI examples discussed so far, only abstract nouns are observed. Our answer is that when *yi* occurs with a concrete noun, it could be ambiguous between E-YI and C-YI. Since people usually do not count abstract notions, when *yi* occurs with an abstract noun, it is unlikely to be C-YI. Thus there is no ambiguity. E-YI may occur with concrete nouns in other contexts, if a C-YI reading is clearly impossible. We will see such a case in Section 4.2.3.

The word *yi* in the following construction may not be replaced by any other numeal and must be followed by the CL *ge*:

(192) *Zanmen   wan   ta   yi   *(ge)   tongkuai!*
     1PL   play   3SG one CL   satisfaction
     'Let's play as much as we like.'

In (192), if *yi* is absent, the sentence is still acceptable, and means the same. This is somehow similar to (*yi*)-*dianr*, where *yi* is also optional (Section 3.3). See Wu (2004: 14–45) and the references mentioned in footnote 19 for studies of the various *ge*-constructions. The *yi* in (192) looks like E-YI.

It introduces an nonspecific state, *yi ge tongkuai* 'one CL satisfaction', and this state is a secondary predicate in the sentence.

E-YI can also be found in reduplicated verbs. Verb reduplication expresses a tentative aspect (Chao 1968: 204). If a mono-syllabic verb is reduplicated, either the perfective aspect marker *le* or *yi* 'one' may occur between the two copies, as seen in (193a) and (194a), respectively. The V-*le*-V form is used in a realis context only, whereas the V-*yi*-V form is used in an irrealis context only, as shown by the acceptability contrast between the a-forms and the b-forms of the two pairs of examples.

(193) a. *Lulu   gangcai   shu-le-shu   qian.*
          Lulu   just.now   count-PRF-count   money
          'Lulu counted the money just now.'
      b. **Lulu gangcai   shu-yi-shu   qian.*
          Lulu   just.now   count-one-count   money

(194) a. *Lulu   xiang   shu-yi-shu   qian.*
          Lulu   want   count-one-count   money
          'Lulu wants to count the money.'
      b. **Lulu xiang   shu-le-shu   qian.*
          Lulu   want   count-PRF-count   money

If the *yi* in the verb reduplication is an E-YI, one can explain its irrealis, and thus indefinite, use (See Basciano & Melloni 2013 for a syntactic analysis of the verb reduplication constructions).

The English word *one* also has both a numeral and a non-numeral use. The latter is called singulative use (labeled as *one*$_s$) in Huddleston & Pullum (2002: 386). *One* in the latter use is similar to E-YI. The two examples in (195) both contain a singulative *one*.

(195) a. *She arrived one rainy morning.*
      b. *For {one/some} reason or another, they didn't charge us.*

Like E-YI, *one* in (195a) does not contrast with a real numeral (**She arrived two rainy mornings*). In (195b), *one* can be replaced with *some*. This is similar to (189a), where E-YI may be replaced with *ji* 'a bit, several'. In English, the singular use of *one* shares properties with the indefinite article *a/an* in rejecting a plural number, unlike a real numeral such as *0.1, 0.5*, and *zero*.

(196) *She arrived one rainy {morning/*mornings}.*

(197) a. *zero unicorns*   b. *0.5 unicorns*   c. *0.1 unicorns*

Huddleston & Pullum (2002: 386) state that "We observed that the indefinite article *a* arose historically by weakening of *one*: *one*ₛ behaves in many respects like a stressed counterpart of *a*." Both E-YI and the singular use of *one* in English seem to under grammaticalization from a cardinal numeral to a D-element. Our observation of E-YI is compatible with Chen's (2003) general claim that the string *yi*-CL in Mandarin Chinese may play the role of an indefinite determiner, although he does not discuss constructions such as (180).

3.5.3. M-YI: *Yi* as a maximal quantifier

The word *yi* 'one' can also occur in constructions such as (198). I call *yi* in this use M-YI (for Maximal *Yi*), since it encodes a maximal or complete reading consistently, seen in the word 'whole' in the translations. The element that immediately follows M-YI, such as *shen* 'body' in (198a) and *lian* 'face' in (198b), is called temporary CL in Chao (1968: 603) and Li & Thompson (1981: 111), although it shares no property with a CL at all, to be shown shortly.

(198) a. *Ta-men {yi/*san}   shen   nitu.*   (M-YI)
         3-PL   one/three body   mud
         'They, their whole bodies are in mud.'
      b. *Ta-men {yi/*san}   lian   you.*   (M-YI)
         3-PL   one/three face   oil
         'They, their whole faces are covered by oil.'

Like G-YI and E-YI, M-YI is not a numeral, either. First, M-YI does not contrast with any other numerals. The examples in (198) already show that *yi* may not be replaced by *san* 'three'. Second, unlike a real numeral, M-YI does not license a numeral-oriented modifier such as *zonggong* 'total' and *yigong* 'totally', or a verb that selects a numeral expression such as *duo-da* 'as many as', as shown in (199).

(199) *Baoyu (*zonggong/*duoda) yi   shen   nitu.*   (M-YI)
        Baoyu   total/as.many.as   one body   mud
        'Baoyu, his whole body is in mud.'

However, M-YI is still different from both G-YI and E-YI. Unlike G-YI, M-YI is compatible with expressions for episodic events, such as *turan* 'suddenly'.

(200) *Ta-men   turen   yi   shen nitu.*   (M-YI)
      3-PL   sudenly   one   body mud
      'Suddenly, their whole bodies are in mud.'

Unlike E-YI, the element following M-YI may not be replaced by *dian*, as shown in (201a). Also, unlike E-YI, M-YI may never be replaced by *ji* 'a bit, several', as shown in (201b).

(201) a. *Baoyu   yi   {shen/*dian}   nitu.*   (M-YI)
         Baoyu   one   body/CL   mud
         'Baoyu, his whole body is in mud.'
     b. *Baoyu   {yi/*ji}   shen   nitu.*   (M-YI)
         Baoyu   one/a.bit   body   mud
         'Baoyu, his whole body is in mud.'

Semantically, unlike G-YI and E-YI, M-YI asserts a sense of completeness. This is attested in the fact that M-YI can be replaced by the word *man* 'full, whole' (Y. M. Li 2000: 54), in the absence of the near synonymous adjective *zheng* 'whole', but the parallel replacement or compatibility is impossible for G-YI or E-YI. (202) shows the contrast. The word *man* functions as a maximal quantifier. If M-YI is also such a quantifier, the replacement by, or its compatibility with, *man* is expected.

(202) a. *Baoyu   gandong-de   {yi/man}   lian   leishui.*   (M-YI)
         Baoyu   be.touched-DE one/whole   face   tear
         'Baoyu was so touched that his whole face was covered by tears.'
     b. *{Yi/*Man}   ke   shu   zong   you   shugen.*   (G-YI)
         one/whole   CL   tree always have   root
         'A tree always has roots.'
     c. *Baoyu   kan-bu-dao {yi/*man}   xian   xiwang.*   (E-YI)
         Baoyu   see-not-to   one/whole   CL   hope
         'Baoyu could not see a hope.'

The adnominal *man* 'full, whole' may precede either a unit word, as in (203a), or a noun, as in (203b) (Lü et al. 1999: 378). In the first use, *man* modifies the unit word, but in the second use, *man* quantifies the noun. In

(203b), *man* is a maximal quantifier. It is in this use that *man* can be replaced with M-YI. (203b) and (204b) mean the same.[30]

(203) a. *Zhuozi-shang   you   liang man   bei   shui.*
   table-on   have two full cup water
   'There are two full cups of water on the table.'

  b. *Man   beizi   dou   shi   mayi.*
   full cup   all be ant
   'The whole cup is covered by ants.'

(204) a. **Zhuozi-shang   you   liang   yi   bei   shui.*
   table-on   have two one cup water

  b. *Yi   beizi   dou   shi   mayi.*
   one cup   all be ant
   'The whole cup is covered by ants.'

(203b) may not be uttered out of the blue. It has to be discourse-linked to a cup identifiable in the context. The same constraint applies to (204b). This also distinguishes M-YI from G-YI, E-YI, and C-YI. Thus, like *man* in its pre-nominal use, M-YI is a maximal quantifier, followed by a noun, instead of a CL.

The maximal quantifier use of *yi* 'one' is also seen in other expressions, as in (205a), which is synonymous to the example in (205b).

(205) a. *yi-xin-yi-yi*   b. *quan-xin-quan-yi*
   one-heart-one-will   whole-heart-whole-will
   'whole-heartedly'   'whole-heartedly'

Other expressions in which *yi* occurs and maximality is expressed include *yi-gai* 'all', *yi-lü* 'all', and *yi-qie* 'all' (see Lü et al. 1999). In these words, the second morpheme never means 'all'. Thus, the maximality meaning of the words comes from *yi* alone.

I propose that the M-YI construction in (206a) has the structure in (206b), where the status of each constituent is labeled by the subscript.

---

30. We do not consider the idiomatic use of *man* 'full'. In the idiomatic expression (i), *xin* 'heart' may not be replaced with any other noun, as shown by (ii). In this case, *man* may not be replaced by M-YI, seen in (iii).

 (i) *Yani man xin huanxi.* (ii) **Yani man nao huanxi.* (iii) **Yani yi xin huanxi.*
  Yani full heart happy Yani full brain happy Yani one heart happy
  'Yani is extremely happy.'

(206) a. *Ta-men   yi   shen   nitu.*   (= (198a))   (M-YI)
    3-PL   one   body   mud
    'They, their whole bodies are in mud.'

  b. *Ta-men*_{matrix subjct} [[*yi*_{maximal quantifier} *shen*_{NP}]_{subject} *nitu*_{pred}]_{matrix pred}
    3-PL   one   body   mud

I claim that in (206), the string *yi shen* 'one body' and the NP *nitu* 'mud'
establish a subject-predicate relation, and *yi* is a maximal or exhaustive
quantifier of the subject. The whole string *yi shen nitu* is in turn a clausal
predicate of the matrix subject *ta-men* 'they'. The structure for (206a) is
parallel to the structures of (207a) and (207b), where the maximal quantifier *quan* 'whole' or *man* 'full, whole' occurs. Such a clausal predicate
structure or double-subject structure is also seen in other constructions of
the language (Zhang 2009).

(207) a. *Ta-men   quan   shen   hong   maofa.*
    3-PL   whole body   red   hair
    'They, their whole bodies have red hairs.'

  b. *Baoyu   man   lian   nitu.*
    Baoyu   whole face   mud
    'Baoyu, his face is covered by mud.'

My predication analysis of the M-YI construction is supported by the
following facts. First, the clausal analysis of the construction is supported
by the possible occurrence of *dou shi* 'all be' between the last two nominals. A maximal or exhaustive quantifier reading is compatible with the
adverb *dou* 'all' (N. Zhang 2008b). In (208), *dou* is optional. If it occurs, it
is licensed by a verb. The occurrence of *shi* 'be' in (209) is thus obligatory.
The M-YI construction in (210a) may host *dou shi*, indicating that the construction patterns with other clausal constructions in which a maximal
quantifier occurs. I use (210b) and (210c) to show that for G-YI and E-YI
constructions, no *dou shi* may intervene between the CL and the noun. This
is because *dou shi* never occurs in a nominal.

(208) a. *Shan-shang daochu   (dou) shi   cao.*
    hill-on   everywhere all   be   grass
    'There is grass everywhere on the hills.'

  b. *Baoyu quan   shen   (dou) shi   han.*
    Baoyu whole body   all   be   sweat
    'There is sweat all over Baoyu's body.'

(209) a. *Shan-shang daocu   dou   *(shi) cao.*
     hill-on   everywhere all   be   grass
     'There is grass everywhere on the hills.'

    b. *Baoyu   quan   shen dou   *(shi) han.*
      Baoyu   whole body all   be   sweat
      'There is sweat all over his body.'

(210) a. *Baoyu   yi   shen (dou shi) han.*   (M-YI)
     Baoyu   one body all be sweat
     'There is sweat all over his body.'

    b. *Yi   ke (*dou shi) shu   zong   you   shugen.*   (G-YI)
      one   CL all be   tree always have root
      'A tree always has roots.'

    c. *yi   xian (*dou shi) xiwang*   (E-YI)
      one CL   all be hope
      'a hope'

Note that if *de* occurs between a subject and its predicate, the whole expression becomes a nominal. We thus see the parallelism between (211a) and (211b) (cf. (207c) and (207a)). This nominalization does not falsify our clause-analysis of M-YI constructions.

(211) a. *Lulu dai-zhe   man lian de nitu zou-jin-le   wuzi.*
     Lulu   bring-DUR   full face DE mud   walk-in-PRF room

    b. *Lulu dai-zhe   yi   lian de nitu zou-jin-le   wuzi.*
      Lulu   bring-DUR   one face DE mud   walk-in-PRF room
      Both: 'Lulu walked into the room with the face covered by mud.'

Second, the adverb *queshi* 'indeed' may precede M-YI, as in (212a). The adverb may precede a predicate, as in (212b), but not a nominal, as shown by (212c).

(212) a. *Baoyu   queshi   yi   shen han.*   (M-YI)
     Baoyu   indeed   one   body sweat
     'There is indeed sweat all over Baoyu's body.'

    b. *Baoyu   queshi   hen   e.*
      Baoyu   indeed   very hungry
      'Baoyu was indeed very hungry.'

    c. **queshi yi   xian xiwang*   (E-YI)
      indeed one   CL   hope

Third, verbs such as *kanqilai* 'appear' may precede M-YI, as seen in (213a). Such a verb may precede another predicate, as seen in (213b), but not a nominal, as shown by (213c).

(213) a. *Baoyu   kanqilai yi   shen da han.*   (M-YI)
       Baoyu   appear   one   body big sweat
       'There seems terrible sweat all over Baoyu's body.'
   b. *Baoyu   kanqilai hen   e.*
       Baoyu   appear   very hungry
       'Baoyu seems very hungry.'
   c. **kanqilai yi   xian xiwang*   (E-YI)
       appear   one   CL   hope

I conclude that the element following M-YI immediately is a nominal, functioning as a subject, instead of a CL. Thus, the term temporary CL in the literature for the element is nothing but a misnomer. If the CL in a numeral expression heads a functional projection (see Section 6.2.1), the element following M-YI is not in that functional head position.

Thus, in addition to (*yi*)-*dian(r)* 'a bit' and (*yi*)-*xie* 'some' (Section 3.3), we have found one more quantifier that is not followed by a CL.

Like (*yi*)-*dian(r)* and any other quantifiers in the language, M-YI shows no selectional restriction on another element. Any noun that can be semantically quantified by a maximal quantifier can go with M-YI.

So far, we have identified four uses of *yi* 'one': a cardinal numeral (C-YI), as in a numeral expression (a numeral expression may also have a specific or definite reading; see Section 5.4.3), a generic quantifier (G-YI), an existential quantifier (E-YI), and a maximal quantifier (M-YI). The last one is not followed by a CL, whereas the other three are. Moreover, the CL with C-YI encodes a counting unit, whereas the one with G-YI and E-YI does not. Since none of G-YI, E-YI, and M-YI licenses numeral-oriented adverbs such as *zuzu* 'as many as', they do not show structural properties of a numeral. This contrast with C-YI is independent of any discourse context and thus the three uses of *yi* are not pragmatic effects of C-YI.

3.6. Chapter summary

This chapter has shown, first, how different types of quantifiers in Mandarin Chinese are sensitive to the occurrence of CLs; and second, for the quantifiers that require a CL, how different types of quantifiers correlate with the different uses of CLs. My conclusions are in (214).

(214) a. Some quantifiers may not be followed by a CL, e.g., *(yi)-dian(r)* 'a bit', *(yi)-xie* 'some', and M-YI;

b. Some quantifiers must be followed by a CL, and the CL contrasts with a CL of a different unit type, e.g., *ji* 'how many', *hao-ji/ji* 'several', *liang-san* 'a couple of', and *ge* 'each';

c. Some quantifiers must be followed by a CL, but the CL does not contrast with a CL of a different unit type (a different CL may not cause a quantificational change or may not be acceptable), although the CL may impose selectional restrictions on the noun, e.g., G-YI and E-YI.

d. The interrogative quantifier *duoshao* 'how many/much' is ambiguous: it belongs to either the group (214a), or the group (214b).

I claim that in the case of (214b), the CLs encode unit in quantification, and therefore, they should have the same syntactic position as those in numeral expressions. However, in the case of (214c), the CLs are simply place-holders of syntactic structures, and thus their function is an extended use of CLs in the language. The chart in (215) is a summary of the differences among the five types of quantifiers discussed in this chapter and the numeral *yi* 'one', i.e., C-YI.

(215) Properties of certain quantifiers in Mandarin Chinese

	C-YI	*ge* 'each'	G-YI	E-YI	*(yi)-dianr*	M-YI
section		3.2	3.5.1	3.5.2	3.3	3.5.3
it contrasts with another numeral	+	+	−	−	−	−
replaceable by *ji* 'several' without meaning change	−	−	−	+	−	−
replaceable by *man* 'full'	−	−	−	−	−	+
it must be followed by a CL(-like) element	CL	CL	CL	CL	DIAN	−
the CL(-like) element denotes a counting unit	+	+	−	−	−	
the CL(-like) element imposes selectional restrictions on the noun	+	+	+	+	−	

Chapter 4
Classifiers and plurality

4.1. Introduction

4.1.1. Number in Mandarin Chinese?

Like the linguistic notions such as gender and person, number has its independent status in grammar. In Chapter 2, we have decomposed countability into two features, Numerability and Delimitability, and also distinguished Numerability from plurality. In this chapter, we explore the property of plurality and its representations in the CL language Mandarin Chinese. CL languages have been generally claimed to have no productive way to encode plurality, however, this chapter falsifies this claim.

The linguistic notion of number is concerned with the morphological contrast between singularity and plurality (including dual and paucal plurality in some languages).[31] Plurality has no semantic dependency on numerals. Whether a plural form is compatible with a numeral in the same nominal is up to the formal properties of the relevant functional categories of the language. In this chapter we show that plurality is compatible with numerals in languages such as English (e.g., *three pianos*), but not in some other languages including Mandarin Chinese. We are going to answer two basic questions: How Mandarin Chinese, a CL language, encodes the number contrast, and why the number markers are optional in the language.

It is well-recognized that personal pronouns in the language have the plural marker -*men*, which is obligatory in use in the case of plural reference.

(216)   SINGULAR   PLURAL

1st person   *wo*   *wo-men*
2nd person   *ni*   *ni-men*
3rd person   *ta*   *ta-men*

---

31. See Corbett (2000: Ch. 7) for other uses of plural forms cross-linguistically, including honorific and exaggerative uses. Other formative forms, such as *yi* 'one' (Section 3.5) and CLs (see Bisang 1993; 1999), may also have special or extended uses beyond their basic uses.

If we consider personal pronouns, kinship terms, and nouns that denote one-to-one natural pairs such as the pair of a husband and wife and the pair of a master and his apprentice, Chinese even seems to have a dual suffix, i.e., *-lia*, as shown by the examples in (217).

(217) a. *ta-lia*
    3-DUAL
    'they two'

    b. *xiong-di-lia*
    elder.brother-younger.brother-DUAL
    'two brothers'

    c. *fu-qi-lia*
    husband-wife-DUAL
    'husband-wife couple'

    d. *shi-tu-lia*
    master-apprentice-DUAL
    'master and apprentice'

(218) a. **shi-sheng-lia*
    teacher-student-DUAL

    b. **guan-bing-lia*
    officer-soldier-DUAL

    c. **yuan-yang-lia*
    mandarin.duck.male-female-DUAL

    d. **ri-yue-lia*
    sun-moon-DUAL

Not distinguishing the post-nominal *lia* from the prenominal one (see Section 6.7.2), Chao (1968: 571) and Lü et al. (1999: 366) claim that *-lia* is a short form of *liang ge* 'two CL', which might function as an appositive, to the right of a compound. However, this claim is not sufficient to explain the unacceptability of the examples in (218). According to the Animacy Hierarchy of number marking (Corbett 2000: 56), personal pronouns and kinship terms are more likely to have number markers than human nouns, and the latter are in turn more likely to have number markers than animate nouns; and inanimate nouns are at the bottom of the hierarchy.

(219) person pronoun > kin > human > animate > inanimate

The restrictive application of the dual marking here seems to follow the hierarchy. The suffix *-lia* occurs freely with personal pronouns and kinship terms; but for other human nouns it is subject to a natural pair constraint. (218a) is not acceptable, probably because one teacher usually has more than one student, and thus the default relation between teachers and students is not one-to-one. The same account might cover the unacceptability of (218b). The non-human nouns in (218c) and (218d) are too low in the hierarchy to allow *-lia*.

Importantly, for personal pronouns, plural marking is obligatory for plural entities. The second person pronoun *ni* in (220a) has neither *-lia* nor *-men*, and thus it refers to a single person only. The two suffixes may also co-occur, as seen in (220b).

(220) a. *Ni   qu   na?*   (✓singular addressee; ✗plural addressee)
        2   go   where
        'Where are you going?'
     b. *Ni-men-lia   qu   na?*
        2-PL-DUAL   go   where
        'Where are you two going?'

Unlike personal pronouns, other types of nominals in the language do not have an obligatory number marker. The most frequently discussed plural-encoding forms are the bound forms *-xie* 'some' (e.g., Iljic 1994) and *-men* (e.g., Li & Thompson 1989: 40, 83; Iljic 1994, 2001; Y.H. Audrey Li 1999; Rijkhoff 2002: 154). However, *-xie* does not morphologically contrast with singularity. We have just seen that in the absence of *-men* or *-lia*, a personal pronoun is singular. The contrast between (221a) and (221b) is not a plural-singular contrast. (221b) is simply not acceptable.

(221) a. *na-xie   shu*   b. **na   shu*
        DEM-XIE   book   DEM   book
        'those books'

Moreover, *xie* may occur with mass nouns such as *shui* 'water' and *mianfen* 'flour' (e.g., *na-xie shui* 'that amount of water', *na-xie mianfen* 'that amount of flour'). Again, it does not contrast with any sense of singularity (in Section 3.3, we discussed the quantifier *(yi)-xie* 'some'). The suffix *-men*, although obligatory for personal pronouns, is restricted to common nouns that are both definite and human-denoting, and thus it is not a productive number marker.[32] Indeed, if we consider *-xie* and *-men* only, we cannot conclude that other than pronouns, there is a systematic number contrast in the language.

However, we argue that the language has a productive formal way to encode plurality, an understanding that has not been reached so far, although the relevant facts have been recognized. Productivity here means the recurrence of a certain morphosyntactic pattern in which lexically different subtypes of elements may occur. If productivity counts as an effective criterion for attesting a certain property (i.e., feature), the investigation of this chapter leads to the conclusion that Mandarin Chinese nominals

---

32. Historically, the plural marker *-men* was found to occur also with non-human nouns such as *ma* 'horse' (Ōta 2003: 316). In some northern dialects of Mandarin, *-men* is used with any nouns, including those for tree, clothes, and meat (Chao 1968: 244: fn. 30).

have the property of number. However, we also show that the identified number markers have a dependency on certain quantificational elements. This dependency may show that the plural markers represent a link of the grammaticalization chain from quantifiers to independent number markers.

In Sections 4.1.2 and 4.1.3, we introduce the notions of general number and abundant plural. Both are identified in the number system of Mandarin Chinese. Then in Sections 4.2 and 4.3, we discuss the plurality and singularity markers in the language, respectively. Section 4.4 is about the correlations between morphological and semantic markedness of number marking, and Section 4.5 is a theoretical discussion of the issue on number in CL languages. Section 4.6 concludes the chapter.

4.1.2. General number and optional number marking

According to Corbett (2000), nominals that are not specified with either singular or plural express the so-called general number. For instance, in the Fouta Jalon dialect of Fula (in Guinea), there is a three-way system of number (Corbett 2000: 12):

(222)	GENERAL		SINGULAR		PLURAL	
a.	*toti*	'toad(s)'	*totii-ru*	'toad'	*totii-ji*	'toads'
b.	*nyaari*	'cat(s)'	*nyaarii-ru*	'cat'	*nyaarii-ji*	'cats'
c.	*boofo*	'egg(s)'	*woofoo-nde*	'egg'	*boofoo-de*	'eggs'
d.	*biini*	'bottle(s)'	*biinii-ri*	'bottle'	*biinii-ji*	'bottles'

Thus, cross-linguistically, the contrast between singular number and plural number can be represented differently. As discussed in Corbett (2000: 9–19), languages such as English do not have general number, and therefore, there is a binary contrast: singular vs. plural, as illustrated in (223a). In languages such as Fula, plurality contrasts with not only singularity, but also the general number, a ternary contrast, as illustrated in (223b). The ternary contrast does not affect the formal status of the number feature in the language (See Rijkhoff 1999; 2002 for a typological study of nouns with general number, "transnumeral nouns" in his term).

(223) a.

singular   plural
(Corbett 2000: 19, Figure 2.4)

b.   general

singular   plural
(Corbett 2000: 11, Figure 2.1)

Many CL languages use bare nouns to express general number. So does Mandarin Chinese (Rullmann & You 2006). Some possible interpretations of the bare noun *xigua* 'watermelon' are listed in (224a), and similarly, some possible interpretations of the bare noun *shui* 'water' are listed in (224b).

(224) a. *Zhuo-shang you   xigua.*
           table-on   have   watermelon
           'There is a watermelon on the table.'
           'There are watermelons on the table.'
           'There is a slice of watermelon on the table.'
           'There are slices of watermelon on the table.'
           'There is a pile of watermelons on the table.'
           'There are piles of watermelons on the table.'

     b. *Zhuo-shang you   shui.*
           table-on   have   water
           'There is a drop of water on the table.'
           'There are drops of water on the table.'
           'There is a cup of water on the table.'
           'There are cups of water on the table.'
           'There is a liter of water on the table.'
           'There are liters of water on the table.'

It has been generally assumed that elements that encode plurality but are optional in use are not real plural markers (e.g., Acquaviva 2008; see also the comment mentioned in Danon 2011: 300 fn. 3). In Rijkhoff (2002: 155), the apparent number markers in some CL languages are analyzed as nominal aspect markers, rather than number markers. In Wiltschko (2009) and Butler (2012) (also see Cowper & Hall 2012), optional plural markers in certain languages are analyzed as adjuncts of certain elements such as DP, n, NP, or nominal root, whereas obligatory ones are analyzed as head elements of an independent functional projection (NumP).

However, such optionality correlates with the availability of general number, as seen in Persian, Korean (Kim 2005), and Indonesian. In Indonesian, bare nouns may express either plural or singular entities (e.g., Dalrymple & Mofu 2012: (2): *telur* 'egg, eggs'), and therefore, plural markings are optional. In the Persian example in (225a), the bare noun *muš* 'mouse' denotes either singular or plural, even though a plural marker *–ha* is available in the language, as seen in (225b) (the examples are cited from Cowper & Hall 2012: 47).

(225) a. *Muš tuye zirzæmin hæst.*   [Persian]
   mouse in basement be
   'There are mice/there's a mouse in the basement.'
  b. *Muš-ha tuye zirzæmin hæst-ænd.*
   mouse-PL in basement be-PL
   'The mice are in the basement.'

If the general number is available in a language, plural marking cannot be obligatory. In such a language, although plurality contrasts with singularity, "the distinction is made 'when it matters' and not automatically, as in languages like English" (Corbett 2000: 14). Corbett (2000: 2) states that "If number forms are available, then surely they must be used? This is an Anglo-centric assumption and is quite false." The number markers in Mandarin Chinese, to be presented in this chapter, have consistent forms and consistent meanings, occurring with all types of unit words, even though they are optional.

4.1.3. Abundant plural

There are different types of plurals, including paucal plural, which encodes small quantity of plurality, and anti-paucal plural. The latter is called abundant plural. This type of plural denotes many instances of x (Corbett 2000: 30, 87).[33]

Abundant plural is found in both material mass nouns and count nouns. For material mass nouns, abundant plural encodes abundant units of the mass. Recall the mass plural examples in (59), repeated here as (226a). As stated in Mathieu, mass plurals "appear neither dividing nor counting. Rather, they appear to denote abundance", and such plural forms are used "when the exact number is impossible to pinpoint or when it is irrelevant" (Mathieu 2012a: 189). Examples of abundant plural of mass nouns have been reported in unrelated languages, including English (226a), French, Hebrew, and Biblical English (see Mathieu 2012a: 189 for examples and references). The Modern Greek example in (226b) is from Alexiadou (2011: 36) (see Tsoulas 2006 for an extensive discussion), and the Niuean example in (226c) is from Massam (2009: 682 fn. 20; C = common). In

---

33. Abundant plural is different from exaggerative plural, since the latter may have just two elements involved (Corbett 2000: 234–235, especially his example (26)).

St'át'imcets (Davis & Matthewson 1999: 61) and Ojibwe (Mathieu 2012a: 184), mass nouns are pluralized freely, to express the abundant meaning. In Persian, mass nouns can also be pluralized to express "a large amount of whatever the noun denotes" (Cowper & Hall 2012: 48; Ghaniabadi 2012). Wiltschko (2012: 153) also reports that mass nouns in Blackfoot and Halkomelem may have plural markers to express this "abundant" meaning.

(226) a. *the (*three) waters of the Nile*
     b. *hithikan nera /hithike   nero   sto   patoma.*   [M. Greek]
        dripped   water.PL/dripped water on.the floor
        'A lot of water dripped on the floor.'
     c. *e   tau vai*   [Niuean]
        ABS.C PL   water

Note that when Mandarin *xie* 'some' occurs with a mass noun, it is not an abundant plural marker, since the nominal *na xie shui* 'that XIE water' may denote any amount of water, including a tiny amount. *Xie* is under-specified with the amount of the quantity (Lü et al. 1999: 581).

For count nouns, the meaning of many instances of x can be found in a bare plural unit word followed by *of* in English, as in (227). The bare plural *years* in (227a), for instance, denotes many years, instead of just a couple of years.

(227) a. *After years of hard work, …*
     b. *There are bottles of wine in the cellar.*
     c. *There are piles of books in the room.*

The meaning of many instances of x can also be expressed by reduplica-tion of bare nouns with *after, by,* or *upon,* as in (228) (Travis 2001, Jacken-doff 2008). This is the so-called NPN construction. Also, as shown in (229a–e), "different size domains can be reduplicated" (Travis 2001: 458), and as seen in (229f), reduplication can apply more than once (i.e., triplica-tion, Jackendoff 2008: 21).[34]

(228) a. *Student after student visited the professor on Monday.*
     b. *Gertrude watched program after program all afternoon.*

---

34. Reduplication is not always iconic. See Travis (1999) for arguments against an iconic approach to reduplication. Also see Jackendoff (2008: 16) and Basciano & Melloni (2013).

    c. *Jon washed plate after plate for hours after the party.*
    d. *Eric can drink mug upon mug of coffee in a single hour.*
    e. *The careful artist completed the mosaic tile by tile.*
    f. *In fairy tale after fairy tale, good triumphs over evil.*
    g. *Bag(s) upon bag(s) of marshmallows were stolen this week.*

(229) a. *cup after cup of coffee*
      b. *cup of coffee after cup of coffee*
      c. *cup after steaming cup of coffee*
      d. *steaming cup after steaming cup of coffee*
      e. *steaming cup of coffee after steaming cup of coffee*
      f. *cup after cup after cup of coffee*

In the NPN constructions, only *upon* allows the reduplicated noun to be plural, as seen in (228g). Polish also has NPN constructions (Jackendoff 2008: 27). In Albanian, reduplicated plural nouns have an abundant reading, such as *gërrica gërrica* 'full of scratches', which is derived from *gërricë* 'scratch'. The plurality is already indicated by the inflectional ending, and the abundance meaning comes from the reduplication alone (Stolz 2012; I thank Guy Emerson for bringing my attention to this fact, and thank Thomas Stolz for explaining the examples to me).

Note that English nouns with [–Numerable, +Delimitable] do not have abundant plural forms. The plurality seen in words such as *clothes* is not abundant plural (Ojeda 2005 calls it "mass plural", but it is different from the mass plural in (226)). Also, **furniture after furniture* or **clothes after clothes* is not acceptable.

The semantic function of abundant plural seems to be similar to the quantifiers such as *a lot of*. Abundant plural is not covered by Harbour's (2011) number features (Singular: [+Singular, -Augmented], Dual: [–Singular, –Augmented], Plural: [–Singular, +Augmented]). A richer feature system is required. But this will not be part of my analysis. Instead, I will report the existence of abundant plurality in Mandarin Chinese.

4.2. Unit plurality

4.2.1. RUWs as unit-plurality markers

In many languages, noun reduplication can express plurality (e.g., Sapir 1921: 76; Rijkhoff 2002: 152). In Mandarin Chinese, however, it is the reduplication of unit words that expresses plurality, and the encoded plurality is unit plurality. This is shown by the underlined parts in (230) (Song 1978: Sec. 5.4; 1980; Li & Thompson 1981: 34; Guo 1999; H. Yang 2005; Hsieh 2008: 66).

(230) a. *He-li   piao-zhe   (yi)   duo-duo lianhua.*
        river-in   float-DUR one   CL-RED lotus
        'There are many lotuses floating on the river.'
    b. *Di-shang   you   yi   dui-dui lianhua.*
        ground-on   have one CL-RED lotus
        'There are piles of lotuses on the ground.'

I will call a reduplicative unit word RUW. Both *duo-duo* in (230a) and *dui-dui* in (230b) are RUWs.

Unlike bare nouns in the language, RUW nominals never allow a singular reading. Song (1978) states that a RUW means many. Therefore, a RUW can be identified as a plural marker. Accordingly, the word *yi* 'one' to the left of a RUW is not a numeral. I will discuss this use of *yi* in Section 4.2.3.1.

RUWs denote plurality of units, rather than plurality of individuals. In (230a), the individual CL *duo* is reduplicated, and thus the plurality of the lotus units overlaps with the plurality of lotus individuals. In (230b), the collective CL *dui* 'pile' is reduplicated, and thus it is lotus piles that are plural.

The plurality type expressed by a RUW is abundant plurality. (230a) may not be accepted if there are only two or three lotuses in the river. I thus add the word 'many' in the translation. Similarly, (230b) may not be accepted if there are only two or three piles of lotuses on the ground.

The combination of the above two properties, unit plurality and abundant plurality, is also found in the English examples in (227).

One difference of RUWs in Mandarin Chinese from the plural markers in some languages is that they do not trigger any kind of number agreement (including disagreement; see Section 6.3) in and out of the nominals, since there is no agreement morphology in the language system.

However, when a CL is reduplicated, its possible co-occurrence restriction on the associated noun remains. For instance, the CL *pi* is for horses, and the CL *tou* is for pigs (Section 5.2.3). The restriction is maintained when the CL is reduplicated to express plurality, as seen in (231) and (232). Thus, unlike quantifiers in the language (Chapter 3), RUWs may exhibit this s-selection restriction. The possible s-selection also entails a complementation relation between a RUW and the noun, which does not support the adjunct analysis of the optional plural markers mentioned in Section 4.1.2.

(231) a. *yi pi-pi ma*   b. **yi pi-pi zhu*
   one CL-RED horse   one CL-RED pig
   'many horses'

(232) a. *yi tou-tou zhu*   b. **yi tou-tou ma*
   one CL-RED pig   one CL-RED horse
   'many pigs'

4.2.2. The productivity

If a certain formal strategy is productive, it is morpho-syntactically systematic. "A productive rule has a variable that can be filled freely by anything that meets its conditions, and so the rule can be applied to novel items" (Jackendoff 2008: 16). All types of mono-syllabic unit words can be reduplicated to express plurality of units in Mandarin Chinese.

(233) a. *Mingtian qiang-shang hui gua-shang (yi) zhan-zhan*
   tomorrow wall-on will hang-up one CL-RED
   ming deng.
   bright light   [Individual CL]
   'There will be many bright lights hung on the wall tomorrow.'
 b. *Yani bei-shang lu-chu (yi) tiao-tiao shang-ba.*
   Yani back-on show-out one CL-RED wound-scar
   'There are many scars on Yani's back.' [Individuating CL]
 c. *Yaunzi-li dui-zhe yi dui-dui xinjian.*
   yard-in pile-DUR one CL-RED letter
   'In the yard, there are piles of letters.'   [Collective CL]
 d. *Panzi-li li-zhe   yi pian-pian xigua.*
   plate-in stand-DUR one CL-RED watermelon
   'In the plate, there stood slices of watermelon.' [Partitive CL]
 e. *Yani ba yi jin-jin rensen cheng-le-you-cheng.*
   Yani BA one catty-RED ginseng weigh-PRF-again-weigh
   'Yani weighed jins of ginseng again and again.' [Standard M.]
 f. *Zhuo-shang fang-zhe yi ping-ping yao-shui.*
   table-on put-DUR one bottle-RED medicine-liquid
   'There are bottles of medicine-liquid on the table.' [Container M.]
 g. *Huojia-shang bai-man-le zhong-zhong guantou.*
   shelf-on   put-full-EXP kind-RED can
   'On the shelf are many kinds of cans.'   [Kind CL]

Among these various types of unit words, at least two of them, i.e., standard measures and container measures, are open class words (see Section 6.5.2); therefore, open-class words may be reduplicated to denote plurality. Moreover, even novel unit words can be reduplicated to express plurality. For instance, if *qiu* 'ball' is used as a unit word in an improvised expression such as *san qiu bingqilin* 'three units of ice-cream', the plurality meaning of *yi qiu-qui* 'one ball-ball' is available, as in *Paizi-li you yi qiu-qiu bingqilin* 'there are many ball-like units of ice-cream in the plate'. It has been found that in some CL languages, certain apparent plural markers are members of a closed class of quantifiers (e.g., Rijkhoff 1999: 240ff; 2002: 153ff). The properties of RUWs in Chinese indicate that they are not quantifiers (although they interact with quantifiers, to be discussed in Section 4.2.3.3). Furthermore, RUWs in Mandarin Chinese may have s-selection with nouns (see (231) and (232)), unlike quantifiers in the language (Chapter 3).

Since all types of unit words can occur in RUWs and a noun of any type may occur with certain types of unit words, RUWs in general may occur with any kind of nouns.

Not only the formation of RUWs is productive and RUW nominals may contain any kind of nouns, but also the distributions of RUW nominals are free. In addition to the above non-initial positions, RUW nominals can also occur at the left-peripheral position of a clause, as seen in (234) (for more examples see Liu 1980: 10; H. Yang 2005: 63; Hsieh 2008: 3):

(234) a. *Ge-ge   xuesheng dou you   ziji   de wangye.*
       CL-RED student   all   have self DE webpage
       'All of the students have their own web pages.'   [Individual CL]

   b. *Yi   gu-gu   zhengqi cong jiqi   pen-le   chulai.*
       one   CL-RED   steam   from machine puff-PRF out
       'Puffs of stream came out of the machine.'   [Individuating CL]

   c. *Shuang-shuang qingren bu-ru   litang.*
       CL-RED   lover   step-in   hall
       'Many pairs of lovers stepped into the hall.'   [Collective CL]

   d. *Pian-pian xigua   dou   hen   tian.*
       CL-RED   watermelon   all   very   sweet
       'Every slice of watermelon is sweet.'   [Partitive CL]

   e. *Cun-cun   jifu   dou   ke   dedao baohu.*
       inch-RED   skin   all   can   get   protection
       'Every inch of the skin can get protected.'   [Standard Measure]

f. *Pan-pan   cai   dou   hen   tebie.*
  plate-RED   dish   all   very   special
  'Every dish is special.'   [Container Measure]

g. *Zhong-zhong   zacao   zhang-man-le   yuanzi.*
  kind-RED   weed   grow-full-PRF   yard
  'Many kinds of weed have grown in the whole yard.'   [Kind CL]

As for the semantic roles of RUW nominals, in addition to possessor, as in (234a), and theme, as in (234b), causer and agent are also possible, as seen in (235a) and (235b), respectively.

(235) a. *Yi   zhi-zhi   fengzheng   la-dao-le   shu-shang   de*
       one   CL-RED   kite   pull-down-PRF   tree-on   DE
       xiao   qizi.
       small   banner
       'Many kites pulled down the banners on the trees.'

      b. *Yi   ge-ge   jizhe   zai yuanzi-li   he-zhe   jiu.*
       one   CL-RED   reporter at yard-in   drink-DUR   wine
       'Many reporters are drinking wine in the yard.'

Note that when RUWs are not followed by a noun, they may function as pronominal subjects, taking other nominals in the context as their antecedent, as in (236a), or as adverbials, expressing the meaning of 'one by one' or 'one after another', as in (236b) (Song 1978, 1980; Guo 1999). In the latter example, the RUW *tiao-tiao* occurs between the subject *e-shang de qing-jin* 'the blue veins on the forehead' and the verb *zhan-chu* 'show-out', a typical position for adverbials of the language.

(236) a. *Zhiyu naxie haizi$_i$,   ge-ge$_i$ dou   hui   Fawen.*
       as.for DEM kid   CL-RED   all   know   French
       'As for those kids, they all know French.'

      b. *E-shang   de qing-jin   tiao-tiao zhan-chu.*
       forehead-on   DE blue-vein   CL-RED   show-out
       'The blue veins on the forehead became visible, one next to another.'

Since it is well-recognized that functional formatives may have multiple grammatical functions, depending on the syntactic contexts, I will not elaborate these usages of RUWs here. Cross-linguistically, plural markers may be used beyond marking plurality. In Mano, a plural marker may have intensificative, contrastive focus, and even mirative uses. In examples such as (237), "plural markers are placed outside the noun phrase and function similar to an adverb." (Khachaturyan 2012)

(237) *lí   gbéípíé ké   vɔ́?*   [Mano]
      2SG   walk   do:IPFV PL
      '(How come,) you are taking a stroll? (I thought you always stay at home)'

One therefore should not use examples like (236a) and (236b) to claim that the RUW to the left of a noun is a floating quantifier.

4.2.3. RUWs, E-YI, and distributivity

A RUW occurs with either an implicit or explicit *yi* 'one', as in (238a), or *dou* 'all', as in (239b). If we remove *yi* or *dou* from the RUW sentences, they may become unacceptable, as seen in (238b) and (239b).

(238) a. *Yi   zhi-zhi mayi pa-dao-le   wo   de beizi-li.*
         one   CL-RED   ant climb-to-PRF   1SG   DE cup-in
         'Many ants climbed into my cup.'
      b. **Zhi-zhi mayi pa-dao-le   wo   de beizi-li.*
         CL-RED ant climb-to-PRF   1SG   DE cup-in

(239) a. *Zhi-zhi mayi dou kang-zhe   dian shenme-dongxi.*
         CL-RED   ant all carry-DUR   a.bit some-thing
         'All the ants are carrying something.'
      b. **Zhi-zhi mayi kang-zhe   dian shenme-dongxi.*
         CL-RED ant carry-DUR   a.bit some-thing

In this subsection, I argue that RUWs can be defective plural markers, since they are related to or licensed by certain quantifiers.

4.2.3.1. RUWs and E-YI

If RUW nominals are plural nominals, as pointed out by Hsieh (2008: 59), it is not clear why *yi* 'one' may occur with them. Unlike other numerals, the *yi* with a RUW may not be replaced by another numeral, as shown in (240) (Steindl 2010: 69).

(240) {*yi*/*wu} *zhi-zhi   xiao   ya*
       one/five CL-RED small duck
       'small ducks'

Thus, as stated by Steindl (2010: 69), the *yi* in a RUW nominal "does not function as a numeral here". I claim that this *yi* is an existential quantifier by default, an E-YI, identified in Section 3.5.2. This assumption explains the fact that if a RUW nominal is initiated with *yi* 'one', it is indefinite, as in (230) and some examples in (233). When a RUW nominal starts with a demonstrative-*yi* string, such as *zhe-yi* 'this-one', the default reading of E-YI is overridden by the demonstrative, and thus a definite reading appears. A similar situation with E-YI has been seen in (190).

However, the occurrence of E-YI with RUWs varies. In certain contexts, e.g., (241) (also (230a)), E-YI is optional, but in some other examples, e.g., (242) (also (230b)) and (238)), it is obligatory.

(241) *Zhe   shi   (yi)   jian-jian wang shi   you   yong-shang xintou.*
       DEM time one   CL-RED   old   event again appear-to mind
       'At this time, many old events appeared in the mind.'

(242) a. *Yan-qian   chuxian-le* *(*yi*) *zhang-zhang shuxi   de miankung.*
          eye-before appear-PRF one CL-RED   familiar DE face
          'Many familiar faces appeared before the eyes.'
      b. *Yani ba na   *(*yi*)   *tou-tou lao-niu gan-ji-le   gucang.*
          Yani BA DEM one   CL-RED   old-cow herd-into-PRF barn
          'Yani herded those many old-cows into the barn.'
      c. *Yani ba* *(*yi*) *jin-jin   rensen   zhuang-jin beibao.*
          Yani BA one catty-RED ginseng put-in   backpack
          'Yani put catties of ginseng into the backpack.'

On the other hand, if a kind CL is reduplicated, E-YI may not occur:

(243) a. *Yani kanjian-le* (*yi)   *zhong-zhong qiguai   de zhiwu.*
          Yani see-PRF   one   kind-RED   strange DE plant
          'Yani saw various kinds of strange plants.'
      b. (*Yi) *zhong-zhong zacao zhang-man-le yuanzi.* (= (234g))
          one   kind-RED   weed grow-full-PRF yard
          'Many kinds of weed have grown in the whole yard.'

I will propose an account of the (possible) occurrence of E-YI with RUWs in (241) and (242), and its impossible occurrence in (243) in Section 4.2.3.3. The issue of the variation seen in (241) will be addressed at the end of Section 4.2.3.3.

4.2.3.2. RUWs and Distributivity

In the literature, the plurality encoded by reduplication has been called 'distributive plural' in Sanches (1973: 13). Similarly, Li & Thompson (1981: 34) claim that reduplication forms "signify 'every'" (also see Steindl 2010: 53). Some grammar books in the late 1950s and the early 1960s (see the review in Song 1980) and Hsieh (2008: 6) also claim that reduplicative CLs have a distributive reading. In Hsieh (2008: 67), based on the assumed distributive reading, RUW nominals without *yi* are claimed to have a singular, rather than plural, feature.

Indeed, the reading of (244), for instance, is that each of the multiple students has his or her own web page. The example does not mean that some students have this property but others do not, although such a meaning is also a plural meaning.

(244) *Ge-ge   xuesheng dou you   ziji   de wangye.*   (= (234a))
CL-RED   student   all   have self DE webpage
'All of the students have their own web pages.'

However, as pointed out by Song (1980: Sec. 2.2.3) and Guo (1999: 7), the distributive or exhaustive meaning comes from the adverb *dou* 'all' in the containing clause, rather than the reduplication itself. They also observe that whenever *dou* is allowed (even though it does not show up), the distributive or exhaustive meaning occurs. In (245), (also (234g), and all of the examples in (233)), there is no *dou* and no exhaustive or distributive reading is attested.

(245) *Shuang-shuang qingren bu-ru   litang.*   (= (234c))
CL-RED   lover   step-in hall
'Many pairs of lovers stepped into the hall.'

Another source for a possible distributive reading of a RUW nominal is the occurrence of certain non-collective adverbials, e.g., *zuge* 'one by one', as in (246). Thus the default plural reading of a RUW nominal can be specified into a distributive plural reading in the context.

(246) *Ta   na   yi   zhuang-zhuang xin-shi   jiu   zheyang*
3SG   DEM   one   CL-RED   heart-thing then so
zhuge   jiechu.
ono.by.one   remove
'His worries are removed one after another in this way.'

The fact that RUW nominals do not have an intrinsic distributive reading is seen in their compatibility with collective verbs or predicates. In (247a), for instance, the RUW nominal *yi ping-ping jiu* 'bottles of wine' is selected by the collective verb *hunhe* 'mix'. Since collective verbs do not select distributive nominals, the RUWs in (247) are not distributive markers.

(247) a. *Yani   ba yi   ping-ping   jiu   hunh zai   yiqi.*
        Yani   BA one   bottle-RED   wine   mix   at   together
        'Yani mixed the bottles of wine together.'
    b. *Yani   ba yi   pian-pian   shuye dui   zai   yiqi.*
        Yani   BA one   CL-RED   leaf gather   at   together
        'Yani gathered many leafs together.'
    c. *Na   yi   zhi-zhi   pangxie   pa-man-le   zhengge chufang.*
        DEM   one   CL-RED   crab   crawl-full-PRF whole   kitchen
        'Those many crabs crawled such as covered the whole kitchen.'

Considering a restricted range of data, Cheng (2009) claims that reduplicative CLs in Mandarin Chinese must occur with *dou* 'all' and that they denote the meaning of 'every'. As shown above, this claim is descriptively inaccurate.

If we consider three aspects, (A) whether both distributive and non-distributive readings are allowed, (B) whether both preverbal and post-verbal positions are allowed, and (C) whether all elements of the type (e.g., all unit words) can be reduplicated, we see that RUWs in Mandarin Chinese are not constrained at all. In contrast, noun reduplication is constrained in the language. Specifically, some non-mass nouns may be reduplicated, as seen in (248a, b). Unlike RUW nominals, such reduplicative nouns never start with *yi*. They must occur with *dou* 'all' and always denote the meaning of 'every' (Sanches 1973: 13) (Aspect A), and they may not occur in a post-verbal position, as seen in (248c) (Aspect B). Moreover, many other non-mass nouns such as *deng* 'lamp' and *shu* 'book' may not be reduplicated, as seen in (248d) (Aspect C) (see Xu 2012 for a general survey of noun reduplication in languages in China).

(248) a. *Zi-zi   dou liulu-chu   tade   chouhen.*
        character-character all reveal-out   his   hatred
        'All characters show his hatred.'
    b. *Cun-cun   dou faxian-le zhe   ge bingdu.*
        village-village   all find-PRF DEM   CL virus
        'This kind of virus has been found in all of the villages.'

    c. **Baoyu   kanjian-le   zi-zi.*
        Baoyu   see-PRF   character-character
        Intended: 'Baoyu saw all the characters.'
    d. **Deng-deng dou hen   liang.*
        lamp-lamp   all   very   bright
        Intended: 'All the lamps are very bright.'

The restriction that only some nouns may be reduplicated to express a plural reading is also seen in other languages (see Rijkhoff 2002: 152). In Kam and Northern Zhuang, reduplication of monosyllabic unit words and monosyllabic non-mass nouns exhibits the same reading and distribution constraints as reduplicative nouns in Mandarin Chinese, but reduplication of disyllabic non-mass nouns may have an abundant plural reading, although they still may not occur postverbally (Gerner 2010: 275).

The fact that RUWs are compatible with distributive readings also indicates that they are not collective markers. This fact, together with the fact that RUWs are not a closed set, also separates RUWs from apparent plural markers in some CL languages, such as *cov* in Hmong Njua, which Rijkhoff (1999) identifies as a collective marker, rather than a real plural marker.

4.2.3.3. RUWs and their licensers

The co-occurrence of E-YI or *dou* 'all' with a RUW leads us to see that RUWs are different from well-recognized plural markers in some other languages. My hypothesis is that RUWs can be defective plural markers and thus may need a formal licenser. E-YI and *dou* are such licensers.

Both E-YI and *dou* are quantifiers. According to Partee (1995), quantifiers can be either D-type or A-type. D-quantifiers are nominal-internal expressions, but A-quantifiers are the ones which typically combine with predicates, e.g., a bound form on a verb stem, an auxiliary, or adverb. Accordingly, E-YI should be a D-type quantifier, and the adverb *dou* should be an A-type quantifier.

In order to capture the observed co-occurrence relation, I claim that RUWs are associated with either an existential quantifier or the distributive quantifier *dou* 'all'. For a non-kind CL RUW, the existential-quantifier is E-YI. Thus, in the RUW nominal *yi zhan-zhan ming deng* 'bright lights', for instance, *yi* is an existential quantifier, which licenses the plural marker *zhan-zhan*. When E-YI is the licenser, the RUW is compatible with either a distributive reading, as in (246), or a collective reading, as in (247). However, when the distributive quantifier *dou* is the licenser of a RUW, a distributive reading is observed.

If a RUW is licensed by E-YI, the licensing is achieved in the nominal locally. Thus such a RUW nominal may occur in any syntactic position possible for a nominal in the language. If a RUW is licensed by *dou*, however, it may not occur to the right of *dou*:

(249) a. **Yani dou   xihuan   pian-pian   wenzhang.*
      Yani all   like   CL-RED   article

    b. *Pian-pian   wenzhang,   Yani dou   xihuan.*
       CL-RED   article   Yani all   like
       'Yani likes all of the articles.'

There are many studies of the syntactic dependency of *dou* and another nominal (e.g, Cheng 1995), and they all recognize that *dou* must be linked to an element to its left, including a null operator (Zhang 1997). The relation between RUWs and *dou* follows this general syntactic constraint on *dou* dependency.

We have observed that for a kind CL RUW, its existential-quantifier licenser is special. E-YI may not occur with such a RUW. The relevant examples are repeated here as (250):

(250) a. *Yani kanjian-le   (*yi)   zhong-zhong   qiguai   de   zhiwu.*
      Yani see-PRF   one   kind-RED   strange DE plant
      'Yani saw various kinds of strange plants.'

    b. *(*Yi) Zhong-zhong zacao   zhang-man-le   yuanzi.*
       one   kind-RED   weed   grow-full-PRF   yard
       'Many kinds of weed have grown in the whole yard.'

I claim that such a RUW can be licensed by the E-closure introduced by a selecting verb, if it is available. In (250a), *zhong-zhong* is in the E-closure introduced by the verb *kanjian-le* 'saw', and thus gets licensed. In (250b), the matrix verb *zhang* 'grow' is an unaccusative verb, taking *zhong-zhong zacao* 'many kinds of weed' as its argument. The licensing of *zhong-zhong* is achieved when the argument is in its base-position, under the E-closure introduced by the verb.

Note that in some situations, an overt *you* 'have' may directly precede a RUW of a kind CL, licensing the latter. (251) is such an example. In this case, the licensing condition is similar to that for the indefinite argument in the language. We leave the specific condition for the choice among the various licensers of RUWs for future research.

(251) (*You*) *zhong-zhong jixiang biaoming jintian yao xiayu.*
     have kind-RED   sign   show   today will rain
     'Various signs indicate that it will rain today.'

Parallel licensing of formatives is also seen in the language. For instance, the word *shenme* 'what' is used as a question word in both (252a) and (252b), but its non-question reading, i.e., indefinite reading, is licensed by the negation in (252b) and the conditional context in (252c) (Y.-H. Audrey Li 1992, among others). In (252a), in the absence of a proper licenser, the non-question reading is not available.

(252) a. *Yani xiang mai sheme*
       Yani want buy what
       'What does Yani not want to buy?'
    b. *Yani bu xiang mai sheme*
       Yani not want buy what
       'What does Yani not want to buy?'
       'Yani does not want buy anything.'
    c. *Ruguo Yani xiang mai sheme …*
       if   Yani want buy what
       'If Yani wants to buy something,' …

It is thus not a surprise that when a special form of a CL plays some role other than a counting unit, it exhibits a certain formal dependency with another element in the context. Our licensing analysis is able to explain why a RUW co-occurs with *dou* or an existential quantifier such as E-YI.

Rijkhoff (1999; 2002) claims that certain apparent plural markers in CL languages should be treated as quantifiers. Our research also shows that there is indeed a close relation between RUWs and quantifiers. Nevertheless, RUWs themselves are not quantifiers; instead, they are licensed by certain quantifiers. It is possible that RUWs in Mandarin Chinese represent a link of the grammaticalization chain from quantifiers to independent number markers.

According to Ōta (2003: 155), after the CL use of nouns or verbs appeared in the history, the use of RUWs developed, and was seen in literary works in the Nan-Bei Dynasty (420–589 AD) and the period of the Tang Dynasty (608–907 AD). Later, the form of a RUW with *yi* 'one' started to appear. He claims that both bare RUWs and those with *yi* had distributive readings in old works. We can seen that since distributivity implies plurality, it is natural that distributive markers can develop into plural markers. The fact that a RUW needs to be licensed shows that it is still under the grammaticalization process to develop into an independent number marker. In the literature, historical development from collective or distributive markers or quantifiers to plural markers in some other languages is addressed in Rijkhoff (1999: 248–249; 2002: 116, fn.21) and Corbett (2000).

The gradient historical change may correlate with the gradient synchronic variations of the dependency of plural markers on quantifiers in the same language. We have seen in Section 4.2.3.1 that the occurrence of E-YI with RUWs varies. Considering the variation, it is possible that there is a certain gradient transition from a quantifier to an independent plural marker, as illustrated in (253).

(253) plural quantifier ⇒ plural marker that must be licensed by a quantifier ⇒ plural marker with the optional occurrence of a quantifier ⇒ independent plural marker

4.2.3.4. RUWs and de

One contrast between RUWs that are licensed by *dou* and those licensed by an existential quantifier is that the former may not be followed by the functional particle *de*, whereas the latter may. This is shown in (254).

(254) a. *Yi   tiao-tiao de shang-ba   chuxian zai   ta   de   ertou.*
    one CL-RED DE wound-scar appear   at   3SG DE forehead
    'Many scars appeared on {his/her} forehead.'
   b. *Tiao-tiao (*de) shang-ba   dou zai   liu-xue.*
    CL-RED   DE   wound-scar all DUR flow-blood
    'All the scars are bleeding.'

Generally speaking, when *de* occurs between two nominal elements, the left one is the modifier of the right one. In (254a), *yi tiao-tiao* 'one CL-RED' is a quantificational modifier of *shang-ba* 'wound-scar'. The acceptability of (254a) is not a surprise, although in this book, as was stated in Section 3.1, we do not discuss modificational quantifiers. But we can offer an account for the unacceptability of the *de*-version of (254b). In such an expression, the licensing relation between *dou* and the RUW *tiao-tiao* is blocked. *Dou* never has a dependency with a nominal to the left of *de*. In (255a), *dou* is associated with *liang jian fangzi* 'two rooms'. In (255b), the same string precedes *de*. *Dou* then fails to link to this string. Instead, it links to *men* 'door'. The meaning of this sentence is that all of the doors of the rooms, rather than all of the rooms, are big.

(255) a. *San   jian   fangzi   dou   hen   da.*
       three   CL   room   all   very   big
       'The three rooms are all big.'
    b. *San   jian   fangzi   de   men   dou   hen   da.*
       three   CL   room   DE   door   all   very   big
       'The doors of the three rooms are all big.'

Thus, since *dou* in (254b) is not able to license the RUW preceding *de*, and there is no existential quantifier to license the RUW, either, the *de*-version of the sentence is not acceptable. We thus see the *dou*-licensing is subject to a certain general locality condition. In (254a), however, the RUW is licensed by the E-YI locally, and thus the licensing is not affected by *de*.

The above discussion also shows that RUW nominals with *de* and without *de* are structurally different. Song (1978) claims that the string of [*yi* XX] is a short form of [*yi* X *yi* X], where X is either a unit word or a noun. In (256a), for instance, *yi* is reduplicated, together with the CL *zhuang*. In (256b), the second *yi* disappears and the first one remains. The two examples basically mean the same.

(256) a. *yi-zhuang-yi-zhuang   de   fangzi*
       one-CL-one-CL   DE   house
       'many houses'
    b. *yi   zhuang-zhuang   (de)   fangzi*
       one   CL-RED   DE   house
       'many houses'

However, as pointed out by Liu et al. (2004: 80), if the string *yi*-CL is reduplicated, it must be followed by *de*. If we remove *de* from (256a), the example becomes marginal. This shows that the two examples have different structures, and thus it is unlikely that the RUW in (256b) is a short form of [*yi* X *yi* X] in (256a). We have also observed that X in [*yi* X *yi* X *de*] can be longer than one syllable, and *de* is required. (257) is an example.

(257) *yi   da   che   yi   da   che   de   liangshi*
     one   big   cart   one   big   cart   DE   foodstuff
     'many big carts of foodstuff'

In (257), both *yi* and the adjective *da* 'big', in addition to the unit word *che* 'cart', are reduplicated. Liu et al. (2004) find that [*yi* X *yi* X de] constructions, compared with the RUWs, are more like descriptive modifiers. I do not discuss quantifying modifiers in this book.

4.2.4. Definiteness and specificity of RUW nominals

If a RUW nominal does not start with *yi*, it can be definite, especially when it occurs in the subject position, as in (244). A RUW nominal can also start with a demonstrative-*yi* string, to encode a definite unit-plurality, as seen in (258) below (also in (242b)). Such examples are parallel to the E-YI example in (190), where the existential quantifier function of E-YI is overridden by the definiteness of the demonstrative. The availability of these various readings of RUW nominals means that the reduplication of a unit word as a morphological strategy to encode unit plurality is underspecified with definiteness, and E-YI, as an existential quantifier, introduces an indefinite reading by default.

(258) a. *Wo   zhongyu kanjian-le   na   yi   zuo-zuo gao-lou.*
     1SG   finally   see-PRF   DEM   one   CL-RED   high-building
     'I finally saw those many high buildings.'
  b. *Ni   yao   ba zhe yi   jin-jin   chaye   fang-dao nali?*
     2SG   want   BA DEM one   catty-RED   tea   put-to   where
     'Where do you want to put these catties of tea?'

RUWs also seem to be underspecified with specificity. In (259a), the RUW nominal *yi ke-ke xingxing* 'many stars' is non-specific (also see (233a)). In (259b), however, the RUW nominal *yi feng-feng xin* 'letter after letter' follows the causative marker BA, which introduces a definite or specific indefinite causee nominal only (also see (233e)). In the existential coda construction in (259c) (Huang 1987; Zhang 2008a), the RUW nominal *yi li-li baoshi* 'diamonds' is the subject of the secondary predicate *shan-shanfaguang* 'shine', and the nominal in this position must be specific indefinite.

(259) a. *Ruguo mei you   yun,   tian-shang jiu   hui   you   yi*
     if   not have   cloud   sky-on   then   will   have   one
     ke-ke   xingxing.
     CL-RED   star
     'If there is no cloud, there will be many stars in the sky.'

b. *Yani ba yi   feng-feng xin   reng-dao-le   huo-li.*
   Yani BA one CL-RED   letter throw-to-PRF   fire-in
   'Yani threw letter after letter into the fire.'

c. *Hezi-li fang-zhe yi   li-li   baoshi   shanshanfaguang.*
   box-in put-DUR one CL-RED   diamond shine
   'In the box, there are many diamonds, which shine.'

4.2.5. The interactions of numerals and number markers

RUWs are incompatible with numerals in Mandarin, as shown by (260):[35]

(260) a. *Zhuo-shang bai-zhe {*jiu/yi}   ben-ben xin   shu.*
         table-on   put-DUR nine/one CL-RED   new   book
         'There are many new books on the table.'

      b. *(*Liu) pian-pian xigua   dou hen   tian.*
         six   CL-RED   watermelon all   very sweet
         'Every slice of watermelon is sweet.'

The unacceptable versions of the two examples in (260) show the inter-action between the RUWs and the numerals. Without the RUWs, the relevant nominals are perfect numeral expressions:

(261) a. *Zhuo-shang bai-zhe jiu   ben xin shu.*
         table-on   put-DUR nine   CL new book
         'There are nine new books on the table.'

      b. *Liu pian xigua   dou hen   tian.*
         six CL   watermelon all   very sweet
         'The six slices of watermelon are all sweet.'

Moreover, without a RUW in a nominal, reduplication itself is not in conflict with numerals. In (262) (Kuo & Yu 2012: 690), the adverbial is in the form of the reduplication of a numeral-CL string *san-ge-san-ge* 'three by three':

---

35. The plural suffix *-men,* which occurs obligatorily with plural pronouns and optionally with plural human-denoting nouns, is also incompatible with numerals, according to Chao (1968: 245). But it may occur with a numeral if the CL is a collective one, e.g., (ib) (Hsieh 2008: 7). See Section 5.2.5.

(i) a. *san   ge laoshi-(*men)*   b. *na   san   qun xuesheng-men*
       three CL teacher-PL   DEM three CL   student-PL
       'three teachers'   'those three groups of students'

(262) *Zhangsan   han   Lisi   ba   xingli-xiang   san-ge-san-ge*
      Zhangsan   and   Lisi   BA   luggage-case   three-CL-three-CL
      ti   jin   lüguan.
      carry   into   hotel
      'Zhangsan and Lisi moved suitcases three by three into the hotel.'

RUWs reject not only numerals, but also elements that must be licensed by numerals, such as *yue* 'roughly (for a numeral)', *zonggong* 'total', and *zuzu* 'as many as':

(263) a. **He-li   piao-zhe   yue   (yi)   duo-duo   lianhua.*
         river-in   float-DUR   roughly   one   CL-RED   lotus
      b. **He-li   piao-zhe   zonggong   (yi)   duo-duo   lianhua.*
         river-in   float-DUR   total   one   CL-RED   lotus

Based on these observations, I propose an account for the incompatibility between a RUW and a numeral: because a RUW is licensed by a certain quantifier (e.g., E-YI or *dou*), it excludes other kinds of quantifiers, in Mandarin Chinese. Cardinal numerals are also quantifiers. If RUWs have a certain dependency with certain types of non-numeral quantifiers, they may not be able to establish a new relation with another kind of quantifiers. In (260a), since the RUW *ben-ben* is licensed by the E-YI, it is not able to establish a new relation with *jiu* 'nine'. In (260b), since the RUW *pian-pian* is licensed by *dou*, it is not able to establish a new relation with *liu* 'six'.

Cross-linguistically, plural markers interact with numerals in various ways. In Purépecha, for instance, the plural marker *-mu* must be hosted by a numeral (Vázquez Rojas 2012: 62). This is a language-specific morphological requirement. In many languages, plural markers are not compatible with numerals. But the incompatibility may have different sources. In the Hungarian examples in (60), repeated here as (264), the plural marker *-k* may not occur with the numeral *három* 'three' (Csirmaz & Dekany 2010: (88)). The same constraint is also found in Turkish, Western Armanian (Bale et al. 2011b), and Bangla (Dayal 2011: 4).[36]

---

36. A related fact is that standard measures tend to lack the plural marker in languages such as Swedish and German. In the German example (1a), *Pfunde* 'pound.PL' is in a plural form, in the absence of a numeral. In (ib), however, the numeral *drei* 'three' occurs, and then only the singular form *Pfund* may show up (Krifka 2007: 26; also see Vos 1999: 52; Acquaviva 2008: 174). This is another case of incompatibility between numerals and plural markers in non-

(264) a. *három takaró-(*k)*   b. *három kutyá-(*k)*   [Hungarian]
three   blanket-PL   three   dog-PL
'three blankets'   'three dogs'

In Oromo, a non-CL language, an apparent plural marker is also incompatible with a numeral. Rijkhoff (1999: 233) argues that the apparent plural marker is in fact a collective marker, and provides his account for the incompatibility. He claims that such an apparent plural marker can be treated as a nominal aspect marker (Rijkhoff 2002: 155). More such languages are listed in Rijkhoff (2002: 38ff).

In Indonesian, a CL language, both mass nouns and non-mass nouns can be reduplicated (Dalrymple & Mofu 2012: 236). Reduplicative mass nouns, as in (265a) and (265b), encode multiple units of massive objects (similar to the examples in (226)), and reduplicative non-mass nouns, as in (266a), encode plurality. Like in Hungarian (see (264)) and Bangla (Dayal 2011), in Indonesian, plurality in the form of reduplication does not go easily with numerals. In (266b) (Sato 2009: 10; also see Dalrymple & Mofu 2012: 234), the numeral *tiga* 'three' may not occur with the reduplicative form.

(265) a. *Mereka telah kemasukan air   laut terlalu   banyak*
3PL   have   ingested   water sea   excessive many
dan air-air   itu   sudah   berhasil   dikeluarkan.
and   water-water that   already successfully PASS.exit.Kan
'They have ingested too much sea water, and those [amounts of] water have successfully been taken away.'
b. *Minyak-minyak itu   muncrat dari manhole kapal dan*
oil-oil   that   stream from manhole ship   and
membeku   setelah   membentuk seperti sabu   dan
solidify   then   form   like   bubble and
mengotori pantai sekitar.
make.dirty beach   around
'The [streams of] oil streamed from the manhole of the ship and solidified, and then formed bubbles and polluted the beach.'

CL languages. See Watanabe (2013: Sec 1) for further discussion of the interactions between standard measures and plural markers.

(i) a. *Peter hat viele Pfunde   verloren.* b. *drei {Pfund/*Pfunde} Papier*
Peter has many pound.PL lost   three pound/pound.PL paper
'Peter lost many pounds.'   'three pounds of paper'

(266) a. *siswa-siswa*   b. *tiga   siswa-(*siswa)*
     student-student   three   student-student
     'students'   'three students'

In Hmong Njua, also a CL language, an apparent plural marker, *cov*, is also incompatible with a numeral. Rijkhoff (1999: 241, and the references therein) shows that *cov* is actually a collective marker, and provides his account for the incompatibility.

Nouns with a plural marker in English may occur with a numeral (Section 2.2.6). One may find a different pattern of interaction between numerals and plural markers in English, however. Examples like those in (267) are mentioned in Saka (1991: 279):

(267) a. *1.0 pianos*   b. **1.0 piano*
    c. **one pianos*   d. *one piano*
    e. *0.5 pianos*   f. *zero pianos*

Saka (1991: 278) states that "[C]ontrary to conventional wisdom, the meaning of plurality is not 'more than one'. Rather, in English it means 'other than one'." But the numerals other than *one*, including *1.0*, do not seem to form a semantic natural class. Recall that *one* can be a singulative (Huddleston & Pullum 2002: 386; cf. Barbiers 2007) (see Section 3.5.2). *One* thus does not represent the general properties of numerals. It is possible that an English numeral must occur with a plural marker in a numeral expression, with *one* as an explainable exception.

Our above explanation predicts that RUWs are not compatible with any quantifiers beyond their licensers. This is true. A RUW nominal may not start with a quantificational D-element such as *suoyoude* 'all', *henduo* 'many', *renhe* 'any', *daliang* 'a lot', *haoji* 'several', and the interrogative *na* 'which'. In (268a), for instance, since the RUW *ben-ben* is licensed by the E-YI, it is not able to establish a new relation with any of these quantificational D-elements.

(268) a. *Zhuo-shang bai-zhe {*suoyoude/ *henduo/ *renhe/ *na/*
    table-on   put-DUR   all/   many/   any/   which/
    yi}   ben-ben   xin   shu.
    one   CL-RED   new   book
    'There are many new books on the table.'
    b. *(*Suoyoude/*Renhe/*Na)   ke-ke   shu   dou   hen   gao.*
      all/   any/   which CL-RED   tree   all   very   tall
      'Every tree is very tall.'

RUWs may not be preceded by any D-cluster that contains the quantifier *xie*, either, e.g, *naxie* 'those', *zhexie* 'these', *yixie* 'some', and *youxie* 'some', as shown in (269). Such a cluster always encodes plurality if it precedes a non-mass noun. Comparing (269) with the examples in (258), we see that it is the occurrence of *xie* that makes the examples unacceptable.

(269) a. **Wo   zhongyu   kanjian-le   naxie   (yi)   zuo-zuo   gao-lou.*
       1SG   finally   see-PRF   those   one   CL-RED   high-building
   b. **Ni   yao   ba zhexie   (yi)   jin-jin   chaye   fang-dao nali?*
       2SG   want   BA this   one   catty-RED   tea   put-to   where

The incompatibility of RUWs with the quantifiers, again, shows that they are different from the plural marker *-s* in English, which is not dependent on a quantifier, and thus is compatible with *all* (e.g., *all books*), *any* (e.g., *any books*), *which* (e.g., *which books*), and so on.

Numerals, non-numeral quantifiers, and number markers are all associated with quantity in language (see Rijkhoff 2012: 5). It is not surprising that different languages show different ways of interactions between these different but also closely related types of formatives.

In summary, a RUW is identified as a plural marker in Mandarin Chinese and it has the following formal properties:

(270) a. It denotes unit plurality, exclusively;
   b. It is attested in all types of unit words;
   c. It is underspecified with definiteness and specificity;
   d. It is not compatible with a numeral.

Other properties include the following:

(271) a. It is licensed in a quantificational context (e.g., with E-YI or *dou* 'all');
   b. If it occurs with *dou*, a distributive meaning emerges;
   c. It never follows a quantificational D-element other than E-YI, such as *suoyoude* 'all', *renhe* 'any', and *na* 'which';
   d. The semantic type of the denoted plurality is abundant plurality.

4.3. Unit singularity

We have just shown that Mandarin Chinese has plural markers, which are special morphological forms of unit words, RUWs, and are not compatible with any numerals. Recall that bare nouns in the language express general number, which is underspecified with either singular or plural reading. In this section, we show that Chinese may encode singularity by forms that are different from both bare nouns and RUWs. Moreover, both singular and plural markers exhibit parallel basic syntagmatic properties, such as incompatibility with numerals.

4.3.1. SUWs as unit-singularity markers

In Mandarin Chinese, a CL that neither shows up in a reduplicative form nor occurs with a numeral encodes singularity consistently, a fact that has been noted by Li & Liu (1978: 4–5), among many others.

Compare the examples in (272) and (273). In (272), the numeral *san* 'three' precedes the CL in all the examples. It is the initial element of the object in (272a), but it follows another element elsewhere: The proximal demonstrative *zhe* in (272b), the universal quantifier *mei* 'each' in (272c), and the interrogative determiner *na* 'which' in (272d). In (273), there is no numeral. In each of the examples in (273), the absence of the numeral to the left of the CL correlates with the consistent singular reading.

(272) a. *Yani mai-le san ben shu.* b. *zhe san ben shu*
Yani buy-PRF three CL   book   DEM three CL   book
'Yani bought three books.'   'these three books'

c. *mei san ben shu*   d. *Na san ben shu?*
every three CL   book   which three CL book
'every three books'   'Which three books?'

(273) a. *Yani mai-le ben shu.*   b. *zhe ben shu*
Yani buy-PRF CL   book   DEM CL   book
'Yani bought a book.'   'this book'

c. *mei ben shu*   d. *Na ben shu?*
every CL   book   which CL book
'every book'   'Which book?'

I will call a simple form of a unit word that is followed by a noun but not preceded by a numeral, such as the CL *ben* in (273a) through (273d),

Simple Unit Word (SUW). In S. Wang (1989: 111), when the CL *ge* starts a SUW nominal, it is treated as an indefinite determiner. But a SUW can be any CL or measure word. I thus give a more general analysis.

In Mandarin Chinese, no noun may be next to a numeral directly (Section 2.3.1). It is a unit word that links a numeral and a noun. In this context, the unit word functions as a counting unit (Chapter 2). In SUW nominals, no numeral occurs, but they encode exactly one unit. In (273), for instance, the CL *ben* occurs, without any numeral, but the meaning of a single book is expressed. I thus claim that the SUW is a singular marker.

According to Bisang (1999, 2012: 19), CLs in CL languages have various extended uses. In the absence of a numeral, a CL can be used as focus markers, a modification marker, or possessive marker (e.g., a CL can be used as a possessive markers in Hmong Njua; see Rijkhoff 1999: 237). This can be a phenomenon of syncretism. The existence of syncretism and the extended uses of elements indicate that the formal features of lexical items can be underspecified, in the absence of a syntactic context. We now see an extended use of CLs in Mandarin Chinese: as a number marker, in the absence of a numeral. In this language, plurality is expressed by the reduplication of CLs and singularity is expressed by the simple form of CLs, in the same syntactic context: i.e., in the absence of a numeral.

It needs to be emphasized that we do not claim that CLs in Mandarin Chinese are singular markers in general. CLs in different syntactic contexts have different syntactic functions. Only in the absence of a numeral does a CL that is followed by a noun function as a singular marker.

Like RUWs, SUWs do not trigger number agreement in the language. Also like RUWs, SUWs keep the possible s-selection of CLs on nouns. We have shown that the CL *pi* is used for horses, and the CL *tou* for pigs, and the RUWs in (231) and (232) are in line with these selectional restrictions. The following example shows us that the same selectional restriction is also maintained in SUWs.

(274) *Yani   mai-le   {pi/*tou}   ma,   Lulu   mai-le   {*pi/tou}   zhu.*
      Yani buy-PRF CL/CL   horse Lulu buy-PRF CL/CL   pig
      'Yani bought a horse and Lulu bought a pig.'

4.3.2. The productivity

A SUW of any kind of unit word may express unit singularity, as shown by (275).

(275) a. *Lulu   mai-le   ben   shu.*   [Individual CL]
        Lulu buy-PRF CL   book
        'Lulu bought a book.'
    b. *Lulu   chi-le   kuai   ji-rou.*   [Individuating CL]
        Lulu eat-PRF chunk chicken-meat
        'Lulu ate a slice of chicken-meat.'
    c. *Lulu   mai-le   ping   jiu.*   [Container M.]
        Lulu buy-PRF bottle wine
        'Lulu bought a bottle of wine.'
    d. *Lulu   mai-le   jin   yangrou.*   [Standard M.]
        Lulu buy-PRF catty mutton
        'I bought a catty of mutton.'
    e. *Lulu   chi-le   pian   xigua.*   [Partitive CL]
        Lulu eat-PRF slice water-melon
        'Lulu ate a slice of water-melon.'
    f. *Lulu   yujian-le   qun   youke.*   [Collective CL]
        Lulu meet-PRF group tourist
        'Lulu met a group of tourits.'
    g. *Lulu   zhaodao-le   zhong   hen   tebie   de   zhiwu.* [Kind CL]
        Lulu find-PRF   kind   very special DE plant
        'Lulu found a kind of very special plant.'

Note that even a standard measure may show up as a SUW, as shown in (275d). More examples of this kind are given in (276) (cf. X. Li & Rothstein 2012: 709).

(276) a. *cun   tu   bu   rang*
        inch land not yield
        'not give up an inch of land'
    b. *Bu   wei   dou   mi   zhe   yao.*
        not for *dou* rice bend waist
        'not bend the back for just a *dou* of rice' (1 *dou* = 10 liters)

In the examples in (275), a SUW occurs in a nominal-initial position. A SUW may also be preceded by a demonstrative, as in (273b), the universal quantifier *mei* 'every', as in (273c) (D. Yang 1996; Cheng & Sybesma

1999: 530; R. Yang 2001: 66, among others), or the question word *na* 'which', as in (273d).

The free combination of a SUW with various kinds of quantifiers reminds us of the constraint on RUWs (see (268)). The asymmetry can be accounted for by the grammaticalization chain illustrated in (253). It is possible that singular markers in the language are more developed and thus more independent number markers than the plural markers in the language. The latter is still dependent on certain types of quantifiers.

The experimental studies of A. Huang (2009) and A. Huang & Lee (2009) show that children between three and a half and five years of age are already sensitive to the quantificational difference between bare nouns and SUW nominals, and they also understand the singular reading of SUW nominals.

The singular interpretation of SUW nominals is also observed in other CL languages or dialects. As in Mandarin Chinese, in the absence of a numeral, when a noun occurs with a unit word, unit singularity is expressed in the Suzhou Wu dialect of Chinese (Shi & Liu 1985), Hmong Njua, Nung, Vietnamese (Rijkhoff 1999: 238), and Thai (Piriyawiboon 2010: 90). In the Bangala example in (277) (Simpson et al. 2011: 188), for instance, in the absence of a numeral, the string *alo-ta* 'light-CL' denotes singularity. Similarly, in another CL language, Hmong, the construction noun-CL-DEM, which contains no numeral, also encodes singularity (Bisang 2012b: 21).

(277) *Tumi ki alo-ta   jele   dite parbe?*   [Bangla]
      2SG Q light-CL turn.on give can
      'Can you turn on the light?'

The form of a SUW is usually monosyllabic, but disyllabic ones are also possible. In (278a), the SUW *bao* 'package' is modified by *xiao* 'small'. In (278b), the SUW *gongjin* 'kilogram' is disyllabic, and in (278c), the SUW *kuødʑ* 'can' in Suzhow Wu dialect of Chinese is also disyllabic (Shi & Liu 1985: 161).

(278) a. *Siyu mai-le   na   xiao bao   chaye.*
         Siyu buy-PRF DEM   small package tea
         'Siyu bought that small package of tea.'
      b. *Siyu jiancha-le   mei   gongjin chaye.*
         Siyu check-PRF   every kilo   tea
         'Siyu checked every kilo of tea.'

c. *kuødʀ   ts'iə?*   [Suzhou Wu Chinese]
   can   paint
   'a can of paint'

A nominal initiates with a SUW may occur in the position of the object a transitive verb, as seen in (275). It can also occur in the position of the direct object a ditransitive verb, as shown by *ba dao* 'CL knife' in (279a). However, it does not occur in the position of a primary subject, as seen in (279c), compared with (279b).

(279) a. *Yani xiang gei wo   ba   dao.*
         Yani want give 1SG CL   knife
         'Yani want to give me a knife.'
      b. *Turan,   yi   ba   dao   chuxian zai yan-qian.*
         suddenly one CL   knife appear at   eye-before
         'Suddenly, a knife appeared before the eyes.'
      c. **Turan, ba dao   chuxian zai yan-qian.*
         suddenly CL knife appear at   eye-before

R. Yang (2001: 72–76) claims that the use of the CL in a SUW is cliticized to the proceding host word, different from the CL in a numeral expression. She shows two parallelisms between SUWs and the English auxiliary clitic *'s*: as a free form, the auxiliary *is* may be stranded by topicalization and VP ellipsis, whereas the clitic *'s* may not. This is shown in (280) and (281).

(280) a. *Going to the party, I believe he is.*
      b. **Going to the party, I believe he's.*

(281) a. *They are going and he is (going), too.*
      b. *They're going and he's *(going), too.*

A similar contrast is seen between the CL in a numeral expression and a SUW, as shown in (282) and (283). In (282a), the CL *ben* in the numeral exprssion is stranded by the topicalization of the noun *shu* 'book', and in (283a), the same CL is stranded by the ellipsis of *shu*, also in a numeral expression. In (282b) and (283b), however, the parallel strandings of the SUW *ben* by the topicalization and ellipsis are not possible.

(282) a. *Shu,   ta   mai-le   yi   ben.*
         book 3SG   buy-PRF   one   CL
         'As for books, he bought one.'

b. **Shu,   ta   mai-le   ben.*
   book 3SG   buy-PRF   CL

(283) a. *Ta   mai-le   yi   ben   shu. Wo   ye   mai-le   yi*
       3SG   buy-PRF one   CL   book 1SG   also buy-PRF   one
       ben   (shu).
       CL   book
       'He bought one book, and I bought one, too.'
   b. *Ta   mai-le   ben   shu. Wo   ye   mai-le   ben *(shu).*
       3SG   buy-PRF CL   book 1SG   also buy-PRF   CL   book

R. Yang's observation shows that SUWs are morphologically different from CLs in numeral expressions. Her clitic analysis of the former explains the unacceptability of examples like (279c).

4.3.3. The problems of the numeral-deletion analysis

It has been generally assumed that a SUW nominal is derived by the deletion of the numeral *yi* 'one' (e.g., Lü 1944; S. Wang 1989: 109), and therefore, clauses containing SUW nominals are treated as *yi*-gapping constructions. Cheng & Sybesma (1999: 525–526) try to falsify the deletion (or called phonological reduction) analysis, but their argument that SUW nominals in Mandarin Chinese cannot be specific is not convincing (see our next subsection). X. Li & Bisang (2012: 344ff) show that SUW nominals have different distributions from numeral expressions, and thus the former cannot be the result of *yi*-deletion from the latter. In this section, new arguments are presented to argue against the *yi*-deletion analysis of SUW nominals, leading to the same conclusion that Cheng & Sybesma and X. Li & Bisang have tried to reach.

First, the assumed deletion has no antecedent, and thus violates the basic identity condition of ellipsis. For instance, the numeral *si* 'four' is available in the first conjunct in (284a), and one thus should expect the deletion of *si* in the second conjunct to be possible, contrary to the fact. On the other hand, SUW nominals may be uttered out of the blue, without a context-support, to encode singularity. In (284b), *yi* does not occur at all, but the SUW nominal *ben shu* 'CL book' denotes singularity exclusively. If deletion needs an antecedent to satisfy the recovery condition (e.g., Chomsky 1965: 144), (284b) cannot be the result of deletion.

(284) a. **Lulu mai-le   si   zhi bi,   Siyu   mai-le   si̶   ben shu.*
      Lulu buy-PRF four   CL   pen   Siyu   buy-PRF four   CL   book
      Intended: 'Lulu bought four pens and Siyu bought four books.'
   b. *Lulu   mai-le   si   zhi bi,   Siyu   mai-le   ben   shu.*
      Lulu   buy-PRF four   CL   pen   Siyu   buy-PRF CL   book
      'Lulu bought four pens and Siyu bought a book.'

Second, the assumed deletion cannot be a lexical-specific operation. Trying to describe SUWs, but realizing the impossibility of the numeral deletion in examples like (284a), R. Yang (2001: 71) states that "as a descriptive generalization, I suggest that the only numeral that can be optionally omitted from the [Num-CL] complex is *yi* 'one'." If one assumes that the numeral *yi* is so special that its deletion does not need an antecedent (as mentioned to me in a conference and also by an anonymous reviewer), we still cannot explain why it may not be deleted in other contexts. One wonders why the deletion fails in the examples in (285).

(285) a. *Yani   chi-le   san-fenzhi-{yi/*_} pian   yao.*
      Yani   eat-PRF   three-part-one   CL   pill
      'Yani took one third of a medicine pill.'
   b. *Yani   ba   chengji tigao-le   {yi/*_}   bei.*
      Yani   BA   score   increase-PRF   one   time
      'Yani doubled the scores.'
   c. *Yani   he-le   di   {yi/*_}   bei   shui.*
      Yani   drink-PRF ORD   one   cup   water
      'Yani drank the first cup of water.'
   d. *Qing   jin   {yi/*_}   hao   fangjian!*
      please   enter   one   number   room
      'Please enter Room No. 1!"

It is clear that the alleged deletion fails exactly in the contexts of numerals. According to Wiese (2003), numerals have three uses: cardinal, as in (285a) and (285b), ordinal, as in (285c), and proper-name-like nominal, as in (285d). Obviously, when *yi* occurs as a real numeral in all of these uses, it may not be deleted.

Numeral deletion is not possible cross-linguistically (Kayne 2012a; Cinque 2012: 180). (286b) is acceptable, but not under the reading of (286a) (Kayne 2012a: 78). Law (2012: 112–115) also shows that numerals may not be deleted in Mandarin Chinese and Naxi.[37]

---

37. However, numeral-initial-*1*, rather than nominal-initial *1*, may take a null form, cross-linguistically (Hurford 1975: 255; 1987; Watanabe 2013). In (ia),

(286) a. *Mary has written four papers, whereas John has only written four squibs.*
   b. *Mary has written four papers, whereas John has only written squibs.*

Third, SUW constructions may not contain numeral-oriented adverbs such as *zuzu* 'as many as', *zhengzheng* 'total', or partitive adverbs such as *duo* 'more' or *ban* 'half', which must be licensed by a numeral. If *zuzu* or *zhengzheng* were syntactically licensed by an implicit *yi*, (287b) would be acceptable, contrary to the fact.

(287) a. *Yani {zuzu/zhengzheng} chi-le   yi   ge dangao.*
   Yani   as.many.as/total   eat-PRF one CL cake
   'Yani ate as much as one whole cake.'
   b. **Yani {zuzu/zhengzheng} chi-le   ge dangao.*
   Yani   as.many.as/total   eat-PRF CL cake

Fourth, a SUW nominal may not be the predicate of a quantity-denoting subject. In (288a), the subject *Lulu de yao-liang* 'Lulu's dosage' is quantity-oriented, and the numeral expression *yi pian zhi-xie-yao* 'one antidiarrheal pill' is a semantically appropriate predicate. In (288b), however, the SUW nominal predicate *pian zhi-xie-yao* 'CL antidiarrheal pill' may not occur as a predicate of the same subject. If the SUW nominal contained an implicit numeral, the sentence would be as good as (288a).

(288) a. *Lulu de yao-liang   shi yi   pian zhi-xie-yao.*
   Lulu DE drug-quantity   be   one CL   anti-diarrheal-drug
   'Yani's dosage is one antidiarrheal pill.'
   b. **Lulu de yao-liang   shi pian zhi-xie-yao.*
   Lulu DE drug-quantity   be   CL   anti-diarrheal-drug

Fifth, a SUW nominal may not be the subject of the secondary predicate *man* 'full' in an amount-oriented V-*man* construction. In (289a), the subject of the resultative *man* is the numeral expression *yi zhang zhi* 'one CL paper'.

---

yi 'one' may not show up, whereas in (ib), *yi* must show up (see Watanabe 2013 for a parallel contrast in Japanese). The (im)possibility for the numeral-initial-*1* to be null under certain conditions has nothing to do with the issue of whether any whole numeral (including *1*) can be null.

(i) *Lulu mai-le (*yi) shi jin dami.*   (ii) *Lulu mai-le *(yi) wan   jin dami.*
   Lulu buy-PRF 1 10 catty rice   Lulu buy-PRF 1 10000 catty rice
   'Lulu bought 10 catties of rice.'   'Lulu bought 10000 catties of rice.'

In (289b), the SUW nominal *zhang zhi* 'CL paper' does not saturate the predicate *man* 'full', and thus the sentence is not acceptable. If the SUW nominal contained an implicit numeral, the sentence would be fine.

(289) a. *Lulu   xie-man-le   yi   zhang zhi,   Yani*
Lulu   write-full-PRF one   CL   paper Yani
xie-man-le   liang   zhang.
write-full-PRF two   CL
'Lulu wrote such that one piece of paper became full of characters, and Yani wrote such that two pieces of paper became full of characters.'
  b. **Lulu xie-man-le   zhang zhi.*
Lulu   write-full-PRF CL   paper

Cross-linguistic facts also falsify the numeral deletion analysis of SUWs. In Suzhou Wu Chinese, SUW nominals may occur in certain positions where no numeral is allowed. One such position is to the right of a reduplicative verb, which denotes a tentative aspect, as in (290a). Since no numeral may follow such a verb, Shi & Liu (1985: 163) point out that there is no numeral deletion for the SUW nominal. Another position where no numeral is allowed but a SUW nominal may occur is to the immediate right of a pronoun or a proper name, as seen in (290b). In this case, the SUW nominal functions as an apposition to the preceding nominal (Shi & Liu 1985: 164).

(290) a. *nɛ   k'ø-k'ø   tsoŋ zãmiɪ k'ø!*   [Suzhou Wu Chinese]
2SG look-look CL   scene look
'Have a look at the scene!'
  b. *nɛ   tsaʔ siœ   ts'iəʔlœ.*
2SG   CL   small devil
'You, small devil.'

We claim that like RUW nominals, SUW nominals do not have a syntactic position for a numeral. Therefore, there is no numeral to be deleted.

In Mandarin Chinese, a CL may follow a demonstrative directly, as seen in (291a). But in a numeral expression, a CL follows a numeral directly, as seen in (291b). With respect to the latter order, Greenberg ([1972] 1990a: 168) states that syntactically, "there is variability in that the classifiers need not be confined to numerical constructions. In Mandarin and other languages the classifier is required with demonstratives even in non-numeral phrases."

(291) a. *zhe   ben   shu*   (= (273b))   b. *zhe   yi   ben   shu*
DEM CL   book   DEM one   CL   book
'this book'   'this book'

However, examples like (291a) show a semantic constraint: their interpretations must be singular. This is pointed out by Greenberg (1990a: 188)
himself: "in Mandarin the classifier *ben* required with *shu* 'book' with any
number (e.g., *i ben shu* 'one book', *san ben shu* 'three books') occurs with
the demonstrative also (*che ben shu* 'this book') but only in the singular."[sic.] In our analysis, such examples are SUW nominals, which are
singular unit-denoting nominals, without a syntactic position for a numeral.[38] Thus, indeed, a CL does not have to follow a numeral. When it
does, as in (291b), it functions as a counting unit. But when it does not, as
in (291a), it is a singular marker instead. In (291a), the number marker
function of the CL is one of the extended uses of CLs.

One supporting fact to distinguish a SUW with a demonstrative, as in
(291a), from a numeral expression with a demonstrative, as in (291b), is
given by an anonymous reviewer and confirmed by my informant: in Mandarin Chinese, both constructions are acceptable, but in the Wu dialect of
Chinese, only the former construction is possible.

4.3.4. Definiteness and specificity of SUW nominals

In Mandarin Chinese, if a nominal is initiated with a SUW, it is indefinite
in general. Chao (1968: 344) and Chen (2003: 1173)'s following examples,
however, indicate that if a CL-initial SUW nominal occurs between the
causative marker BA and a kinship term, a definite reading is possible in
Mandarin Chinese.

---

38. A demonstrative may also combine with a reduced *yi* 'one', deriving *zhei* (*zhe*
    + *yi* 'this + one') and *nei* (*na* + *yi* 'that + one') (Zhu 1982: 85). However, be-
    cause of reanalysis, *zhei* and *nei* can also function as pure demonstratives, fol-
    lowed by a numeral other than *yi* 'one'. So (i) is acceptable. The opaque func-
    tion of *yi* in *zhei* in (i) is similar to the opaque function of *et* 'and' in the phrase
    and etcetera, where two conjunctions (*and, et*) occur in a row, and *cetera*
    means 'the rest'.

    (i) *zhei   san   feng xin*
        DEM   three   CL   letter
        'these three letters'

(292) a. *Ta   ba   ge   zhangfu   si-le.*
       3SG   BA   CL   husband   die-PRF
       'She suffered her husband to die on her.'
  b. *Ta   bei   pengyou   ba   ge   taitai   gei   pian-zou-le.*
       3SG   PASS   friend   BA   CL   wife   PASS   cheat-away-PRF
       'He was cheated by his friend out of his wife' or 'He suffered from
       his friend cheating his wife away from him.'

In Suzhou Wu Chinese (Shi & Liu 1985), Cantonese, Vietamese (Daley 1998), and Yongren Lolo (Gerner 2003: 993–994), a CL-initial SUW nominal can be either definite or indefinite (see Simpson et al. 2011: 169, and the references thereof).[39] If a SUW nominal starts with a demonstrative, as in (291), it is definite. Since SUWs may occur in either definite or indefinite nominals, they themselves are not specified with any definiteness feature.

An indefinite SUW nominal can also be either specific or non-specific. In (279a), the SUW nominal is clearly nonspecific.[40] Data like (293) show that the claim that CL-initial nominals must be non-specific in Mandarin Chinese (Cheng & Sybesma 1999: 526; Hsieh 2008: 126–127; X. Li & Bisang 2012: 345; Huang & Ochi 2012: (18)) is not accurate. First, the causee position following the causer marker *ba* is a typical position for a definite or specific indefinite nominal. Since a SUW nominal may occur in this position, as seen in (293a), it can be specific (see Chen 2003: 1178 for more examples of this kind). Second, the subject of a secondary predicate in an existential coda construction (Huang 1987) must be a specific indefinite. Since a SUW nominal may also occur in this position, as seen in (293b), it can be specific. Third, an indefinite nominal occurring between *you* 'have' and a modal is always interpreted as being specific (Tsai 2010:

---

39. In Suzhou Wu Chinese, when a SUW nominal is definite, it exhibits the same tone sandhi as when it is preceded by the demonstrative *gəʔ* 'this', and thus Shi & Liu (1985: 165) claim that the definite use is the result of the phonological deletion of the demonstrative in the context.
40. Li & Thompson (1981: 130) claim that "nonreferential noun phrases never take classifier phrases"; "if a noun phrase has a classifier phrase, it must be a referential noun phrase". In (i), the CL expression *liang ba dao* 'two knives' is non-specific. A CL also follows G-YI in a generic noun phrase (Section 3.5.1). I thus guess their use of "non-referential", whatever it means, does not mean unspecific or generic.
  (i) *Wo xiang mai liang ba dao.*
     1SG want buy two CL knife
     'I want to buy two knives.'

210). Since a SUW nominal may also occur in this position, as seen in (293c), it can be specific. Thus the singular marker is not specified with any specificity feature.

(293) a. *Shouwei ba ge cong nanfang lai   de xiaotou fangpao-le.*
       guard   BA CL from south   come DE thief   release-PRF
       'The guard got released a thief who had come from the south.'
    b. *Lulu mai-le   zhang zhuozi san   tiao tui.*
       Lulu buy-PRF CL   table   three CL   leg
       'Lulu bought a table which has three legs.'
    c. *Zhe   ci   you   ge ren   {keneng/yiding} hui lai.*
       this   time   have   CL person   possibly/surely   will come
       'This time, a certain person will {possibly/surely} come.'

Cross-linguistically, the string CL-NP is not restricted in definiteness and specificity. X. Li & Bisang (2012: 340) report that in the object position, the string is indefinite in both Mandarin and Wu, but it is either definite or indefinite in Cantonese. In the subject position, the string is indefinite in Yi (Jiang & Hu 2010), but definite in both Wu and Cantonese. Liu's (2006: 74) following summary also shows that in three CL languages, namely, Yi, Mandarin and Cantonese, there is no general constraint on the definiteness and specificity of SUW nominals (see his work for examples in Yi and Cantonese).

(294)   SUWs in Yi, Mandarin and Cantonese (Liu 2006 : 74)

	SUBJECT POSITION	OBJECT POSITION
Yi	specific indefinite	specific, non-specific indefinite
Mandarin	*	specific, non-specific indefinite
Cantonese	definite	definite, specific, non-specific indefinite

In summary, the following four major properties are shared by the plural number feature of RUWs and the singular number feature of SUWs:

(295) a. The number feature denotes the number of the unit, rather than that of the individual denoted by the associate noun;
    b. It is attested in all types of unit words;
    c. It is underspecified with definiteness and specificity;
    d. It is not compatible with a numeral.

4.4. Morphological and semantic markedness

I have identified the unit word that is not preceded by a numeral as a number marker in Mandarin Chinese. The newly identified number markers share properties with well-recognized number markers in languages such as English. First, they have stable morphological forms. Plural markers are reduplicative unit words, and singular markers are non-reduplicated unit words. Second, they are productive and systematic. They are found with all types of unit words. Third, they are underspecified with either definiteness or specificity properties. Fourth, they show consistent syntagmatic properties. In English, number markers are compatible with numerals and trigger agreement on verbal elements, whereas in Mandarin Chinese, number markers block the occurrence of numerals, and may exhibit s-selection on nouns.

According to Greenberg Universal 35, in many languages, the singular feature is not associated with any overt phonological content but the plural is. In both English and Mandarin Chinese, plural forms are morphologically marked. In English, the suffix -*s* is used for regular plural forms, in contrast to the unmarked forms for singularity. In Mandarin Chinese, the reduplicative forms of unit words for plurality contrast with the simple forms of unit words for singularity. In some languages, however, both singular and plural number are overtly expressed, e.g., in Babungo, Bukiyip, Kisi, Nasimo, and Ngiti (cited in Rijkhoff 2002: 150), and Ojibwe (Mathieu 2012a). In the following Kisi examples (Childs 1995: 14), the number marking is related to class membership. This is different from the general pattern found in English and Chinese.

(296) a. *nì-léŋ*   b. *nì-láŋ*   [Kisi]
      ear-CL.SG   ear-CL.PL
      'ear'   'ears'

However, in my understanding, one contrast of the plurality-marking between English and Mandarin Chinese is the pattern of the semantic markedness of the plural feature (Bale et al. 2011a). As shown in Bale et al. (2011a), English plural forms are semantically unmarked, although they are morphologically marked. Therefore, a nominal with a plural marker may denote a singular element, element smaller than one, and even zero, as shown in (267), some of them are repeated here in (297) (in fact, English plurals may even occur with non-count nouns e.g., *clothes*; see McCawley 1979; Ojeda 2005).

(297) a. *1.0 eggs*   b. *0.5 eggs*   c. *zero eggs*

The semantic unmarkedness of plurals in English is also seen in the so-called "inclusive plural". In (298), the plural noun *children* in A is not interpreted as plural, and therefore, the answer in B is appropriate, but the answer in C is not (Krifka 1989, 2008: Sec. 5.1; see Bale et al. 2011a: 203, 209 for further discussion of cross-linguistic variations and some pragmatic constraints on such singular interpretations of plural nominals in English).

(298) A. *Do you have children?*
      B. *Yes, one.*
      C. **No, (just) one.*

(299) A. *Do you have two or more children?*
      B. **Yes, one.*
      C. *No, (just) one.*

In (298), no numeral occurs in A's question. Therefore, counting is not an issue. A only asks for the existence of children. B's affirmative answer, followed by the quantity information "one" is appropriate. But C's negative answer followed by the quantity "one" is self-contradictory. In (299), a numeral occurs in A's question, and thus counting is an issue here. Therefore, B's affirmative answer followed by the information that is not compatible with the numeral given by A is not acceptable; but C's negative answer followed by the numeral that is not compatible with the numeral given by A is an appropriate one.

This "inclusive plural" is also found in Indonesian (Dalrymple & Mofu 2012: 251).

In Mandarin Chinese, however, plural forms are semantically, as well as morphologically, marked. Since general number is available in the system, a plural marker is used only when the singular-plural contrast matters in the context. It thus never occurs in a nominal that does not denote plurality. For instance, question A in (300) may not be answered by the positive answer in B, if there is only one light. Instead, only C is the appropriate answer, with a stress on the numeral *yi* 'one' (The stress is marked by the capital letters) (In this aspect, Mandarin plural forms are like plural forms in Western Amenian; see Bale & Khanjian 2008: 73; also Bale et al. 2011a: 209).

(300) A. *Shu-shang   shi-bu-shi   gua-zhe   zhan-zhan   ming   deng?*
         tree-on   be-not-be   hang-DUR   CL-RED   bright light
         'Are there bright lights hung on the tree?'

   B. **Dui, shu-shang gua-zhe yi zhan ming deng.*
      right, tree-on   hang-DUR one CL bright light
   C. *Bu dui, shu-shang gua-zhe YI zhan ming deng.*
      notright, tree-on   hang-DUR one CL bright light
      'No, there is ONE bright light hung on the tree.'

In contrast, singular forms are semantically, as well as morphologically, unmarked. This can be seen in the fact that a form usually interpreted as a singular may get a plural reading in an irrealis context, as shown by (301b):[41]

(301) a. *Wo mai-le ben shu.*   b. *Wo xiang mai ben shu.*
       1SG buy-PRF CL book   1SG want buy CL book
       'I bought a book.'   'I want to buy {a book/books}.'

This contrast in the markedness pattern is consistent, and is observed also in the systems of third person pronouns. Number marking in pronouns is obligatory in both English and Chinese. However, in colloquial English, the third person plural pronoun can take a singular antecedent, so long as it does not refer to an identified referent (this is a similar non-specific condition for number flexibility in (301b)):

(302) a. *Someone left their jockstrap in the locker room.* (Rullmann 2003)
     b. *Someone came this morning, but I didn't see them.*
     c. *There's someone at the door. Go see what they want.*

(303) a. **Bill left their jockstrap in the locker room.*
     b. **The man came this morning, but I didn't see them.*

In Chinese, however, the third person singular pronoun *ta* 'he/she/it' can take a plural antecedent, as seen (304).

(304) *Zhexie jiahuo, zhineng dui ta bukeqi.*   (Xu 1999: 7)
     these chap cannot.but to 3SG impolite
     'As for these chaps, (we) cannot but be impolite to them.'

Recall that if *-men* occurs with a common noun, the noun must refer to definite persons. The referent or antecedent of a *-men* pronoun is also subject to the human constraint (Zhu 1982: 82). Therefore, although *-men* is

---

41. According to Rullmann & You's (2006: 184) judgment, (301a) also allows a plural reading. Our judgment is different from theirs.

obligatory for a pronoun that has a plural antecedent, *ta*, instead of *ta-men* is used in each of the examples in (305), where its antecedent is plural and inanimate. The number mismatch between the antecedent and the pronoun in such cases is not an issue of semantic markedness, unlike the one in (304).

(305) a. *Zhexie shu,* wo   *yiqian meitian wanshang dou kan   ta.*
        these   book 1SG   before   every   evening   all   read   3SG
        'These books, I read them every evening in the past.'
    b. *Zhexie dengpao* dou *huai-le,   ba ta   reng-le   ba.*
        these   bulb   all   bad-PRF   BA 3SG   dump-ASP   PRT
        'These bulbs are all defective, let us dump them.' (Zhu 1982: 82)
    c. *Wo xiang xie   ji   feng xin,   ranhou ba ta   ji-chuqu.*
        1SG want   write   several CL   letter   then   BA 3SG mail-out
        'I want to write several letters, and mail them.'   (Julia Su, p.c.)

4.5. Number marking in CL languages

Number is expressed by morphological forms of nominal-internal elements (in addition to agreement markers on nominal-external elements in some languages). The morphological strategies include affixation, reduplication, and other inflectional operations. Different languages may mark number information on different types of elements. In English and Lezgain, for instance, nouns are marked for number by suffixation (Corbett 2000: 179); in Bambara, plural markers occur as phrase-final enclitical elements (Rijkhoff 2002: 32); in Mokilese (Corbett 2000: 212) and St'át'imcets (Davis & Mathewson 1999: 61), nouns are marked for number through demonstrative or determinative affixes; in spoken French (Corbett 2000: 179; Bouchard 2002) and Haitian Creole (Deprez 2006), number contrast is basically marked on articles (e.g., *le voiture* 'the car', *les voiture(s)* 'the cars' in French, where the *-s* with the noun is optional in spoken form, but obligatory in writing); and in Purépecha (Vázquez Rojas 2012) and Slovenian (Herrity 2000), number is marked on numerals, as well as other elements including nouns. In languages such as Niuean (Massam 2009: 676) and Hawaiin (Dryer 2005), plural markers can be independent free forms.

We have shown that in Mandarin Chinese, plurality can be expressed by reduplication of unit words. In other numeral CL languages reported in Gerner (2006) (see (307)–(309)), number is also encoded by special morphological forms of CLs.

In Mandarin Chinese, SUWs express singularity. This extended use of CLs, however, is not seen in Japanese (Satoshi Tomioka, p.c.; Watanabe

2012: 4). Similarly, in Purépecha, a CL can occur only in the presence of a numeral or an interrogative quantifier meaning 'how many'. As expected, "Although in Purépecha bare nouns can occupy argumental positions, they cannot do so if they are preceded only by a classifier, because classifiers require a numeral" (Vázquez Rojas 2012: 89). Similarly, in Niuean, a CL occurs only in the presence of a numeral or quantifier (Massam 2009). Thus the form of a SUW nominal is simply unacceptable in the languages. No example of RUW nominal is seen in the languages, either. The languages have systematic plural markers. Thus, number is expressed by strategies other than any (special form of) CLs, unlike in Mandarin Chinese.

In some Kam-Tai languages, plurality can be expressed by the reduplication of nouns or CLs (Gerner 2006: 255). In Indonesian, plurality is expressed by reduplication of nouns (Dalrymple & Mofu 2012), as seen in (306):

(306) a. *siswa-siswa*   b. *pulau-pulau*   [Indonesian]
      student-RED   island-RED
      'students'   'islands'

As in Chinese, the plural reading of reduplicative nouns does not have to be connected to either definiteness or distributivity (Dalrymple & Mofu 2012: 232–234). Moreover, in both languages, the plural encoded by reduplicated forms is abundant plural (Section 4.2.1 and Dalrymple & Mofu 2012: 234). Furthermore, plural markings in RUW nominals reject numerals (Section 4.2.5), and in Indonesian, "the use of reduplicated nouns with numerals (with or without classifiers) is possible but dispreferred" (Dalrymple & Mofu 2012: 243, 257). These shared properties distinguish the two languages from languages such as Haitian Creole. In Haitian Creole, indefinite nominals may remain unmarked for number, whereas definite ones must have number specification (Deprez 2006).

In the same language, different nominal systems may also mark number information in different ways. In English, plural marking in pronouns is different from that in nouns. In Mandarin Chinese, for personal pronouns, the plural marker is the suffix *-men*. But RUWs are words. The difference correlates with Corbett's (2000: 75) claim that of the two ways of number marking, i.e., direct morphological operations and number words, the former is more likely used for personal pronouns than for other types of nominals.

The fact that Mandarin Chinese, as a numeral CL language, has plural markers is theoretically significant. The so-called Sanches-Greenberg Generalization states that "[N]umeral classifier languages generally do not have compulsory expression of nominal plurality, but at most facultative expression." (Greenberg 1974: 25; also see Sanches 1973) Indeed, in CL languages such as Japanese, Thai, and Korean, reported plural markers are not systematic (Mizuguchi 2004: 18, 145, among others). The Sanches-Greenberg Generalization has been extended into a complementary distribution relation between CLs and plural markers in T'sou (1976), Doetjes (1996, 1997), and Chierchia (1998). It has been assumed that a language has either CLs or plural markers, and if a language has both systems, a CL does not occur with a plural marker in the same construction (e.g., Borer 2005: 95). However, it has been observed that there are numeral CL languages in which number marking is obligatory, e.g., Ejagham (Watters 1981) and Kana (Ikoro 1994, 1996) (see Bisang 2012a: Sec.1). In Northern Kam, CLs must have number inflection, regardless of whether a numeral occurs, as in (307), or no numeral occurs, as in (308) and (309) (Gerner 2006: 243–244, 249), although general number is expressed by bare nouns in the language (Bisang 2012a: Sec. 3).

(307) a. i^{45} jiu^{22} na^{45} b. ham^{11} t_iu^{22} na^{45} [Norther Kam]
        one CL:SG river   three CL:PL river
        'one river'   'three rivers'

(308) a. $wəi^{31}$ tu^{33} b. $məi^{31}$ tu^{33}
        CL:SG garment   CL:PL garment
        'a garment'   'garments'

(309) a. γa^{55} $hoŋ^{22}$ b. $ʔa^{55}$ $hoŋ^{22}$
        CL:SG loom   CL:PL loom
        'a loom'   'looms'

    Allan (1977: 294) and Aikhenvald (2003: 100–101; 249) also report cases where CL languages have number markings. See Bisang (2012a) for further discussion of the issue.
    Although, as pointed out by Doetjes (2012: 2), the Sanches-Greenberg generalization does not go the other way, i.e., it does not make any claim about non-CL languages, one still finds the co-occurrence of CLs and plural marking in non-CL languages. Krifka (2008: 7) claims that the German examples in (310) show this. It has also been claimed that Persian (Ghomeshi 2003: 55–56; Gebhardt 2009: 191–192), Hungarian (Csirmaz & Dékány 2010: 13), and Purépecha (Vázquez Rojas 2012) allow a plural marker and a CL to occur in the same nominal, regardless of whether they

are CL languages. If these claims are true, the allegedly complementary distribution between CLs and plural markers is also weakened.

(310) a. *zwanzig Stück Semmel-n*   [German]
         twenty   CL   bread.roll-PL
         'twenty bread-rolls'
     b. *fünf Mann Mensch-en*
         five   CL   person-PL
         'five people' (title of a play by Jandl & Mayröcker)

There are also languages that have neither CLs nor plural markers, such as Karitiana (Müller et al. 2006) and Dëne (Wilhelm 2008). The existence of such languages goes beyond the empirical coverage of the allegedly complementary distribution between CLs and plural markers.

If bare nouns express general number, as we mentioned in Section 4.1.2, plural marker on nouns cannot be compulsory. Nevertheless, it is still possible in these language to encode the contrast between singularity and plurality systematically in certain morpho-syntactic ways (e.g., on CLs). We have used Chinese to show this possibility.

We have shown that CL languages may have a productive way to encode the notion of plurality. Cognitively speaking, the fact that CL languages also have productive ways to encode the notion of nominal plurality indicates that the contrast between singularity and plurality is not restricted to non-CL languages. Acquisition studies also show that Mandarin Chinese and Japanese children "were not delayed relative to English-learning children for 1 versus 4 comparisons" (Li et al. 2009b: 1651), suggesting that children of the CL languages are conceptually sensitive to the semantic contrast of singularity and plurality.

In contrast to the Sanches-Greenberg Generalization, which tries to link the lack of obligatory number markers with the availability of CLs, Bošković (2012: 5) tries to link the lack of obligatory number markers with the lack of articles in the relevant languages. The new link implies that articleless languages may have general number. Indeed, Mandarin Chinese has no articles, indicating a support to Bošković's new generalization.

4.6. Chapter summary

In this chapter, we have identified the number system in Mandarin Chinese, a CL language. The system can be summarized in (311):

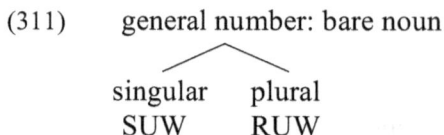

(311)   general number: bare noun

singular   plural
SUW   RUW

The existence of general number, which is encoded by bare nouns, means that in this language, plural entities do not have to be expressed by plural markers. When the contrast between plurality and singularity of units is salient in the context, the former is expressed by RUWs and the latter is expressed by SUWs, in the absence of any numeral. Salient plurality is also related to the fact that the plurality is an abundant one. The basic properties of the number markers are summarized in (312):

(312) a. The number feature denotes the number of unit;
      b. It is attested in all types of unit words;
      c. It is underspecified with definiteness and specificity;
      d. It is not compatible with a numeral;
      e. Plural markers are structurally licensed by certain quantifiers;
      f. Unlike in English, there is no negative correlation between morphological and semantic markedness of number marking.

The facts discussed in this chapter show that first, CL languages may have systematic ways to encode the contrast between singularity and plurality. Second, the function of number marking of CLs is one of the extended functions of CLs. Plural markers also have extended usages in other languages. For instance, in Mano, plural markers can be used as adverbials (see (237)); and in Irish, plural markers may even be used as counting units, like CLs in CL languages (Acquaviva 2006: 1879; 2008: 188–194). Third, when the same formatives occur in different syntactic structures and thus have different functions, they exhibit different formal properties. Although CLs in Mandarin Chinese have [+Numerable] in numeral expressions, they have [−Numerable] when they function as number markers.

Chapter 5
The syntactic constituency of numeral expressions

5.1. Introduction

This chapter addresses one of the most fundamental issues of the syntax of
numeral expressions: constituency. Such expressions contain three basic
elements in Mandarin Chinese, i.e., a numeral, such as *san* 'three' in (313),
a noun, such as *putao* 'grape' in (313), and a unit word between them, such
as the CL *ke* in (313a), the standard measure *gongjin* 'kilo' in (313b), and
the container measure *wan* 'bowl' in (313c). Among the three elements, is
there any syntactic hierarchy? Since the unit word surfaces between the
other two elements in Mandarin Chinese, the question is whether the unit
word c-commands the noun.

(313) a. *san   ke putao*   b. *san   gongjin   putao*
         three CL grape   three kilo   grape
         'three grapes'   'three kilos of grapes'
      c. *san   wan   putao*
         three bowl   grape
         'three bowls of grapes'

Greenberg (1990b [1975]: 227) makes the following statement, without
specifying the "many indications":

> There are many indications that in the tripartite construction consisting of
> quantifier (Q) [= numeral], classifier (Cl), and head noun (N), Q is in direct
> construction with Cl and this complex construction, which will be called the
> classifier phrase, is in turn in construction with N.

What is stated here is that if the order of a numeral expression is Nu-
meral-CL-NP, it has a unified left-branching structure, in which the numeral
and the unit word form a constituent first, excluding the noun, as in (314a).
In this structure, the unit word never c-commands the NP. Similar proposals
have been made in Li & Thompson (1981: 105), Paris (1981: 105–117),
Tang (1990a), Croft (1994: 151), Lin (1997: 419), R. Yang (2001: 58), and
Hsieh (2008). In contrast, Tang (1990b: 413; 2005), Cheng & Sybesma

(1998, 1999), and Y.H. Audrey Li (1999), among others, have proposed a unified right-branching structure, in which a unit word and the noun form a constituent first, excluding the numeral, as in (314b). In this structure, the unit word may c-command the NP (UW = unit word).

(314) a.

		NP		b.	numeral		
numeral	UW	putao			san	UW	NP
san	ke	grape			three	ke	putao
three	CL					CL	grape

In contrast to both schools, X. Li (2011a: 118) proposes that both left- and right-branching structures are possible, and that the former and the latter are mapped to a measure reading and a count reading, respectively. For instance, *liang ping jiu* 'two bottle wine' has a measure reading in (315a), but a count reading in (315b). It is claimed that (315a) has a structure like (314a), and (315b) has a structure like (314b).

(315) a. *Ta   de   wei   neng zhuangxia liang ping   jiu.*
   3SG DE stomach can   contain   two   bottle wine
   'His stomach can contain two bottles of wine.'

   b. *Ta   ling-le   liang ping jiu,   zuo-shou yi   ping,*
   3SG lift-PRF two   bottle wine left-hand one bottle
   you-shou   yi   ping.
   right-hand   one   bottle
   'He carried two bottles of wine, one in the left hand and the other in the right hand.'

Although not many arguments have been provided for any of the above three approaches, I will examine all that I have found. I will propose that unit words exhibit two different patterns of constituency. On the one hand, numeral expressions of container and standard measures, and partitive and collective CLs have a left-branching structure, as in (314a). On the other hand, numeral expressions of individual, individuating, and kind CLs have a right-branching structure, as in (314b). The proposal is based on arguments from four aspects: the scope of a left-peripheral modifier; the effect of modifier association; the semantic selection relation between a unit word and a noun, and the order of shape and size modifiers.

The constituency issue is the first step in analyzing the syntactic structures of numeral expressions. The categorial labels of the constituents identified in this chapter will be specified in the next chapter.

In addition to this introductory and the final summary section (Section 5.6), the organization of the chapter is the following. Section 5.2 presents the four arguments for a non-unified analysis of the constituency of numeral expressions, and makes the proposal that the left- and right-branching structures correlate with different types of unit words. Section 5.3 discusses several invalid arguments in the constituency study. Section 5.4 discusses whether there is any mapping between readings and the syntactic structures of numeral expressions. Finally, Section 5.5 discusses the occurrence of the functional particle *de* following a unit word, with respect to the constituency issue.

5.2. Four arguments for the non-unified analysis

In numeral expressions, different types of unit words do not behave the same syntactically. In this section, I present four differences, and link the differences to the constituency contrasts.

5.2.1. The scope of a left-peripheral modifier

Two incompatible modifiers may co-occur if they have scope over separate constituents. In each of the examples in (316), through (319), two incompatible modifiers co-occur. In (316a), for instance, the square shape expressed by the left-peripheral modifier *fangfangzhengzheng* 'square' is not compatible with the triangle shape expressed by the post-unit-word modifier *sanjiaoxing* 'triangle', but the whole nominal is acceptable.

(316) a. *fangfangzhengzheng* de liang bao   *sanjiaoxing* de binggan
        square   DE two package triangle   DE cookie
        'two square packages of triangle cookies'
     b. *yuanyuan* de yi   guan *fang*-tang
        round   DE one can square-sugar
        'a round can of sugar cubes'

(317) a. *houhou* de yi luo *bo*   bing
        thick   DE one pile thin pancake
        'a big pile of thin pancakes'

    b. <u>*hen*</u>   <u>*chang*</u> *de*   *yi*   *pai*   <u>*chao-duan*</u> *de xiao   qiche*
       very   long   DE   one   row   super-short DE small car
       'a very long row of super-short small cars'

(318) <u>*hen*</u>   <u>*duan*</u> *de yi*   *duan*   <u>*chang*</u> *de kewen*
       very   short DE one paragraph long   DE text
       'a very short paragraph of long text'

(319) <u>*zhengzheng*</u> *de yi*   *gongjin* <u>*sui*</u>   *hetao*
       full   DE one kilo   broken   walnut
       'a full kilo of walnut pieces'

The acceptability of this type of data indicates that the scope of the left-peripheral modifier excludes the NP, which has its own modifier. This fact shows that the two modification domains are separate constituents, and that the first constituent is composed of a numeral and a unit word, as well as the modifier. Putting the categorial labels of the constituent nodes aside, among the three structures in (320), only (320a) can capture the fact that the left-modifier does not have scope over the NP. This is a left-branching structure. Thus, data like (316), (317) and (318) should have a left-branching structure for the three basic elements of the constructions.

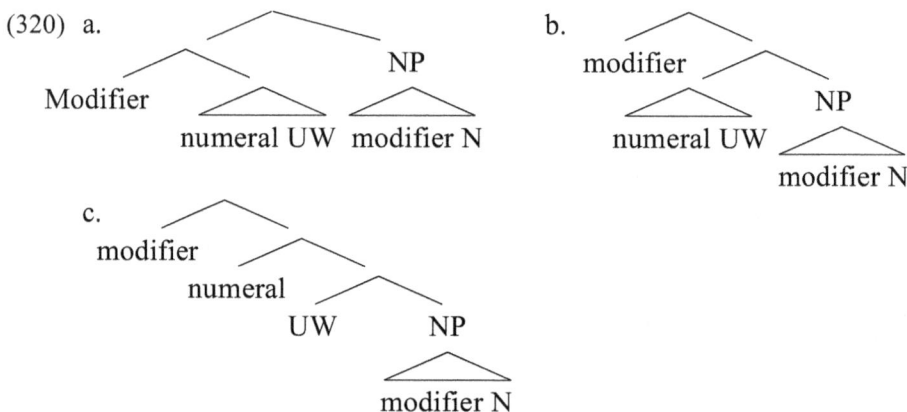

(320)

The unit words are container measures in (316), collective CLs in (317), a partitive CL in (318), and a standard measure in (319). Other types of unit words may not have modifiers that are not compatible with the modifiers of the associated nouns, as seen in (321). The unit word is the individual CL *gen* in (321a), the individuating CL *di* in (321b), and the kind CL *zhong* 'kind' in (321c). In each example, if either of the two modifiers were absent, the expression would become acceptable. For instance, the two forms in (322) are both acceptable, compared with (321a).

(321) a. **changchang* de san gen *duan* de huanggua
       long   DE three CL short DE cucumber

   b. **hen ganjing* de yi di *gangzang* de shui
       very clean   DE one CL dirty   DE water

   c. **hen bai* de yi zhong *heise* de yu
       very white DE one kind   black DE fish

(322) a. *changchang* de san gen *huanggua*
       long   DE three CL cucumber
       'three long cucumbers'

   b. *san gen duan de huanggua*
       three CL   short DE cucumber
       'three short cucumbers'

However, the structure of the unacceptable examples in (321) can be either (320b), a left-branching structure, or (320c), a right-branching structure. In both structures, the left-modifier c-commands the modifier of N. The incompatibility of the two modifiers could be captured by either structure. Therefore, such unacceptable examples cannot be used to distinguish a left-branching structure from a right-branching one.

It is necessary to clarify that the occurrence of the left-peripheral modifier cannot be the result of movement from a position between the numeral and the unit word. This is because the modifier must be followed by *de*. However, an adjective next to a unit word may not occur with *de*, as shown in (323) (Tang 1990b: 418; see Section 6.4 of this book for a discussion). If *de* emerges during the alleged movement, the derivation violates the Inclusiveness Condition (Chomsky 1995: 228), which bans the insertion of any new element during movement.

(323) **yi* [*yuanyuan* de] guan fang-tang
     one round   DE can square-sugar

In our argumentation, we use only incompatible modifiers to test their scopes. If there is only one modifier, as in (322) above, or if there are two compatible modifiers in a numeral construction, it is impossible to use them to distinguish between the structures in (320). Examples like (324), where the modifiers are associated with the NPs, rather than the unit words, do not tell us whether the structure is (320b), which is left-branching, or (320c), which is right-branching, since the modifier c-commands the NP in both cases. Moreover, in (325), *zhengzheng* 'whole' is associated with the numeral. In all of the three structures in (320), the left-peripheral modifier c-commands the numeral. Therefore, these examples neither challenge the analysis here (cf. X. Li & Rothstein 2012: 720), nor can they be used to distinguish the structures in (320) (cf. X. Li & Rothstein 2012: 723).

(324) a. *hei-huhu de yi   wan   Yidali   mian*
         black   DE one bowl Italian noodle
         'a bowl of Italian noodles'
      b. *hen   meiwei   de yi   zhuo cai*
         very delicious DE one CL   dish
         'a table of very delicious dishes'

(325) *Ta   zhong-le zhengzheng wu-bai   ke (de) shu.*
      3SG plant-PRF whole   five-hundred CL DE   tree
      'He planted five hundred trees in total.'

I conclude that numeral expressions with a container measure, a collective CL, or a partitive CL, have a left-branching structure, in which the numeral and the unit word form a constituent, excluding the noun. In this structure, the unit word does not c-command the noun.

5.2.2. The effect of modifier-association

A delimitive modifier of a noun can modify an individual CL (Zhu 1982: 52; see my Section 2.4.6). Lu (1987: 64) lists several adjectives that may do so, including *da* 'big', *xiao* 'small', *chang* 'long', *hou* 'thick', *bo* 'thin', and *zheng* 'full'. (326a) and (326b) differ in the position of the delimitive adjective *chang* 'long': it precedes the CL *tiao* in (326a), but follows the same CL in (326b). The two numeral expressions basically mean the same, regardless of the position of the adjective (the different word orders naturally introduce different information structures, which is not at issue here). Other examples in (327) and (328) show the same pattern.

(326) a. *yi   chang tiao xianglian*
         one long   CL   necklace
      b. *yi   tiao chang xianglian*
         one CL   long   necklace
         Both: 'one long necklace'

(327) a. *yi   bo   ce   tongsu   duwu*
      one thin CL popular book

    b. *yi   ce   bo   tongsu   duwu*
      one CL thin popular book

    Both: 'one thin popular book'

(328) a. *yi   hou   ben   jiaoke-shu*
      one thick CL   text-book

    b. *yi   ben   hou   jiaoke-shu*
      one CL thick text-book

    Both: 'one thick text-book'

However, such an association is not seen in the numeral expressions of a collective CL, partitive CL, and container and standard measure, as shown in (329) through (332). In these examples, the readings of the a-examples are different from those of the b-examples. In Section 2.4.3, we used this contrast to distinguish individual CLs from collective and partitive CLs. We now see that container and standard measures pattern with collective and partitive CLs in this aspect.

(329) a. *yi   da   dui   maozi*   [Collective CL]
      one big CL hat

    'one big pile of hats'

    b. *yi   dui   da   maozi*
      one CL big hat

    'one pile of big hats'

(330) a. *yi   da   pian   xigua*   [Partitive CL]
      one big CL   watermelon

    'one big slice of watermelon'

    b. *yi   pian   da   de   xigua*
      one CL   big DE watermelon

    'one slice of big watermelon'

(331) a. *yi   xiao   he   kouzi*   [Container Measure]
      one small box button

    'one small box of buttons'

    b. *yi   he   xiao   kouzi*
      one box small button

    'one box of small buttons'

(332) a. *yi   zheng jin   hetao*   [Standard Measure]
      one full   catty walnut
      'one full catty of walnuts'
   b. *yi   jin   zheng hetao*
      one catty full   walnut
      'one catty of whole walnuts'

The possible displacement of the modifier in (326) through (328) indicates that the unit word c-commands the noun, so that the modifier of the former can be semantically related to the modifier of the latter. The c-commanding relation can be represented by the right-branching structure in (314b), but not (314a). In (329) through (331), however, as mentioned above, the readings of the a-examples are different from those of the b-examples. If the structure of these examples is left-branching, as in (314a), the unit word does not c-command the noun; the structure captures the fact that the modifier of the former does not interact with the modifier of the latter.

For the rest two types of unit words, the test does not apply, since no acceptable minimal pair can be found. A mass noun may not be modified by any delimitive adjective (Section 2.2.2), and thus the individuating CL construction in (333b) is not acceptable for an independent reason. As for kind CLs, when adjectives such as *da* 'big' and *xiao* 'small' precede them, the size reading disappears, and thus the acceptability of (334a) and (334b) has a different nature from that of the examples in (326) through (332).

(333) a. *yi   da di shui*   b. **yi   di   da   shui*
      one big CL water   one   CL big   water
      'one big drop of water'

(334) a. *yi   da lei shuiguo*   b. *yi   lei   da   shuiguo*
      one big CL fruit   one   CL   big fruit
      'one major type of fruit'   'one type of big fruit'

The effect of modifier-association is similar to the effect of Neg-Raising. One reading of (335a) is synonymous to (335b). In this reading of (335a), it seems that the meaning of the negation is "raised" from the lower clause to the matrix clause. Importantly, Neg-Raising is attested in complementation structures only. The higher position of the negation must c-command the lower position of the negation.

(335) a. *I don't think she is at home.*   b. *I think she is not at home.*

My conclusion to this subsection is that individual CL constructions have a right-branching structure, and container and standard measure constructions, and collective and partitive CL constructions have a left-branching structure.

5.2.3. Semantic selection

It is well-known that there is a semantic selection relation between CLs of certain types and their associated nouns. We have addressed the syntagmatic nature of selection in Section 2.2.1. According to Bloomfield (1933: 165), "The features of selection are often highly arbitrary and whimsical." See Ramchand (2008) for an extended discussion of semantic selection. In this subsection, we examine the selection of different types of unit words.

5.2.3.1. *Individual CLs*

Many individual CLs show selection relation with the associated nouns. In (336a), for instance, the individual CL *pi* may occur with *ma* 'horse', but not with *zhu* 'pig'.

(336) a. *san   pi   {ma/*zhu}*
        three CL   horse/pig
        'three horses'

    c. *san   sou   {chuan/*feiji}*
        three CL   ship/airplane
        'three ships'

    e. *san   tiao   {*xiaohua/jianyi}*
        three CL   joke/suggestion
        'three suggestions'

b. *san   zhan {deng/*lazhu}*
   three CL   lamp/candle
   'three lamps'

d. *san   ze {xiaohua/*jianyi}*
   three CL joke/suggestion
   'three jokes/suggestions'

The use of the CL *pie* also shows s-selection. When a person uses a brush pen to write a stroke which looks like a slash sign /, the stroke is called *pie*. *Pie* is also used as a CL. According to Lü et al. (2002: 974), this CL is used for things that look like such a stroke, e.g., *huzi* 'mustache'. However, the CL seems to occur with *huzi* only, as in (337a) (I thank Guy Emerson for bringing my attention to this CL) (precisely speaking, only the left mustache looks like a *pie*, and the right one actually looks like a *na* 'a stroke that resembles a backslash sign \') . Leaves may also have a shape like a stroke written with a brush pen, but *pie* may not occur with *shu-ye* 'tree-leaf', as seen in (337b).

(337) a. *Ta   you   liang pie   xiao   huzi.*
    3SG   have   two   CL   small mustache
    'He has two small strips of mustaches.'
  b. **Nali you   liang pie   shu-ye.*
    there have   two   CL   tree-leaf

Even the more general individual CLs such as *jian* have selectional restrictions. *Jian* may occur with *liwu* 'gift', *shi* 'matter', *yifu* 'clothes', *jiaju* 'furniture', *zuopin* 'literature or art product', but not with nouns such as *zhuozi* 'table', *shu* 'book', *deng* 'lamp', *qianbi* 'pencil', or *men* 'door'.

In the modern poet Yu Kwang-Chung's (1999) poem, the same CL *pi* in (336a) is used with the noun *taiyang* 'sun', as in *yi pi taiyang* 'one CL sun', to describe the sudden rising of the sun in a dawn, in which the sun looks like a galloping horse. The occurrence of such an effect in turn shows the existence of s-selection of the CL. Cases like this, as pointed by T'sou (1976: 1224), "are instances of intentional violation of selectional restrictions. They are very much in evidence and the ability to produce them is part of linguistic competence and must be accounted for in an adequate grammar."

The same noun may be selected by different CLs in different dialects of Chinese. *Qiao* 'bridge' occurs with the CL *zuo* or *jia* in Beijing dialect (see (134)), with the CL *ge* in Xi'an dialect, with the CL *ding* in Suzhou dialect, with the CL *du* in Nanchang dialect, with the CL *tiao* in Fuzhou dialect, and with the CL *jian* in Xiamen dialect (Qian et al. 2002: 171).

5.2.3.2. Individuating CLs

Semantic selection is also found in individuating CLs, which occur with mass nouns. In (338a), for instance, the individuating CL *ji* may occur with *yao-shui* 'medicine-liquid', but not with *ji-tang* 'chicken-soup'.

(338) a. *liang ji {yao-shui/*ji-tang}*
    two   CL   medicine-liquid/chicken-soup
    'two doses of liquid medicine'
  b. *liang pao {niao/*ji-tang}*
    two   CL   urine/chicken-soup
    'the amount of pee of two peeing events'

c. *liang {pian/*zhang} yun*
two CL/CL cloud
'two pieces of cloud'

d. *liang {gu/*tiao} zheng-qi*
two CL/CL steam-air
'two puffs of steam'

e. *liang pi {bu/*zhi}*
two CL cloth/paper
'two units of cloth'

f. *liang zhang {*bu/zhi}*
two CL cloth/paper
'two units of paper'

The acceptability contrasts in (338) show that like other nouns, mass nouns may also occur with particular CLs (contra Chao 1968: 508 "Mass nouns do not have specific classifiers"; also p. 503; Hundius & Kölver 1983: 168; Krifka 2008: Sec. 2).

5.2.3.3. Kind CLs

A less discussed fact is that kind CLs also show selectional restrictions. Huang & Ahrens (2003: 362) list as many as fourteen kind CLs in Mandarin Chinese, and describe their compatible nouns (although no unacceptable forms are given for comparison). Our following examples show the acceptability contrast between different kind CLs occurring with different nouns.[42]

(339) a. *san kuan {*shi/shouji/*xuesheng/*lilun}*
three CL matter/cellphone/student/theory
'three kinds of cellphones'

b. *san dangzi {shi/*shouji/*xuesheng/*lilun}*
three CL matter/cellphone/student/theory
'three kinds of things'

c. *san tao {*shi/*shouji/*xuesheng/lilun}*
three CL matter/cellphone/student/theory
'three kinds of theories'

---

42. The 14 kind CLs are: *zhong, ban, pai, ma, mazi, dang, dangzi, deng, lei, kuan, hao, shi, se,* and *yang.* We can add another one: *tao* for abstract nouns, as seen in (339c), although this CL is used as a collective one when it occurs with non-mass concrete nouns, e.g., *san tao youpiao* 'three sets of stamps'.

5.2.3.4. Other types of unit words

Unlike individual, individuating and kind CLs, other types of unit words do not show selectional restrictions on nouns. In (340a), the container measure *chexiang* 'cattle-car (of a train)' is blind to the semantic distinction between *ma* 'horse' and *zhu* 'pig'. The lack of selectional restriction is also seen in the examples of the standard measure in (341), the collective CLs in (342), and the partitive CL in (343) (Note: it is the semantic conflict rather than the arbitrary selectional restrictions that accounts for the constraint that standard and container measures do not occur with immaterial notions, as shown in Section 2.2.1).

(340) a. *san   chexiang {ma/zhu}*   [Container M.]
         three cattle.car horse/pig
         'three cattle-cars of {horses/pigs}'
     b. *san   wan   {yao-shui/ji-tang}*
         three bowl medicine-liquid/chicken-soup
         'three bowls of {liquid-medicine/chicken-soup}'

(341) *san   sheng {yao-shui/ji-tang}*   [Standard M.]
       three liter   medicine-liquid/chicken-soup
       'three liters of {liquid-medicine/chicken-soup}'

(342) a. *yi   dui   {shu/shoujuan}*   [Collective CL]
         one pile book/handkerchief
         'one pile of books/handkerchiefs'
     b. *yi   qun   {shagua/feiji/daoyu/gao lou/shanmai}*
         one group fool/aircraft/island/tall building/mountain
         'one group of {fools/aircrafts/islands/tall buildings/mountains}'

(343) *san   pian {xigua/huluobo/juzi/xiangchang}*   [Partitive CL]
       three CL   watermelon/carrot/orange/sausage
       'three slices of {watermelon/carrot/orange/sausage}'

Long & Ma (2008) claim that standard measures never occur with animate nouns. But this constraint simply reflects our conventional world knowledge, since we usually do not measure animate entities with standard measures. Thus the constraint is pragmatic, rather than a case of co-occurrence restriction. If a proper context is found, the constraint disappears. Imagine that the total weight of some students is 550 kgs, then (344) is perfectly fine:

(344) *Zhuangzai-zhe <u>550   gongjin   xuesheng</u> de na   ge qiqiu*
    load-DUR   550   kilogram student   DE DEM CL balloon
    manman de sheng-qilai le.
    slow   DE rise-up   PRT
    'The balloon that carries students, who are 550 kilograms in totoal, is
    rising slowly.

5.2.3.5. Selection and constituency

A selection relation must be represented in a local syntactic relation, i.e.,
the two elements that hold the relation must form a constituent, excluding
other elements. The right-branching structure, as in (314b), captures the
selection relation of the individual, individuating, and kind CL constructions, since the unit word and the noun form a constituent. The absence of
the selection relation in other types of unit word constructions indicates that
the unit words do not interact with the nouns syntactically. The left-
branching structure, as in (314a), correctly captures the absence of the interaction.

   In Hsieh (2008: 47 fn. 15), a unified left-branching structure is proposed.
In order to explain the semantic selection between an individual CL and a
noun, a feature-percolating theory is mentioned. However, since the CL in
the assumed left-branching structure does not c-command the noun, the
assumed percolation is hard to be maintained.

   Based on the semantic selection of a unit word on its associated noun, I
conclude that individual, individuating and kind CL constructions have a
right-branching structure, in which the unit word and the noun form a constituent, excluding the numeral. In contrast, container measure, standard
measure, collective CL, and partitive CL constructions have a left-
branching structure, since they do not show semantic selection.

5.2.4. The order of size and shape modifiers

When a shape and a size modifier co-occur with the same noun, the shape
adjective should be closer to the modifiee than the size adjective (Vendler
1968), regardless of how this order constraint is syntactically represented
(see McKinney-Bock 2010 and the references therein). In Chinese, this
default order is observed in the absence of the functional particle *de* (Sproat
& Shih 1988, 1991). In our following discussion, we use examples without

de to see the effect of the default order. In (345), both the size adjective *xiao* 'small' and the shape adjective *yuan* 'round' occur to the right of the CL, and in (346), the same two adjectives occur both to the left of the CL. Compared with (345a), (345b) is not acceptable. Similarly, compared with (346a), (346b) is not acceptable.

(345) a. *si   pian xiao   yuan   shuye*   [pre-NP Adj]
        four   CL   small round leaf
        'four small round leaves'
    b. **si   pian   yuan   xiao   shuye*
        four   CL   round small leaf

(346) a. *si   xiao   yuan   pian   shuye*   [pre-CL Adj]
        four   small round CL   leaf
        'four small round leaves'
    b. **si   yuan   xiao   pian   shuye*
        four   round small CL   leaf

If two delimitive adjectives do not occur in a row in a numeral expression, the above order constraint is still observed in individual CL constructions. In (347), where the individual CL *pian* occurs, the size adjective *xiao* 'small' must precede the shape adjective *fang* 'square'. (348) shows a similar contrast.

(347) a. *si   xiao   pian fang   binggan*   [Individual CL]
        four   small CL   square   cookie
        'four small round cookies'
    b. **si   fang   pian   xiao   binggan*
        four   square CL   small cookie

(348) a. *san   xiao   pian yuan   shuye*   [Individual CL]
        three small CL   round   leave
        'three small round leaves'
    b. **san   yuan   pian   xiao   shuye*
        three round CL   small leave

We now examine a different group of data. In (349), where the container measure *pan* 'plate' occurs, the order of the two adjectives is free, although different orders correlate with different meanings. The same situation is seen in the collective CL *dui* 'pile' in (350), and the partitive CL *kuai* in (351).

(349) a. *si   xiao   pan   yuan   binggan*   [Container Measure]
          four   small   plate round   cookie
          'four small plates of round cookies'
      b. *si   yuan   pan   xiao   binggan*
          four   round   plate small   cookie
          'four round plates of small cookies'

(350) a. *si   xiao   dui   chang   qiezi*   [Collective CL]
          four   small   pile long   eggplant
          'four small piles of long eggplants'
      b. *si   chang   pai   xiao   qiezi*
          four   long   row   small   eggplant
          'four long rows of small eggplant'

(351) a. *si   da   kuai chang   qiezi*   [Partitive CL]
          four   big   chunk long   eggplant
          'four big chunks of long eggplants'
      b. *si   fang   kuai da   qiezi*
          four   square chunk big   eggplant
          'four square chunks of big eggplants'

Such a comparison between the two orders of adjectives is impossible
for other types of unit words. Kind CLs and standard measures may not be
modified by size and shape adjectives, and the noun following an individuating CL may not be modified by these types of adjectives, either. Thus the
test of the adjective order does not apply to the numeral expressions of
these unit words.

The contrast in the adjective order indicates that in a numeral expression, an individual CL, as well as its modifier, c-commands the modifier of
the associate NP, and therefore, they are all in the same domain, in which
the two types of adjectives follow the Vendler order. Our right-branching
structure captures this adjective order fact. In contrast, for container measures, collective CLs, and partitive CLs, their modifiers do not interact with
the modifiers of the NP, and therefore the Vendler order is not enforced.
The absence of the interaction indicates the absence of a c-command relation between the two adjectives. Our left-branching structure captures this
adjective order fact. The two adjectives have no c-commanding relation in
the left-branching structure. Therefore, the lack of the Vendler's order effect is explained.

5.2.5. Two possible structures

In this section, I have presented four arguments to distinguish a left-branching structure from a right-branching structure. They are summarized in (352).

(352) a.
Argument A: The combination of a numeral and a unit word as the scope of a left-peripheral modifier ⇒ Left-branching (+A)
Argument B: The effect of modifier association:
The presence of the effect ⇒ Right-branching (+B)
The absence of the effect ⇒ Left-Branching (−B)
Argument C: Semantic selection of a unit word on a noun
The presence of the effect ⇒ Right-branching (+C)
The absence of the effect ⇒ Left-Branching (−C)
Argument D: The Vendler's size-shape modifier hierarchy
The presence of the effect ⇒ Right-branching (+D)
The absence of the effect ⇒ Left-Branching (−D)

b.

	Left-branching	*Right-branching*
Container Measure	Argument +A, −B, −C, −D	
Standard Measure	Argument +A, −B, −C	
Collective CL	Argument +A, −B, −C, −D	
Partitive CL	Argument +A, −B, −C, −D	
Individual CL		Argument +B, +C, +D
Individuating CL		Argument +C
Kind CL		Argument +C

From the four constituency tests listed in (352a), we can conclude that the constructions of the first four types of unit words listed in (352b), i.e., container measures, standard measures, collective CLs, and partitive CLs, have a left-branching structure, in which the numeral and the unit word form a constituent, excluding the noun, as shown in (353a), and that the constructions of individual, individuating, and kind CLs have a right-branching structure, in which the CL and the noun form a constituent, excluding the numeral, as shown in (353b).

(353) a.

san	ping	shui
three	bottle	water

'three bottles of water'

b.

san	di	shui
three	CL	water

'three drops of water'

In addition to the above four main arguments, three more facts further support our syntactic division of two types of unit words. One of them will be added in Section 6.5.3, after certain background information has been introduced. The other two are the following. First, the plural-denoting suffix -*men,* which occurs obligatorily with plural pronouns and optionally with plural human-denoting nouns, is generally incompatible with an individual CL (Lü et al. (1999: 385), as shown in (354a). But -*men* may occur with a collective CL, as shown in (354b) (Hsieh 2008: 7).

(354) a. *san ge laoshi-(*men)*   b. *na san qun xuesheng-men*
     three CL teacher-PL   DEM three CL student-PL
     'three teachers'   'those three groups of students'

This contrast indicates that -*men* interacts with individual CLs, but not collective ones. The interaction is possible if the CL c-commands -*men,* which has a local relation with the noun.[43] If an individual CL construction has the right-branching structure in (353b), the c-command relation is captured. In contrast, the lack of the interaction suggests that there is no such c-command relation for a collective CL construction. If a collective CL construction has the left-branching structure in (353a), the absence of the c-command relation between the CL and the noun can be captured.

Second, the formal division between the group of individual, individuating, and kind CL constructions on the one side, and the remaining types of unit words on the other side is supported by the fact that the default CL *ge* may alternate with the unit words of the former group only (see Section 2.4.5). This is shown by the contrast between (355) and (356).

---

43. In Y.H. Audrey Li's (1999) analysis of (354a), the CL *ge* blocks the head movement that derives the N-*men* string. In her analysis, the CL c-commands the noun, similar to my analysis. She does not discuss examples like (354b).

(355) a. *san*   {*tai/ge*}   *dianshi-ji*   [Individual CL]
         three   CL/CL   TV-set
         'three television sets'

   b. *san*   {*xiang/ge*}   *yuanze.*   [Individuating CL]
         three   CL/CL   principle
         'three principles'

   c. *Mei   ge cunzi   dou faxian-le zhe   liang* {*zhong/ge*}
         every CL village all   find-PRF   DEM two   CL/CL
         bingdu.   [Kind CL]
         virus
         'These two kinds of virus have been found in every village.'

(356) a. *san*   {*pian/*ge*}   *xiangjiao*   [Partitive CL]
         three   CL/CL   banana
         Intended: 'three slices of banana'

   b. *san*   {*dui/*ge*}   *xiangjiao*   [Collective CL]
         three   CL/CL   banana
         Intended: 'three piles of bananas'

   c. *san*   {*lan/*ge*}   *xiangjiao*   [Container M.]
         three   basket/CL   banana
         Intended: 'three baskets of bananas'

   d. *san*   {*bang/*ge*}   *xiangjiao*   [Standard M.]
         three   pound/CL   banana
         Intended: 'three pounds of bananas'

5.3.   Invalid arguments

In this section, I falsify a few arguments that have been used in the literature in analyzing the constituency of numeral expressions.

5.3.1. The adjacency of a numeral and a unit word

In CL languages such as Chinese, a numeral and a CL are adjacent. Greenberg (1972) thus claims that the two elements should form a constituent. Similarly, Croft (1994: 151; also see Wilhelm 2008: 60) claims that since a CL and a numeral co-occur, they must form a constituent. Thus a unified left-branching structure for all types of CL constructions is proposed from this co-occurrence perspective.

   This is not an effective argument for the constituency of the string numeral-CL. In English, an auxiliary (e.g., *have* or *be*) needs to occur with a subject or expletive, but the two elements never form a constituent. Also, as pointed out by Krifka (2008: Sec. 6.3), although the co-occurrence of two elements might lead to a certain morphological combination, this does not mean in itself that the two elements form a constituent in the syntactic structure. It is well-known that the fusion of a preposition and its following article in French *aux* (= *à les* 'to the') and German *beim* (= *bei dem* 'at the') does not mean that the preposition and the article form a syntactic constituent, excluding the noun. Similarly, the cliticalization of a CL to a numeral to the right, as seen in the Lhiimaqalhqama' example in (357) (Kung 2007: 189), does not imply that the numeral and the CL form a syntactic constituent. The surface adjacency can be the result of certain morphosyntactic operations.

(357) a. *puma-t'útu*   *lapanák*   b. *'aqx-tam*   *'alhik*
      CL:human-three people   CL:flat-one paper
      'three people'   'one sheet of paper'

In Mandarin Chinese, contraction is found between a demonstrative and the numeral *yi* 'one', as in (358a), and between the numeral *liang* 'two' or *san* 'three' and the CL *ge*, as in (358b) and (358c), respectively (Chao 1968: 570; see Section 4.1.1 for the suffix use of *lia*).

(358) a. *zhe* *yi* *ge* *pingguo* ⇒ *zhei*   *ge* *pingguo*
      DEM one CL apple   DEM.one CL apple
      'this apple'
    b. *liang* *ge* *pingguo*   ⇒ *lia*   *pingguo*
      two   CL apple   two.CL apple
      'two apples'
    c. *san* *ge* *pingguo*   ⇒ *sa*   *pingguo*
      three CL apple   three.CL apple
      'three apples'

The morphological operation is not seen in other numerals. This is similar to the case that the numerals 1–3 may undergo certain phonological changes in Tlingit, but other numerals may not do so (Cable 2012: Sec. 3).

A numeral and a CL may also form a phonological phrase, triggering tone sandhi in Mandarin Chinese (Gil 1994). For instance, the citation third tone of the numeral *wu* 'five' is uttered as the second tone, when it is followed by the third tone CL *ba* in (359).

(359) a. *wu³ ba³ cha²-hu²*   ⇒   b. *wu² ba³ cha²-hu²*
          five CL   tea-pot
          'five tea pots'

However, as is well-known, phonological phrases are not necessarily isomorphic to syntactic constituents. For instance, the syntactic constituency of (360a) is not reflected in the phonological grouping in (360b) (Jackendoff 1997: 26) (ω marks a prosodic word boundary).

(360) a. [_DP *a* [_NP [_AP *big*] *house*]]   b. [_φ [_ω *a big*] [_ω *house*]]

Phonological words do not always correlate with syntactic constituents, either. For instance, the underlined parts of the examples in (361) are not syntactic constituents at all.

(361) a. *That man over <u>there's</u> working this morning.*
        b. *You <u>aren't</u> helping.*
        c. <u>*You're*</u> *not helping.*

Moreover, it is not true that a CL is always next to a numeral, cross-linguistically. As pointed out by Bisang (2012a: fn.1), Greenberg's con-stituency is challenged by the fact that in languages such as Ejagham (Benue-Congo) (Watters 1981: 310; see Aikhenvald 2003: 99 and Simpson 2005: 809), all numerals may be found non-adjacent to the CL (NC = noun class marker):

(362) *a-mege*   '   *i-cokud*   *a-bae*
        NC-CL   GEN   NC-orange seed   NC-two
        'two orange seeds'

5.3.2. Syntactic operations on NPs

One argument that has been used to support the unified left-branching con-stituency of a numeral expression in Mandarin Chinese is that certain syn-tactic operations may be applied to the NP alone, excluding the string of a numeral and a unit word. In (363a), the NP *rou* 'meat' is topicalized, stranding the numeral *shi* 'ten' and the unit word *bang* 'pound'. In (363b) the NP *rou* is preposed to the left of the subject *ta* '3SG', and in (363c), *rou* is preposed to the position between the subject and the verb.

(363) a. *Rou   ta   mai-le   shi   bang.*
        meat 3SG   buy-PRF ten   pound
        'As for meat, he bought ten pounds.'

    b. *Lian rou   ta   ye   mai-le   shi   bang.*
        even meat 3SG also   buy-PRF ten   pound
        'He even bought ten pounds of meat.'

    c. *Ta   rou   zhi   mai   yi   bang.*
        3SG   meat only buy   one pound
        'He bought only one pound of meat.'

This argument was offered to David Gil in his internet conversation on the constituency of numeral expressions in Mandarin Chinese and other CL languages (Gil 1994). The argument is not effective, since a possible syntactic operation applied on X shows the constituent status of X only, not the constituent status of any other elements of the construction. Parallel to this, one does not claim that the combination of a subject and a transitive verb is a constituent simply because the object may move. For instance, there is no evidence for the constituent status of the string *ta mai-guo-le* 'he has bought' in (364).

(364) *Rou   ta   mai-guo-le.*
     meat 3SG   buy-EXP-PRF
     'As for meat, he has bought.'

We now clarify a related issue. In Mandarin Chinese, the combination of a numeral and a unit word may not be fronted. We can see that if we move the numeral *san* 'three' and the CL *ben* in (365a) to the left of the subject *Yani*, as in (365b), the result is not acceptable. (366b) shows a similar result with the standard measure *jin* 'catty'.

(365) a. *Yani mai-le   san   ben   shu.*
        Yani buy-PRF three CL   book
        'Yani bought three books.'

    b. **San   ben,   Yani mai-le   shu.*
        three   CL   Yani buy-PRF book

(366) a. *Yani mai-le   san   jin   niurou.*
        Yani buy-PRF three catty beef
        'Yani bought three catties of beef.'

    b. **San   jin,   Yani mai-le   niurou.*
        three   catty Yani buy-PRF beef

This is different from the following Japanese examples, where the combination of the numeral *san* 'three' and the CL *satu* may be separated from the associated noun *hon* 'book' in (367b):

(367) a. *Taroo-wa   san-satu   no   hon-o   katta.*
        Taroo-TOP   three-CL   NO   book-ACC   bought
   b. *San-satu, Taroo-wa   hon-o   katta.*
        three-CL   Taroo-TOP   book-ACC   bought
        Both: 'Taroo bought three books.'

Saito et al. (2008: 260) use the contrast between (365) and (367) to show that the CL construction in Chinese is right-branching and thus the combination of the numeral and the CL may not move, whereas the CL construction in Japanese is left-branching and thus the combination of the numeral and the CL can move (see Watanabe 2010 for more discussion of the syntax of Japanese CL constructions). In this chapter, I have also argued that individual CL constructions in Chinese have a right-branching structure, in which the numeral and the unit word do not form a constituent excluding the NP, and thus the unacceptability of (365b) is expected. Our conclusion is compatible with Saito et al.'s claim on Mandarin. However, if the constructions of some other types of unit words, such as the standard measure in (366a), have a left-branching structure, as we have proposed, how is it that the combination of the numeral and the unit word may still not move, as seen in (366b)?

The unacceptability of (366b) does not falsify my analysis, however. It is obvious that not all syntactic constituents may move. One account of the unacceptability is that the parallel left quantity-denoting constituent of a nominal may not move in Chinese, either, as seen in (368b). The constituency status of the string *hen duo* 'very many' is not controversial. The fact that the string may not move does not affect its constituent status.

(368) a. *Yani   mai-le   hen   duo   (de)   shu.*
        Yani   buy-PRF   very   many   DE   book
        'Yani bought many books.'
   b. **Hen   duo   (de),   Yani   mai-le   shu.*
        very   many   DE   Yani   buy-PRF   book

In Section 6.5.3, I will give a unified treatment of the unacceptability of (366b) and (368b).

5.3.3. NP ellipsis

In Mandarin Chinese, an NP can be elided after a unit word, regardless of
the type of the unit word, as shown in (369).

(369) *Yani you yi ba shanzi, Lulu ye you yi ba* ~~shanzi.~~
     Yani have one CL fan   Lulu also have one CL fan
     'Yani has one fan and Daiyu also has one.'

Ellipsis examples like this have been assumed to show that the string
that is unaffected by the deletion should form a constituent, i.e., the numeral *yi* 'one' and the CL *ba* in this example should form a constituent.
This is another argument offered by some linguists in Gil's (1994) internet
conversation on the constituency of numeral expressions in Mandarin Chinese, and is also seen in Her (2012: 1234). However, this ellipsis fact simply
shows that the unit word surfaces at a head position and the NP surfaces to
the right of the head. As we know, the availability of VP ellipsis does not
mean that the stranded part, e.g., the combination of an subject and an auxiliary, is a constituent. For instance, there is no evidence for the constituent
status of the string *Lulu ye hui* 'Lulu will also' in (370).

(370) *Yani hui qu mai shanzi, Lulu ye hui* ~~qu mai shanzi.~~
     Yani will go buy fan   Lulu also will go buy fan
     'Yani will go to buy fans and Lulu will do so, too.'

This ellipsis possibility in examples like (369) just tells us that unit
words are not phrases, which do not license ellipsis in the language (see
Section 6.2.1). The possibility tells us nothing about whether a numeral
construction is left-branching or right-branching.

5.3.4.   The positions of the partitives *duo* 'more' and *ban* 'half'

5.3.4.1. The position of duo *'more'*

In Mandarin Chinese, *duo* 'more' may follow a unit word. The unit word
can be ten or the multiples of ten (called *wei-shu* 'position number' in Zhu
1982: 45; e.g., 10, 100, 1000), as well as a measure word. Lü et al. (1999:
184) claim that *duo* 'more' may follow a measure word, but not a CL in
general.

(371) a. *liu jin   duo   putao*   b. *liang xiang duo   shu*
      six catty more grape   two   box   more book
      'six and more catties of grapes'   'two and more boxes of books'

Wang (1994: 35) uses the occurrence of the post-unit word *duo* to distinguish CLs from measure words. In Hsieh (2008: 46; also X. Li 2011a: 114; Her 2012: 1235), it is assumed that if *duo* follows a unit word, the unit word and its preceding numeral should form a constituent. If so, the structure should be left-branching.

However, the position of *duo* is not a reliable argument in judging the constituency of the containing structure, for the following reason. *Duo* is an additive partitive quantifier, scoping over the single unit-morpheme to its immediate left. In (372), for instance, the unit morpheme to the immediate left of *duo* is *shi* 'ten', which is the second morpheme of the word *wu-shi* 'fifty'. The quantity expressed by this example is 50 plus a part of *shi* 'ten'. It can be any number between 50 and 60. More precisely, the use of *duo* here is similar to that of the post-numeral *odd* or *some* in English (e.g., *fifty-some, fifty-odd*).[44]

(372) *wu-shi   duo   feng   xin*
     five-ten   more   CL   letter
     'fifty-odd letters' (50 < x < 60)

---

44. The distributions of the partitive markers *duo* 'more', *ban* 'half', and *ji* 'a few, several' are different. Although *duo* may follow either a numeral or a unit word, as seen in (373) and (374), *ban* follows a unit word only, rather than a numeral, as seen in (i); and *ji* may follow a numeral, but not a unit word, as seen in (ii). But *ji* may also precede a numeral, whereas the other two may not, as seen in (iii). Like *duo*, *ji* may be next to ten or the multiples of ten only, as seen in (iv).

(i) a. *shi mi   ban*   b. **shi ban mi*
    10 meter half   10 half meter
    '10 and more meters'

(ii) a. **shi mi   ji*   b. *shi ji   mi*
     10 meter several   10 several meter
     '10.5 meters'

(iii) a. *ji   shi mi*   b. **duo shi mi*   c. **ban shi mi*
      several ten meter   more ten meter   half ten meter
      'several dozen meters'

(iv) a. **shi-wu duo mi*   b. **shi-wu ji   mi*   c. **ji   wu mi*
      ten-five more meter   ten-five several meter   several five meter

Importantly, *duo* does not scope over the two-morpheme string *wu-shi* 'fifty' in (372), since the reading of the phrase may not cover figures such as 70, which is 50 plus 20 (20 is part of 50). The following minimal pair is telling (from Lü et al. 1999: 184; 1 *mu* = 6.666 m^2). With different positions of *duo*, (373a) and (373b) cover different ranges.

(373) a. *shi   duo   mu   di*
         ten   more   mu   land
         Lit. '10 and more *mu* (of) land' ($10 < x < 20$)
    b. *shi   mu   duo   di*
         ten   mu   more   land
         Lit. '10 *mu* and more (of) land' ($10 < x < 11$)

In (373a), *duo* 'more' is adjacent to *shi* 'ten' to its left. In this case, it means part of ten. The quantity expressed by the whole phrase is 10 plus a part of 10, i.e., any figure between 10 and 20 (e.g., 12 *mu*). In (373b), *duo* is adjacent to the standard measure *mu* to its left. In this case, it means part of one *mu*. The quantity expressed by the whole phrase is 10 plus a part of one *mu*, i.e., any figure between 10 and 11 *mu* (e.g., 10.6 *mu*).

Similarly, the reading of (374a) is 30 plus part of 10. The quantity expressed by the whole nominal is thus any number between 30 and 40, e.g., 33 *mu*. In contrast, the reading of (374b) is 30 plus a part of one *mu*. The quantity expressed by the whole nominal is any number between 30 and 31 *mu*, e.g., 30.4 *mu*.

(374) a. *san-shi   duo   mu   di*
         three-ten   more   mu   land
         '30-some *mu* (of) land' ($30<x<40$)
    b. *san-shi   mu   duo   di*
         three-ten   mu   more   land
         '30 *mu* and more (of) land' ($30<x<31$)

Therefore, if *duo* follows a unit word, as in (373b) and (374b), it scopes over the unit word only, excluding the numeral. Recall that in Chapter 2, we claimed that a unit word expresses a counting unit. If *duo* follows a unit word, its partitive meaning scopes over the one unit encoded by the unit word. Thus, the constituency of (374b) is [*san-shi* [*mu duo*] *di*], which does not show whether the numeral and the unit word form a syntactic constituent.

The above generalization receives a critical comment from X. Li & Rothstein (2012: 714). They claim that the observed scope of *duo* is prag-

matically driven, instead of being semantically entailed. They claim that the
scope of *duo* is cancelled in (375).

(375) a. *Ta   zuiduo   zhi   neng   he   san   ping   jiu.   Jintian*
        3SG   at.most only   can   drink three bottle wine   today
        ta   he-le   <u>san   ping   duo</u>, jieguo   hezui   le.
        3SG   drink-PRF three bottle more consequently drunk PRT
        Zixi   suansuan, te   he-le   zuzu   you si   ping ban.
        careful count   3SG drink-PRF enough have four bottle half
        Translation cited: 'He can drink three bottles of wine at most.
        Today he drank <u>more than three bottles</u>, so finally he got drunk.
        To be more precise, he drank four and half bottles.'
        My translation: 'He can drink three bottles of wine at most.
        Today he drank <u>three bottles and more</u>, so finally he got drunk.
        To be more precise, he drank four and a half bottles.'
    b. *Wo   jintian shangjie yi   kou qi   mai-le   <u>shi</u>*
        1SG   today go.street one CL   breath buy-PRF   ten
        <u>*duo   shuang wazi.*</u> *Hui   jia   yi-kan, jieguo   you*
        more   CL   sock go   home   look   consequently have
        ershi-san   shuang.
        twenty-three CL
        Translation cited: 'Today, I went to buy <u>more than ten pairs of</u>
        <u>socks</u> at one go. After getting back home, I found that (I bought)
        twenty three pairs.'
        My translation: 'Today, I went to the street and bought <u>ten and</u>
        <u>more pairs of socks</u> at one go. After getting back home, I found
        that (I bought) twenty-three pairs.'

One can see from the underlined part that there is a translation disagreement between the translations given by X. Li & Rothstein (i.e., the cited
translation) and my translations. If we translate their English sentences
back into Chinese, the phrase *san ping duo* 'three bottle more' in (375a)
should be replaced with (376a), and the phrase *shi duo shuang wazi* 'ten
more pair sock' in (375b) should be replaced with (376b):

(376) a. *bu zhi   san   ping*   b. *zhi-shao shi shuang wazi*
        not only three bottle   at-least   ten CL   sock
        'more than three bottles'   'at least ten pairs of socks'

In (376a), the quantity expressed by *bu zhi san ping* 'at least three bottles' is vague. It can be any amount that is more than three bottles, including any amount that is between three bottles and four bottles (i.e., the meaning of *san ping duo* 'three bottles and more'). This last reading is canceled by the last sentence of (375a). We indeed see the semantic cancellation if (376a) replaces the underlined part in (375a). The same is true of (375b).

Let us now return to the X. Li & Rothstein's original Chinese examples in (375). In (375a), instead of an implicature cancellation, what we see is a denial relation between the two sentences of the example. The two sentences are linked by the null form of the corrective adversative coordinator *danshi*, which is the counterpart of the corrective *but* in English (Vicente 2010). Importantly, what is denied is indeed semantically entailed. If a proposition is denied by another proposition, the two propositions are not compatible with each other. The constructions of corrective adversative coordinators have their own formal properties (Vicente 2010). The same analysis applies to (375b). Thus, a cancellation effect is seen if the expressions in (376) occur (it is also seen in their English translations of the two examples in (375)), but not in their original Chinese examples in (375). The formal properties of *duo* are different from those of *zhishao* 'at least' and *bu zhi* 'not only'. We therefore do not think the scope of *duo* is determined pragmatically. If it were, we would expect to see some specific pragmatic conditions for the observed readings in (373) and (374). As said above, the use of *duo* is similar to the post-numeral *some* or *odd* in English. The expression *sixty-some* may mean any number between 61 and 69, but not 70 or higher. In contrast, the expression *more than sixty* may mean any number higher than 60, including 70 and any number higher than 70. The contrast between *sixty-some* and *more than sixty* is not pragmatic.

X. Li & Rothstein (2012: 714) also use (377) to argue against my above generalization on the scope of *duo* in numeral constructions, claiming that such an example supports the constituency of [[[Numeral CL] *duo*] N], instead of my [numeral [CL duo] N].

(377) *ban   mu   duo   di*
      half   mu   more   land
      'a piece of land between 0.5 and 1 mu'

If *duo* in (377) scopes over the combination of *ban* and *mu*, it is still not clear why the example does not mean any amount over 1 mu. Even if some new evidence is found to show that (377) indeed has a left-branching structure, my constituency analysis is supported rather than being challenged.

This is because standard measure constructions have a left-branching structure in my analysis (Section 5.2.4). My discussion of the *duo* facts above is intended to show that the position of *duo* alone is not a valid argument for the constituency of numeral constructions, without making any claim on the exact constituency of various *duo* constructions.[45]

5.3.4.2. *The position of* ban *'half'*

Lü et al. (1999: 60) claim that *ban* 'half' may follow a measure word, but not a CL in general.

(378) a. *liu jin   ban putao*   b. *liang xiang ban shu*
        six catty half grape   two   box   half book
        '6.5 catties of grapes'   '2.5 boxes of books'

In Hsieh (2008: 46) and Her (2012: 1235), it is assumed that if *ban* follows a unit word, the unit word and its preceding numeral should form a constituent. The argument is not valid.

Like *duo* 'more', *ban* 'half' is also a partitive quantifier, scoping over one single adjacent morpheme. When *ban* follows a unit word, it scopes over the unit word only, excluding the numeral. For instance, in the three examples in (379), *ban* follows *mi* 'meter'. The reading of (379a) is 5 plus plus half a meter, i.e., 5.5m. The reading of (379b) is 13 plus half a meter, i.e., 13.5m. This example never means the half of 13 (i.e., 6.5). Similarly, the reading of (379c) is 300 plus plus half a meter, i.e., 300.5m.

---

45. I have discussed X. Li & Rothstein's (2012) analysis of *duo* to the right of a unit word. Their analysis of the construction in which *duo* precedes a unit word, such as (ia) and (ib) (= their (32a)), is not clear to me, either.

    (i) *er-shi   duo ben shu*   b. *shi duo feng xin*
        Two-ten   more CL letter   ten more CL   letter
        'twenty and more books'   'ten and more letters'

    They claim that the construction has either a measure or count reading (Claim A) (p. 713). They also claim that "*duo* is a modifier which modifies the constituent immediately preceding it" (Claim B). Based on Claim B, (ib) should have the structure [[*shi duo*] *feng xin*]. However, they claim that on the measure reading, the constituency is [[Numeral *duo* CL] N], but on the count reading, the constituency is [Numeral *duo* [CL N]] (Claim C). However, neither Claim A nor Claim B, or even the combination of the two claims, may lead to the two structures in Claim C.

(379) a. *wu   mi   ban*   b. *shi-san   mi   ban*
      five meter   half   ten-three meter half
      '5.5 meters'   '13.5 meters'
  c. *san-bai   mi   ban*
     three-hundred   meter   half
     '300.5 meters'

Since *ban* never scopes over the combination of a numeral and a unit word, its position does not show whether the combination is a constituent or not.

It needs to be pointed out that the similar scope of *duo* 'more' and *ban* 'half' indicates a systematic property of the partitives in the language. The consistency does not support X. Li and Rothstein's (2012) pragmatic analysis of the issue.

In addition to *duo* and *ban*, the word *zuoyou* 'approximate' may also occur between a unit word and a noun, as seen in (380) (X. Li & Rothstein 2012: 715). However, since the particle *de* is obligatory in the *zuoyou* construction, I do not think such a construction can be used to analyze the constituency of numeral expressions, which do not contain *de*. For the derivations of various *de* versions of numeral expressions, see Section 5.5.

(380) *san   gongjin   zuoyou   *(de) dami*
      three kilogram approximate DE   rice
      'approximately three kilos of rice'

5.3.4.3. The condition for the occurrence of post-unit duo *and* ban

Lü et al. (1999) claim that *duo* 'more' and *ban* 'half' generally may not follow a CL, but they also report some exceptions. We have shown that when these two partitive markers follow a unit word, they scope over the unit word only, introducing an additional fractional quantity. My own observation is that if the nominal is the internal argument of an incremental theme verb (Dowty 1979, 1991; Tenny 1987; Krifka 1989) (e.g., verbs of consumption), it may contain a fractional numeral, or the partitive marker *duo* 'more' or *ban* 'half'. In other words, if a context allows the occurrence of a fractional numeral, it also allows the occurrence of *duo* or *ban* after a unit word, including a CL. In (381a), the verb *yong* 'use' takes the object that has the fractional numeral 3/4. In (381b) and (381c), we see that in the same context, the object may contain the partitive marker *duo* and *ban*, respectively. Our observation shows that Wang (1994: 35) and X. Li & Rothstein's (2012: 712) claim that *duo* may not follow an individual CL such as *ge* is not true. In (382a), however, the verb *zhaixia* 'pick' may not take the object that has the fractional numeral 3/4. Then in (382b) and (382c), in the same context, the object may not contain the partitive marker *duo* and *ban*, respectively. The examples in (383) and (384) show the same kind of contrast.

(381) a. *Zuo   zhe   ge dangao wo   yong-le   3/4 ge pingguo.*
           make DEM CL cake   1SG   use-PRF   3/4 CL apple
           'I used three quarters of an apple to make this cake.'

     b. *Zuo   zhe   ge dangao wo yong-le yi   ge duo   pingguo*
           make DEM   CL cake   1SG use-PRF one CL more apple
           'I used one apple and (some) more to make this cake.'

     c. *Zuo   zhe   ge dangao wo   yong-le yi   ge ban pingguo*
           make DEM CL cake   1SG use-PRF one CL half apple
           'I used one and a half apples to make this cake.'

(382) a. **Ta   cong   shu-shang   zhaixia-le 3/4 ge pingguo.*
           3SG   from   tree-on   pick-PRF   3/4 CL apple

     b. **Ta   cong   shu-shang   zhaixia-le yi   ge duo   pingguo.*
           3SG   from   tree-on   pick-PRF   one CL more apple

     c. **Ta   cong   shu-shang   zhaixia-le yi   ge ban   pingguo.*
           3SG   from   tree-on   pick-PRF   one CL half apple

(383) a. *Na   zhi yang yao-sui-le   3/4   zhi   qianbi.*
           DEM CL goat chew-broken-PRF 3/4 CL   pencil
           'That goat chewed three quarters of a pencil into pieces.'

     b. *Na   zhi yang yao-sui-le   san   zhi   duo   qianbi.*
           DEM CL goat chew-broken-PRF three CL   more pencil
           'That goat chewed three and more pencils into pieces.'

     c. *Na   zhi yang yao-sui-le   san   zhi ban qianbi.*
           DEM CL goat chew-broken-PRF three CL half pencil
           'That goat chewed three and a half pencils into pieces.'

(384) a. **Wo   mai-le   3/4 zhi   qianbi.*
           1SG   buy-PRF 3/4 CL   pencil

     b. **Wo   mai-le   san   zhi duo   qianbi.*
           1SG   buy-PRF three CL more pencil

     c. **Wo   mai-le   san   zhi ban qianbi.*
           1SG   buy-PRF three CL half pencil

The same numeral expression may occur in one context, but not another. The acceptability contrast exhibited in the above data is neither a contrast between CLs and measure words (as claimed by Lü et al. 1999 and Wang 1994), nor a contrast in the nominal-internal constituency (as claimed by Hsieh 2008, and X. Li 2011a). As existential verbs may not take a definite argument in the VP domain, certain verbs may be sensitive to other formal properties of nominal arguments. Thus, it is possible that non-incremental verbs such as those in (382) and (384) disallow their internal argument to have a fractional number. Instead, only integers are allowed.

5.3.5. Other invalid arguments

Her (2012: 1234) lists five other arguments for the unified left-branching analysis of the constituency of numeral expressions in Mandarin Chinese. They are not valid.

The first argument is that CLs and measure words seem to be mutually exclusive and thus seem to occupy the same position. It is true that all unit words surface at the same syntactic position (Unit, see Chapter 6), but this does not mean that they have the same syntactic relation with the associated numerals and the same syntactic relation with the associated nouns, in every step of the derivation. Numeral expressions do not have two unit words in a row, as in (385a), or two strings of numeral-unit word in a row, as in (385b), simply because counting the same entity may not have different counting units at the same time. In the two unacceptable examples in (385), both the CL *tao* and the CL *ben* occur with the same noun *shu* 'book'. This constraint applies regardless of the types of the unit words.

(385) a. **Ta   mai-le   liang tao   ben   shu.*
　　　　3SG   buy-PRF two   CL   CL   book
　　 b. **Ta   mai-le   liang tao   wu   ben   shu.*
　　　　3SG   buy-PRF two   CL   five   CL   book

The second argument is that the whole string of a unit word and a noun can be elided if the numeral is a high and round number such as 400, regardless of the type of the unit word. In (386), the numeral *si-bai* 'four-hundred' is stranded. A plausible analysis of such an example is that the final morpheme of the numeral, *bai* 'hundred' in (386), is reanalyzed as a collective CL, similar to *shuang* 'pair' or *da* 'dozen' (see our discussion of (77) in Section 2.3.1). Since the morpheme plays the role of a unit word, it may license the ellipsis of the whole string to its right, regardless of the syntactic structure of the string. This ellipsis possibility does not show whether a numeral construction is left-branching or right-branching.

(386) *Baoyu   mai-le   san-bai   {ge/jin}   pinguo,   Daiyu*
   Baoyu   buy-PRF three-hundred CL/catty apple   Daiyu
   mai-le   si-bai.
   buy-PRF   four-hundred
   'Baoyu bought 300 {apples/catties of apples}, and Daiyu bought 400.'

The third argument is that all types of unit words may be followed by the functional particle *de*. In Section 5.5, I give an explanation why the occurrence of *de* does not tell us the constituency of numeral constructions.

The fourth argument is that for all types of unit words, if the numeral is *yi* 'one', it is claimed to be optional. As the discussion in Section 4.3.3 shows, there is no numeral deletion operation. Therefore, numerals, including *yi* 'one', are never optional. When a unit word occurs without a numeral (SUW), the nominal encodes unit singularity. Therefore, the absence of a numeral is not an argument for the internal structure of a numeral expression.

The fifth argument is that in a numeral expression, the semantic features of the noun can satisfy the s-selection of the verb that takes the whole numeral expression as its complement. In fact, both the unit word and the noun can satisfy the s-selection of the verb, as shown in (387). In Zhang (2012a), it is shown that this s-selection issue does not help us to see the constituency of the nominal, since semantic features can be percolated from non-head elements.

(387) a. *Yani   he-le   liang ping   niunai.*
         Yani   drink-PRF two   bottle milk
         'Yani drank two bottles of milk.'
      b. *Yani   dapo-le   liang ping   niunai.*
         Yani   break-PRF two   bottle   milk
         'Yani broke two bottles of milk.'

5.4. Constituency and the readings of numeral expressions

I have argued that the division of the left-branching and right-branching structure of numeral expressions correlates with the differences between two types of unit words. In this analysis, the contrast between a left-branching and right-branching structure of numeral expressions of Mandarin Chinese is not that between count and mass nouns, since there is no count nouns in Chinese (Chapter 2). Moreover, my conclusion that individuating and individual CL constructions have an identical constituency shows that there is no constituency difference between numeral expressions of mass and non-mass nouns in the language. In this section, I discuss other possibilities of mapping of different readings of numeral expressions with their structure constituency.

5.4.1. Count and measure

X. Li (2011a: 113–117; 119–120) and X. Li & Rothstein (2012) claim that for a numeral expression in Mandarin Chinese, a measure reading is mapped to the left-branching structure, whereas a count reading is mapped to the right-branching structure. Putting aside the problematic *duo*-argument (X. Li & Rothstein 2012: 712) (see Section 5.3.4.1 above), and leaving the *de*-argument (X. Li & Rothstein 2012: 709) to Section 5.5, I discuss X. Li's two remaining arguments in this section:

(A) the drop of a numeral (the argument is also seen in X. Li & Rothstein 2012: 709);

(B) the deletion of the noun after a reduplicative container measure word.

In addition to these arguments, X. Li (2011a) also mentions another argument: RUWs (e.g., *ping-ping* 'bottle-bottle') may not take a nominal in a measure reading as its antecedent (p. 115–116, 120). A similar observation has been reported in Rothstein (2009), and Y.H. Audrey Li (1998: 698) for a quantity reading of numeral expressions. But it is hard to see how this fact is related to the internal constituency of a numeral expression. I thus ignore this final argument.

X. Li (also X. Li & Rothstein 2012: 709) claims that only the right-branching structure allows the numeral to be dropped. Recall that X. Li assumes that the right-branching structure has the semantics of counting, rather than measuring. This argument for the measure-count mapping of constituency is based on the examples like (388), assuming the numeral *yi* 'one' is dropped in the position marked by __.

(388) *Lao Li mai-le*   __ *ben shu.*
     Lao Li buy-PRF   CL book
     'Lao Li bought a book.'

In Section 4.3.3, I have argued that such a SUW nominal has no position for a numeral (Note that even standard measures may occur in SUW nominals; see (275d, e)). In this new understanding, nominals like *ben shu* 'CL book' in (388) do not have a numeral in their syntactic structure. Therefore, one should not use such examples to discuss whether a unit word is merged with a numeral first (to derive a left-branching structure), or with a noun first (to derive a right-branching structure).

X. Li (p. 120) also claims that when a container measure is reduplicated, the noun to its right may not be deleted if the whole nominal has an anaphoric relation to an antecedent that is a numeral expression. His example is (389) (his judgment):

(389) *zhe   ge   tong   zhuang-le <u>san   ping   jiu,</u>   <u>ping-ping</u>*
DEM   CL   bucket   hold-PRF   three   bottle   wine   bottle-RED
*(<u>jiu</u>)   dou   hen   gui.
wine   all   very   expensive
'This bucket holds three bottles of wine, each of which is expensive.'

According to X. Li, *san ping jiu* 'three bottle wine' in this sentence has a measure reading. Under his hypothesis, the nominal should have a left-branching structure, and the string *san ping* 'three bottle' is a modifier of the noun. If so, he claims, the impossible deletion can be accounted for, assuming the modified noun may not be deleted. However, first of all, if *san ping jiu* in the first clause of (389) has a measure reading, it should not function as an antecedent of another form (his p. 111; 116; note the occurrence of *dou* 'all' in the example). Second, the assumption that a modified noun may not be deleted is problematic. The following sentence also has a measure reading, but the noun to the right of the unit word, which is assumed to be a modified noun in his analysis, is deleted:

(390) *Baoyu   yao   mai   san   bang   yingtao,   Daiyu   yao   mai*
Baoyu   want   buy   three   pound   cherry   Daiyu   want   buy
wu   bang.
five   pound
'Baoyu wants to buy three pounds of cherries, and Daiyu wants to buy five pounds.'

In X. Li (2011a), individual CL constructions have a default counting reading (p. 121), and such a reading has a right-branching structure. For the possible measure reading of such constructions, he resorts to the operation of semantic shift (p. 137). Since measure reading has a left-branching structure in his analysis, the assumed semantic shift must correlate with a change in the syntactic structure. However, no syntactic evidence has been shown to support a left-branching structure for individual CL constructions (see Section 5.2 for our arguments for the right-branching structure of such constructions).

We conclude that the above arguments for the measure-count mapping of constituency of numeral expressions in Mandarin Chinese are not convincing.

Rothstein (2009), X. Li (2011a), and X. Li & Rothstein (2012: 708, 719) also use numeral expressions with a container measure to support their constituency analysis.

(391) a. *John carried three bottles of water home.*
     b. *John poured three bottles of water into the soup.*

The expression *three bottles of water* has a container reading in (391a), but a containee reading in (391b). They correlate the container reading with a count or individual reading, which they assume to have a right-branching structure; and correlate the containee reading with a measure reading, which they assume to have a left-branching structure. The correlations have been challenged in Zhang (2012a). In Zhang's analysis, the two readings correlate with the two sources of the semantic features that satisfy the s-selection of the verb. In (391a), the semantic features of the container-denoting element, i.e., *bottle*, are projected to the whole nominal, satisfying the s-selection of *carried*. In (391b), in contrast, the semantic features of the containee-denoting element, i.e., *water*, are projected to the whole nominal, satisfying the s-selection of *poured*. She shows that the constituency of the whole expression *three bottles of water* is the same in the two readings.

Rothstein (2009) presents a few contrastive properties of the two readings of a container measure expression. She (p. 110) also mentions that in English, "[O]n the measure reading, the suffix *-ful(s)* can often be added to the classifier, but this is inappropriate for the individuating reading." The examples in (392) are given to show the contrast:

(392) a. *Add two cup(ful)s of wine to the soup.*   [Measure]
     b. *Bring two cup(#ful)s of wine for our guests.*   [Individual]
     c. *We needed three bucket(ful)s of cement to build that wall.*
                                                     [Measure]
     d. *Three bucket(#ful)s of mud were standing in a row against the wall.*
                                                   [Individual]

According to Akmajian & Lehrer (1976: 412), "[T]he suffix *-ful* added to nouns is a partially productive way of converting nouns to quantifiers." If a speaker chooses the quantifier version of an expression (i.e., the *-ful* form), instead of the simple noun version, the intended meaning must be a measure one, instead of a count one. Rothstein further reports certain morphological contrasts of the two readings in Hebrew. However, no syntactic constituency contrast is presented.

If we talk about the interpretations of nominals in context, however, Partee & Borschev (2012) show that container measure constructions can be classified into four readings, rather than two. (A) Container + Contents reading: a predicate true of a container together with a substance that fills it. The reading of *three bottles of water* in (391a) is an example. (B) Concrete Portion reading. The English version of a Russian container measure construction is (393), where *two pots of soup* has this concrete portion reading.

(393) *He cooked two pots of soup, a big one for us and a small one for the cat.*

(C) Ad Hoc Measure reading: a measure predicate true of a quantity of the substance, corresponding to some container of the given sort. The reading of *three bottles of water* in (391b) is an example. (D) Standard Measure reading: a measure predicate true of a standard quantity of the substance, corresponding to a conventional standard size of containers of the given kind. Partee & Borschev elaborate that "In English, *a cup of milk* has a reading in which *cup* is a standard unit of measure (two cups make a pint, two pints make a quart): *cup* as a unit of measure has become lexicalized as a specific volume." (p. 469)

Partee & Borschev doubt whether there are any direct syntactic mappings for the four possible readings of container measure expressions. They (2012: 474) state that in their analysis, "the Concrete Portion reading is close to the measure readings and involves the same syntax but does not express measure."

Moreover, consider the examples of modification constructions discussed before. One of the examples is repeated here as (394) (= (316a)). Zhang (2006) shows that if a construction has a pre-numeral modifier, it has a specific and thus counting reading, but the modification evidence shows that in such examples, the construction clearly has a left-branching structure. This is unexpected if counting readings are to correlate with a right-branching structure.

(394) <u>*fangfangzhengzheng*</u> *de liang bao*   *sanjiaoxing de binggan*
       square   DE two   package triangle   DE cookie
       'two square packages of triangle cookies'

5.4.2. Individual and quantity

A contrast related to X. Li's count-measure contrast is Y.H. Audrey Li's (1998) individual-quantity contrast of numeral expressions. In order to complete our discussion, we now show that the different types of constituency argued in my Section 5.2 do not correlate with this individual-quantity contrast, either. We have concluded in Section 5.2.5 that individual, individuating, and kind CL constructions have a right-branching structure and other types of unit word constructions have a left-branching one. Both structures may have the individual and quantity readings. In (395), the individual CL *duo* and the noun *hua* 'flower' form a constituent first, excluding the numeral *san* 'three' (i.e., right-branching structure). Now we see that (395a) has an individual reading and (395b) has a quantity reading. In (396), the kind CL *zhong* 'kind' and the noun *yu* 'fish' also form a constituent first, excluding the numeral *san* 'three'. (396a) has an individual reading and (396b) has a quantity reading. In (397), the container measure *ping* 'bottle' and the numeral *san* 'three' form a constituent first, excluding the noun *jiu* 'wine' (i.e., left-branching structure). (397a) has an individual reading and (397b) has a quantity reading.

(395) a. *Wo ba* <u>*liu duo hua*</u>   *dou fang zai zhuozi-shang le.*
        1SG BA six CL   flower all   put   at   table-on   PRT
        'I put all of the six flowers on the table.'   [Individual]
    b. *Zheli zhi*   *neng fang*   <u>*liu duo hua*</u>.
        here   only can   put   six CL   flower
        'Only three flowers can be put here.'   [Quantity]

(396) a. *You*   <u>*san*   *zhong yu*</u>   *you*   *de hen*   *kuai.*
        have   three   kind   fish   swim DE very   fast
        'There are three fishes which swim very fast.'   [Individual]
    b. *Ni*   *zuiduo zhi neng tiao*   <u>*san*   *zhong yu*</u>.
        you   most   only can   choose   three   kind   fish
        'You can choose only three kinds of fish at most.'   [Quantity]

(397) a. *Wo ba liu ping jiu   dou fang zhuozi-shang le.*
1SG BA six bottle wine all   put   table-on   PRT
'I put all of the six bottles of wine on the table.'   [Individual]
b. *Zhe   zhi bing-tong zhi   neng fang liu ping jiu.*
DEM CL ice-bucket only   can   put   six bottle wine
'This ice-bucket can hold only three bottles of wine.'   [Quantity]

In Y. H. Audrey Li (1998), a pure quantity reading of a numeral expression is represented by a functional projection NumP (note that this projection is for quantity, rather than the morphological number), and an individual reading is represented by DP. The latter has one more layer of functional projection than the former. The contrast between the two readings has nothing to do with the nominal-internal constituency.

Furthermore, English numeral-initial NPs such as *three small children* have no CL, but they also have the two readings (Y. H. Audrey Li 1998: 695). The numeral-initial nominals in (398a) and (398b) both have a quantity reading, whereas the one in (399) has an individual reading. There is no evidence for a difference in the c-command relation of *three* and *small children* between (398a) and (399).

(398) a. *That bed sleeps three small children.*
b. *That hotel suite accommodated 100 guests.*

(399) *Three small children* have arrived. *They are all in the kitchen.*

I thus claim that the contrast between a left- and right-branching structure of numeral constructions does not correlate with the contrast between quantity and individual readings.

5.4.3. Definiteness and specificity

Numeral expressions can have non-specific indefinite readings, as seen in (400); they can also have specific and definite readings. In (401a) and (401b), *san zhi bi* 'three CL pen', in which *bi* 'pen' is elided, is linked to the expresion *wu zhi bi* 'five CL pen' in the context, and is thus partitively specific (See Zhang 2006 for more examples of specific indefinite readings of numeral expressions).

(400) *Yani xiang mai wu   zhi bi.*
Yani want buy five   CL   pen
'Yani wants to buy five pens.'

(401) a. *Yani mai-le wu zhi bi, <u>san zhi b̶i̶</u> huai-le.*
    Yani buy-PRF five CL pen three CL pen break-PRF
    'Yani bought five pens, but three of them are broken.'
 b. *Yani mai-le wu zhi bi, wo zhi kanjian <u>san zhi b̶i̶</u>.*
    Yani buy-PRF five CL pen I only see three CL pen
    'Yani bought five pens but I only saw three of them,

M. Wu (2006, contra Li & Thompson 1989: 130; Cheng & Sybesma 1999: 528–530; 2009: 144; 2012: 645) shows that numeral-initial nominals in Mandarin Chinese can also yield a definite reading (numeral-initial nominals can also be definite in the CL languages Japanese and Korean; see Downing 1996: 163 and Yi 2012: 149). In (402a) (M. Wu 2006: 129), *dou* 'all' does not show up, therefore, Cheng & Sybesma's (1999: 539) hypothesis that the definite reading of a numeral-initial nominal is related to *dou* does not apply here. The preposed object *san ben shu* 'three CL book' in (402b) is also definite (Liao & Wang 2011: 158).

(402) a. *San ge wen guan xia-de zhi daduosuo.*
    three CL rotten official scare-DE keep shiver
    'The three rotten officials were shivering with fear.'
 b. *Wo san ben shu kan-wan yihou, you mai-le*
    1SG three CL book read-finish after then buy-PRF
    ling yi ben.
    another one CL
    'After I read the three books, I bought another one.'

Numeral expressions with measure words, which have a left-branching structrure, may also have specific and definite readings. In (403a), *san wan* 'three bowl', which is followed by the elided *jiu* 'wine', has a specific in-definite reading, and in (403b), *san wan jiu* 'three bowl wine' has a definite reading.

(403) a. *Lulu he-le liu wan jiu, san wan shi jia de.*
    Lulu drink-PRF six bowl wine three bowl be fake DE
    'Lulu drank six bowls of wine, but three of them were fake.'
 b. *Lulu san wan jiu he-wan yihou, you he-le*
    three CL bowl wine drink-finish after then drink-PRF
    yi wan.
    one bowl
    'After Lulu drank the three bowls of wine, she drank another one.'

Since individual CL constructions and measure word constructions behave the same in allowing various types of readings, the different syntactic
constituency patterns of the two constructions do not correlate with a reading
contrast.

5.5.   Constituency and the occurrence of *de* following a unit word

5.5.1. Background

In Mandarin Chinese, the functional element *de* is an enclitic (Huang
1989), although it is usually called a particle. It may introduce a modifier to
the left of another element (e.g., *sanjiaoxing de binggan* 'triangle cookie',
where *sanjiaoxing* 'triangle' is a modifier of *binggan* 'cookie'). *De* may
also surface between a unit word and a noun. If the unit word is an individual or individuating CL, there are certain constraints, which will be explained as we progress. However, in general, all types of unit words may be
followed by *de*, as observed in Tang (2005: 444), Hsieh (2008: 42), X. Li
(2011a), Her & Hsieh (2010: 540), and Her (2012: 1223), as shown in
(149), repeated here as (404).

(404) a. *Lulu   chi-le   yi-bai   {ge/gongjin/bao/pian/dui/zhong}*
          Lulu   eat-PRF one-hundred CL/kilo/bag/slice/pile/kind
          de   pingguo.
          DE   apple
          'Lulu ate 100 apples or 100 {kilos/bags/slices/piles/kinds} of
          apples.'
      b. *Lulu   chi-le   san-fen-zhi-yi li   de ganmao-yao.*
          Lulu   eat-PRF one-third   CL DE cold-pill
          'Lulu took one third of a cold pill.'
      c. *Yi   liang tiao de maojin   ni   zong   mai-de-qi   ba!*
          one   two   CL   DE towel   2SG   after.all buy-can   PRT
          'You should be able to afford to buy one or two towels!'

In this chapter, I do not consider numeral expressions that express an
intrinsic or individual-level property of the entity denoted by the noun, such
as the underlined part in (405) (Tang 2005: 434). The syntactic structure of
such constructions will be discussed in Section 6.6.

(405) *Ta   mai-le   liang tao* [*wu   ben de shu*].
       3SG   buy-PRF two   CL   five CL   DE book
       'He bought two sets of five volume books.'

Hsieh (2008: 45) claims that "The use of *de* calls for the organization of all the relevant information in an N-C sequence as a constituent" (her N = numeral; C = CL). The same idea is found in X. Li (2011a: 119) and X. Li & Rothstein (2012: 709). They thus all argue for a unified left-branching structure from this *de*-perspective. However, we have shown that an individual CL construction may not have two incompatible modifiers (see Section 5.2.1). In (406a), *hen da* 'very big' is not compatible with *hen xiao* 'very small'. If *de* follows the CL, as in (406b), the constraint remains. The consistency does not support a left-branching structure for the numeral expression, in which *de* is supposed to mark the boundary of two constituents [*yi-bai ge*] and [*hen xiao de pingguo*].

(406) a. **Lulu chi-le   hen da de yibai ge hen xiao de pingguo.*
          Lulu   eat-PRF very big DE 100   CL very small DE apple
   b. **Lulu chi-le   hen da de yibai ge **de** hen xiao de*
          Lulu   eat-PRF very big DE 100   CL DE   very small DE
          pingguo.
          apple

Moreover, if an individual or individuating CL s-selects a noun, it does so regardless of the presence of *de*. In (407), *pingguo* 'apple' may occur with the CL *ge*, but not the CL *zhan*. The latter is for lamps. The selection restriction is not affected by the presence of *de*. The selection supports a right-branching structure, rather than a left-branching one (Section 5.2.3). This consistency does not support a left-branching structure for the numeral expression.

(407) *Lulu   chi-le   yibai {ge/*zhan} (de) pingguo.*
     Lulu   eat-PRF 100   CL/CL   DE apple
     'Lulu ate 100 apples.'

We thus need a more plausible analysis of the *de* versions of numeral expressions in which different types of unit words occur.

5.5.2. The quantity-reading condition

Hsieh (2008: 40, 45) observes that *de* may follow an individual CL, as in (407), when the quantity is emphasized. We further find that in a context where the quantity is not emphasized, *de* may not follow an individual CL, individuating CL, or kind CL, but may follow a unit word of other types, i.e., a partitive or collective CL, container or standard measure.

(408) a. **Zhuozi-shang you san ge de pingguo.*   [Individual CL]
      table-on   have three CL DE apple
  b. **Zhuozi-shang you san di de you.*   [Individuating CL]
      table-on   have three CL DE oil
  c. **Zhuozi-shang you san kuan de fuzhuang.*   [Kind CL]
      table-on   have three kind DE clothes

(409) a. *Zhuozi-shang you san pian de xiangjiao.* [Partitive CL]
      table-on   have three CL   DE banana
      'There are three slices of banana on the table.'
  b. *Zhuozi-shang you san dui de yingtao.* [Collective CL]
      table-on   have three pile DE cherry
      'There are three piles of cherries on the table.'
  c. *Zhuozi-shang you san bao de pingguo.* [Container M.]
      table-on   have three bag DE apple
      'There are three bags of apples on the table;
  d. *Zhuozi-shang you san bang de yingtao.*   [Standard M.]
      table-on   have three pound DE cherry
      'There are three pounds of cherries on the table.'

The division between (408) and (409) coincides with the one between the right- and the left-branching numeral expressions. Specifically, the individual CL *ge* in (408a), the individuating CL *di* in (408b), and the kind CL *kuan* in (408c) have a right-branching structure (see Section 5.2.5). They all disallow *de* in the same context where no clue shows that the quantity is emphasized. In contrast, the partitive CL *pian* in (409a), the collective CL *dui* 'pile' in (409b), the container measure *bao* 'bag' in (409c), and the standard measure *bang* 'pound' in (409d), all have a left-branching structure; they all allow *de* in the same context.

If the same right-branching type of numeral expressions occurs in a context where quantity is emphasized, their acceptability improves significantly. In (410), the quantity reading is attested in the presence of the adverb *yigong* 'total', and in (411), the quantity reading is attested in the predicate *zugou* 'enough'.

(410) a. *Zhuozi-shang yigong you 300 ge de pingguo.*
      table-on   total   have 300 CL DE apple
      'There are 300 apples in total on the table.'

b. *Zhuozi-shang yigong you 300 di de you.*
   table-on   total   have 300 CL DE oil
   'There are 300 drops of oil in total on the table.'

c. *Zhuozi-shang yigong you jin   300 kuan de fuzhuang.*
   table-on   total   have about 300 kind DE clothes
   'There are about 300 kinds of clothes in total on the table.'

(411) a. *Yi   liang ge de pingguo jiu zugou le.*
   one two CL DE apple   just enough PRT
   'Just one or two apples are enough.'

b. *Yi   liang di de you jiu   zugou   le.*
   one two CL DE oil just enough PRT
   'Just one or two drops of oil are enough.'

c. *Yi   liang kuan de fuzhuang jiu   zugou   le.*
   one two   kind DE clothes   just   enough PRT
   'Just one or two kinds of clothes are enough.'

Note that when a quantity is emphasized, the quantity does not have to be a precise one. Hsieh (2008: 37) lists some examples in which an estimated quantity is expressed by an individual CL and *de*. Our examples in (410c) and (411) show this point. Based on the above acceptability contrast, we propose the following generalization:[46]

(412) The particle *de* may follow an individual, individuating, and kind CL if the quantity reading of the numeral expression is salient.

This generalization is further supported by three more facts. First, in the presence of a demonstrative, where an individual rather than a quantity-reading is more prominent, the acceptability contrast between the *de*-versions of the left- and right-branching numeral expressions emerges. (Cheng & Sybesma 1998: 393 claim that no demonstrative may occur with a post-unit *de*. However, I find the examples in (413) natural. All of the nominals in (413) can be found via an internet search. The acceptability judgment on the examples is also shared by an anonymous reviewer).

---

46. Hsieh (2008: 39) claims that *de* may follow an individual CL if the quantity expressed by the numeral is either approximate or emphasized, but she does not discuss the case in which the encoded quantity is approximate but not emphasized. The investigation reported here shows that the quantity emphasis is a necessary condition for *de* to follow an individual CL.

(413) a. *Ni   ba na   san   xiang de shu   qingli-diao!*
     2SG   BA DEM three box   DE book clear-away
     'Clear away those three boxes of books!'   [Container M.]

    b. *Ni   ba   na   yi   dui de lüyou-shu   qingli-diao!*
       2SG   BA DEM one   pile DE travel-book clear-away
       'Clear away that pile of travel books!'   [Collective CL]

    c. *Ni   ba   na   san   jin   de fanqie   qingli-diao!*
       2SG   BA DEM three catty DE tomato clear-away
       'Clear away those three kilos of tomatoes!'   [Standard M.]

    d. *Ni   ba   na   liang bufen de kewen   bei   yixia!*
       2SG   BA DEM two   part DE text   recite once
       'Recite those two parts of the text!'   [Partitive CL]

(414) a. **Ni ba na   san   ge de pingguo qingli-diao* [Individual CL]
     2SG BA DEM three CL DE apple   clear-away

    b. **Ni ba na   san   di de you qingli-diao*   [Individuating CL]
       2SG BA DEM three CL DE oil clear-away

    c. **Ni ba na   san   zhong de niu-rou   qingli-diao* [Kind CL]
       2SG BA DEM three kind   DE cow-meat clear-away

Second, we find that the presence of *de* to the right of an individual CL and the presence of a quantity adverb both make an exclusively individual-denoting expression unacceptable. Although a numeral expression such as (415a) may have either a quantity reading (Q-R) or an individual reading (I-R) (Y.H. Audrey Li 1998), it can be disambiguated in various ways. In (415b), the modifier occurs to the left of the numeral *100*. Such a construction always has a specific and thus an individual reading (Zhang 2006). In (415c), the word *yigong* 'altogether, total' signals a quantity context. Since the two ways disambiguate numeral expressions in the opposite directions, they may not be used at the same time, as shown by the unacceptability of (415d). Note that in the examples in (415), no *de* follows the CL *ge*.

(415) a. *100 ge [Lulu mai] de xigua*   ✓I-R, ✓Q-R
     100 CL Lulu buy   DE watermelon
     '100 watermelons that Lulu bought'

    b. *[Lulu mai]   de 100 ge xigua*   ✓I-R, ✗Q-R
       Lulu buy   DE 100 CL watermelon
       'the 100 watermelons that Lulu bought'

    c. *Ta   yigong chi-le   100 ge xigua.*   ✗I-R, ✓Q-R
       3SG   total   eat-PRF   100 CL watermelon
       'He ate 100 watermelons in total.'

    d. **Ta   yigong   chi-le   [Lulu mai] de 100 ge xigua.*
        3SG   total   eat-PRF Lulu buy DE 100 CL watermelon

The contrast in (416) below shows that when *de* follows an individual CL, the pre-numeral modifier construction in (416b) is as bad as (415d), although no quantity adverb such as *yigong* 'total' shows up.

(416) a. *100 ge de xigua*
        100 CL DE watermelon
        '100 watermelons'
    b. **[Lulu mai] de 100 ge de xigua*
        Lulu buy DE 100 CL DE watermelon

A pre-numeral modifier occurs in (416b), but not in (416a). We can see that the *de* construction may not host a pre-numeral modifier (see Cheng & Sybesma 1998: 394; Tang 2005: 448 for more examples that show the constraint). (416b) is different from (415b) only in the presence of *de* to the right of the CL *ge*. The constraint seen in (416b) is parallel to the one in (415d). In both cases, the exclusive individual reading of the pre-numeral modifier construction is in conflict with something: it is in conflict with the adverb *yigong* 'total' in (415d), and with the post-CL *de* in (416b). It is plausible to assume that like the adverb, the post-CL *de* in (416b) also provides a quantity context. Accordingly, the *de* version of the right-branching numeral expression is associated with a quantity reading.

    Third, if a nominal has an exclusive non-quantity reading in a certain context, *de* may not follow the CL in such a nominal. According to Y.H. Audrey Li (1998), the Chinese operator *dou* 'all' ranges over an entire set of individuals to derive a universal-quantificational expression, and the operator *you* 'exist, have' asserts the existence of individuals. "The number expression occurring with *dou* and *you* must be interpreted as denoting individuals, rather than quantity." (p. 697) (417a) has *dou* and (417b) has *you*. Neither has a quantity reading.

(417) a. *300 ge xuesheng dou lai   zher le.*
        300 CL student   all   come here PRT
        'The 300 students all came here.'
    b. *You 300 ge xuesheng lai   zher le.*
        have 300 CL student   come here PRT
        'There are 300 students that came here.'

As expected, *de* may follow neither the CL of the nominal that is in construal with *dou*, as seen in (418a), nor the CL of the nominal that is in construal with *you*, as seen in (418b). This contrasts with the examples in (410) and (411), in which a quantity context is provided and *de* may occur.

(418) a. *300 ge (*de) pingguo dou lan   le.*
       300 CL   DE   apple   all   rotten PRT
       'The 300 apples all got rotten.'
   b. *You   300 ge (*de) pingguo lan   le.*
       have 300 CL   DE   apple   rotten PRT
       'There are 300 apples that got rotten.'

The above facts tell us that with respect to the occurrence of *de* to the right of a unit word, the left-branching type is not constrained, whereas the right-branching type is licensed only in a quantity context. We try to explain this contrast in the next subsection.

In Section 5.4, we have seen arguments against the claim that a left-branching structure encodes a quantity reading exclusively and a right-branching structure encodes a non-quantity reading exclusively. The pattern observed here further falsifies the claim.

5.5.3. Different sources of *de*

It is possible that there are two different sources of *de* that follows a unit word in a numeral expression. The one with a left-branching construction is structurally ambiguous, but the one with a right-branching construction is not ambiguous. In the latter case, the *de* construction is exclusively related to a quantity reading.

5.5.3.1. *Source A: comparative modification construction*

In this sub-section, I show that the *de* version of an individual CL construction is a quantity-comparative modification construction. The modification claim on the *de* version of measure word constructions has been seen in Cheng & Sybesma (1998: 393) and Tang (2005). In X. Li (2011a), the *de* construction is called the as-many/much-as construction. I now combine these insights and propose that the construction is a specific type of modification construction: elliptical comparative modification construction.

Elliptical comparative modification constructions are independently observed in Mandarin Chinese. In this language, a gradable adjective can follow the word *name* 'that', and a string such as *name da* 'that big' or *name duo* 'that many' needs a discourse or linguistic antecedent. In (419a), the cluster *name da* 'that big' takes *zhima* 'sesame seed' as its antecedent. In such a construction, the word *name* 'that' can be deleted. (419a) and (419b) have the same reading. In this construction, *de* introduces a comparative modifier. (419c) is my analysis of (419b).

(419) a. *Lulu mai-le* [*yi ge* [[*zhima name da*] *de wanju*]].
      Lulu buy-PRF one CL sesame that big DE toy
    b. *Lulu mai-le yi ge zhima da de wanju.*
      Lulu buy-PRF one CL sesame big DE toy
      Both: 'Lulu bought a toy as big as a sesame seed.'
    c. *Lulu mai-le* [*yi ge* [[*zhima ~~name~~ da*] *de wanju*]].
      Lulu buy-PRF one CL sesame that big DE toy

Similarly, I claim that *de* in (420a) also introduces a comparative modifier. The full form of (420a) is (420b), where the first *pingguo* 'apple' and *name duo* 'that many' are deleted at PF. (421) shows the same point. In the following, I discuss (420) only.

(420) a. *Lulu chi-le yibai ge de pingguo.*
      Lulu eat-PRF 100 CL DE apple
      'Lulu ate 100 apples.'
    b. *Lulu chi-le* [[[*yibai ge ~~pingguo~~*] ~~*name duo*~~] *de pingguo*].
      Lulu eat-PRF 100 CL apple that many DE apple

(421) a. *Lulu chi-le san-fen-zhi-yi li de ganmao-yao.*
      Lulu eat-PRF one-third CL DE cold-pill
      'Lulu took one third of a cold-pill.'
    b. *Lulu chi-le* [[[*san-fen-zhi-yi li ~~ganmao-yao~~*] ~~*name duo*~~]
      Lulu eat-PRF one-third CL cold-pill that much
    de ganmao-yao].
    DE cold-pill

In (420b), the antecedent of *name duo* 'that many' is the numeral expression *yi-bai ge pingguo* 'one hundred CL apple', which is a syntactic constituent.[47] The deletion of the noun, i.e., *pingguo* 'apple' in (420b), is an

---

47. *Name* 'so, that' has a distal feature, in contrast to *zheme* 'this', which has a proximal feature. The latter may not be bound (cf. Ducceschi 2012), and therefore, *name* in all of the examples discussed here may not be replaced by *zheme*.

instance of Backward Deletion, in which the licensing string ("antecedent") occurs to the right of the ellipsis site, and both the licensing string and the ellipsis site must be right-peripheral in their respective domains (Wilder 1997: 92). In (422), for instance, Backward Deletion of *any of our sales people*, which is the object in the relative clause of the subject, is licensed by the object of the verb *like* (Wilder 1997: 87):

(422) [*Anyone* [*who meets* ~~*any of our sales people*~~]]
       [*really comes to like* <u>*any of our sales people*</u>]

Similarly, in (420b), the ellipsis site of *pingguo* is right-peripheral in the domain of [*yi-bai ge* ~~*pingguo*~~], and its licensing string *pingguo* is right-peripheral in the domain of the object of the verb *chi-le* 'eat-PRF'. The deletion of the string *name duo* 'that many' in (420b) is parallel to the deletion of *name* in (419c). There are non-parallel details of the two deletion operations, but they can be explained. In (419c), the adjective *da* 'big' may not be deleted with *name* 'that', since its absence will lead to a different reading. Compare (419b) with (423).

(423) *Lulu   mai-le   yi   ge   zhima   de   wanju.*
       Lulu   buy-PRF   one CL   sesame   DE   toy
       'Lulu bought a toy that is made of sesame seeds.'

Following the same recoverability principle in deletion (Hankamer 1973; Chomsky 1965), the adjective *duo* in (420b) must be deleted together with *name*, since its presence may lead to a partitive reading of *duo* (see Section 5.3.4), which is not the intended reading. Compare (420a) with (424).

(424) *Lulu   chi-le   yi-bai   ge   <u>duo</u>   de   pingguo.*
       Lulu   eat-PRF   one-hundred   CL   more   DE   apple
       'Lulu ate more than 100 apples.'

It is thus the general recovery condition of PF deletion that explains why the adjective must not be deleted in (419), and must be deleted in (420).

In this elliptical comparative perspective, *de* introduces a modifier to the left of another element (i.e., the modifiee). The surface order can be further derived by ellipsis. The syntactic position of *de* to the right of an individual, individuating, or kind CL is the same as that of (419c). Crucially, the noun following *de* is not in a numeral expression at all. The noun that is in a numeral expression has been deleted, and the containing numeral expression is embedded in the modifier. Thus the position of *de* in this case does not show the constituency of the elements within a numeral expression (contra Hsieh 2008: 45; X. Li 2011a: 115; 119; X. Li & Rothstein 2012: 709).

5.5.3.2. Source B: constituent boundary

We have seen that the *de* version of the right-branching structure is constrained by the quantity-reading condition, but for the *de* version of the left-branching structure, this condition is not observed. This contrast can be explained by the hypothesis that when *de* occurs in a left-branching numeral expression, it is ambiguous between the *de* that introduces a comparative modifier and the *de* that does not. It is in the latter case that *de* occurs between the two syntactic constituents, i.e., between the numeral-unit-word string and the NP. In the former case, *de* is a comparative modification marker, which is external to the numeral expression. The two analyses of the same string *san bei de jiu* 'three cup *de* wine' are seen in (425a) and (425b).

(425) a. [[*san bei ~~jiu~~ ~~name duo~~*] *de jiu*]
    three cup wine that much DE wine
    'three cupfuls of wine'
  b. [[*san bei*] *de jiu*]
    three cup DE wine
    'three cups of wine'

In (425a), *de* is out of the numeral expression *san bei jiu* 'three cup wine', whereas in (425b), *de* occurs between two syntactic constituents of a numeral expression, *san bei* 'three cup' and *jiu* 'wine'.

5.5.3.3. A comparison with two alternative analyses

I have proposed a fine-grained analysis of the *de* versions of numeral expressions, to capture the constraint on the occurrence of *de* to the right of an individual, individuating, and kind CL, and the absence of the constraint on the other types of unit words, in numeral expressions. The empirical coverage of this analysis does not exclude fractional and low-number expressions (see (404b) and (404c)) (cf. X. Li and Rothstein 2012). We have tried to explain the acceptability of various kinds of relevant facts, and their possible derivations, leaving aside an account of some unacceptable cases, such as (148b). Additional constraints are needed to explain such idiosyncratic cases.

Our analysis is different from Cheng & Sybesma's (1998) relativization analysis and Tsai's (2003: 173) NP-internal DP analysis. In Cheng & Sybesma (1998: 406), the *de*-less numeral expression (426a) has the structure in (426b), where a container measure word moves from N to Cl. The structure is a right-branching one, which I have argued against in Section 5.2.

(426) a. *san   wan   tang*
      three bowl soup
      'three bowls of soup'

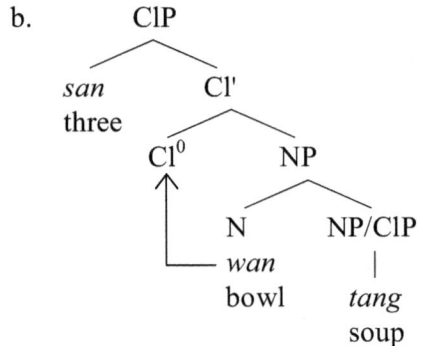

b.
```
              ClP
            /     \
          san      Cl'
         three    /   \
               Cl⁰     NP
                ↑     /   \
                 |   N    NP/ClP
                 |  wan     |
                 └─ bowl   tang
                          soup
```

In their relativization analysis of the *de* version of numeral expressions, (427a) has the structure in (427b) (Cheng & Sybesma 1998: 398), where *de* is always base-generated between *san wan* 'three bowl' and *tang* 'soup'. This is compatible with my (425b), but not (425a).

(427) a. *san   wan   de tang*
      three bowl DE soup
      'three bowls of soup'

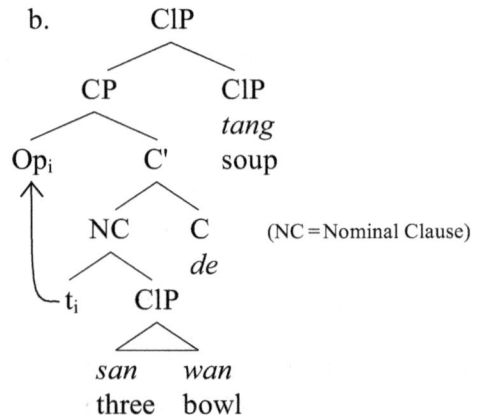

b.
```
              ClP
            /      \
          CP        ClP
         /  \       tang
       Opᵢ   C'     soup
        ↑   /  \
        |  NC   C        (NC = Nominal Clause)
        |  /\   de
        └tᵢ  ClP
             / \
           san  wan
          three bowl
```

In Tsai's (2003: 173) NP-internal DP analysis, (426a) and (427a) have the structures in (428a) and (428b), respectively. Both structures are right-branching, which cannot capture the facts presented in Section 5.2 of this book.

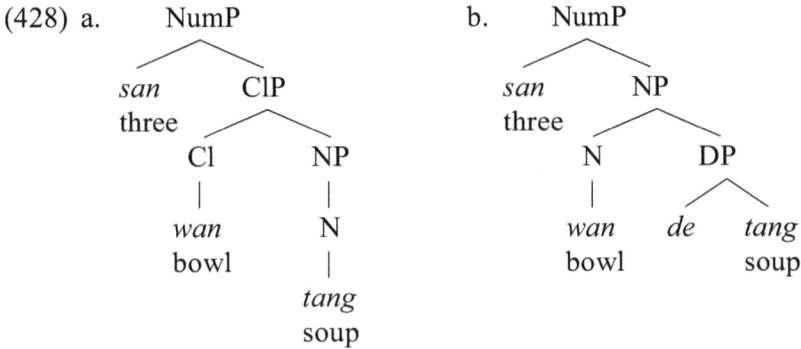

(428) a.
```
        NumP
       /    \
     san     ClP
    three    /  \
          Cl     NP
          |      |
         wan     N
         bowl    |
                tang
                soup
```

b.
```
        NumP
       /    \
     san     NP
    three    /  \
          N      DP
          |     /  \
         wan   de   tang
         bowl       soup
```

Neither of the two analyses considers the *de* constructions of other types of unit words. Accordingly, the facts reflected in the generalization in (412) are not discussed in these analyses.

5.6. Chapter summary

In this chapter I have investigated the constituency of numeral expressions in Chinese. I have argued that the constituency of the numeral expression with an individual, individuating, and kind CL is different from that of the constructions with other types of unit words.

I have discussed four issues: the scope of a left-peripheral modifier, the effect of modifier association, the semantic selection of a unit word on a noun, and the order of the size and shape modifiers. Based on the different behaviors of the different types of unit words, I have identified two structures: a left-branching structure for numeral expressions of container and standard measures, partitive and collective CLs; and a right-branching structure for numeral expressions of individual, individuating, and kind CLs. In the former structure, the unit word does not c-command the NP, whereas in the latter structure, the unit word c-commands the NP.

I have falsified invalid arguments such as the adjacency of a numeral and a unit word and the position of the partitive markers *duo* 'more' and *ban* 'half'. I have also argued against the measure-count semantic mappings with the different syntactic structures. Finally, I have presented a comparative deletion analysis of the constructions in which the functional particle *de* follows a unit word.

A further issue to be studied is the categorial labels of the nodes of the different structures. This issue will be discussed in the next chapter.

Chapter 6
The syntactic positions of classifiers

6.1. Introduction

The goal of this chapter is to identify the details of the syntactic structures of CL constructions in Mandarin Chinese, compared with some types of non-CL languages.

In Chapter 5, we have reached the conclusion that there are two basic configurations of numeral expressions in Mandarin Chinese: a left-branching structure for constructions of container and standard measures, and partitive and collective CLs, and a right-branching structure for constructions of individual, individuating, and kind CLs. The unit word does not c-command the NP in the former structure, but it does so in the latter structure. Thus the basic hierarchical relations have been identified, but neither the syntactic labels for the constituents of the structures, nor the possible derivations of the structures have been discussed.

In this chapter, we argue for a functional projection below DP: UnitP, in addition to NumP (or called #P or $\#^{max}$), which represents number (e.g. Ritter 1991, 1995), and QuantP, which hosts quantifiers such as *much* (Borer 2005). Theoretically, we adopt the assumption that each syntactic head represents one and only one feature (Kayne 2005b; Szabolcsi 2011: 2), although a morph that realizes the head may bear two or more different features. With UnitP, we will present our derivations of the left- and right-branching structures of Chinese numeral expressions, and address the realizations of the head of UnitP in different constructions in Chinese and in various types of non-CL languages.

We argue that a numeral and a unit word hold a Spec-Head relation of UnitP in a certain step of the derivation, and thus the occurrence of a numeral alone results in the projection of UnitP. But the occurrence of a plural marker correlates with the projection of NumP, rather than UnitP. This analysis is thus different from Borer (2005) with respect to the base-position of numerals, and to the syntactic relation between number markers and the CLs of numeral expressions. In discussing the cross-linguistic variation between CL and non-CL languages, our analysis also challenges Wilhelm's (2008) numeral-oriented analysis.

The chapter is organized as follows. Section 6.2 argues that the unit word in a numeral expression heads UnitP. Section 6.3 identifies the syntactic positions of various types of quantifiers and number markers that were discussed in Chapter 3 and Chapter 4. Section 6.4 addresses the morphosyntactic properties of pre-unit-word adjectives that have been introduced in 2.4.7. Section 6.5 presents possible derivations of left- and right-branching numeral constructions that were discussed in Chapter 5. Section 6.6 discusses the structure of attributive numeral expressions. Section 6.7 explores various kinds of null versions of individual and individuating CLs in different types of languages. Section 6.8 provides a brief summary.

6.2.   The projection of UnitP

6.2.1. Unit words in numeral expressions and the head of UnitP

We have seen in Chapter 2 that a unit word in a numeral expression is [+Numerable] and is thus always countable. It has been proposed by many syntacticians that the countability of human language is represented by a functional projection. Chinese CLs in numeral expressions have been generally considered to be the realization of the head of this functional projection. However, different scholars give different labels to the functional category, e.g., CLP or Borer's (2005) DivP. As I argued in Section 2.6.2, the general function of CLs in numeral expressions is to represent a unit for counting. This general function of CLs is not dividing elements. Collective CLs, for instance, group individuals into a single unit, rather than divide elements. I thus do not use the label DivP.

CLs in numeral expressions have been treated as nominal auxiliaries in Chao (1948, 1968: 584), Gao (1948: Ch. 4, *fu-mingci* 'auxiliary noun'), Lu (1951: 42), and Blühdorn (2006, "auxiliar-substantive"), as numeral auxiliaries in Ōta (2003: 146), as light nouns in Wiltschko (2005) and Huang (2009), and as "bleached grammaticalized nouns" in Gerner (2010: 275). Bowers (1991: 19) assumes that in numeral expressions in Mandarin Chinese, "the classifiers are phonetic realizations of Nm", which is a functional head parallel to the functional head of a clause. In all of these works, CLs of numeral expressions are claimed to be parallel to functional elements such as auxiliaries of clauses, although no systematic argument has been given.

Before we show the similarities between verbal auxiliaries and CLs, let us review our understanding of the notion of verbal auxiliary or auxiliary of a clause. It is generally recognized that a word that "helps" the main verb of a clause in expressing certain moods, aspects, tenses or voices, is an auxiliary verb. For instance, *was* in (429a) is a passive auxiliary, *has* in (429b) is a perfect auxiliary, and *should, have* and *been* in (429c) are a modal, perfect and passive auxiliary, respectively.

(429) a. *Greg was defeated.*
b. *Miguel has defeated Greg.*
c. *Erik should have been present.*

We find at least five shared properties between auxiliaries of clauses and CLs of numeral expressions (an additional one, a place-holder property, will be presented in the next chapter). If the former may head a functional projection, so may the latter.

First, neither auxiliaries of clauses nor CLs of numeral expressions may function as an argument or predicate. The apparent predicate use of the modal in B's answer in (430) can be the result of ellipsis of the following VP. Specifically, in B's answer, the VP *youyong* 'swim' is elided to the right of *keyi* 'may'; the ellipsis is semantically licensed by the availability of the overt element *youyong* in A's question.

(430) A. *Wo   keyi   youyong ma?*   B. *Keyi.*
        1SG   may   swim   Q   may
        'May I swim?'   'You may.'

Second, neither auxiliaries of clauses nor CLs of numeral expressions may have any thematic relation to any nominal. In this respect, CLs are different from light verbs and their nominalized version, light nouns, since it is generally assumed that light verbs have thematic relations with an external or causer argument of a clause.

Third, both auxiliaries of clauses and CLs of numeral expressions select substantive categories. The former selects verbal phrases and the latter selects nominal phrases.

Fourth, they can both be absent or have null forms in certain constructions and in certain languages. Not all clauses have overt auxiliaries (Kayne 2012b: Sec. 4). Similarly, in idiomatic expressions and list contexts in Chinese, no CL occurs between a numeral and a noun (Section 2.3.1), as seen in (431).

(431) *si   hai   wei   jia*   [idiomatic expression]
      four   sea   become home
      'take everywhere as one's home'

Fifth, they both license ellipsis, like many other head elements.[48] As in other languages (e.g., Hankamer 1971; Sag 1980; Lobeck 1987, 1995; Chao 1988, Zagona 1988), head elements in Chinese may license the ellipsis of the string to their right, whereas phrasal elements may not. In (432a), the modal *hui* 'will' licenses the VP ellipsis , whereas in (432b), the adverbial NP *jin-nian* 'this year' does not license the VP ellipsis (in B's answer in (430), the modal *keyi* 'may' also licenses the VP ellipsis).

(432) a. *Lulu hui   mai baoxian, Yani ye   hui   mai   baoxian.*
         Lulu will   buy insurance Yani also   will   buy   insurance
         'Lulu will buy insurance, and Yani will also buy insurance.'
      b. **Lulu qu-nian mai-le   baoxian, Yani jin-nian ye   mai-le*
         Lulu   last-year buy-PRF   insurance Yani this-year also buy-PRF
         baoxian.
         Insurance

Parallel to the head elements that license ellipsis, the CL *ben* in the second conjunct of (433) also licenses the ellipsis of the NP to its right, and the meaning of the NP can be recovered from *shu* 'book' in the first conjunct.

(433) *Lulu mai-le   liu ben shu, Yani ye   mai-le   liu ben shu.*
      Lulu buy-PRF   six CL book Yani also buy-PRF   six CL   book
      'Lulu bought six books, and so did Yani.'

Head elements may not only license ellipsis, but also be stranded. In (434a), the modal *keyi* 'can' is stranded. The missing VP has a dependency with the left-peripheral *mai xiaoshuo* 'buy novel'. In (434b), the word *nali* 'there' is not a head element and thus it may not be stranded. Similar to the head element in (434a), the CL *ben* in (434c) is also stranded, and the

---

48. Head elements may license ellipsis, but not all kinds of head elements may do so. The complememtizer *for*, the determiner *the*, and the non-finite Infl *to* in ECM and raising constructions do not license the ellipsis of their complements. See Thoms (2010) and Bošković (2012) for discussions on what kinds of heads may license ellipsis.

missing NP has a dependency with the topic *xiaoshuo* 'novel'. This fact shows that CLs in numeral expressions are head elements.[49]

(434) a. *Mai   xiaoshuo, Baoyu (dangran) keyi.*
        buy   novel   Baoyu   sure   can
        'Buy novels, Baoyu surely can.'
    b. **Mai xiaoshuo, Baoyu (danran) keyi zai nali.*
       buy novel   Baoyu   sure   can   at   there
    c. *Xiaoshuo, Baoyu yinggai mai   wu   ben.*
       novel   Baoyu should   buy   five CL
       'Novels, Baoyu should buy five copies.'

The five shared properties show that CLs in numeral expressions behave like auxiliaries, although they are in the nominal domain.[50] Nevertheless, CLs also have certain properties that seem to be shared with substantive elements, rather than functional elements.

The most telling fact in this respect is that individual, individuating, and kind CLs have semantic selectional restrictions (Section 5.2.3). In the literature, it has been claimed that elements with s-selectional properties should be treated as substantive, rather than functional elements (Cardinaletti & Giusti 2006: 52). According to Ramchand (2008: 117), "Selection can be achieved via category labels on lexical items plus a constrained theory of lexical insertion (which we need anyway)." It is plausible that a certain functional category represents the syntactic position of counting units, and various CLs are just the lexical realizations of the category. It is then possible that various CLs have their own combination properties, which are lexical.

But still, one wonders why there are so many CLs of the same type, especially individual CLs. As we know, all CLs have developed from substantial elements such as nouns and verbs. As realizations of a functional head, CLs

---

49. The string *de jiu* in (ia) may not move, although the unit word *bei* 'cup' is a head element, as seen in (ib). One account is that *de* is an enclitic. Also, *de* and the element to its right never form a maximal projection (Zhang 1999; 2010), thus such a string may not move (Chomsky 1994; 1995: 253).
   (i) a. [[*san bei*] *de   jiu*] (= (425b))   b. *[*de jiu*]ᵢ ...... [[*san   bei*] tᵢ]
       three cup DE wine   DE wine   three cup
       'three cups of wine'
50. The similarities between auxiliaries and CLs indicate that CLs are more qualified to be treated as nominal auxiliaries than articles (cf. Roehrs 2009). Articles may not have a null form and do not license ellipsis. The same is true of demonstratives, another kind of functional elements in nominals.

seem to keep the selectional restrictions of the original source (Section 2.6.3.4). This suggests that grammaticalization does not affect all formal features of a lexical item in the same speed. From a different perspective, if linguistic formatives are clusters of formal features, and if formal features of various types can be bundled in various ways, it should not be surprising that there are gradient differences between substantive and functional elements. CLs may belong to what Borer (2005: 100) calls "twilight zone between the substantive and the functional", or semi-lexical category in the sense of Corver & van Riemsdijk (2001), or functional category in the faculty of language in the broad sense, rather than in the narrow sense (see Déchaine & Tremblay 2011). In any case, the fact that CLs exhibit selectional restrictions may enrich our current understanding of the contrasts between functional and substantive elements.

A further discussion of a relevant issues is in order here. CLs have been claimed to be an open system (T'sou 1976: 1217; Loke 1997; Aikhenvald 2003: 99; H. Zhang 2007: 57; Wu & Bodomo 2009: 490). My own examination tells me that in Mandarin Chinese, the alleged open system is usually seen in standard measures (e.g., *bang* 'pound' did not exist in old days, and *qian*, which was equivalent to 5 grams, has disappeared in the modern standard measure system) and container measures (e.g., *san CD wenjian* 'three CDs of files'). Many of Chao's (1968) so-called temporary measures are emerging container measures (others are nouns with M-YI; see Section 3.5.3). Such unit words occur in the left-branching types of numeral expressions only. In my analysis to be presented in Section 6.5.2 (also Cheng & Sybesma 1998: 406; see (426b) above), such unit words are base-generated at N and they surface at the same position as other unit words by movement. Since the elements base-generated at N come from an open system, it is natural that these unit words look like elements of an open system. Gebhardt (2011: 127) is right in saying that CLs like *ben* (for books) and container measures such as *bao* 'bag' "should not be lumped together", when we decide whether unit words are functional or lexical. On the other hand, occasionally, we see new individual or individuating CLs (e.g., *san qiu bingqilin* 'three CL ice-cream', where the CL *qiu* is derived from the noun *qiu* 'ball'). In such cases, we see an on-going grammaticalization process from a noun to a CL. The new function of a lexical item emerges when the item shows up in the new syntactic position (i.e., occurring between a numeral and a noun in the language).

I adopt the well-established theory that CLs are realizations of an independent functional head. I label the projection UnitP, and go ahead to examine its structural properties.

6.2.2. The Spec-Head relation of a numeral and a unit word

A numeral and a unit word exhibit a dependency relation in a numeral expression. Counting makes sense only when we know what counts as one unit. The quantity of *two bags of apples* is different from *two slices of apples*, although the numerals are the same. As early as the 1920s, Li ([1924] 1992: 81) noted that a CL in a numeral expression encodes a counting unit. From a semantic perspective, a numeral needs an operator to access the unit for counting. In Krifka (1995: 400), the operator is called OU (for Object Unit), and a unit word such as a CL is a linguistic form of OU. In Kobuchi-Philip (2007), a unit word is the semantic argument of a numeral.

This semantic dependency in counting, regardless of whether it is a variable-operator relation or predicate-argument relation, is between a numeral and one and only one counting unit. This accounts for Ratliff's (1991: 696; see also Bisang 1993: 24) "double classifier constraint", since each instance of counting may have only one counting unit.[51]

The main semantic function of CLs in numeral expressions is to specify a unit for counting, rather than to make a semantic classification (see Section 2.6.3). Therefore, the co-occurrence of CLs with numerals distinguises the CLs in numeral expressions from other types of CLs that are incorporated into verbal expressions in sign languages (e.g., Sandler & Lillo-Martin 2006) or noun CLs in Bantu languages (e.g., Aikhenvald 2003; Svenonius's 2008 SortP).

In Mandarin Chinese, a CL licenses the occurrence of a numeral in a nominal (Ōta 2003: 146 call CLs numeral auxiliaries), although CLs may have other uses in other constructions. In languages such as Purépecha (Vázquez Rojas 2012: 87) and Niuean (Massam 2009: 682), a numeral licences the occurrence of a CL, and thus CLs are used only in numeral expressions. Thus, there is a general dependency between numerals and CLs in numeral expressions.

In the last subsection, I have argued for the head position of CLs, and the above discussion shows the dependency between numerals and CLs in numeral expressions. I now turn to the syntactic position of numerals.

---

51. Counting may use a complex unit, e.g., *kilometer per hour,* or *liang-ci* 'unit of vehicle per time' (Zhang 2002), but not two different units. When multiple CLs occur in a numeral expression, only one of them functions as a counting unit. See Chapter 7 for my research of double CL constructions in Mandarin Chinese, and Piriyawiboon (2010: 110) for an analysis of multiple CL constructions in Thai.

Cross-linguistically, numerals have been identified as NPs or APs (e.g., Zweig 2006, Corver & Zwarts 2006, Corver et al. 2007: 755; Stavrou & Terzi 2008).[52] Numerals in nominal expressions have been assumed to be base-generated at a Spec position (Borer 2005: 96), and the relation between a numeral and a CL is represented as a Spec-Head relation in Cheng & Sybesma (1998: 406). Danon (2012) claims that both a Spec and a head position are possible for the base-position of numerals, cross-linguistically and even in the same language. In Aboh et al. (2011: 8), it is assumed that numerals are phrasal in English but are heads in Mandarin Chinese. Their theoretical assumption is that modification possibility can show the phrase level of an element. Their only argument is that in (435a) the numeral is modified by *exactly*, but in its Chinese counterpart, (435b), however, the modifier *jiu* 'exactly' must precede the whole VP, rather than the numeral *san* 'three'. This argument is weak. In (435c), any of the three modifiers, *zonggong* 'total', *dayue* 'about', and *zuzu* 'as many as', may occur to the immediate left of the numeral (also see (153) and (325)). The constraint on *jiu* 'exactly' is lexical, and thus does not apply to other numeral-oriented modifiers. Therefore, numerals in Chinese, as in English, can be modified.

(435) a. *I bought exactly three books.*
　　　 b. *Wo   jiu   mai-le   san   ben   shu.*
　　　　　 1SG   exactly   buy-PRF   three   CL   book
　　　　　 'I bought exactly three books.'
　　　 c. *Wo   mai-le   {zonggong/dayue/zuzu}   san   ben   shu.*
　　　　　 1SG   buy-PRF   total/about/as.many.as   three   CL   book
　　　　　 'I bought {three books in total/about three books/as many as} three books.'

The non-head status of numerals in Mandarin Chinese is supported by the fact that unlike head elements in the language (see Section 6.2.1 above), numerals neither license ellipsis nor are strandable. In (436), the numeral

---

52. H. Yang (2005: 45) also claims that numerals are phrasal. But her two arguments are either incomplete or unconvincing. One argument is that a numeral can be replaced by *ji* 'how many'. But in order to show that the numeral replaced by *ji* is phrasal, we need to see that *ji* is phrasal. Another argument is that numerals can be conjoined. But conjuncts do not have to be phrasal (Zhang 2010).

san 'three' does not license the ellipsis of the string to its right, i.e., *ben shu* 'CL book' (also see our discussion of (386)).[53]

(436) *Baoyu   mai-le   san   ben shu, Daiyu   ye   mai-le   san*
     Baoyu   buy-PRF   three   CL   book   Daiyu   also   buy-PRF   three
     *(ben shu).
     CL   book
     'Baoyu bought three books, and so did Daiyu.'

To represent the dependency between a numeral and a unit word, and the non-head status of numerals, I assume that a numeral is base-generated at the Spec of UnitP and an individual, individuating, or kind CL is the realization of Unit. The base-positions of the elements in (437a) are shown in (437b):

(437) a. *san   ge xuesheng*   b.   UnitP
       three CL student
       'three students'   *san*   Unit'
                      three
                           Unit   NP
                           ge   *xuesheng*
                           CL   student

---

53. Examples such as (i) show that elements to the right of a numeral in English can be deleted (see Kayne 2005a: Ch. 10; Thoms 2010: Sec. 4.4):

(i)   *Bill bought five books and Kim bought six ~~books~~.*

Nominal-internal ellipsis is subject to language-specific, as well as universal restriction (Cinque 2012, and the references thereof). In West Flemish, a noun after an adjective may be elided, as seen in the string *een witte* 'a white' in (ii) (Alexiadou et al. 2007: 263), whereas this is impossible in English. In the English translation of (ii), the word *one* must show up.

(ii)   *Marie eet een zwarte katte en   ik   een   een witte.*
      Marie has a   black   cat   and   1SG   have   a   white
      'Marie has a black cat and I have a white *(one).'

The fact that in English, non-head elements may also license ellipsis is seen in sluicing. Assume sluicing is derived by deletion in English (Merchant 2001). In (iii), the string after *which model*, which is not a head element, is deleted.

(iii) *They discussed a certain model, but they didn't know which model.*

In (437b), the numeral c-commands the CL. The locality of the dependency between the two elements is reduced to the "closest c-command" (Chomsky 2000: 122). This Spec-head relation between a numeral and a CL is also seen in Cheng & Sybesma (1998: 406) and Watanabe (2006; 2010).

If a numeral and a unit word hold a Spec-Head relation in certain steps of the derivation, UnitP is projected whenever a numeral occurs, regardless of whether there is any overt form for the head of this projection. But the occurrence of a plural marker does not correlate with the projection of UnitP. Accordingly, for a numeral expression without a plural marker and a CL, UnitP is still projected. In this case, the head of Unit is null. Both the Dëne example in (438a) (Wilhelm 2008: 46) and the idiomatic Chinese example in (438b) illustrate this. The base-positions of the elements *wu ti* 'five body-parts' in (438b) are represented in (438c). See Section 6.7.1 for a discussion of null Unit in non-CL languages. One might assume that in Chinese idiomatic constructions, an individual CL shows up in the form of a zero-allomorph.

(438) a. *solághe   dzól*   [Dëne]
      five   ball
      'five balls'

    b. *wu   ti   tou   di*   [Chinese idiomatic expression]
       five   body.part reach ground
       'the five body parts (the four limps and the head) touch the
       ground (as a gesture of respect).'

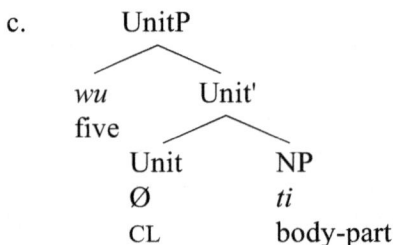

    c.   UnitP
          /‾‾‾‾‾\
    wu   Unit'
    five   /‾‾‾‾‾\
       Unit   NP
       Ø   *ti*
       CL   body-part

I put aside the details of the categories of the Spec of Unit. Such details do not affect the argumentation of this book. Further studies are needed to determine whether the numerals in Chinese numeral constructions are nominal or adjectival (see Zweig 2006; Danon 2009).[54]

---

54. In Wu & Bodomo's (2009: 500) structure of numeral expressions, it is not
    clear where the syntactic position for a numeral is.

6.2.3.   The surface position of numerals and QuantP

6.2.3.1. QuantP in the absence of UnitP

The quantifier (*yi*)-*dianr* 'a.little' may not be followed by a unit word, as seen in (439) (Section 3.3). This quantifier is not used for counting.

(439) (*yi*)-*dianr* (**kuai*) *bing*
       one-DIAN   CL   ice
       'a little ice'

   Following Borer (2005) and Watanabe (2010: 46), I assume that all kinds of quantifiers surface at Spec of QuantP. QuantP can be projected without UnitP. If there is neither a numeral nor a unit word for counting, as in (439), UnitP is not projected. In Section 3.3 we also saw that (*yi*)-*dian* licenses ellipsis, and thus *dianr* in this expression can be at a head position. We claim that the structure of (439) is (440):

(440)   QuantP
         /   \
   (*yi*)-   Quant'
    one   /   \
         Quant   NP
         dianr   *bing*
                     ice

   This use of *yi* is in fact similar to E-YI (to be discussed shortly), except that it is optional. Also, *dianr* in the structure occurs in the same structure position as the CL after E-YI, although it has no s-selection with the NP. The structure positions for the elements of an (*yi*)-*xie* nominal are the same as those of an (*yi*)-*dian* nominal.
   The Spec of QuantP is also the position of the quantifier M-YI, identified in Section 3.5.3. Thus, the structure of the constituent bracketed in (441a) is (441b):

(441) a. *Tamen* [{*yi/man*} *shen   nitu*].   (M-YI)
         3PL   one/full   body mud
         'They, their whole bodies are in mud.'

b.

```
              ┌─────────────┐
      SUBJECT    ┌──────────┐
      QuantP        PREDICATE
     ┌──────┐         NP
  yi/man   Quant'    nitu
  one/full ┌──────┐  mud
      Quant    NP
            shen
            body
```

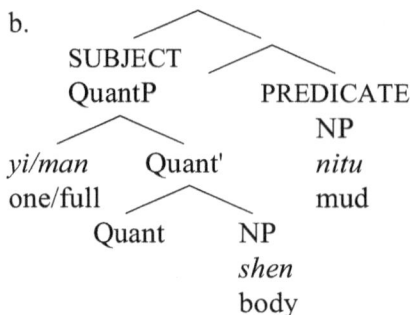

As elements at Spec, quantifiers of various kinds have no selectional restrictions on other elements.

QuantP encodes quantity in general, but UnitP encodes counting. Only counting needs numerals and a counting unit. QuantP does not host a formative used as counting unit, whereas UnitP does. Some animals are able to discriminate between different quantities without counting (see Agrillo et al. 2011 and the references thereof). Moreover "some developmental studies indicate that infants may also preferentially use continuous variables in quantity discrimination" (Agrillo et al. 2011: 281). In Feigenson et al. (2002), for example, 12-month-old children were allowed to choose one of the containers, after they saw crackers placed sequentially into two containers, and it is observed that infants were able to choose the larger quantity when comparing one cracker versus two, and two crackers versus three, however, when crackers were of different sizes, the choice was determined by total surface area or total volume (Agrillo et al. 2011: 282). Thus the separation of a quantity-denoting category (QuantP) and a counting-denoting category (UnitP) has its cognitive foundation.

Syntactically, as we mentioned in Section 3.1, numerals license numeral-oriented adverbs such as *zhengzheng* 'whole', *zonggong* 'total', *dayue* 'about', and *zuzu* 'as many as', whereas quantifiers do not. Thus the adverbs are licensed by UnitP, but not QuantP.[55]

In Chapter 3, we have also distinguished the non-counting-unit use of CLs from the counting-unit use of CLs in quantifier constructions. The CL *jia* and the CL *sou* in (442a) (= (174b)), and the CL *pian* in (442b) (= (180b)) do not encode a counting unit.

---

55. See Watanabe (2010: 45) for a claim that all non-numeral quantifiers (i.e., vague-quantity expressions, in his term) in Japanese are merged in Spec of QuantP.

(442) a. *Yi   jia   feiji   de sudu   bi   yi   sou lunchuan*
      one CL   airplane DE speed than one CL   ship
      de   sudu kuai.
      DE speed fast
      'An airplane's speed is faster than a ship's.'
  b. *Baoyu gandao yi   pian mangran.*
      Baoyu feel   one CL   confusion
      'Baoyu felt confused.'

I claim that the quantifier G-YI and the CL *jia,* or *sou,* in (442a) are in a Spec-head relation of QuantP, as shown in (443a). Similarly, the E-YI and the CL *pian* in (442b) are also in a Spec-head relation of QuantP, as shown in (443b). In these two structures, the CL is not a formative used as a counting unit. But the CL in both G-YI and E-YI constructions is obligatory and shows selectional restrictions with the noun (Sections 3.5.1 and 3.5.2). This indicates that the CL and the noun are in a head-complement relation. The two structures in (443) capture the relation.

(443) a.   QuantP   (G-YI)   b.   QuantP   (E-YI)

      yi   Quant'   *yi*   Quant'
      one   one
         Quant   NP   Quant   NP
          | *feiji* | *mangran*
        jia   airplane   *pian*   confusion
        CL   CL

6.2.3.2. *QuantP and UnitP*

I have argued that the base-position of a numeral in a numeral expression is Spec of UnitP. I extend this claim to all quantifiers that occur with a unit word that denotes a counting unit, as in (444a). I claim *haoji* 'several' in (444a) is base-generated at Spec of UnitP, as shown in (444b).

(444) a. *haoji   *(kuai) bing*
      several   CL   ice
      'several chunks of ice'

b.   UnitP
        ╱‾‾‾‾‾╲
    haoji   Unit'
    several   ╱‾‾‾‾‾╲
          Unit   NP
           | *bing*
          kuai   ice
          CL

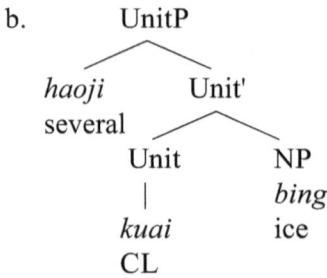

I adopt Borer & Ouwayda (2010: 12) and Watanabe's (2010: 46) claim that a numeral must move from its base-position to Spec of QuantP. A numeral never occurs with another quantifier such as *many*, although it may occur with a D-element such as *every* or *all*, which are base-generated in DP. The incompatibility between a numeral and quantifier is captured if they compete for the same surface position.

A numeral does not have to surface next to a unit word, whereas the base-generated Spec-Head relation may not be intervened by any other element (e.g., an adjective). From this perspective, the raising of a numeral away from UnitP captures the possible separation of a numeral from a unit word. Accordingly, a more complete form of (437b) should be (445).

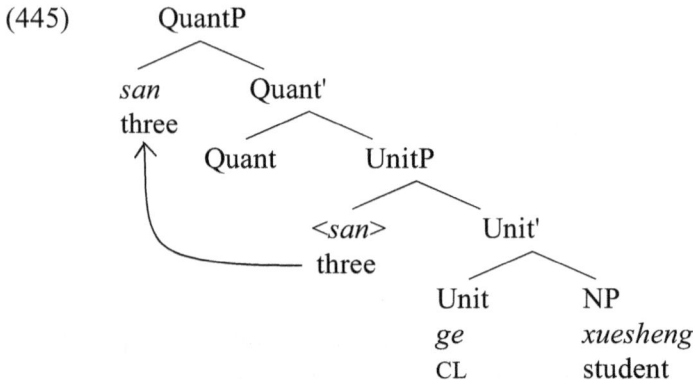

(445)   QuantP
         ╱‾‾‾‾‾╲
      san   Quant'
      three   ╱‾‾‾‾‾╲
         ↑   Quant   UnitP
         | ╱‾‾‾‾‾╲
         | <*san*>   Unit'
         └──── three   ╱‾‾‾‾‾╲
                     Unit   NP
                     ge   *xuesheng*
                     CL   student

Parallel to a numeral, quantifiers like the one in (444) may also move to Spec of QuantP.

QuantP may have dependency with DP, to encode definiteness and specificity. See Section 5.4.3 for examples of numeral expressions with such readings. If numeral-initial nominals, as well as CL-initial nominals (Section 4.3.4) and bare nouns, may have either definite or indefinite readings in dialects of Chinese, it is unlikely that CLs alone may play the role of D-elements in CL languages (pace Cheng & Sybesma 1999, 2012: 647). Ndayiragije & Nikema's (2011) study shows that in some languages with both determiners and CLs, a CL may occur with a determiner in the same nominal. It is possible that in Chinese, definiteness is encoded by elements that merge at various points along the spine of DP, similar to the syntax of plurality in various languages proposed in Butler (2012).[56]

6.3. The co-occurrence of QuantP, UnitP, and NumP

Adopting Ritter (1991), I assume that NumP (or called #P or $\#^{max}$) hosts the number feature, which is the locus of the contrast between morphological singularity and plurality. The syntactic structure of the English plural noun in (446a) is represented in (446b).

(446) a. *students*

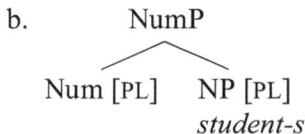

b.
```
        NumP
       /    \
  Num [PL]   NP [PL]
            student-s
```

The head of NumP can be realized by an independent word, such as *tau* in the Niuean example in (447a) (Massam 2009: 676) and *mau* in the Hawaiian example in (447b) (Dryer 2005).

(447) a. *e tau tagata*   [Niuean]
   ABS.C PL person
   'the people'

  b. *'elua a'u mau i'a*   [Hawaiian]
   two my PL fish
   'my two fish'

The structure in (446b) is independent of UnitP, and therefore it can also represent the so-called mass plurals (Sections 2.2.6, 2.5.3, and 4.1.3).

---

56. In English, numerals may also exhibit properties of a high syntactic position. The numeral *zero* in English may move through DP to license a NPI in the clause, as in (i) (cited from Postal 2002).

 (i) *Hector sent zero presents to any of his ex-wives.*

Moreover, although NumP is an independent functional projection, it is possible for a plural marker to host other features such as gender features in addition to a number feature. It is also possible for some other element such as an adjective or a determiner to exhibit number features. In the Walloon example in (448a) (cited from Berstein 2001), the plural marker –*ès* (feminine) is attached to the adjective, and in the German example in (448b), we see the plural article *die* (also, the English indefinite article *a* has [–PL] feature; see Danon 2011: 309 for further discussion).

(448) a. *dès   vètès-   ouh*   [Walloon]
          some green.FEM.PL door
          'some green doors'
      b. *die   Bücher*   [German]
          the.PL book.PL
          'the books'

Thus, the same φ-features often appear on multiple forms within the same DP, a phenomenon of agreement (Danon 2011: 303). Moreover, if a nominal-external element shows number-agreement with the nominal, it should also have number features (unvalued features) (Harbour 2011: 567).

Bare nouns in Mandarin Chinese encode general number, and they thus express either singular or plural entities (Section 4.1.2). Following Bale (2011: Sec. 4), I assume that the structure of a bare noun in the language does not contain a phonologically null NumP.

However, Num can host a SUW or RUW. The structure of the internal argument of (449a) is represented in (449b) (the possible DP projection dominating NumP is omitted).

(449) a. *Yangtai-shang you   pian shuye.*
          balcony-on   have CL   leaf
          'There is a leaf on the balcony.'

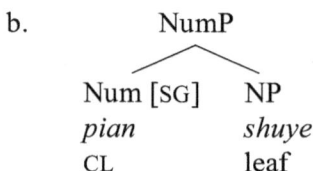

      b.   NumP
              ⌒⎯⎯⌒
          Num [SG]   NP
          pian   *shuye*
          CL   leaf

As we show in Chapter 4, plural markers in the language are licensed by quantifiers. Thus, QuantP is projected above plural NumP in the language. The structure of the internal argument of (450a) is represented in (450b).[57]

(450) a. *Yangtai-shang you   (yi)   pian-pian shuye.*
        balcony-on   have one CL-RED   leaf
        'There are many leaves on the balcony.'

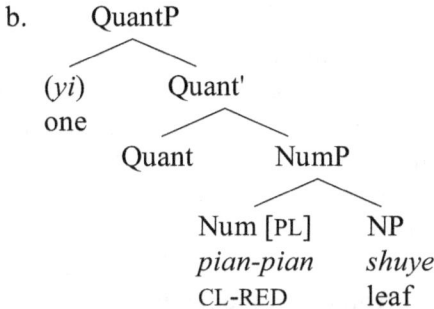

    b.   QuantP

          (yi)   Quant'
          one

                Quant   NumP

                        Num [PL]   NP
                        pian-pian *shuye*
                        CL-RED   leaf

In the NumP structures in (449b) and (450b), the CL realizes Num, and it exhibits selectional restrictions on the NP (see Section 4.2.1 for RUWs and Section 4.3.1 for SUWs). The head-complement relation between Num and NP captures the selection relation.

The unit words that realize Num may also either directly move to D or have a certain dependency with D, exhibiting their interactions with the feature of definiteness or specificity (Sections 4.2.4 and 4.3.4).

So far, we have identified three syntactic positions for CLs: Unit, as in (445), Quant, as in (443), and Num, as in (449b).

In (450b) above, both QuantP and NumP are projected for the same nominal. The English example in (451a) also has both a non-numeral quantifier *many* and a plural noun *books* (another example is the Walloon example in (448a)). The quantifier is hosted by QuantP and the number marker is licensed by NumP. Since there is neither a numeral nor a unit word, UnitP is not projected. The structure for (451a) is (452b).

(451) a. *I bought many books.*   b. *I bought so much clothes.*

---

57. In H. Yang (2005: 85 fn. 19), NumP is projected above CLP. In order to generate a reduplicative CL form, a CL moves from the head of CLP to the head of NumP, and then moves further to D. At D, it is spelled out as a reduplicative form. My analysis does not have the CL-to-Num movement.

(452)   QuantP
         ╱   ╲
    many   Quant'
            ╱   ╲
       Quant   NumP
              ╱   ╲
         Num [−PL]   NP
                    books [−PL]

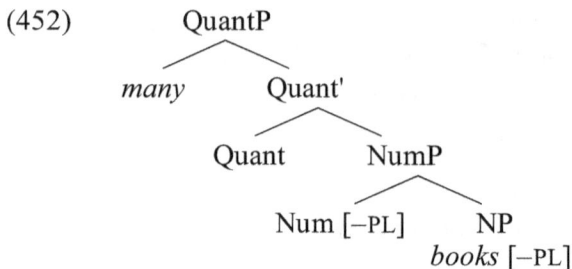

UnitP and NumP may also both be projected in the same nominal. We discuss two such constructions. First, for constructions that have both a numeral and a plural marker, both UnitP and NumP are projected, although the head of Unit can be null. UnitP is projected above NumP (Duffield 1995: 266–332; Svenonius 2008; Gebhardt 2009; Ott 2011). The base-positions of the two words in (453a) are represented in (453b), where UnitP is added to the structure in (446b), to host the numeral. The plural feature hosted by Num licenses the number features of the noun, and is responsible for the possible number agreement with any other element in the context (e.g., D-element, verb). The example in (447b) has a structure similar to (453b), with the plural marker *mau* as a realization of Num.

(453) a. *three students*

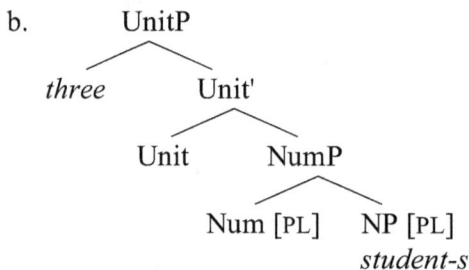

b.   UnitP
      ╱   ╲
   three   Unit'
          ╱   ╲
     Unit   NumP
           ╱   ╲
      Num [PL]   NP [PL]
                 student-s

Second, for constructions that have a CL, a number marker, and a numeral, both UnitP and NumP are projected. In this case, since a unit word is higher than a plural marker, as in (453b), UnitP is projected above NumP. In my analysis, the base-positions of the elements in (454a) (Gebhardt 2009: 227) are represented in (454b). A similar Persian example, *se-ta ketab-ha* 'three-CL book-PL', is found in Ghomeshi (2003: 59 (36b)).

(454) a. *car   ta   deræxt-ha*   [Persian]
          four CL   tree-PL
          'four trees'

b.   UnitP

    car   Unit'
    four

        Unit   NumP
        ta

        CL   Num [PL]   NP [PL]
                          derœxt-ha
                          tree-PL

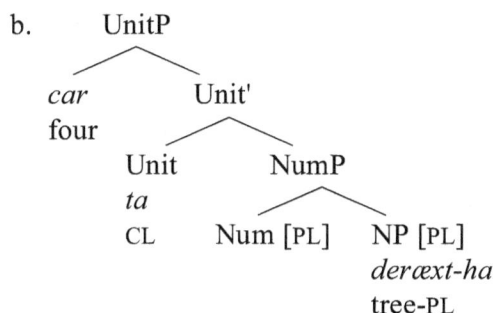

UnitP and NumP also interact in various ways. We have claimed that the occurrence of a numeral signals the projection of UnitP. In Chapter 4 we have shown that no numeral occurs with a RUW or SUW. Thus, in Chinese, Unit never takes NumP as its complement. The co-occurrence of a numeral and a plural marker is also not possible in languages such as Hungarian or Bangla (Section 2.2.6).

In languages such as Oromo and Lango, however, numerals trigger singular number agreement (Rijkhoff 1999: 234; 2002).

(455) *gaala lamaa sookoo d'ak'-e.*   [Oromo]
     camel two   market go-3SG:MASC:PAST
     'two camels went to the market'

In Finnish, no plural noun occurs with a numeral, as seen in (456a); but if a demonstrative precedes the numeral, it must be plural, as seen in (456b) (Brattico 2010).

(456) a. *Kolme auto-a   aja-a   tiellä.*   [Finnish]
       three   car-PART.SG drive-SG road
       'Three cars drive on the road.'
    b. *Ne   kaksi   pien-tä   auto-a   seiso-ivat*
       those.PL two.SG small-PART.SG car-PART.SG stand-PST.3PL
      tiellä.
      road.ADESS
      'Those two small cars stood at the road.'

In all of these cases, the numeral is hosted in UnitP, and number agreement, regardless of whether it is singular or plural agreement, is licensed by the projection of NumP (cf. Danon 2011: 301). If the occurrence of a numeral consistently triggers singular number, Unit selects singular Num.

Recall our discussion that the occurrence of a real numeral triggers plurality in English (Section 4.2.5). It is possible for Unit to select plural Num in English.

(457a) is an English example in which a quantifier, a kind CL, and a PL marker co-occur, without a numeral. In the Ahmao example in (457b) (Wang 1986: 76), similarly, the quantifier *pidzan* 'several' and a portmanteau morph *dzhai*, which contains a CL and a singular (SG) number morpheme, occur together, without a numeral. In such examples, the quantifier is hosted by QuantP, the CL hosted by UnitP, and the plural marker is licensed by NumP. The basic structure of (457a) is (458) (we ignore the position of *of* here).

(457) a. *many kinds of books*
　　　b. *pidzau　　dzhai　　　　　　　tci*　　　[Ahmao]
　　　　　several　CL.MED.SG.INDEF　road
　　　　　'several roads'

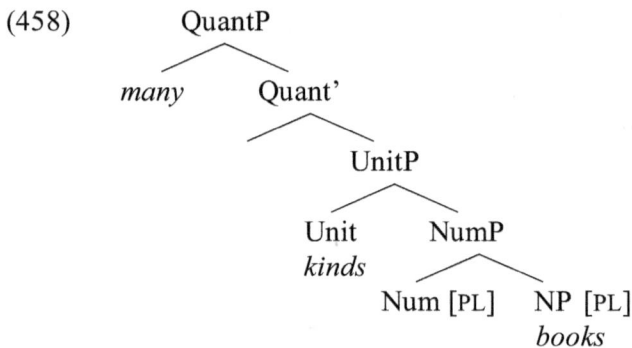

(458)

```
            QuantP
           /      \
       many       Quant'
                 /      \
              UnitP
             /      \
        Unit        NumP
        kinds      /    \
               Num [PL]   NP [PL]
                          books
```

This approach is different from Borer (2005) in the base-position of numerals and in the syntactic relation between number markers and CLs. First, numerals are base-generated in Spec of $\#^{max}$ in Borer (2005: 96; also Li 1999: 86; Huang et al. 2009: 312), as in (459a), but in Spec of UnitP in the present approach, as in (459b).[58] In both approaches, the CL is hosted by a functional projection: CL^{max} in (459a) and UnitP in (459b). However,

---

58. In Huang et al. (2009: 312), numerals are base-generated at Spec of NumP, but on page 296 of the same book, numerals are generated at the head of NumP. See Bartos (2011: 317) for a critical comment on the inconsistency.

(459b) captures the formal dependency between a CL and a numeral (Section 6.2.2), but (459a) does not.[59]

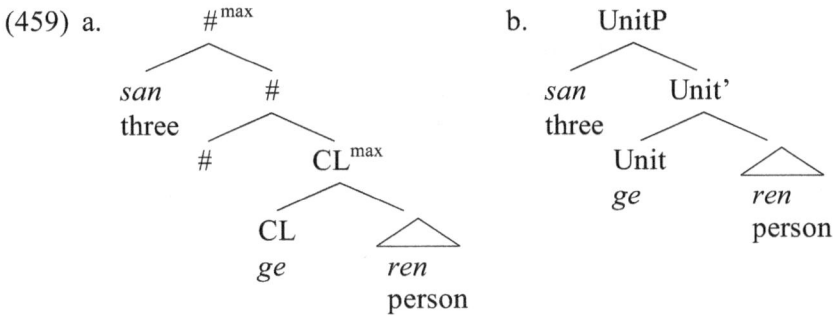

(459) a.

```
            #max
          /      \
      san          #
    three        /    \
              #         CLmax
                       /     \
                    CL        △
                    ge     ren
                          person
```

b.

```
              UnitP
            /       \
        san          Unit'
      three        /      \
               Unit         △
                ge      ren
                      person
```

Second, a plural marker and a CL are hosted in the same functional head, CL or Div, in Borer (2005), but in the present analysis, the projection of NumP is independent of the projection of UnitP. In my analysis, the CL of a numeral expression is hosted by Unit, but a plural marker is related to Num. This analysis, as well as Gebhardt (2009), is able to cover the possible co-occurrence of a CL and a number marker in the same construction, as in (454) and (457) (also see Allan 1977: 294; Aikhenvald 2003: 100–101, 249; Gerner & Bisang 2008; Ueda 2009: 123; Csirmaz & Dékány 2010: 13, among others). Moreover, in my analysis, the occurrence of a numeral leads to the projection of UnitP, even without a plural marker or a CL.

6.4. The morphosyntactic properties of pre-unit word adjectives

In Mandarin Chinese, not only non-mass nouns, such as *pangxie* 'crab' in (460a), but also unit words, such as the CL *zhi* in (460b), can be modified by delimitive adjectives (Sections 2.4.7 and 5.2.2).

---

59. My analysis is compatible with Munn and Schmitt's (2005: fn. 5) claim that "Num may not be the locus for overt numerals, which may be higher in the structure". Massam (2009: 675) also points out that "in Niuean, it is clear that number and numerals are not in the same projection, as argued by Pearce (2007) also for various Oceanic languages." Similarly, Espinal's (2010: 987 fn. 8) analysis of Catalan and Spanish indicates that, in addition to Num, a different function must be attributed to numerals. According to her, semantically, numerals introduce a cardinality function over singularities or pluralities.

(460) a. *san   zhi   da   pangxie*   b. *san   da   zhi   pangxie*
      three CL big   crab   three big CL   crab
      'three big crab'   'three big crab'

One might claim that the adjective in (460b) has moved from the position in (460a). However, it is not always possible to associate a pre-CL adjective to a post-CL adjective, since mass nouns reject delimitive adjectives, as shown in (461b) (Chapter 2). In (461a), the adjective *xiao* 'small' has to be base-generated above UnitP. Moreover, a pre-CL delimitive adjective may occur with a post-CL delimitive adjective, as shown in (461c, d).

(461) a. *san   xiao   di   shui*
        three small CL water
        'three small drops of water'
   b. **san   di   xiao   shui*
        three CL small water
   c. *san   da   ke   fang   xigua*
        three big CL square watermelon
        'three big square watermelons'
   d. *san   xiao   pian   yuan   shuye*
        three small CL   round leave
        'three small round leaves'

Therefore, a delimitive modifier may be directly adjoined to UnitP if it immediately precedes a unit word. According to McNally (to appear), modifiers do not change the semantic type of the associated element. In Section 2.4.7, we reported that various types of unit words may be preceded by a delimitive adjective, except kind CLs. The semantic type of a unit word is not affected by the adjective. Thus, *xiao* 'small' in (461a, d) and *da* 'big' (461c) are modifiers and occur at an adjunct position.

The two examples in (460) mean the same. This semantically transparent relation is compatible with the right-branching structure in which the position of a pre-CL adjective is in the position of an adjunct of UnitP, and thus c-commands a possible post-CL adjective (the representation of a left-branching structure is discussed in the next section).

We now examine the category-level of pre-unit-word modifiers. When a delimitive adjective modifies a noun, it can be followed by the functional particle *de*, as seen in (462). In addition to the simple form of the adjective in (462a), a pre-*de* adjective can also be in a reduplicative form, as in (462b), in a coordinate construction, as in (462c), or it can occur with a degree word *hen* 'very', as in (462d) (Wang 1995: 306, 314). The three complex forms must be followed by *de*.[60]

(462) a. *chang de xianglian*
        long   DE necklace
        'long necklace'
   b. *changchang *(de) xianglian*
        long   DE necklace
        'long necklace'
   c. *chang erqie cu   *(de) xianglian*
        long   and   thick DE necklace
        'long and thick necklace'
   d. *hen   chang *(de) xianglian*
        very long   DE necklace
        'very long necklace'

However, when an adjective modifies a unit word, no *de* is allowed to intervene between them, as seen in (463a) and (463b) (note that we are talking about the *de* to the left of a unit word, not to the right of a unit word; the latter issue is discussed in Section 5.5). As expected, none of the three complex forms may precede a unit word. (463c) shows this constraint.

(463) a. *san   chang (*de) tiao xianglian*
        three long   DE   CL   necklace
        'three long necklaces'
   b. *san   da (*de) xiang xianglian*
        three big   DE box   necklace
        'three big boxes of necklaces'
   c. **san changchang (de) tiao xianglian*
        three long   DE CL   necklace

The ban of *de* in data like (463a) has been noted since Tang (1990b: 419). In Cheng & Sybesma (1999: 529 fn.16), it is conjectured that "[T]his may be due to some obligatory cliticalization of CL to Numeral" (also see

---

60. Y.H. Audrey Li (2012: 32) claims that in *hui-meng-meng zhaopian* 'grey misty photo', no *de* occurs between the reduplicative adjective and *zhaopian* 'photo'. The example is marginal to me. Even if it is acceptable to others, it seems that this is the only example in which a noun is modified by a complex adjective without *de*. The idiomatic usage thus does not challenge the generalization stated in the text.

R. Yang 2001: 72). However, in the presence of *chang* 'long', the CL *tiao* in (463) is not next to a numeral. Moreover, it is well recognized that a clitic may be hosted by a cluster that is composed of another clitic and its host (e.g., both *'d* and *'ve* are clitics and the latter is hosted by *I'd* in *I'd've brought some for you, if I'd known*). Thus, if a CL is an enclitic and *de* is also an enclitic (Huang 1989), why can the CL not take the cluster *chang de* 'big DE' as its host in (463a)? It is clear that the constraint in (463) goes beyond the alleged clitic status of the CL.

It is well-recognized that pre-*de* modifiers are phrasal (e.g., Fan 1958, C. Huang 1989, Tang 1990b: 420). So the constraint under discussion is the following generalization:

(464) An adjective to the left of a unit word is not phrasal.

But such an adjective does not show properties of syntactic head elements. For instance, it does not license ellipsis:

(465) **Baoyu mai-le san da kuai doufu, Daiyu mai-le*
     Baoyu buy-PRF three big CL tofu Daiyu buy-PRF
     si xiao ~~kuai doufu~~.
     four small CL tofu

I have just clarified that a pre-unit word adjective is not raised from a lower position. Also, there is no selection relation between an adjective and a unit word, in either direction. Therefore, it is unlikely that an Adj-CL cluster is formed in syntax. I therefore do not adopt Tang's (1990: 418) claim that the cluster *chang-tiao* in (463a) is a complex head cluster. Instead, extending Matushansky's (2006) theory, I assume that the pre-unit-word adjective is syntactically an adjunct of UnitP, but it undergoes a morphological merger operation and is thus adjacent to the unit word at PF.

An adjective to the immediate left of an individual or individuating CL behaves like a phrasal prefix or proclitic morphologically. Phonologically, any such adjective in this position must be monosyllabic (Liu 1980: 10; Zhu 1982: 52). This constraint rules out reduplicative adjectives, as in (466a), and adjectives that are modified by another element, as in (466b).

(466) a. **san changchang tiao feizao*
        three long CL soap
        Intended: 'three long soaps'

    b. **san   quantou-da kuai bing*
       three fist-big   CL   ice
       Intended: 'three chunks of ice and each as big as a fist'

Moreover, some types of clitics do not bear stress, but some other types may (e.g., in African French; see Salvesen 2011). A pre-unit word adjective may bear contrastive stress, as in (467) (stressed elements are in capitals):

(467) *Ta zhua-le   san   DA tiao yu, bu shi san XIAO tiao yu.*
      3SG catch-PRF three big CL   fish not be three small CL   fish
      'He caught three BIG fish, not three SMALL ones.'

Two delimitive modifiers can occur with the same unit word (I have not seen any example in which there are more than two delimitive adjectives to the left of a unit word), if each of them is monosyllabic. In each example in (468), two delimitive adjectives occur in a row ((468c) and (468e) are cited from Y. Li 2000: 57). The modifiers are all adjuncts of UnitP.

(468) a. *si   xiao   yuan pian shuye*
         four   small round CL   leaf
         'four small round leaves'
    b. *si   xiao   fang   kuai bing*
         four   small square CL   ice
         'four small square chunks of ice'
    c. *si   xiao   bo   pian mianbao*
         four   small thin   CL   bread
         'four small thin slices of bread'
    d. *si   da   hou   pian luobo*
         four   big   thick CL   turnip
         'four big thick slices of turnip'
    e. *si   da   chang chuan tang-hulu*
         four   big   long   CL   sugar-fruit
         'four big long strings of sugared fruit'

If there are two adjectives to the left of a unit word, neither of them may occur with *de*, as seen in (469a), and thus neither of them may surface as a phrase, as stated in (412). They all undergo morphological merger with the unit word. The situation for an adjective to the right of a CL, as in (469b), is different. In this case, there is no special morphological constraint on the form of the delimitive adjectives, and no morphological merger is seen.

(469) a. *si   xiao (*de) yuan (*de) pian shuye*   [pre-CL Adj]
        four small   DE   round   DE   CL   leaf
        'four small round leaves'
    b. *si   pian xiao (de) yuan (de) shuye*   [pre-NP Adj]
        four   CL   small DE   round DE   leaf
        'four small round leaves'

6.5.   The right- and left-branching numeral constructions

Having established UnitP, in addition to NumP and QuantP, we are ready
to label the nodes of the two syntactic structures argued for in Chapter 5: a
right-branching structure and a left-branching structure.

6.5.1. The representations of the right-branching structure

Numeral expressions with an individual, individuating, or kind CL have a
right-branching structure (Section 5.2.5). The individual CL expression in
(470a) has the structure in (470b). The individuating CL expression in
(471a) has the structure in (471b). The kind CL expression in (472a) has
the structure in (472b). In the three examples, there is no structural difference among the three types of CLs: the CLs are all base-generated at Unit,
c-commanding the NP.

(470) a. *san   xiao   duo   hua*   [Individual CL]
        three small CL   flower
        'three small flowers'

    b.

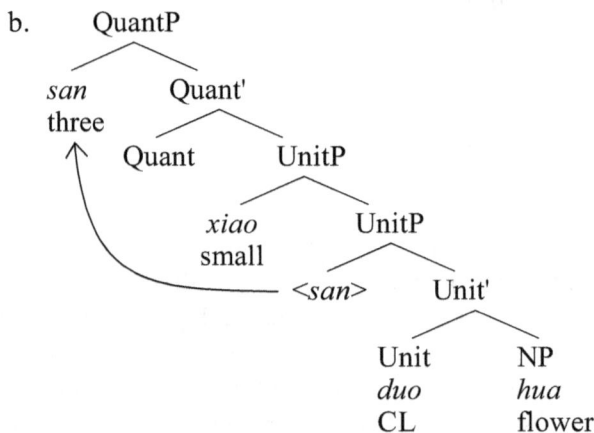

(471) a. *san   xiao   duo   yun*   [Individuating CL]
　　　three small CL   cloud
　　　'three small pieces of cloud'

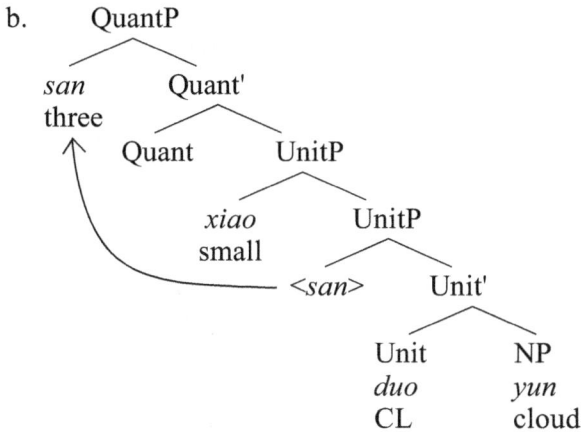

b.　　　QuantP
　　┌───┴───┐
san　　　Quant'
three　　┌──┴──┐
　　↑　Quant　　UnitP
　　│　　　┌───┴───┐
　　│　　*xiao*　　UnitP
　　│　　small　┌──┴──┐
　　└──────── *<san>*　　Unit'
　　　　　　　　　　┌──┴──┐
　　　　　　　　　Unit　　NP
　　　　　　　　　duo　*yun*
　　　　　　　　　CL　　cloud

(472) a. *san   lei xigua*   [Kind CL]
　　　three CL watermelon
　　　'three kinds of watermelons'

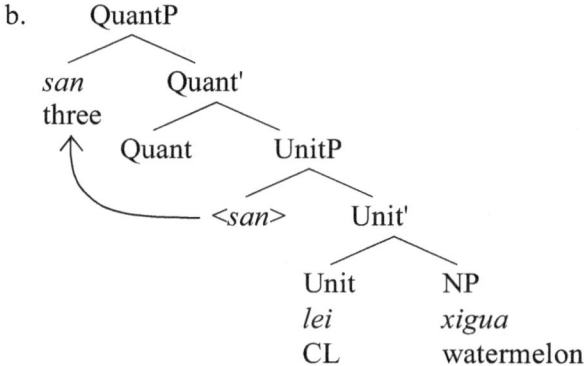

b.　　　QuantP
　　┌───┴───┐
san　　　Quant'
three　　┌──┴──┐
　　↑　Quant　　UnitP
　　│　　　┌───┴───┐
　　└──── *<san>*　　Unit'
　　　　　　　　　┌──┴──┐
　　　　　　　　Unit　　NP
　　　　　　　　lei　*xigua*
　　　　　　　　CL　　watermelon

6.5.2. The representation of the left-branching structure

A left-branching structure is for numeral expressions of container and standard measures, and collective and partitive CLs (see Section 5.2.5). In this structure, the unit word does not c-command the associated NP. Therefore, the unit word and the NP may have incompatible adjectives, and the former does not have a selection relation with the latter (Section 5.2).

However, the unit words of the left-branching structure, such as the standard measure *gongjin* 'kilo' and container measure *bei* 'cup' in *san bei cha* 'three cups of tea' also share formal properties with CLs of the right-branching structure. We have seen the ellipsis and stranding examples of individual CL constructions in (433) and (434) above. Similarly, the container measure *wan* 'bowl' in the second conjunct of (473a) may also license an empty NP to its right, and the meaning of the NP can be recovered from an NP in the first conjunct, i.e., *tang* 'soup'. Also, the container measure *wan* 'bowl' in (473b) is stranded, and the missing NP has a dependency with the topic *niurou-tang* 'beef soup'.

(473) a. *Baoyu   he-le   san   wan   tang, Daiyu ye   he-le*
　　　　 Baoyu   drink-PRF three   bowl   soup   Daiyu also   drink-PRF
　　　　 san   wan   ~~tang~~.
　　　　 three   bowl   soup
　　　　 'Baoyu ate three bowls of soup, and so did Daiyu.'
　　 b. *Niurou-tang, Baoyu yinggai he   wu   wan.*
　　　　 beef-soup   Baoyu should   drink five bowl
　　　　 'Beef soup, Baoyu should eat five bowls of it.'

I claim that all unit words in numeral expressions surface at the same syntactic position, i.e., the head of UnitP, but the unit words of the left-branching structure are base-generated at N, and then undergoes head movement and surfaces at Unit. Moreover, in the left-branching structure, the QuantP, which contains the UnitP headed by the unit words, and the NP, are integrated together by MonP (for Monotocity Phrase), in the sense of Schwarzschild (2006: 100; also see Cornilescu 2009). For instance, the structure for (474a) is (474b). In this structure, the locality between the numeral *san* 'three' and the unit word *sheng* 'liter' is achieved derivationally, after the latter has moved to Unit and before the former moves to Spec of QuantP, as illustrated by the encircled part.

(474) a. *san   sheng you*　　　　　　　　　 [Standard Measure]
　　　　 three   liter oil
　　　　 'three liters of oil'

b.

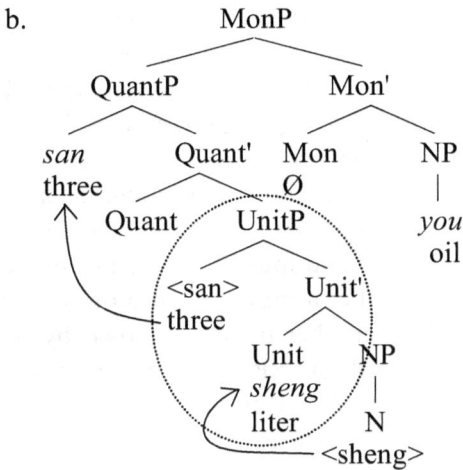

Similarly, the structure for (475a) is (475b).

(475) a. *liang da pian xiao   qiche*   [Collective CL]
        two   big CL   small car
        'two big groups of small cars'

b.

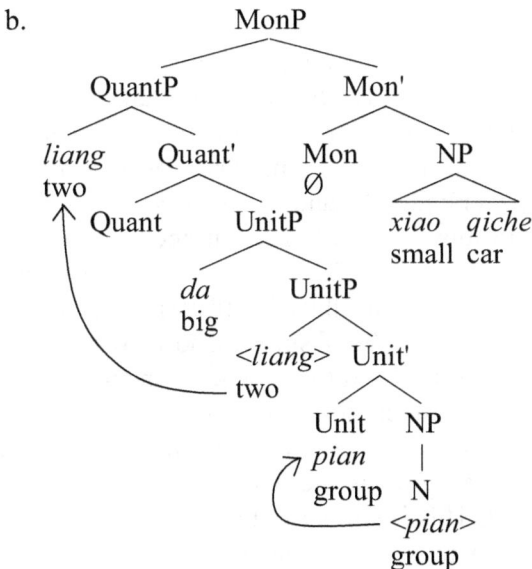

   In this analysis, collective CLs, partitive CLs, standard CLs, and container CLs are all base-generated at N, and surface at Unit; and the QuantP and the NP are Spec and Comp of Mon, respectively.

Three characteristics of the proposed derivation of the left-branching structure are as follows. First, there is a head movement from N to Unit in the derivation. A similar head movement from N to a functional head is proposed in Cheng & Sybesma (1998: 406; see (426b) above) for container measure constructions. Tang (2005: 452–453) presents three arguments against this kind of movement, trying to show that nouns such as *beizi* 'cup' and *benzi* 'notebook' are different from unit words such as the container measure *bei* 'cup' or *wan* 'bowl' and thus they may not move to the position of a unit word. (A) Unlike either a measure word or an individual CL, a noun may not be followed by another noun, as shown by the noun *wan* in (476a). (B) Unlike a unit word, an NP can occur at an argument position, as shown by *da de wan* 'big DE bowl' in (476b). (C) A noun "cannot appear alone with numerals like *yi* 'one'," as in (476c).

(476) a. *yi   ge wan (*shui)*
      one CL bowl water
      'one bowl'

    b. *Da de wan   hen   gui.*
      big DE bowl very expensive
      'Big bowls are expensive.'

    c. *yi *(ge) wan*
      one CL bowl
      'one bowl'

However, all of the three arguments simply show that nouns and unit words have different syntactic positions. Unit words in numeral expressions are defined by their syntactic local relation to a numeral. Their surface positions can be the result of syntactic operations. One can claim that if the word *wan* 'bowl' is base-generated at N, and if the CL *ge* is base-generated at Unit, *wan* has no way to move to Unit. The surface order of (476a) is thus derived. Thus, there is no position for another noun such as *shui* 'water'. In (476b), no numeral occurs and thus UnitP is not projected. Then there is no N-to-Unit movement. (476c) simply shows that the head of UnitP cannot be empty in Chinese. Therefore, the movement analysis is not challenged. An element has the function of counting unit only when it occurs in a specific syntactic position, i.e., syntactically local to a numeral. In none of the three examples in (476), is the word *wan* local to a numeral, and thus it is not a unit word. This is similar to the situation that Infl can be realized by an auxiliary or a raised verb, but the possibility of the verb movement does not blur the distinction between auxiliaries and verbs.

Following Roberts (2010), Branigan (2011: 40), Hartman (2011), and Stepanov (2012), I assume that head movement can be an operation in narrow syntax. The N-to-Unit movement in the left-branching structure of numeral expressions in Mandarin Chinese is an instance of nominal-internal head movement. Nominal-internal head movement has been independently attested in Modern Hebrew (Borer 1999, Ritter 1991), Irish (Duffield 1996), Welsh (Rouveret 1991), and Romance languages (Longobardi 1994), among other languages. Such head movement is parallel to the head movement in the verbal domain (Pollock 1989). In line with the literature cited above, this study of nominal-internal head movement shows the cross-categorial symmetry in displacement phenomena (Chomsky 1970).

In both left-branching and right-branching structures of numeral expressions in Mandarin Chinese, the unit word surfaces at a head position, therefore, the string to its right can be elided, regardless of the syntactic relation between the unit word and the string. We have seen such examples in (433) and (473).

Second, in the left-branching structure of numeral expressions in Mandarin Chinese, the unit word starts from the position of N, which is not a position for a functional element. Recall that the CL *ge* may alternate with an individual, individuating, or kind CL, but not with a unit word of any other type, in a numeral expression (Section 5.2.5). The contrast matches the contrast between the unit words that occur in the right-branching structure and the unit words that occur in the left-branching structure. This restriction on the function of *ge* indicates that this CL is base-generated at the head of UnitP, rather than N, in a numeral expression.

Like other nouns, container measures exhibit substantive properties. Such unit words may have complex forms, containing a non-delimitive modifier, such as *ma* 'horse' in (477a), and *suliao* (or *sujiao* in Taiwan Mandarin) 'plastic' in (477b). It is plausible that the complexes are base-generated at N and move to a functional position. In contrast, individual and individuating CLs may not have such complex forms, as seen in (477c). They are more like intrinsic functional elements, base-generated at a functional head.

(477) a. *liu ma-che   liangshi*   b. *liu suliao-tong   qiyou*
       six horse-cart food   six plastic-bucket gasoline
       'six horse-carriages of food'   'six plastic buckets of gasoline'
   c. **liu suliao-duo hua*
       six plastic-CL flower

Note that *de* may not intervene between a modifier and a unit word. The constraint that a modifier to the left of a unit word may not surface as a phrase (Section 6.4) is consistent, regardless of the type of the unit word, and regardless of how this constraint is analyzed.

(478) a. **liu   ma   de   che   liangshi*
　　　　 six   horse DE   cart   food
　　 b. **liu   suliao   de   tong   qiyou*
　　　　 six   plastic DE   bucket gasoline

Third, the MonP structure for the left-branching numeral expressions is compatible with the properties of MonP stated in Schwarzschild (2006) and Cornilescu (2009). For instance, the Spec of MonP is always a quantifier phrase such as *a bit* (Schwarzschild 2006: 100) or a measure phrase such as *two meters* (see Cornilescu 2009). The Spec-Complement relation of a QuantP and a NP represents the semantics that the interpretation "in which the dimension is monotonic on the relevant part-whole relation in the domain given by the noun" (Schwarzschild 2006: 73). Moreover, the unit word of the measure phrase exhibits properties of nouns, crosslinguistically (See Watanabe 2012 for further noun properties of measure words). Furthermore, the associated noun can be either a mass or non-mass noun (Schwarzschild 2006: 69; Cornilescu 2009: 45).

MonP can be below DP. If a demonstrative occurs with a numeral expression that has a MonP structure, it is hosted at the DP level. In Mandarin Chinese, a numeral expression with any kind of unit word may be either individual-denoting or quantitiy denoting, even in the absence of an overt D-element (see (395)–(397)). Moreover, numeral expressions with measure words may also have specific and definite readings (see (403)). These readings are licensed by DP.

In my analysis, the contrast between the unit words that are base-generated at a functional head and those that start out in N has nothing to do with the contrast between count and mass status of nominals. My analysis is different from Cheng & Sybesma (1998, 1999), where it is claimed that the alleged count unit words are base-generated at the functional head Cl, whereas the alleged mass unit words start out in N and then undergo N-to-Cl movement in my analysis (see (426b)).

6.5.3. MonP and *de*

In this subsection, I address the occurrence of the particle *de* to the right of a unit word, with respect to the contrast between the left- and right-branching structures. The fact further supports my syntactic analysis of numeral constructions.

In Section 5.5, I have analyzed the availability of the particle *de* to the right of a unit word: it is available for the left-branching structure in general, and for the right-branching structure, it is available in the quantity reading, but not in the non-quantity reading. In that section, I have also argued that if *de* occurs in a right-branching construction, it is in fact out of the numeral expression, since the surface order is the result of deletion from a comparative modification construction.

From the structure in (475) we can see that the constituent boundary between the Spec of Mon and the complement of Mon makes the occurrence of *de* always possible. *De* can simply surface at the position of Mon. This captures the fact that there is no forced quantity-reading if *de* occurs in the left-branching structure.

In contrast, there is no syntactic position parallel to Mon in the right-branching structure of a numeral expression. No MonP is projected for such an expression. Therefore, the possible *de* construction must be constructed differently. In Section 5.5.3, I proposed that such a construction is derived by comparative deletion, from a quantity-denoting construction. Therefore, such a *de* construction always has a quantity reading.

Certain quantifiers are always followed by *de*. Such quantifiers may not be followed by a CL. In Section 3.1, I mentioned a few such quantifiers, e.g., *daliang* 'a lot', *suoyou* 'all', *quanbu* 'all', *daduoshu* 'most', *dabufen* 'most'. In (479a), *dabufen* 'most' may not be followed by the CL *wei*, and in (479b), *daduoshu* 'most' is subject to the same constraint.[61]

(479) a. *dabufen (*wei) laoshi*   b. *daduoshu (*wei) laoshi*
        most   CL   teacher   most   CL   teacher
        'most teachers'   'most teachers'

---

61. *Dabufen* 'most' may occur with any noun, while *daduoshu* 'most' may not occur with material mass nouns. In (ib), the material noun *moshui* 'ink' may not follow *daduoshu*.

(i) a. *{dabufen/daduoshu} shu diao-dao di-shang le.*
     most/most   book fall-to ground-on PRT
     'Most of the books fell on the ground.'

   b. *{dabufen/*daduoshu} mo-shui liu-dao di-shang le.*
      most/most   ink-water flow-to ground-on PRT
      'Most of the ink flew to the ground.'

   c. *{dabufen/daduoshu} qingkuang dou hen hao.*
      most/most   situation   all   very good
      'Most of the situations are very good.'

It is possible that each of such quantifiers is a QuantP or quantificational AP, and it is linked to the NP by Mon, which is realized by *de*. Therefore, there is no syntactic position for a unit word. The absence of the CL *wei* in (479) is accounted for. The structure of (479a) is (480):

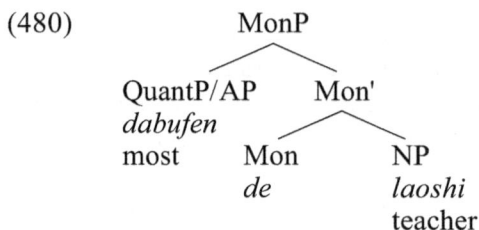

(480)

```
                    MonP
                   /    \
        QuantP/AP        Mon'
        dabufen         /    \
        most        Mon       NP
                    de        laoshi
                              teacher
```

Note that we do not assume that the particle *de*, as well as other functional formatives, has a unique syntactic position (contra X. Li & Rothstein 2012). Although the formative *de* may be a realization of the functional head Mon, it may also surface in other syntactic positions (see Y. H. Audrey Li 2012). The *de* at Mon and the *de* in another position exhibit different structural properties. For instance, the *de* at Mon may not be stranded, either by NP ellipsis or NP topicalization, whereas the *de* that introduces a modifier may be. The ellipsis contrast is shown in (481). In the quantifier constructions (481a) and (481b), *de* does not license the NP ellipsis, but in the non-quantifier construction (481c), *de* licenses the ellipsis of *zhima* 'sesame'. The parallel topicalization contrast is shown in (482). It has been realized that not all head elements license ellipsis or stranding. The English infinitive T element *to* may do so in control constructions, but not in ECM and raising constructions. See footnote 48.

(481) a. **Baoyu   renshi   suoyou   de laoshi,   Daiyu   renshi*
        Baoyu   know   all   DE teacher   Daiyu   know
        dabufen de ~~laoshi~~.
        most   DE teacher
    b. **Baoyu   mai-le   san   jin   de zhima,   Daiyu   mai-le*
        Baoyu   buy-PRF three   catty DE sesame   Daiyu   buy-PRF
        si   jin   de ~~zhima~~.
        four   catty DE sesame
    c. *Baoyu   mai-le   hese   de zhima,   Daiyu   mai-le   baise*
        Baoyu buy-PRF black   DE sesame   Daiyu   buy-PRF white
        de ~~zhima~~.
        DE sesame
        'Baoyu bought black sesame seeds and Daiyu bought white ones.'

(482) a. **Laoshi, Daiyu renshi dabufen de.*
　　　 teacher　Daiyu　know　most　DE
　　 b. **Zhima, Daiyu mai-le si jin de.*
　　　 sesame　Daiyu　buy-PRF　four catty DE
　　 c. *Zhima, Daiyu mai-le baise de.*
　　　 sesame　Daiyu　buy-PRF　white　DE
　　　 'As for sesame seeds, Daiyu bought white ones.'

MonP is different from other categories in that not only the complement may not be empty, but also the Spec may not move. If *de* occurs, it is expected that an element to its left may not be moved away, since *de* is an enclitic. But we have observed that a quantifier may not move even in the absence of *de*. We have seen the acceptability contrast between the a-forms and the b-forms of (483) and (484) (Section 5.3.2).

(483) a. *Yani mai-le san jin niurou.*
　　　 Yani buy-PRF three catty beef
　　　 'Yani bought three catties of beef.'
　　 b. **San jin, Yani mai-le _ niurou.*
　　　 three catty Yani buy-PRF　beef

(484) a. *Yani mai-le hen duo shu.*
　　　 Yani buy-PRF very many book
　　　 'Yani bought many books.'
　　 b. **Hen duo, Yani mai-le _ shu.*
　　　 very many Yani buy-PRF　book

Like the *de* following quantificational modifiers, the *de* following outer modifiers, which precede a numeral, does not license NP ellipsis and the NP may not move, either. In (485a), both the modifier *guanyu Xizang* 'on Tibet' and the modifier *guanyu Taiwan* 'on Taiwan' follow the CL *ben*, and they are thus inner modifiers. In this example, the *de* following *guanyu Taiwan* licenses the ellipsis of *shu* 'book, in the second conjunct. In (485b), the two modifiers, *guanyu Xizang* and *guanyu Taiwan,* both precede the numeral *liu* 'six', and they are thus outer modifiers. In this example, the string after *de* in the second conjunct may not be elided.

(485) a. *Yani mai-le liu ben guanyu Xizang de shu,*
　　　 Yani buy-PRF six CL on Tibet DE book
　　　 Lulu mai-le liu ben guanyu Taiwan de.
　　　 Lulu buy-PRF six CL on Taiwan DE
　　　 'Yani bought six books on Tibet, and Lulu bought six books on Taiwan.'

    b. **Yani mai-le   guanyu Xizang de liu ben shu,*
       Yani buy-PRF on   Tibet DE six CL   book
       Lulu mai-le   guanyu Taiwan de.
       Lulu buy-PRF on   Taiwan   DE

In (486a), the modifier *guanyu Xizang* 'on Tibet' follows the CL *ben*, and it is thus an inner modifier. In (486b), the *de* following *guanyu Xizang* licenses the movement of the NP *shu* 'book. In (487a), the modifier *guanyu Xizang* precedes the numeral *liu*, and it is thus an outer modifier. One can see that in (487b), the string *liu ben shu* 'six CL book' may not move away from *de*.

(486) a. *Yani mai-le   liu ben guanyu Xizang de shu.*
       Yani buy-PRF six CL   on   Tibet   DE book
       'Yani bought six books on Tibet.'
    b. *Shu, Yani mai-le   liu ben   guanyu Xizang   de.*
       book Yani buy-PRF six CL   on   Tibet   DE
       'As for books, Yani bought six on Tibet.'

(487) a. *Yani mai-le   guanyu Xizang de liu ben shu.*
       Yani buy-PRF on   Tibet   DE six CL   book
       'Yani bought six books on Tibet.'
    b. **Liu ben shu, Yani mai-le   guanyu Xizang de.*
       six   CL   book Yani buy-PRF on   Tibet   DE

The above examples show that when *de* follows an outer modifier, it shows similar properties as the one follows a quantificational modifier, as in (483) and (484). Zhang (2006) claims that outer modifers are exclusively specific. Presumably, outer modifiers and quantificational modifiers are followed by the same *de*, which is different from the *de* that follows a regular modifier. The contrastive properties of *de* for modifiers in different positions remain to be visible in the presence of the demostrative *na* 'that', as seen in (488) through (491).

(488) a. *Yani mai-le   na   liu ben guanyu Xizang de shu.*
       Yani buy-PRF DEM six CL   on   Tibet   DE book
       'Yani bought those six books on Tibet.'
    b. *Shu, Yani mai-le   na   liu ben guanyu Xizang de.*
       book Yani buy-PRF DEM six CL   on   Tibet   DE
       'As for books, Yani bought those six on Tibet.'

(489) a. *Yani mai-le guanyu Xizang de na liu ben shu.*
     Yani buy-PRF on   Tibet DE DEM six CL book
     'Yani bought those six books on Tibet.'

    b. **Na liu ben shu, Yani mai-le guanyu Xizang de.*
     DEM six CL book Yani buy-PRF on   Tibet DE

(490) a. *Yani mai-le na liu ben erzi xihuan de shu.*
     Yani buy-PRF DEM six CL son like DE book
     'Yani bought those six books that her son likes.'

    b. *Shu, Yani mai-le na liu ben erzi xihuan de.*
     book Yani buy-PRF DEM six CL son like DE
     'As for books, Yani bought those six that her son likes.'

(491) a. *Yani mai-le erzi xihuan de na liu ben shu.*
     Yani buy-PRF son like DE DEM six CL book
     'Yani bought those six books that her son likes.'

    b. **Na liu ben shu, Yani mai-le erzi xihuan de.*
     DEM six CL book Yani buy-PRF son like DE

In my analysis, two types of quantifiers have different syntactic positions. Quantifiers that may not be followed by *de* occur at Spec of QuantP, and those that are followed by *de* occur at Spec of MonP. The head of MonP can be realized by *de*. Neither the Spec nor the complement of Mon may be empty in Mandarin Chinese.

6.6. The structure of attributive numeral expressions

So far, we have discussed the syntactic structures of numeral expressions for quantification (counting or measuring). We now move to attributive numeral expressions, which express an intrinsic, classifying, or individual-level property of the entity denoted by the noun, as shown by the underlined part in (492).

(492) a. *Ta mai-le liang tao [wu ben de shu].*
     3SG buy-PRF two CL five CL DE book
     'He bought two sets of five-volume books.'

    b. *Ta mai-le san kuai [liang ceng de boli].*
     3SG buy-PRF three CL two layer DE glass
     'He bought three pieces of two-layer glass.'

    c. *Ta   mai-le   liang mi   [yi gongfen de shengzi].*
       3SG   buy-PRF two   meter one cm   DE rope
       'He bought two meters of the rope that is 1 cm thick.'
    d. *san   ge shi bang de xigua*
       three CL ten pound DE watermelon
       'three ten pound watermelons'
    e. *Ni   yao   liang he   20 bao de chaye, haishi liang*
       2SG   want   two box 20 bag DE tea   or   two
       he   30 bao de?
       box 30 bag DE
       'Do you want two boxes of tea that contain 20 bags each, or two
       boxes that contain 30 bags each?'

In such constructions, the lower unit word can be an individual CL, such as *ben* in (492a), an individuating CL, such as *ceng* in (492b), a standard measure, such as *gongfen* 'centimeter' in (492c) and *bang* 'pound' in (492d), or a container measure, such as *bao* 'bag' in (492e); and the higher unit word can be either a CL, such as the collective CL *tao* in (492a), the individuating CL *kuai* in (492b), and individual CL *ge* in (492d), or a measure word, such as *mi* 'meter' in (492c), and *he* 'box' in (492e) (contra Her & Hsieh 2010: 536).

The attributive numeral constructions are discussed in many works (e.g., Tang 2005: 434; Schwartzchild 2006; Hsieh 2008; Corver 2009: 125; Cornilescu 2009; Her & Hsieh 2010; Liao & Wang 2011: Sec. 5; X. Li 2011a). Semantically, such attributive constructions are used for classifying, rather than counting. The former and the latter belong to Rijkhoff's (2002) quality and quantity modifiers, respectively. Crucially, unlike pseudo-partitive (i.e., counting) constructions, attributive numeral expressions do not encode a monotonic ordering relation. For instance, for (492a), regardless how many *tao*s 'sets' of the books are bought, each set is always composed of five volumes. The external counting with the unit *tao* does not track any part-whole relation inside the nominal *wu ben de shu* 'five-volume book'.

Semantically, attributive numeral constructions answer the questions regarding the quantity characteristics of the entities (e.g., *shenmeyang-de*? 'what characteristics?' or *na-zhong-de* 'which type?'), rather than the questions regarding the counting (e.g., *duoshao* 'how many?'). Syntactically, attributive numeral constructions are different from the pseudo-partitive constructions discussed in previous chapters, as follows. First, the functional particle *de* must occur to the right of the attributive, i.e., the right of the second unit word in (492) (contra Her & Hsieh 2010: 536). This makes the construction pattern with other constructions that contain a complex attributive (see (462b–d)), rather than numeral expressions for counting.

Second, attributive numeral expressions behave like bare nouns in the language, in the following senses. They can be preceded by another unit word and numeral, as seen in the examples in (492). They also allow two or more numeral-unit word strings introduced by *de*, as seen in (493).

(493) *Wo   yao   liang ge <u>san   cheng de   liu   cun   de   dangao</u>.*
     1SG want two CL three CL   DE six inch DE cake
     'I want two three-layer and six-inch cakes.'

In contrast, non-attributive numeral expressions do not have two strings of the combination of a numeral and a unit word in a row, since counting never has different counting units at the same time (see Section 6.2.2).

Third, the obligatory particle *de* can be stranded, either by ellipsis of the noun or the topicalization of the noun. One ellipsis example is seen in the second conjunct of (492e). A topicalization example is seen in (494).

(494) *Chaye,   wo   mai-le   liang he   <u>30 bao de</u>.*
     tea   1SG buy-PRF two   box 30 bag DE
     'As for tea, I bought two boxes that contain 30 bags each.'

In contrast, if *de* follows the unit word in a non-attributive numeral expression, it may not be stranded. We have seen this constraint in (481b) and (482b). The contrast indicates that the *de* in attributive constructions is similar to the one occurring in regular modification constructions, different from the one in non-attributive numeral expressions.

The counterpart of *de* here in other languages is analyzed as a nominal copula in Corver (2009). In both English and Dutch, measure words may not be plural when they occur in attributive constructions (e.g., *a ten pound(*s) watermelon*). In Swiss German and Russian, a unit word is followed by an adjective suffix in attributive constructions (Schwarzschild 2006: 84). In Romanian, a numeral and a unit word precede the associate noun in pseudo-partitive constructions, but they follow the noun in the attributive constructions (Cornilescu 2009: 44). Following Schwartzchild (2006) and Cornilescu (2009), I treat attributive numeral expressions as ordinary modifiers of nominals.

Semantically, a modifier is "an expression that combines with an unsaturated expression to form another unsaturated expression of the same type" (McNally. To appear: (4)). Syntactically, it is generally assumed that modifiers are not complements. In the underlined part *wu ben de shu* 'five CL book' in (492a), for example, both *shu* and the whole string are unsaturated expressions, like other bare nouns in the language. In the structure of (492a), the underlined part has the same syntactic status as a bare noun, i.e., an NP, which is selected by the collective CL *tao*. In the NP, the numeral *wu* 'five' and the unit word *ben* form a QuantP, and the QuantP is a modifier of the NP *shu* 'book'.

6.7. Various realizations of the head of UnitP

According to Chomsky's (2001: 2) Uniformity Principle, "[I]n the absence of compelling evidence to the contrary, assume languages to be uniform, with variety restricted to easily detectable properties of utterances". In line with this principle, I assume that universally, UnitP is projected for numeral expressions, and a unit word surfaces at the head of UnitP. I also assume that the numeral of such an expression is hosted at Spec of UnitP. I have argued that a numeral expression in Mandarin Chinese has either a left-branching or right-branching structure, depending on the type of the unit words. It is possible that numeral expressions in other languages have different structures. According to Borer (1984), functional categories are the locus of parametric variations. We thus expect Unit, as a functional head, to be the locus of some parametric variations. In this subsection, I discuss some different properties of Unit and their realizations in certain types of languages, and in different types of numeral constructions in the same language.

6.7.1. Major typological patterns of the null Unit

Following Croft (1994: 151–152), I assume that standard measures (e.g., *kilo*), container measures (e.g., *bottle* in *three bottles of milk*), kind CL (*kind* in *three kinds of chocolate*), partitive CLs (e.g., *section* in *three sections of orange*), and collective CLs (e.g., *group* in *three groups of students*) are available in both CL and non-CL languages. The following Dëne examples in (495) (Wilhelm 2008: 47), and the Karitiana examples in (496) (Müller et al. 2006: 133) show the availability of measure words in the non-CL languages, in addition to English.

(495) a. *solághe* <u>*nedádhi*</u> *bër*   b. *náke* <u>*tutılı*</u> *tł'ólátúé*
         five   pound   meat   two   bottle beer
         'five pounds of meat'   'two bottles of beer'

(496) a. *Myhin-t* <u>*kilo*</u>-*t*   *ouro na-aka-t*   *i-'ot-<o>t*
    one   kilo-OBL gold DECL-AUX-NFUT   part-fall-RED-NFUT
    'One kilogram of gold fell.'

    b. *jonso   naka-ot-Ø*   *sympom-t* <u>*byt*</u>-*ypip ese.*
       woman   DECL-bring-NFUT two-OBL   bowl-in water
       'The woman brought two bowls of water.'

In another non-CL language, Yudja (Lima 2010: 10–11), the partitive CL *txa* is available, to distinguish the part of an entity (e.g., pieces of meat from an animal) from the whole body of the entity (e.g., the whole animal).

In my analysis, these measure words and CLs all surface at the head of UnitP. We now address the cross-linguistic variations in the properties of the head of UnitP in other types of numeral expressions, specifically, the counterparts of Chinese individual and individuating CL constructions.

In Chinese, the head of UnitP is always realized by an overt element, in regular productive phrasal nominals: individual CLs select nominals with [+Delimitable] and individuating CLs select nominals with [−Delimitable].

In a different pattern, a silent Unit correlates with both individuating and individual CLs in Mandarin Chinese. The silent Unit in Yudja (Lima 2010, 2012), Ojibwe (Mathieu 2012a), and Halkomelem Salish (Wilhelm 2008: 64) selects a nominal with either [+Delimitable] or [−Delimitable]. In other words, any noun may be next to a numeral directly, including a mass noun, as shown in (497) (Lima 2010: 7; 2012), (498), and (499) (Mathieu 2012a: 186) (IN = inanimate; parallel examples in Halkomelem and Blackfoot can be found in Wiltschko 2012: (33), (34)). In (497) and (498), where the nouns are mass nouns, the silent Unit is a covert counterpart of an individuating CL in Chinese; in (499), where the noun is a non-mass noun, the silent Unit is a covert counterpart of an individual CL in Chinese.

(497) *txabïa apeta*   (= (57))   [Yudja]
     three   blood
     'three units of blood' (the exact unit is decided by the context: drops, puddles, or containers)

(498) a. *bezhig azhashki*   b. *niizh azhashki-n*   [Ojibwe]
     one   mud   two   mud-PL.IN
     'one chunk of mud'   'two chunks of mud'

(499) a. *bezhig baagan*   b. *niizh baagan-an*
     one   nut   two   nut-PL.IN
     'one nut'   'two nuts'

In a third possible pattern, the silent Unit correlates with Chinese individual CLs only, but not with individuating CLs. The silent Unit in Dëne (Wilhelm 2008), Karitiana (Müller et al. 2006), and Haitian Creole (Deprez 2005: 861), selects only nominals with [+Delimitable], i.e., non-mass nouns. In (500a) (Wilhelm 2008: 46), the non-mass noun *dzól* 'ball' combines with the numeral *solághe* 'five' directly, whereas in (500b) (Wilhelm 2008: 47), the mass noun *bër* 'meat' may not do so. The same contrast is reported in Karitiana (Müller et al. 2006).

(500) a. *solághe dzól*   b. **solághe bër*   [Dëne]
          five   ball   five   meat
          'five balls'

Some Formosan languages in Taiwan seem to behave like Dëne and Karitiana in this respect (Tang 2004). They have no individual or individuating CLs, and numerals can combine with non-mass nouns directly, but not with mass nouns. Wilhelm (2008: 48) also reports that in Dëne, not only concrete nouns such as the one in (500b), but also abstract nouns that encode unbound concepts may not combine with a numeral directly.

A fourth possible pattern is seen in Jingpo (Cheung 2003: 28), where CLs are required for mass nouns, but optional for non-mass nouns, as seen in (501). A similar CL optionality for non-mass nouns is also seen in Vietnamese (Bisang 1999: 145).

(501) a. *udi (hkum) sanit*   b. *n-gu *(tum) sanit*   [Jingpo]
          egg   CL   seven   rice   CL   seven
          'seven eggs'   'seven grains of rice'

Languages like English may represent the fifth possible pattern. In this language, generally speaking, the silent Unit selects nominals with [+Numerable], whereas an overt Unit selects nominals with [−Numerable]. In (502a) and (502b), where the two nouns *belief* and *book* are [+Numerable], the Unit is silent. In contrast, in (502c) and (502d), where *paper* and *furniture* are [−Numerable], the Unit is realized by *piece*. Both *belief* and *paper* are [−Delimitable], whereas both *book* and *furniture* are [+Delimitable].

(502) a. *three (*pieces of) beliefs*   b. *three (*pieces of) books*
      c. *three *(pieces of) paper*   d. *three *(pieces of) furniture*

Since Unit is always [+Numerable], we can see that in English, Unit as a bearer of the feature also takes nominals that have this feature as its complement. Therefore, there is a [+Numerable]-agreement relation between the silent Unit and its selected noun, in English.

The sixth possible pattern is found in Purépecha. In the numeral constructions of this language, [–Delimitable] nouns must occur with a measure word, rather than any CL (Vázquez Rojas 2012: 57). This contrast is shown in (503) (Vázquez Rojas 2012: 90). On the other hand, all [+Delimitable] nouns may combine with a numeral directly; but they are divided into the wasp or fly-group and the log or corncob-group. The former rarely occurs with a CL, as seen in (504), where as the latter may optionally take a CL, as seen in (505) (Vázquez Rojas 2012: 88–90).

(503) a. *Jimíni   jarhá-h-ti   má   tsuntsu   kamáta.*
there   be-PFVE-3IND   one   cup   corn.beverage
'There is a cup of corn beverage there'

b. **Jimíni   jarhá-h-ti   má   erhákwa   kamáta*
there   be-PFVE-3IND   one   CL.round   corn.beverage

(504) a. *Jáma-sha-ti=ksï   tanímu   tsïtsïsï-cha.*
be.around-PROGR-3IND=3PL   three   wasp-PL
'There are three wasps flying around'

b. **Jáma-sha-ti=ksï   tanímu   {ichákwa/erhákwa}*
be.around-PROGR-3IND=3PL   three   CL.long/CL.round
tsïtsïsï-cha.
wasp-PL

(505) *Paku-a-s-ka-ni=ya   tanimu   ichákwa   chkari   naná*
take-DIST-PFVE-1/2IND-1SG=ADV   three   CL.long   wood   HON
Camerí-ni.
Camerina-OBJ
'I already took three logs to Camerina'

In Niuean, mass nouns neither combine with a numeral directly nor occur with any CL, whereas non-mass nouns are linked to numerals by the CL *e* (Massam 2009). The pattern seems to be similar to but simpler than that of Purépecha.

The above six patterns are summarized in (506). The symbol ∅ means a null head, and * means that in syntax, the type of Unit does not merge with the type of nouns.

(506) Patterns of the head of UnitP

	standard/container M, kind/collective/ partitive UWs	other UWs that select [–Delimitable] N	other UWs that select [+Delimitable] N
Chinese	overt	individuating CL	individual CL
Yudja	overt	∅	∅
Dëne	overt	*	∅
Jingpo	overt	overt	optional
English	overt	∅ for [+Numerable] N	∅ for [+Numerable] N
		overt for [–Numerable] N	overt for [–Numerable] N
Purépecha	overt	*	∅ for the fly-type
			optional for the corncob-type

The above classification of the patterns of Unit is made on the consideration of the combination possibility of certain type of Unit and certain type of nouns, the overtness of Unit when the combination is possible in syntax, the value of Delimitability selected by Unit, and the value of Numerability selected by Unit.

The idea that languages may have silent elements to encode counting units is not new. For example, Sharvy (1978) states that English might have empty CLs correlating to Chinese individual CLs. Thus *three books* contains a silent individual CL, the sentence *Open three beers* contains a silent container measure, and the sentence *We tasted three Canadian beers* contains a silent kind CL. In Bowers (1991: 19), the functional head Nm, which is realized by a CL in Mandarin Chinese, is labeled by an empty category *e* for the structure of the English nominal *these three good books* (in his structure, the numeral is an adjunct of NmP). Csirmaz & Dékány (2010: 11) also argue for the existence of zero CLs in Hungarian. Moreover, Delsing (1993), Van Riemsdijk (2005), and Vangsnes (2008) claim that kind readings of numeral expressions in Germanic languages have a silent CL, and thus when *three wines* means 'three kinds of wine', a silent kind CL occurs. The analysis of this book has developed the idea of silent

Unit, and further identified the possible conditions for a silent Unit to occur.

From (506) and above discussion, we see that language variations are observed in the counterparts of Chinese individuating, individual, and kind CLs. We have argued that these CLs are functional elements, base-generated at the functional head Unit. In this approach, the division between CL and non-CL languages, and the division between different types of non-CL languages are understood in terms of properties of functional elements. The formal features of functional elements and their overtness at PF are subject to language variation, as expected (Borer 1984, Chomsly 1995, Kayne 2012b). This contrasts with the approaches in which the divisions are understood in terms of either nouns (e.g., to assume that all nouns in CL languages are mass nouns, see Section 2.6), or numerals (see next subsection).

Grammatical formatives such as tense markers, definiteness markers (e.g., articles), and counterfactual markers (e.g., subjunctive mood markers) are found to be overt in many languages, but not in Chinese. In contrast to this pattern, individual CLs as unit words in numeral expressions are obligatorily overt in Chinese, but not overt in some other languages. Moreover, the effects of Universal Sorter and Universal Packager, which contain covert kind CLs and covert container measures, respectively, are also absent in Chinese (Section 2.2.5). All of these observations indicate that Chinese does not show context-dependent flexibility in certain constructions. With more and more studies of syntactic issues, we cast a reasonable doubt on the belief that Chinese syntax is more discourse-dependent than other languages, and the claim that Chinese is a discourse-oriented language (e.g., Tsao 1977).

6.7.2. A comparison with numeral-oriented approaches

The proposed unit-word-oriented analysis of language variation in the syntax of numeral expressions is different from both the noun-semantics-oriented analysis (Section 2.5.2) and the number-morphology-oriented analysis (Section 2.5.3). My analysis is also different from the numeral-oriented analysis proposed in Wilhelm (2008) (adopted in Hsieh 2008: 36–37).

Following Krifka (1995: 400), Wilhelm (2008: 54) first introduces an operator or function that specifies the objects to be counted as atoms. This atom-accessing function is called OU (short form for Object Unit). She then makes the following statement (p. 56):

in general, counting involves an atom-accessing function OU. Languages differ in whether OU is part of the meaning of numerals or expressed separately by numeral CLs. In other words, I propose that there is crosslinguistic variation in the semantics of numerals, and that this variation is responsible for the difference between Chinese and Dëne/English.

According to this numeral-oriented approach, in languages such as Dëne and English, the unit meaning of CLs is integrated into numerals, countability correlates with atomicity of the element denoted by a noun, therefore only count nouns may semantically be compatible with a numeral. In Chinese, however, unit meanings are expressed by CLs, rather than numerals. But it is unlikely that unit meanings are part of the meanings of numerals for non-CL languages. First, the five types of unit words listed at the beginning of Section 6.7.1 also exist in non-CL languages. If a numeral always contains unit information in such languages, an additional operation is necessary to get rid of the information when the numeral occurs with any unit word of the five types. This is because a numeral is in construal with one unit only. For instance, when the meaning of 'five groups of students' or 'five boxes of books' is expressed, the numeral for 'five' in a non-CL language must exhibit the same properties of the corresponding numeral in a CL language. It is not clear how this is achieved in this numeral-oriented approach.

Second, in non-CL languages such as Yudja (Lima 2010, 2012) and Halkomelem Salish (Wilhelm 2008: 64), a numeral may occur with a mass noun, as in (497). Thus, if the unit meaning is integrated into the numerals in such languages, the theory cannot explain why the combination of a numeral with a mass noun is impossible in Dëne, but possible in Yudja and Halkomelem Salish. In my unit-word-oriented approach, both types of languages may have silent Unit and they differ in the selection of the Delimitability feature by the silent Unit. The variation correlates exactly with that between individual and individuating CLs in CL languages. In Wilhelm (2008), the pattern of Halkomelem Salish is mentioned, without an analysis (her p. 64).

Third, if English numerals contain the meaning of unit, why is the CL *time* still necessary for a numeral expression in a verbal domain (see Section 2.6.1)?

Fourth, the two arguments used to support the idea that unit meanings are integrated into numerals in non-CL languages are weak. Both arguments are intended to show that numerals in non-CL languages are different from those in CL-languages. The first argument is that some numerals in Dëne are specifically for human beings, which might mean that "Dëne basic numerals contain a general classifier that accesses the atoms or object sic numerals contain a general classifier that accesses the atoms or object units in the denotation" (Wilhelm 2008: 58). However, in the CL language Niuean, when the numerals qualify over a human noun, they are prefixed with the person marker *toko-*, as seen in (507) (*e* is a CL, marked as DIV) (Massam 2009: 679). So the form of the numeral is also specifically for human. Thus this CL language is similar to the non-CL language Dëne in this respect.

(507) *toko-lima   e   tagata   loloa*   [Niuean]
       PERS-five   DIV   person   tall
       'five tall people'

The second argument to support the idea that unit meanings are integrated into numerals in non-CL languages is that "In English and Dëne, but not in Mandarin and other languages with obligatory numeral classifiers, numerals can be used pronominally. In the latter, only the numeral-classifier combination can be used pronominally." In (508), *one* alone can mean 'one new blanket', whereas in the Mandarin Chinese examples in (509), *yi* 'one' alone may not stand for 'one new blanket'.

(508) *I bought two new blankets. <u>One</u> is black and <u>one</u> is red.*

(509) a. *Wo   mai-le   liang   tiao   xin   tanzi.   <u>Yi   tiao</u>   hei*
        1SG   buy-PRF   two   CL   new   blanket   one   CL   black
        de,   <u>yi   tiao</u>   hong   de.
        DE   one   CL   red   DE
        'I bought two new blankets. One is black and one is red.'
   b. **Wo   mai-le   liang   tiao   xin   tanzi.   <u>Yi</u>   hei   de,   <u>yi</u>*
        1SG   buy-PRF   two   CL   new   blanket   one   black   DE   one
        hong   de.
        red   DE

The data indeed show that numerals in the two languages behave differently. However, I doubt that the contrast can show that a numeral contains unit information in non-CL languages. Data like (508) and (509a) can be derived by deletion. In (508), the NP *new blanket* is deleted after each instance of *one* (see Section 6.2.2).[62] In (509a), the NP *xin tanzi* 'new blanket'

---

62. The word *one* in (508) is different from the pronominal use of *one* in data like (i) or (37a). In (i), the word *one* cannot be followed by a noun such as *car*.
   (i) *John bought a big car and Mary bought a small one* (**car*).

is deleted after each instance of *yi tiao* 'one CL'. The deletion is licensed by the CL *tiao*, which is a head element (Section 6.2.1). (509b) is not acceptable simply because in this language, ellipsis is licensed by the occurrence of a head element and a numeral is not a head element, which cannot license the deletion of the string *tiao xin tanzi* 'CL new blanket'. (See footnote 53 for more discussion of ellipsis in English).

The two approaches, the unit-word-oriented and the numeral-oriented approach to numeral expressions, have been seen in Quine (1969: 36), in a slightly different version. Quine states that a CL in a CL language can be treated as a constituting part of a numeral, so that a numeral is sensitive to the semantic type of the noun when it applies to the noun. On the other hand, a CL can also be treated as a unit word for the noun, so that a numeral can apply to the noun. Quine does not make a choice between the two approaches. The present approach to individual and individuating CLs argues for the second one.

In addition to Wilhelm's (2008) semantically numeral-oriented approach, Lehmann (2008) proposes a morphologically numeral-oriented approach to the existence of CLs in CL languages. In the latter approach, "[T]he primary function of numeral classifiers is to serve as dummy nouns that those numerals which are affixes can attach to." (Lehmann 2008: 5) However, numerals in Mandarin Chinese, regardless how long they are, always require the occurrence of a CL when counting. In (510), the numeral *yi-bai-wu-shi-san* 'one hundred and fifty-three' has five syllables. It does not look like an affix, but the CL *zhang* is obligatory.

(510) *yi-bai-wu-shi-san* *(*zhang*)   *zhuozi*
     1-100-5-10-3   CL   table
     '153 tables'

Second, as shown in Section 2.6.1, when a numeral occurs in a verbal expression in English, a CL is required. If numerals do not need CLs in nominals in English, they should not require the occurrence of CLs in verbal expressions, either. One should not expect the same numerals to behave differently in terms of their morphological behavior in the same language.

6.8. Chapter summary

In this chapter, I have argued for a new projection between DP and NP: UnitP, in addition to NumP and QuantP. The projection represents Numerability, one of the two features identified in Chapter 2. Numerals are argued to be base-generated at Spec of Unit and a unit word such as a CL heads UnitP. Thus UnitP is projected if a numeral occurs, regardless of whether there is any overt form for the head of this projection.

The quantifiers G-YI, E-YI, and M-YI are hosted by the Spec of QuantP, and the obligatory CL following G-YI and E-YI are at the head of QuantP.

Plural markers, including RUWs in Mandarin Chinese, are hosted in NumP, which is different from UnitP. Thus, the occurrence of a plural marker does not correlate with the projection of UnitP.

In the proposed analysis, countability is represented by functional structures, rather than substantive properties of nouns or numerals. In this aspect, the analysis is compatible with Borer's (2005) syntactic approach to countability, although the details of our functional structures are different.

Using the new categorial label UnitP, I have also presented the derivations of the left- and right-branching structures of Chinese numeral expressions, established in Chapter 5. Then, based on the selections of the two features, Numerability and Delimitability, I have identified various ways of realization of the head of UnitP in different types of languages, and within the same language. The null Unit in Yudja is a covert counterpart of either an individual or individuating CL in Chinese. The null Unit in Dëne is a covert counterpart of individual CL in Chinese. I have also argued against numeral-oriented analyses of the existence of CLs in numeral expressions. In this analysis, language variations are represented by fine, yet discrete, graduations of properties of overt and covert functional elements.

Chapter 7
Noun-classifier compounds

7.1. Introduction

In Mandarin Chinese, a compound can be made up of a noun and a CL, as shown by the underlined parts in the examples in (511). If such a compound occurs in a numeral expression, there are two CLs. I will call the compound-internal CL lower CL, and the one out of the compound higher CL. In (511b), for instance, *qun* is the lower CL and *ge* is the higher one.

(511) a. *yi   di   shui-di*
         one CL   water-CL
         'one drop of water'

     c. *yi   zu   xian-tiao*
         one CL   line-CL
         'one group of lines'

     b. *yi   ge   yang-qun*
         one CL   sheep-CL
         'one flock of sheep'

One goal of this chapter is to show that even for a nominal that has a built-in element to denote unit, another unit word is still required to link the nominal to a numeral in Chinese. Thus the occurrence of a CL between a numeral and a nominal in the language is a syntactic requirement. It reflects a syntagmatic relation between a numeral and a nominal in the language, as claimed in Chapter 2.

Another goal of the chapter is to show that CLs exhibit different syntactic properties in different syntactic positions. In addition to realizing Unit, Quant, and Num (Chapter 6), we argue that the lower CL, if it is not a kind CL, realizes the head of a functional projection DelP, and the higher CL in cases such as (511a) and (511b) is a place-holder of Unit, without semantic content. I argue that the structure of the numeral expression that has a place-holder CL is always right-branching, i.e., the higher CL always c-commands the comound.

Identifying the possible place-holder function of the higher CL in numeral expressions is significant in at least two aspects. First, the surface position of a unit word in a numeral expression must be the position of a functional head. Second, CLs provide one more instance of evidence for the parallelism between the syntax of nominals and the syntax of verbal or clausal constructions: both may have X^0 place-holders.[63]

The chapter is organized as follows. Section 7.2 presents new data to show the syntactic similarities and differences between N-CL compounds and bare nouns in the language. Section 7.3 reports on how the lower CL decides the Delimitability of the compound, and plays a role in establishing the non-mass status of the compound when the noun root is a mass noun. Section 7.4 reports, however, on how the lower CL has no influence on the non-count status of the compound. In Section 7.5, various relations between the higher CL and the lower CL are discussed. The section shows that if there is no place-holder CL, although there are two CLs, only the lower one can be an individuating CL, and only the higher one encodes a counting unit. The two CLs also interact with respect to delimitive modifiers. In Section 7.6, I present the semantic emptiness of the higher CL, if it is *ge* or a copy of the lower CL, arguing for their place-holder status. In Section 7.7, I present my proposed syntactic derivations of different numeral expressions that contain an N-CL compound, including those containing a place-holder. Section 7.8 provides a brief summary.

7.2. Basic properties of N-CL compounds

7.2.1. The components of N-CL compounds

In some languages, one can find the so-called singulatives (e.g., Mathieu 2012b), as shown by the suffixes in (512b), (513b) (Acquaviva 2008: 237; 2010: 7), and by the right morpheme of the examples in (514) (Yi 2010: 94):

(512) a. *hteb*   b. *hteb-a*   [Moroccan Arabic]
         'fire wood'   'piece of firewood'

(513) a. *glao*   b. *glav-enn*   [Breton]
         'rain'   'raindrop'

---

63. A place-holder of a different kind in Mandarin Chinese is reported in Hurford (1975: 246). His example is the element *ling* 'zero' in the numerals in (i) (cited from Chao 1968: 575).

   (i) a. *yi-qian-ling-er-shi-si*   b. *er-bai-ling-er*
           1-1000-0-2-10-4   2-100-0-2
           '1024'   '202'

(514) a. *mwul-pangwul*   b. *pis-pangwul*   c. *kilum-pangwul*   [Korean]
water-drop   rain-drop   oil-drop
'water drop'   'rain drop'   'oil drop',

Similar complex words are found systematically in Mandarin Chinese, with the following characteristics. First, the counterparts of singulatives are just CLs. Any type of CL may follow a noun, forming a compound, as seen in (515) (see Loke 1997 for a discussion of the historical origin of such compounds in Mandarin Chinese).

(515) a. *shui-di*   *zhi-zhang*   *tu-dui*   [Individuating CL]
water-CL   paper-CL   earth-CL
'water-drop'   'paper-piece'   'earth-pile'
   b. *hua-duo*   *shu-ben*   *ma-pi*   [Individual CL]
flower-CL   book-CL   horse-CL
'flower'   'book'   'horse'
   c. *huluobo-pian*   *pingguo-kuai*   *hua-ban*   [Partitive CL]
carrot-CL   apple-CL   flower-CL
'carrot-slice'   'apple-chunk'   'flower-petal'
   d. *yang-qun*   *yaoshi-chuan*   *shu-dui*   [Collective CL]
sheep-CL   key-CL   book-CL
'sheep-flock'   'key-bunch'   'book-pile'
   e. *shu-zhong*   *dongwu-lei*   *shipin-lei*   [Kind CL]
tree-kind   animal-kind   food-kind
'tree-type'   'animal-type'   'food-type'

CLs are thus systematically able to occur in an N-CL compound. Although accidental gaps occur (e.g., the CL *ge* may not occur in such a compound), the pattern of the compound is an attested construction in the language, and its generality should not be ignored in analyzing the formal properties of CLs (cf. Cheng 2012: 202 fn. 3). This is parallel to the situation that although not all verbs may occur with the past tense suffix *-ed* in English, the formal status of the suffix is well-recognized; similarly, although the combinations such as /k'u²/, /ku²/, and /su³/ do not exist in Mandarin Chinese, one does not deny the availability of consonant-vowel combination in the language.

Second, not only all types of CLs, but also all types of nouns may occur in an N-CL compound. The noun root *shui* 'water' in (515a) is a mass noun, but the noun root *hua* 'flower' in (515b) is a non-mass noun. As for abstract nouns, *kuan* 'money' in the N-CL compound in (516) is a mass noun, whereas *shi* 'event' in the N-CL compound in (517) is a non-mass noun.

(516) a. *liang ge kuan-xiang*
     two CL money-CL
     'two units of money'

    b. *liang xiang zhuan   kuan*
      two CL   special money
      'two units of special money'

(517) a. *liang ge shi-jian*
     two CL event-CL
     'two events'

    b. *liang jian shi*
      two CL   event
      'two events'

Third, the selection of the Delimitability of a CL in an N-CL compound is identical to that of the corresponding free form CL. The individual CL *zhi*, but not the individuating CL *di*, occurs with the non-mass noun *qiang* 'gun' in (518a). The contrast remains visible in the N-CL compound in (518b). On the other hand, the individuating CL *di*, rather than the individual CL *zhi*, occurs with the mass noun *you* 'oil' in (518c). The contrast also remains visible in the N-CL compound in (518d).

(518) a. *san*   *{zhi/*di} qiang*
     three CL/CL   gun
     'three guns'
   c. *san*   *{*zhi/di} you*
     three   CL/CL oil
     'three drops of oil'

    b. *qiang-{zhi/*di}*
      gun-CL/CL
      'gun'
    d. *you-{*zhi/di}*
      oil-CL/CL
      'oil-drop'

Fourth, the s-selection of a CL in an N-CL compound is also identical to that of the corresponding free form CL. The individual CL *li*, but not *duo*, occurs with the non-mass noun *huasheng* 'peanut'. We see the selectional restriction in both the free form CL in (519a) and the compound-internal CL in (519b). In contrast, the individual CL *duo*, but not *li*, occurs with the non-mass noun *hua* 'flower'. We see the selection restriction in both the free form CL in (519c) and the compound-internal CL in (519d). The examples in (520) show the same point.

(519) a. *san*   *{li/*duo} huasheng*
     three CL/CL   peanut
     'three peanuts'
   c. *san {*li/duo} hua*
     three CL/CL flower
     'three flowers'

    b. *huasheng-{li/*duo}*
      peanut-CL/CL
      'peanut'
    d. *hua-{*li/duo}*
      flower-CL/CL
      'flower'

(520) a. *san* {*zhang/*pi*} *zhi*
  three CL/CL   paper
  'three pieces of paper'
  c. *san* {**zhang/pi*} *bu*
  three CL/CL   cloth
  'three pieces of cloth'

b. *zhi-*{*zhang/*pi*}
  paper-CL/CL
  'paper'
  d. *bu-*{**zhang/pi*}
  cloth-CL/CL
  'cloth'

The above two points show that a CL has its consistent co-occurrence restriction pattern, regardless of whether it occurs in a compound or not.

Fifth, compound-internal CLs have a consistent position: they always surface at the end of a word in Chinese. The underlined morphemes in (521), which are not the last morphemes of the words, are lexical roots, not CLs, although they share forms with the nominal or verbal CLs in (522).

(521) a. *ge-zi*
  height-suffix
  'tallness'
  b. *ben-zi*
  book-suffix
  'writing book'
  c. *yi-xia-zi*
  one-down-suffix
  'immediately'

(522) a. *san ge haizi*
  three CL kid
  'three kids'
  b. *liu ben shu*
  six CL book
  'six books'
  c. *Pai wo san xia!*
  pat 1SG three CL
  'Pat me three times!'

All CLs in Chinese have developed from other substantive categories such as nouns and verbs (e.g., Li 1924; Peyraube 1998). Thus the form-sharing is not surprising.

This fixed final position of CLs in the compounds distinguishes them from regular nominal components of a compound, which are not restricted to a specific position:

(523) a. *dao-di   ~ di-dao*
  road-earth earth-road
  'real'   'real'
  c. *cha-hua ~ hua-cha*
  tea-flower flower-tea
  'tea flower' 'scented tea'
  b. *ren-qing   ~ qing-ren*
  person-love   love-person
  'human relation' 'lover'
  d. *he-fan   ~ fan-he*[64]
  box-meal   meal-box
  'meal in boxes' 'meal box'

---

64. The two forms *he-fan* 'box-meal' and *fan-he* 'meal box' are Beijing Mandarin. Their Taiwan Mandarin counterparts are *he-can* 'box-meal' and *can-he* 'meal box', respectively.

7.2.2. The distributions and readings of N-CL compounds

The distributions of N-CL compounds are similar to those of bare nouns. Like a bare noun, an N-CL compound can occur in an argument position, as in (524a), and a predicate position, as in (524b):

(524) a. *Kefei   kanjian-le hua-duo.*   b. *Zhe   shi hua-duo.*
       Kefei   see-PRF   flower-CL   DEM be   flower-CL
       'Kefei saw (the) flowers.'   'This is a flower.'
       'Kefei saw {the/a} flower.'   'These are flowers.'

    Like a bare noun, the interpretation of an N-CL compound can be indefinite, as seen in (525a), definite, or generic, as seen (525b), or kind, as seen in (526). Also like a bare noun, such a compound does not have to denote plural or collective entities (contra Li & Thompson 1981: 82). Singular readings of (525a) and (525b) are possible. The context of *zhuan-zhi* 'boat-CL' in (527) indicates that the nominal has a singular reading exclusively (the example is from the Taiwan newspaper *Lianhe Bao*, Nov. 17, 2012).

(525) a. *Ta   xiang yao   hua-duo.*
       3SG   want   want flower-CL
       'He wants to have {a flower/flowers}.'
       'He wants to have the flower(s).'
    b. *Hua-duo   hui diaoxie.*
       flower-CL can wither.'
       '{That flower/Those flowers/Flowers} can wither.'

(526) a. *Zhang Zhongjing faxian-le   shancha hua-duo.*
       Zhang Zhongjing discover-PRF camellia flower-CL
       'Zhang Zhongjing discovered camellia.'
    b. *Zai zhe ge dao-shang, ma-pi   yijing   miejue-le.*
       at DEM CL island-on   horse-CL already   extinct-PRF
       'On this island, horses have become extinct.'

(527) *2008 nian, Shawudi-Alabo chaoji-you-lun   zai Suomali wai-hai*
       2008 year Saudi-Arabia   super-oil- tanker at Somali out-sea
       zao jie,   wei lilai bei jie de zuida chuan-zhi.
       suffer hijack be   so.far PASS rob DE largest ship-CL
       'In 2008, a Saudi Arabian oil tanker was hijacked off the coast of Somali. It is the largest ship being hijacked so far.'

But, as noted in X. Li (2011a: 53), if the compound-internal CL is a kind CL, the compound is different from a bare noun. Such a compound shows properties of kind-denoting nominals only, whereas a bare noun can be ambiguous between a kind and a non-kind reading. (528) shows that the compound *niao-lei* 'bird-kind' may not be the argument of the presentational verb *fei-zhe* 'fly-DUR', whereas the bare noun *niao* 'bird' can.

(528) *Tian-shang fei-zhe* {*niao*/*niao-lei}.
     sky-on   fly-DUR   bird/bird-kind
     'Birds are flying in the sky.'

If the kind meaning of the compound-internal kind CL is projected to the whole compound, the exclusive kind reading of the compound is expected.

7.3.   DelP and N-CL compounds

7.3.1. Compound-internal CL as a realization of Del

Among the various types of CLs, kind CLs may not be modified by a delimitive adjective, whereas all other types may (Section 2.4.7). This contrast remains to be seen in N-CL compounds. In (529a) and (530a), we see that the kind CLs *lei* and *zhong* may not be modified by *da* 'big'. If the compound-internal CL is a kind CL, consistently, the whole compound may not be modified by a delimitive adjective, as seen in (529c) and (530c). Thus, if the feature [−Delimitable] of the compound-internal kind CL is projected to the whole compound, the same feature is expected to be found in the compound.

(529) a. *yi da lei hua   b. *hua-lei*
         one big type flower   flower-type
                                             'flower type'
     c. *da hua-lei
       big flower-type

(530) a. **yi da zhong shu*   b. *shu-zhong*
         one big type   tree   tree-type
                                             'tree type'
     c. *da shu-zhong
       big tree-type

However, if the compound-internal CL is not a kind CL, the whole compound may always be modified by a delimitive adjective, regardless of whether the noun-root itself may be modified by such an adjective in other contexts. In (531a), *hua* 'flower' is modified by *da* 'big', and thus it is not surprising to see that in (531b) *da* occurs with the compound *hua-duo* 'flower-CL'. In (532a), however, *xue* 'blood' may not be modified by *da* 'big', but the compound *xue-di* 'blood-CL' can be modified by *da* in (532b).

(531) a. *da   hua*
      big flower
      'big flower'

    c. *yi   da   duo hua*
      one big CL   flower
      'one big flower'

    b. *da hua-duo*
      big flower-CL
      'big flower'

(532) a. **da xue*
      big blood

    c. *yi   da   di xue*
      one big CL blood
      'big blood-drop'

    b. *da xue-di*
      big blood-CL
      'big blood-drop'

In (532b), *xue* 'blood' is [−Delimitable], as seen in (532a), but *di* is [+Delimitable], as seen in (532c). The whole compound can be modified by a delimitive adjective and thus is [+Delimitable]. Therefore, if the feature [+Delimitable] of the compound-internal CL is projected to the whole compound, the same feature is expected to be found in the compound.

The effect of the compound-internal CL is seen not only in modification, but also in predication. In (533a) and (533b), the mass noun may not be the subject of the delimitive predicate *hen da* 'very big'. In (534a) and (534b), however, the corresponding N-CL compound, which has the same mass noun root as in (533), can be the subject of the delimitive predicate.

(533) a. **You hen   da.*
      oil   very big

    b. **Qi   hen   da.*
      air   very big

(534) a. *You-di hen   da.*
      oil-CL very big
      'The oil drop is big.'

    b. *Qi-tuan hen   da.*
      air-CL   very big
      'The (ball-like) air-unit is big.'

The above facts show that a lower CL contributes its Delimitabilty to the whole compound. I thus claim that if a lower CL is not a kind CL, it is a realization of the head of a functional projection, DelimitP, shortened as DelP; the compound is thus a non-mass noun, with the feature [+Delimit-able]. I further assume that Del takes NP as its complement. This head-complement relation captures the selection relation between the CL and the noun in a N-CL compound (Section 7.2.1). Moreover, the surface order is derived by the raising of N to Del. We will elaborate this movement in Section 7.7.1. The derivation of (535a) is (535b).

(535) a. *da   bing-kuai*
       big   ice-CL
       'big ice-chunk'

   b.   DelP

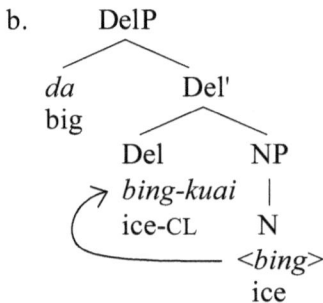

In (535b), the delimitive adjective *da* 'big' is hosted by Spec of DelP. In Cinque (1994), a functional projection may license a particular type of modifiers. The projection of DelP licenses delimitive modifiers only, but not any other types of modifiers. In (536a), for instance, the noun *xue* 'blood' may not be modified by the adjective *shan* 'kind, nice', and the occurrence of the CL *di* to the right of the noun in (536b) does not make the string acceptable. *Shan* is not a delimitive adjective, and thus it is not licensed by DelP.

(536) a. **shan xue*   b. **shan xue-di*
       kind blood   kind blood-CL

The function of a delimitive adjective such as *da* 'big' and the function of the CL of an N-CL compound are different. They make different contri-butions to the interpretation of nominals. All delimitive adjectives are predicative (an unsaturated expression), exhibiting intersective properties. When such an adjective modifies a noun, which is also unsaturated, it restricts the meaning of the noun (e.g., *cat* ⇒ *big cat*). According to McNally (To appear: (4)), a modifier is an expression that combines with an unsaturated expression to form another unsaturated expression of the same type. Both *cat* and *big cat* are [+Delimitable], as well as unsaturated. The semantic type of the two expressions is the same. The CL of an N-CL compound, however, may combine with a [−Delimitable] noun such as *xue* 'blood' to form a [+Delimitable] nominal, e.g., *xue-di* 'blood-CL' in (532b). The semantic types of *xue* and *xue-di* are different. Thus the CL is not a modifier. Instead, it heads a functional projection, and its Spec may host a certain type of modifier, i.e., a delimitive modifier.

On the other hand, if the compound-internal CL is a kind CL, since it does not have a [+Delimitable] feature, it is base-generated simply at N, instead of Del. Presumably, (537a), for instance, is derived by a direct merger of two Ns, as illustrated in (537b). As we discussed in Section 7.2.2, the kind meaning of the kind CL is projected to the whole compound.

(537) a. *shu-zhong*
     tree-kind
     'tree types'

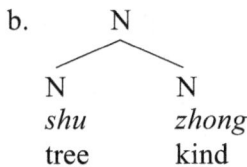

   b.   N
           ╱‾‾╲
     N   N
    shu   *zhong*
    tree   kind

So far, we have identified four functional positions of CLs: first, as a realization of Unit, when it is in a simple free form with a numeral (Section 6.2.1); second, as a realization of Quant, when it occurs with a quantifier but does not denote any counting unit (Section 6.2.3); third, as a realization of Num, when it is in the form of a RUW or SUW (Section 6.3); and fourth, as a realization of Del, when it is in a compound. So the syntactic status of a CL is context-dependent.

7.3.2. DelP and delimitable markers

In Chapter 2, two features, Numerability and Delimitabilty, are identified. In the last chapter, I argue that Numerability is represented by UnitP. I have just proposed that Delimitability may project another functional projection DelP. In de Belder (2011a,b), a more specific projection, SizeP, is proposed.

We have seen in Chapter 2 that Delimitability is related to not only size information such as big and small, but also shape information such as thin and round, and boundary information such as whole or partial. I thus extend de Belder's SizeP into DelP.

A functional projection is attested if certain formatives are shown to be the realizations of the functional head. The projection of DelP is attested not only in compound-internal CLs in Mandarin Chinese, but also in diminutive markers, as argued by de Belder (2011b). The occurrence of a diminutive marker indicates atomicity and thus a non-mass reading.

(538) a. *pane*   b. *panino*   [Italian]
         bread   bread-DIM
         'bread'   'bread roll'

(539) a. *Brot*   b. *Brötchen*   [German]
         bread   bread-DIM
         'bread'   'bread roll'

In Gan, the diminutive suffix *tsi7* can follow various types of elements: N, Adj, V, CL, and D (proper names) (X. Li 2011b). The free selection of the diminutive marker is not a typical property of a substantive element. See Fortin (2011: Chapter 2) for a discussion of the properties of such affixes. It is possible that like CLs in numeral expressions, diminutive affixes are semi-functional heads or nominal-internal auxiliaries.

Nominals with [–Delimitable] reject delimitive adjectives, and therefore, no DelP is projected in their structures. Neither mass nouns such as *xue* 'blood' and *xinqin* 'mind, mood', nor nouns like *suggestion* have DelP.

7.4. The non-count status of N-CL compounds

Like other nouns in Chinese, N-CL compounds may not combine with a numeral directly, as seen in (540). A unit word is required for such a combination, as in (541). So N-CL compounds are also non-count nouns.

(540) a. **san shui-di*   b. **san hua-duo*
         three water-CL   three flower-CL

(541) a. *san ge shui-di*   b. *san   chuan shui-di*
         three CL water-CL   three CL   water-CL
         'three drops of water'   'three rows of water-drops'

As expected, when quantifiers that need to occur with a unit word (see Chapter 3) combine with such compounds, a unit word must occur, as seen in (542a); and when quantifiers that reject a unit word combine with such compounds, no unit word may occur, as seen in (542b).

(542) a. *Nali you ji   *(ge) shui-di?*
      there have how.many CL water-CL
      'How many water drops are there?'
   b. *Yusan-shang juran mei-you (yi)-dianr (*ge) shui-di.*
      umbrella-on even not-have some   CL water-CL
      'There is not even any water drop on the umbrella.'

Therefore N-CL compounds behave the same as regular nouns in the language, when they occur with numerals and various quantifiers. Such a compound is a non-count noun, with the feature [–Numerable].

With the two features, [+Delimitable] and [–Numerable], compounds like *shui-di* 'water-CL' are non-mass and non-count nouns, similar to *pingguo* 'apple' and the English word *furniture*. An N-CL compound contains a CL, i.e., a unit-denoting element. It expresses atomicity morphologically. But still, it requires the help of another unit word in order to show up with a numeral. Moreover, like simple nouns in the language, such compounds also reject the shifts of Universal Packager and Universal Sorter (Section 2.2.5), since there is no context in which they may combine with a numeral directly. This contrasts with languages such as Yudja (Lima 2010, 2012) and Karitiana (Müller et al. 2006). In the latter type of languages, any noun can combine with a numeral directly (Section 2.3.1). The obligatory presence of a unit word between a numeral and a N-CL compound tell us that the occurrence of a CL in a numeral expression in Chinese is a syntactic requirement.

7.5. The relations between the higher and the lower CLs

7.5.1. No multiple individuating

If an N-CL compound is [+Delimitable], it is a non-mass noun. Non-mass nouns do not occur with individuating CLs. Thus if the lower CL is an individuating CL, the higher one cannot be another different individuating CL. Both *di* and *tan* are unambiguously individuating CLs, as seen in (543a) and (543b). The examples in (543c) and (543d) show that they cannot co-occur in the same numeral expression. So, semantically, only one individuating CL is allowed for one mass noun.

(543) a. *yi   di   shui*
　　　　 one   CL   water
　　　　 'one drop of water'

　　　b. *yi   tan   shui*
　　　　 one   CL   water
　　　　 'one puddle of water'

　　　c. **yi   di   shui-tan*
　　　　 one   CL   water-CL

　　　d. **yi   tan   shui-di*
　　　　 one   CL   water-CL

Other CLs such as *tiao, zhang, pian* can be ambiguous. *Tiao* is an individual CL when it occurs with a [+Delimitable] noun such as *yu* 'fish', but an individuating CL when it occurs with a [–Delimitable] noun such as *bu* 'cloth'; *zhang* is an individual CL when it occurs with *zhuozi* 'table', but an individuating CL when it occurs with *zhi* 'paper'; *pian* is an individual CL when it occurs with *shuye* 'leaf', but an individuating CL when it occurs with *bing* 'ice'. If such a CL occurs as a higher CL, as in (544), one cannot exclude the possibility that the CL is an individual CL, representing the unit established by the lower CL. Thus, there is no case in which one mass noun occurs with two individuating CLs.

(544) a. *san   tiao   mu-pian*
　　　　 three   CL   wood-CL
　　　　 'three pieces of wood strips'

　　　b. *san   pian   mu-tiao*
　　　　 three   CL   wood-CL
　　　　 'three pieces of wood strips'

　　　c. *san   zhang   xiao   zhi-pian*
　　　　 three   CL   small   paper-CL
　　　　 'three small pieces of paper'

7.5.2. No multiple counting-units

If the higher CL and the lower CL have different forms, and the higher one is not *ge*, it is the higher one that encodes the counting unit. In (545a), there is only one CL, *juan*, which denotes a counting unit in a roll shape. In (545b), the lower CL is the same as the one in (545a), but the counting unit is the higher CL, *dui,* which is a collective CL. One uses this expression to count piles of paper-rolls, rather than individual paper rolls. The examples in (546) show the same point.

(545) a. *san   juan   zhi*
　　　　 three   CL   paper
　　　　 'three rolls of paper'

　　　b. *san   dui   zhi-juan*
　　　　 three   CL   paper-CL
　　　　 'three piles of paper-rolls'
　　　　 Not: 'three rolls of paper'

(546) a. *si   duo   hua*   b. *si   pai   hua-duo*
      four   CL   flower   four   CL   flower-CL
      'four flowers'   'four rows of flowers'
                                  Not: 'four flowers'

    c. *si   zhong hua-duo*
      four   kind   flower-CL
      'four kinds of flowers'
      Not: 'four flowers'

Since each counting operation allows only one counting unit, based on the readings of the examples in (545) and (546), we conclude that it is the CL that is local to the numeral that denotes the counting unit, for this type of examples. So the higher one is consistently a realization of Unit, as claimed in Chapter 6. The lower one, as claimed in Section 7.3 above, is a realization of Del, rather than that of Unit.

7.5.3. The semantic interactions between the two CLs

A higher CL and a lower CL may interact in different ways, semantically. The shape meaning of the whole numeral expression can be either the combination of the meanings of the two CLs, or the hierarchical combination of the meanings of the two CLs. In (547a) and (547b), for instance, both the flat-thin shape denoted by the CL *pian* and the narrow-strip shape denoted by the CL *tiao* are accessible, regardless of which one is the higher one. The two examples mean the same (note that *pian* is not a collective CL in (547)).

(547) a. *san   pian mu-tiao*   b. *san   tiao mu-pian*
      three CL   wood-CL   three CL   wood-CL
      Both: 'three wood units that are flat-thin and narrow'

In Zhang (2012a), it is argued that s-feature projection is flexible, if the sources of the features are not in a thematic relation. Here we see that the shape features of the two CLs can both be projected. Since the features from the two CLs are compatible, their combination is expected. If the semantic features of two CLs are not compatible, they may not be combined. In the unacceptable (548), the CL *li*, which is used for ball-shaped small entities, is in conflict with the CL *tiao*, which is used for narrow-strip shaped entities.

(548) a. **san li mu-tiao*   b. **san tiao mi-li*
      three CL wood-CL   three CL   rice-CL

Also, as expected, conflict modifiers in the shape composition are not allowed, either, as seen in (549). In this example, *pian* is intended to be an individual CL, rather than a collective CL.

(549) **san da pian xiao mu-tiao*
      three big CL   small wood-CL

Recall that individual and individuating CL constructions are right-branching (Chapter 5), and thus a higher modifier and a lower modifier are in the same domain, which may not hold conflicting semantics. In (547a), the higher CL *pian* is an individual CL. The impossibility for conflict modifiers to occur between the higher CL and the nominal, as seen in (549), is expected in the right-branching structure.

In (550a), however, the higher CL is the collective CL *dui* 'pile'. Conflicting modifications are possible, as seen in (550b), since the modifiers have different scopes. Recall that collective CL constructions are left-branching, and thus the two modifiers are not in the same domain (Section 5.2.1).

(550) a. *san   dui mu-tiao*
          three CL   wood-CL
          'three piles of wood-strips'
      b. *san   da   dui xiao mu-tiao*
          three big CL small wood-CL
          'three big piles of small wood-strips'

In this section, I have discussed various relations between the higher CL and the lower CL in a numeral expression that contains a N-CL compound. I have shown that although there are two CLs, only the lower one is an individuating CL, and only the higher one encodes a counting unit. The shape meanings of the two CLs can also both be projected in a right-branching structure, if they are semantically compatible.

7.6. The place-holder CLs

So far, in all of the examples discussed above, the higher CL is neither *ge* nor a copy of the lower CL. In this section, we show that if the higher CL is *ge* or a copy of the lower CL, it functions as a place-holder of a syntactic position. Thus the upper CL in such constructions has no semantics.

7.6.1. *Ge* as the higher CL

If the higher CL is *ge*, the meaning of the lower CL is projected. First, the real counting unit is the lower one, rather than *ge*. In both (551a) and (551b), the higher CL is *ge,* but the encoded water-units are different. In (551a), the lower CL denotes a unit in a drop shape, and the counting unit denoted by the whole numeral expression is also in a drop shape, identical to the one denoted by the lower CL. In (551b), the lower CL denotes a unit in a puddle shape, and it is this unit that is the unit expressed by the whole numeral expression.

(551) a. *san   ge shui-di*   b. *san   ge shui-tan*
        three CL water-CL   three CL water-CL
        'three drops of water'   'three puddles of water'

Moreover, in the following three groups of examples, although *ge* follows the numeral immediately in all of the cases, the readings of the a-forms are decided by the lower CLs, and are thus different from the meanings of the b-forms, where *ge* is the only CL (the b-forms are typically found in Northern Mandarin).

(552) a. *san   ge luobo-pian*   b. *san   ge luobo*
        three CL carrot-CL   three CL carrot
        'three carrot-slices'   ≠   'three carrots'

(553) a. *san   ge yang-qun*   b. *san   ge yang*
        three CL sheep-CL   three CL sheep
        'three flocks of sheep'   ≠   'three sheep'

(554) a. *san   ge shu-zhong*   b. *san   ge shu*
        three CL tree-type   three CL tree
        'three kinds of trees'   ≠   'three trees'

If there is only one CL in a numeral expression, the unique CL encodes the counting unit. This is the case for the b-forms of (552), (553), and (554). We have just seen in Section 7.5.2 that generally, the higher CL denotes the counting unit. We now see that if the higher CL is *ge*, however, it is the lower CL that denotes the counting unit.

Second, if *ge* is the higher CL, it has no effect on the s-selection of the verb that takes the numeral expression as its argument. In (555a), the CL *juan*, which denotes a unit in a roll-shape, satisfies the s-selection of the complex verb *ya-bian* 'press-flat', whereas the CL *pian*, which denotes a unit in a flat shape, does not. In (555b), although the higher CL is *ge*, we see the same s-selection pattern. In this example, the selection is satisfied by the lower CL, an element that is not local to the verb. The examples in (556) show the same point.

(555) a. *Daiyu ya-bian-le   yi   xiao {*pian/juan} zhi.*
         Daiyu press-flat-PRF one   small CL/CL   paper
         'Daiyu pressed a small {*piece/roll} of paper flat.'
     b. *Daiyu ya-bian-le   yi   ge xiao zhi-{*pian/juan}.*
         Daiyu press-flat-PRF one CL small paper-CL/CL
         'Daiyu pressed a small {*piece/roll} of paper flat.'

(556) a. *Lu-shang ji-le   yi {*di/tan} shui.*
         road-on   accumulate-PRF one   CL/CL   water
         'A {*drop/puddle} of water has accumulated on the road.'
     b. *Lu-shang ji-le   yi ge shui-{*di/tan}.*
         road-on   accumulate-PRF one CL water-CL/CL
         'A {*drop/puddle} of water has accumulated on the road.'

Therefore, the higher CL *ge* in a numeral expression has no semantic function, behaving like a place-holder of certain syntactic positions.

7.6.2. The CL copying constructions

If the higher CL has the same form as the lower CL, it is also semantically vacuous. For instance, if it is a copy of a collective CL, it does not behave like a collective CL. This can be seen in two aspects.

First, if the higher CL is a copy of a collective CL, the scope of a left-peripheral modifier is the whole numeral expression, rather than the combination of the numeral and the higher CL. If there is only one collective CL, the left-peripheral modifier may be incompatible with the modifier of the NP, as in (557) (Section 5.2.1). In (557b), the left-peripheral modifier is *dada* 'big', which is in conflict with the adjective preceding the NP, *xiao* 'small'. However, if the higher CL is a copy of the lower collective CL, the left-peripheral modifier may not be incompatible with the modifier of the compound. In (558b), the left-peripheral modifier is still *dada* 'big', and the adjective preceding the compound is *xiao* 'small'. This example is not acceptable.

(557) a. *san   qun   yang*
      three CL   sheep
      'three flocks of sheep'
   b. *dada de san   qun xiao   yang*
      big   DE three CL   small sheep
      'three big flocks of small sheep'

(558) a. *san   qun   yang-qun*
      three CL   sheep-CL
      'three flocks of sheep'
   b. **dadade san   qun   xiao yang-qun*
      big   DE   three CL   small sheep-CL

In Chapter 5, I used the acceptability of data like (557b) to argue for the grouping of the numeral with the CL, and thus for the left-branching structure of a collective CL construction. The acceptability contrast between (557b) and (558b) indicates that if the higher CL is a copy of a collective CL, it does not behave like a collective CL. Instead, since the scope of the left-peripheral modifier interacts with the NP in the CL copying construction, a right-branching structure is possible.

Second, if the higher CL is a copy of a collective CL, the effect of modifier-association is also changed. In Section 5.2.2, I have shown that if a CL is a collective CL, there is no correlation between the different positions of the same modifier: immediately before the noun and immediately before the CL, as seen in (559a) and (559b), respectively. The two examples do not mean the same.

(559) a. *san   qun   <u>da</u> yang*   b. *san   <u>da</u> qun   yang*
      three CL   big   sheep   three big   CL   sheep
      'three flocks of big sheep' ≠ 'three big flocks of sheep'

However, if the higher CL is a copy of the lower CL, a correlation between the different positions of the same modifier emerges. In (560a) the adjective *da* 'big' immediately precedes the compound, whereas in (560b), the same adjective immediately precedes the higher CL *qun*. The two examples mean the same.

(560) a. *san   qun   <u>da</u> yang-qun* b. *san   <u>da</u> qun yang-qun*
      three CL   big sheep-CL   three big   CL sheep-CL
      'three big flocks of sheep' = 'three big flocks of sheep'

Thus, the higher copy of a collective CL does not exhibit the distinctive formal properties of a collective CL. The correlation is similar to the semantic correlation between (561a) and (561b), discussed in Section 5.2.2. Crucially, the CLs in (560) are collective CLs and the ones in (561) are individual CLs.

(561) a. *san   tou   da   niu*   b. *san   da   tou   niu*
      three   CL   big   cow   three   big   CL   cow
      'three big cows'   =   'three big cows'

The above two points show that if the higher CL is a copy of the lower one, it heads a right-branching structure consistently, c-commanding the NP. It has no semantics, like a place-holder. It is the lower CL that plays the semantic role of the higher one, and is the associate of the place-holder.

7.6.3. The alternation possibility

The above two subsections show that if the higher CL is *ge* or a copy of the lower one, it has no semantics, behaving like a place-holder of certain syntactic positions. In this subsection, we provide further evidence for the place-holder status of such CLs. Specifically, if they are exchangeable, they must be place-holders of the same syntactic position.

In (562), the forms in the three columns in each row mean the same. The higher CL is *ge* in column A, and a copy of the lower CL in column B. The forms in column C have only one CL each, which is identical to the lower CL in the other two columns. In the first row, for instance, in the example in column A, the higher CL is *ge* and the lower one is *di*; in the example in column B, the two CLs are identical: *di*; and in the example in column C, only one CL, *di*, occurs. Nevertheless, the three examples all mean 'six drops of water'.

(562) A   B   C

       [Individuating CL]

a.   *liu ge shui-di*   *liu di shui-di*   *liu di shui*
       six CL water-CL   six CL water-CL   six CL water
       A/B/C: 'six drops of water'

       [Individual CL]

b.   *liu ge hua-duo*   *liu duo hua-duo*   *liu duo hua*
       six CL flower-CL   six CL flower-CL   six CL flower
       A/B/C: 'six flowers'

[Partitive CL]

c. *liu ge luobo-pian*   *liu pian luobo-pian*   *liu pian luobo*
   six CL carrot-CL   six CL   carrot-CL   six CL   carrot
   A/B/C: 'six carrot-slices'

[Collective CL]

d. *liu ge yang-qun*   *liu qun yang-qun*   *liu qun yang*
   six CL sheep-CL   six CL   sheep-CL   six CL   sheep
   A/B/C: 'six flocks of sheep'

[Kind CL]

e. *liu ge shu-zhong*   *liu zhong shu-zhong*   *liu zhong shu*
   six CL tree-kind   six kind   tree-type   six kind   tree
   A/B/C: 'six kinds of trees'

The alternation between the forms in column A and the forms in column B is always possible. If the higher CLs in both columns are semantically vacuous, the alternation possibility is expected.

Moreover, either group may always be changed into the corresponding simple forms in column C. If the higher CLs in column A and column B are all place-holders, this possibility of change is also expected. The semantics of a place-holder construction can be expressed by a construction without the place-holder. The change in the opposite direction is not always possible, however. But this is explainable. Not all CLs may occur in a N-CL compound, as mentioned in Section 7.2.1. For instance, (563a) may not be changed into either (563b) or (563c).

(563) a. *liu du qiang*   b. **liu ge qiang-du*   c. **liu du qiang-du*
      six CL wall   six CL wall-CL   six CL   wall-CL
      'six walls'

The alternation among the three constructions is not found in other kinds of compounds, such as *xizao-jian* 'bath-room', *you-tiao* 'oil-stick' (a kind of fried food), *ruan-jian* 'soft-ware', and *jiu-bei* 'wine-cup'. For instance, the CL *ge* in (564a) may not be replaced by a copy of the second morpheme of the compound, as in (564b); and (564a) has a different reading from (564c).

(564) a. *liu ge jiu-bei*   b. **liu bei jiu-bei*
      six CL wine-cup   six   cup   wine-cup
      'six wine-cups'

     c. *liu bei jiu*
      six cup wine
      'six cups of wine'

The contrast between the possible alternation of N-CL compound constructions and the impossible parallel alternation of other types of compounds supports a syntactic analysis of N-CL compounds.

7.6.4. The significance of place-holder CLs

I have shown that if the higher CL is *ge* or a copy of the lower one, it is a place-holder of a certain syntactic position. We have seen that in (562), a place-holder CL may occur with all possible types of CLs. This consistency indicates that the occurrence of place-holder CLs is systematic in the language.

Place-holders are semantically vacuous. The possibility to have a place-holder shows that the presence of a CL between a numeral and a noun in Chinese is a syntactic requirement. It further falsifies the assumption that the existence of CLs is caused by the alleged mass status of nouns in the language.

Moreover, the possibility for a place-holder to occur in the position of a regular CL of a numeral expression means the position must be a functional head position. I have argued that the syntactic position for a CL that occurs between a numeral and a nominal is Unit (Chapter 6). We now see that Unit can be realized by a place-holder.

A well-known place-holder of a functional head position is the English auxiliary *do*, which occurs in a clausal structure, regardless of how one analyzes the condition for its occurrence (see e.g., Bruening 2010). Japanese also has a similar empty verb, *suru* 'do', functioning as a place-holder (Kishimoto 2011). We now find similar place-holders in the nominal domain (See Aboh et al. 2010: 782 and the references thereof for a summary of more parallelisms between nominal and clausal constructions, with respect to the structural makeup and syntactic operations). *Do* and *suru* are place-holders in verbal domains. The finding of the place-holders in nominal constructions supports the cross-categorial symmetry in syntax (Chomsky 1970).

7.7.   Syntactic representations of N-CL numeral expressions

7.7.1. The constructions without a place-holder CL

According to our conclusion reached in Section 7.3.1, the lower CL, if it is not a kind CL, is a realization of Del. In order to derive a possible N-CL compound, I have claimed that the N head of an NP moves to the head of DelP. The derivation of (565a) is (565b):

(565) a. *da   bing-kuai*   (= (535))
       big ice-CL
       'big ice-chunk'

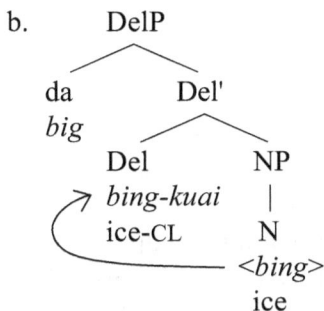

   b.   DelP
           ⌒
        da   Del'
        big   ⌒
              Del   NP
            bing-kuai |
             ice-CL   N
            _____ <*bing*>
                          ice

Since the landing site of a specific type of movement is consistent, nouns move to the left of the lower CL, resulting the consistent N-CL order of such compounds. This captures the position consistency of the lower CL, mentioned at the end of Section 7.2.1.

After the N-to-Del movement, the noun alone may not have a syntactic dependency with another element anymore. The N-CL *hua-duo* 'flower-CL' in (566a) is derived by the raising of *hua* at N to *duo* at Del. After the raising, *hua* alone may not be related to the topic *hua* at the sentence-initial position, as shown in (566b). However, the whole compound *hua-duo* may be topicalized, as seen in (566c). The topicalization in (566c) is parallel to that in (567b), where the noun *hua* 'flower' alone does not undergo any head movement. The restriction follows the well-recognized constraint on head movement, which Platzack (2010: 8) formalizes as "If a head β moves to α, the {α + β} acts as one constituent." Of course, the effect of this constraint is the same effect as that of the traditional Lexical Integrity (e.g., Di Sciullo & Williams 1987), although the latter is challenged, for instance, by the existence of the V-*le*-V and V-*yi*-V verbs in Mandarin (see (193a) and (194a); Basciano & Melloni 2013).

(566) a. *Lulu mai-le   san   ge hua-duo.*
         Lulu buy-PRF three CL flower-CL
         'Lulu bought three flowers.'
    b. **Hua, Lulu mai-le san   ge <hua>-duo.*
         flower Lulu buy-PRF three CL flower-CL
    c. *Hua-duo, Lulu mai-le san   ge <hua-duo>.*
         flower   Lulu buy-PRF three CL flower-CL
         'Flowers, Lulu bought three.'

(567) a. *Lulu   mai-le   san   ge   hua.*
   Lulu   buy-PRF   three   CL   flower
   'Lulu bought three flowers.'
  b. *Hua,   Lulu   mai-le   san   ge.*
    flower   Lulu   buy-PRF   three   CL
    'Flowers, Lulu bought three.'

Now let us see the structure of a numeral expression that contains an N-CL compound. We have argued that the higher CL heads UnitP and the lower one, if it is not a kind CL, heads DelP. It is possible that both the higher CL and the compound each have a delimitive adjective, as seen in (568a). The derivation of (568a) is (568b). Note that the two CLs are different in this example and the higher one is not *ge*. Thus there is no placeholder CL in the structure. The higher CL *tiao* is the counting unit, which heads UnitP. As argued in Section 6.2.3, a pre-unit adjective is an adjunct of UnitP. Thus *chang* 'long' in this example is an adjunct of UnitP. As for the lower adjective, *bo* 'thin', it is licensed by the lower CL *pian*, and is thus hosted by the Spec of DelP headed by *pian*.

(568) a. *san   chang   tiao   bo   mu-pian*
   three   long   CL   thin   wood-CL
   'three long and thin wood pieces'

  b.

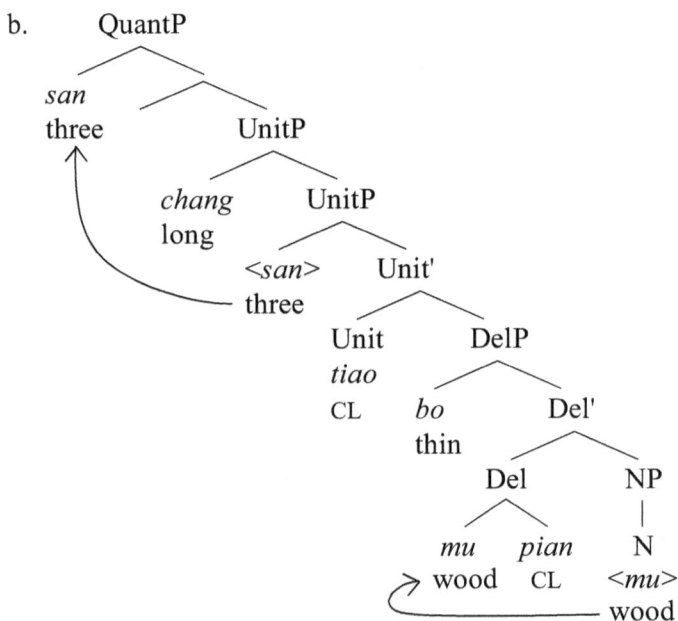

In this structure, DelP is below UnitP. This analysis is similar to the one proposed in de Belder (2011a,b), where SizeP is always under DivP (≈ my UnitP).

If the higher CL is a collective CL, as we argued in Chapter 5, the construction has a left-branching structure. (569b) is the structure of (569a). The higher CL *dui* is a counting unit, surfacing at the head of UnitP.

(569) a. *liang da   dui xiao   mu-tiao*
      two   big CL   small wood-CL
      'two big piles of small wood strips'

b.

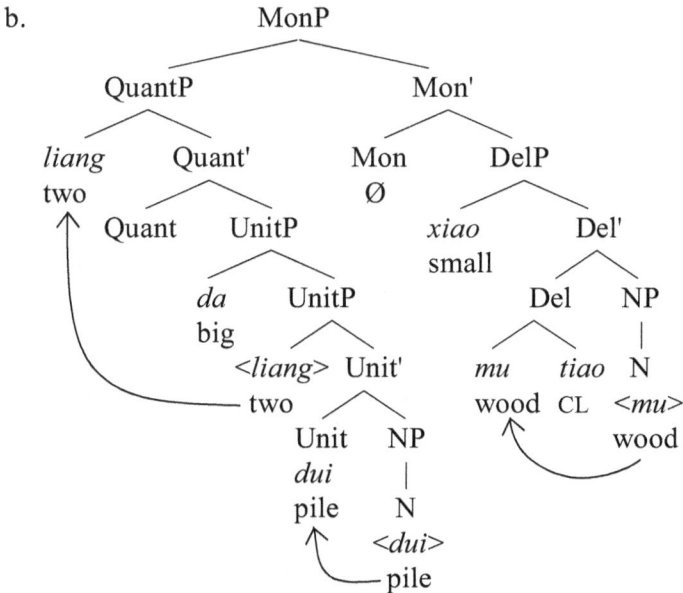

7.7.2. The constructions with a place-holder CL

If the higher CL is either *ge* or a copy of the lower CL, it is a place-holder of Unit (Section 7.6). In (570a), *ge* may alternate with *kuai*. The structure of (570a) is (570b).

(570) a. *wu   {ge/kuai} da   bing-kuai*
      five CL/CL   big   ice-CL
      'five big ice-chunks'

b.   QuantP

  wu   Quant'
  five
         ↑ Quant   UnitP

              <*wu*>   Unit'
              five
                     Unit   Del
  PLACE-HOLDER ⇨   *ge/kuai*
                       CL   *da*   Del'
                            big
                                 Del   NP
                                                |
                              bing   *kuai*   N
                              ice   CL   <*bing*>
                                                 ice

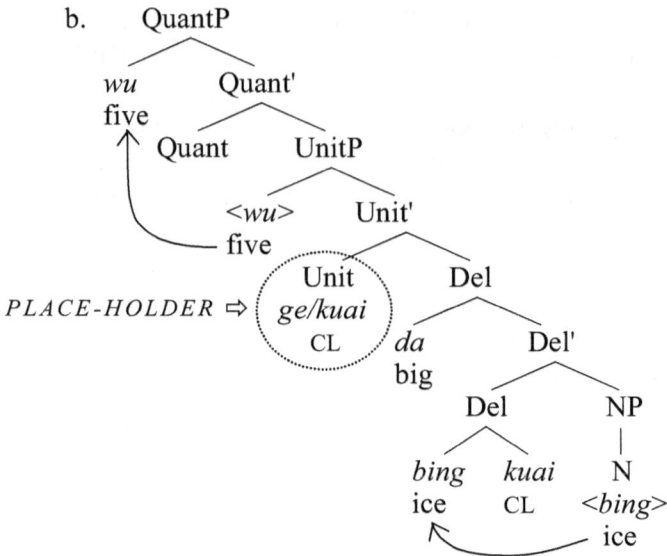

Recall that if ther is no N-CL compound, constructions of collective CLs have a left-branching structure, and the constructions of individual CLs have a right-branching structure (Chapter 5). (571b) is the structure of (571a), where the collective CL *qun* occurs. (572b) is the structure of (572a), where the individual CL *tou* occurs. There is no place-holder CL in the two structures.

(571) a. *san   qun yang*
         three CL   sheep
         'three groups of sheep'

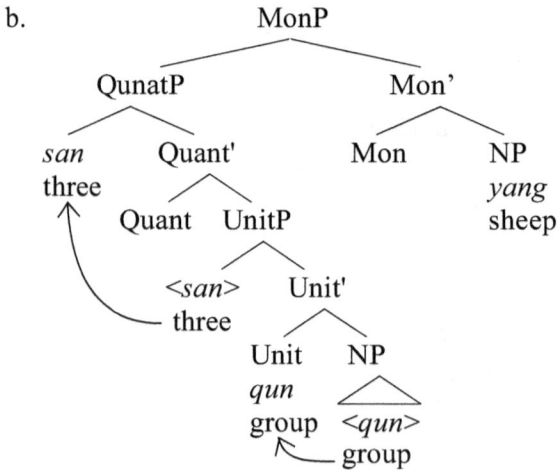

b.   MonP

      QunatP   Mon'

  san   Quant'   Mon   NP
  three   *yang*
         ↑ Quant UnitP   sheep

              <*san*>   Unit'
              three
                      Unit   NP
                      qun
                      group <*qun*>
                             group

(572) a. *san   tou   yang*
　　　　three CL   sheep
　　　　'three sheep'

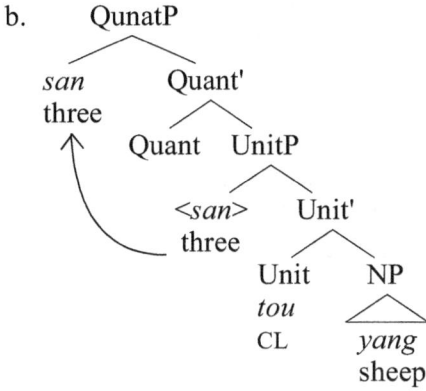

b.　　　QunatP

```
         QunatP
        /\
   san       Quant'
  three      /\
        Quant   UnitP
              /\
         <san>    Unit'
         three    /\
              Unit    NP
              tou    /\
              CL    yang
                    sheep
```

In Section 7.6.2 above, we concluded that if the higher CL is a copy of the lower CL, the structure of the whole numeral expression is always right-branching, regardless of the type of the CL. (573b) is the structure of (573a) (= (558a)), in which the higher CL is a copy of the a collective CL, and it may alternate with the CL *ge*. The structure is right-branching.

(573) a. *san   {ge/qun} yang-qun*
　　　　three CL/CL   sheep-CL
　　　　'three groups of sheep'

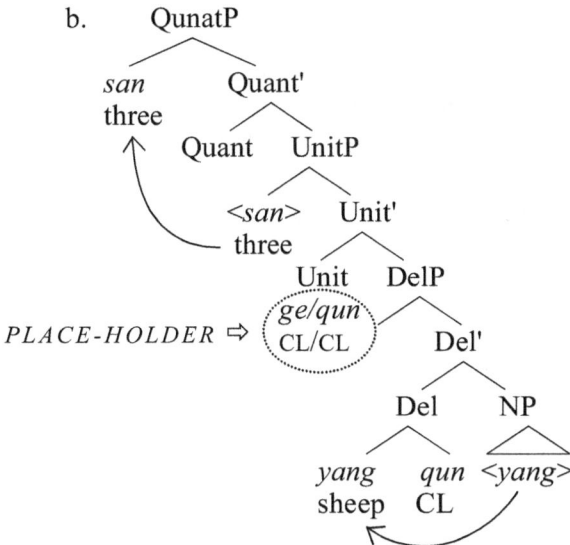

b.　　　QunatP

```
         QunatP
        /\
   san       Quant'
  three      /\
        Quant   UnitP
              /\
         <san>    Unit'
         three    /\
              Unit    DelP
            ge/qun    /\
PLACE-HOLDER ⇨ CL/CL    Del'
                       /\
                    Del    NP
                    /\    /\
                yang    qun <yang>
                sheep   CL
```

Since numeral expressions with a place-holder CL have a consistent right-branching structure, we see the similarity in configuration between (573b) and (572b) or (568b). The consistent right-branching structures are expected if place-holders must c-command their associates. In (573b), the place-holder CL *ge/qun* c-commands the lower CL *qun*.

One can see that CLs display different properties in different syntactic contexts. It is common for the same formative to play different roles in different contexts. Not only the syntactic category of a CL varies (Unit, Quant, Num, and Del), but also the structure of a numeral expression varies, depending on the status of the CL: if the higher CL is a place-holder of Unit, the structure of the numeral expression is always right-branching, regardless of the type of the lower CL.

7.8. Chapter summary

In this chapter, I have shown that even for a nominal that has an internal element to denote unit, another unit word is still required to link the nominal to a numeral in Chinese. Thus the presence of a CL with a numeral and a nominal in Chinese is a syntactic, rather than semantic, requirement.

I have also shown that the presence of a lower CL decides the Delimitability of the compound on the one hand, and the presence of the unit word does not make a non-count nominal a count one, on the other hand. These two facts have led us to see that a lower CL is a realization of a functional head Del, rather than Unit. Therefore, in addition to Unit, Quant, and Num, there is a fourth functional position for CLs: Del.

I have also shown that if the higher CL is *ge* or a copy of the lower CL, it is a place-holder of Unit, without semantic contents. In this case, the structure of the construction may be different from that of the corresponding construction in which the same CL is not a place-holder. N-CL constructions thus tell us more about the syntactic nature of CLs, the syntactic positions of various types of CLs, and the cross-categorial availability of place-holders for functional heads.

Chapter 8
Conclusions

This book has aimed to clarify four major empirical issues with respect to the syntax of CL constructions in Mandarin Chinese, a CL language, compared with non-CL languages:

I. The countability issue, i.e., the relationship between CLs and the count-mass contrast;

II. The number issue, i.e., possible systematic morpho-syntactic ways to express the contrast between singularity and plurality;

III. The structure issue, i.e., the constituency and thus the syntactic structures of numeral constructions;

IV. The position issue, i.e., the structural positions of CLs in different constructions.

I. The countability issue has been investigated from the following two aspects.

I-A. The relation between count and mass, from a syntagmatic perspective

We have concluded that the contrast between count and mass is not a dichotomous contrast. Instead, there are two features to make the relevant distinctions: Numerability and Delimitability. [+Numerable] means that a noun may combine with a numeral directly, and [+Delimitable] means that a noun may be modified by a size (e.g., *big*), or shape (e.g., *round*), or boundary (e.g., *whole*) modifier. Like agentivity of VPs (i.e., whether an agent-oriented adverb is allowed) and gradability of APs (i.e., whether a degree word is allowed), Numerability and Delimitability are defined syntagmatically. The two newly identified features can be attested in the co-occurrence restrictions of articles, quantifiers, adverbs, and CLs, in pronominalization, and in the input or output of the Universal Grinder, Universal Packager, and Universal Sorter.

I have claimed that a count noun is defined exclusively by [+Numerable]. It is generally recognized that such a combination possibility is the most reliable grammatical property of count nouns (e.g., Chierchia 2010: 104). This book has further argued that this is the only defining grammatical property of a count noun, cross-linguistically. The syntagmatic property of count nouns is clearly linguistic, rather than extra-linguistic. It is thus not surprising that countability is expressed in various ways, cross-linguistically. For example, in Chinese, no noun may combine with a numeral directly, and therefore, no noun is a count noun (e.g., *san ba shanzi* 'three CL fan' vs. **san shanzi*). Numerability of the language is instead represented exclusively by unit words, including CLs and measure words. In languages such as Ojibwe (Mathieu 2012a: 186), Yudja (Lima 2010, 2012), Halkomelem Salish (Wilhelm 2008: 64), and Hopi (Whorf 1956 [1941]: 141), every noun can combine with a numeral directly, and thus every noun is a count noun. Between these two patterns, in languages such as English, in an unmarked situation, words like *cat* and *belief* are [+Numerable], and words like *oil* and *furniture* are [–Numerable].

On the other hand, the notion of mass is not the direct negation of count. I claim that it is the combination of two syntagmatic properties that defines mass: [–Numerable] and [–Delimitable]. Words such as *oil* in English and their counterparts in Chinese are mass nouns. This refined analysis makes it possible to precisely identify elements that may not combine with a numeral directly but allow a delimitive adjective, e.g., *furniture* in English, and *shanzi* 'fan' in Chinese. They are non-count and non-mass nouns. Since such words may have size information but are still non-count, this book argues against de Belder's (2011a,b) claim that size features entail the count status.

In all languages that have adnominal numerals and delimitive modifiers, we are able to identify count and mass elements, with the same criteria.

(574) a. count elements: [+Numerable]
       b. mass elements: [–Numerable, –Delimitable]

This book also shows that in Chinese, even for a nominal that has a built-in unit-denoting element, i.e., a noun-CL compound, an independent unit word is still required to link the nominal to a numeral (*san ge hua-duo* 'three CL flower-CL' vs. **san hua-duo*). Thus countability is a syntagmatic relation between a numeral and a nominal in the language, rather than a semantic property of nouns.

I-B. The distinctive property of CL languages, compared with non-CL languages

This book also presents a new study of language variation with respect to CLs in numeral expressions. Although every language has five types of unit words: standard measures (e.g., *kilo* in *three kilos of apples*), container measures (e.g., *bottle* in *three bottles of milk*), kind CLs (*kind* in *three kinds of chocolate*), partitive CLs (e.g., *section* in *three sections of orange*), and collective CLs (e.g., *group* in *three groups of students*), not every language has individuating CLs (e.g., *drop* in *three drops of oil*) and individual CLs (e.g., *ba* in *san ba shanzi* 'three fans').

With the two newly identified features, and thus the understanding that not all nouns in Chinese are mass nouns, I have argued that the function of individual CLs, which distinguish numeral CL languages from other languages, is not dividing or individuating. The popular belief that it is the individuating (discrete set-creating) function of CLs that is special in CL languages is wrong. Instead, numeral CL languages are different from other languages in that they have overt forms to represent the natural units of the elements denoted by non-mass nouns (i.e., [+Delimitable] nouns). Like other types of unit words, individual CLs in numeral expressions express counting units. English verbal numeral expressions also require the presence of an individual CL (*Bill traveled to Paris three *(times)*; see Krifka 2007: 39; Moltmann 2013: 21). Thus precisely speaking, both English and Chinese are numeral CL languages if we consider verbal expressions.

II. The number issue has been probed from the following three aspects.

II-A. The relation between the count-mass contrast and morphological number

Numerability, which is one of the two features responsible for the mass-count contrast, is different from morphological number, which is concerned with the contrast between singularity and various kinds of plurality. In this new perspective, nouns that have plural markers but reject numerals, such as *clothes, oats, grits,* and *masses* (McClawley 1979 [1975]: 172; Huddleston & Pullum 2002: 342), are [+Plural, -Numerable]. Plurality is also seen in mass plurals, which remain to be mass nouns, since they reject delimitive modifiers. Nouns that reject both plural markers and numerals, such as *furniture* are [-Plural, -Numerable]. There is no direct correlation between plurality and the count status of a noun. The new theory also covers various interactions between countability and number.

II-B. Expressing plurality in Mandarin Chinese

We have reported that all types of CLs and measure words in Mandarin Chinese can be reduplicated to express unit-plurality, such as *duo-duo* in (575a).

(575) *Tian-shang piao-zhe (*san) duo-duo bai yun.*
     sky-on   fly-DUR   three   CL-RED white cloud
     'Many pieces of white cloud are flying in the sky.'

Such plural markers are not specified with definiteness or specificity. The semantic type of the encoded plural is abundant plural. The optionality of the plural markers is predicted because the language has general number, in the sense of Corbett (2000). General number, as claimed by Rullmann & You (2006), is expressed by bare nouns in the language.

We have also shown that plural markers in the language may exhibit a dependency on certain quantifiers (e.g., the existential quantifier *yi* 'one' or *dou* 'all'), explicitly or implicitly. The dependency makes the markers reject other quantifiers, including a numeral, as seen in (575). Moreover, if a plural marker is licensed by *dou*, the nominal has a distributive reading. Otherwise, it is underspecified with either a distributive or collective reading.

II-C. Falsifying the numeral-deletion analysis of singular-denoting elements

It has been widely assumed that the numeral *yi* 'one' is deleted in a bare CL nominal, such as *duo bai yun* 'CL white cloud' in (576). However, such a nominal does not license any numeral-oriented modifier, such as *zuzu* 'as many as', and fails to establish a predication relation with a numeral-oriented element. Falsifying the assumption, we have argued that the CL in this use is a singular marker. A nominal like *duo bai yun* 'CL white cloud' in (576) denotes unit-singularity. It contrasts with both a nominal with a reduplicative CL, such as *duo-duo bai yun* 'CL-RED white cloud' in (575), which denotes plurality, and a bare noun nominal, such as *bai yun* 'white cloud', which denotes general number.

(576) *Tian-shang fei-zhe <u>duo</u> bai yun.*
      sky-on   fly-DUR CL   white cloud
      'A piece of white cloud is flying in the sky.'

III. The structure issue has been studied from the following three aspects.
III-A. The constituency of numeral expressions

This book has examined the constituency of a numeral expression, which contains three basic elements: a numeral, a unit word, and an NP in Mandarin Chinese. It identifies two structures: a right-branching structure for constructions of individual, individuating, and kind CLs, and a left-branching structure for constructions of partitive and collective CLs, and container and standard measures. In the right-branching structure, the unit word c-commands the NP, whereas in the left-branching structure, the unit word does not c-command the NP. The identification of the two structures is mainly based on the contrastive properties of the two types of unit words: the scope of a left-peripheral modifier, the effect of modifier-association, the semantic selection of a unit word on a noun, and the order of size and shape modifiers.

III-B. The projection of UnitP

We have shown that in a numeral expression, individual, individuating, and kind CLs behave like auxiliaries in a clause. We thus assume that they are base-generated at the head of a functional projection, UnitP. They consistently denote counting units. Their close relation with numerals is represented as Head-Spec relation in their base-positions. Other unit words also surface at Unit, keeping a syntacally local relation with numerals.

III-C. The variation in the realization of the head of UnitP

I have proposed that the projection of UnitP for numeral expressions is universal. In the presence of a numeral, the head of UnitP can be null in non-CL languages. This book has presented various patterns of the null forms of Unit, based on the newly identified two features. In languages such as Chinese, the head of UnitP is always realized by an overt element such as a CL, in regular productive phrasal nominals. In languages such as Karitiana (Müller et al. 2006), Ojibwe (Mathieu 2012a), Yudja (Lima 2010, 2012), Halkomelem Salish (Wilhelm 2008: 64), Dëne (Wilhelm 2008), and Haitian Creole (Deprez 2005: 861), the head of UnitP is not realized by an overt element other than the five types of unit words mentioned in I-B above. However, the silent Unit in Yudja and Halkomelem Salish selects a nominal with either [+Delimitable] or [–Delimitable]. So it is a covert counterpart of either an individual CL or individuating CL in Chinese. In contrast, the silent head of UnitP in Dëne selects only nominals with [+Delimitable]. Thus, it is a covert counterpart of a Chinese individual CL, but not that of an individuating CL. In languages such as English, generally speaking, the silent Unit selects nominals with [+Numerable], whereas the overt Unit selects nominals with [–Numerable]. In *three books*, where *books* is [+Numerable], Unit is silent; in *three pieces of paper* or *three pieces of furniture*, where *paper* or *furniture* is [–Numerable], however, Unit is realized by *pieces*. This book also argues against numeral-oriented theories of the cross-linguistic variation.

IV. The syntactic positions of CLs in various constructions have been identified as the following positions

IV-A. Unit

As we stated in III-B above, in a numeral construction, the numeral and the CL are Spec and head of UnitP, respectively. Individual, individuating, and kind CLs are realizations of the head of UniP. Other unit words such as partitive and collective CLs, as well as standard and container measures, are base-generated at N and move to Unit, and thus exhibit properties of both nouns and functional elements.

IV-B. Quant

If a CL follows the generic quantifier *yi* 'one', as in (577a), or the existential quantifier *yi* 'one', as in (577b), it heads QuantP. In both cases, the occurrence of the CL is obligatory, and the CL may exhibit selectional restrictions on the NP. In the structures of the constructions, since no numeral occurs, no UnitP is projected.

(577) a. *Yi*   <u>*zhi*</u>   *niao keyi fei de   hen   gao.*
       one   CL   bird can   fly DE   very high
       'A bird can fly very high.'
   b. *Yani sihu   kandao-le yi   <u>xian</u> xiwang.*
       Yani seem see-PRF   one CL   hope
       'Yani seems to have seen a hope.'

IV-C. Num

If a pre-NP CL is reduplicated, or occurs without any numeral, as in (575) and (576), respectively, it heads NumP. A reduplicative CL has [+PL], and the bare CL has [−PL].

IV-D. Del

If a non-kind CL surfaces in a compound, such as *di* in (578), it heads DelP. In (578), it is the compound-internal CL *di* that licenses the delimitive modifier *xiao* 'small'.

(578) *Zhuo-shang you   xiao   shui-<u>di</u>.*
      table-on   have small water-CL
      'There are small drops of water on the table.'

IV-E. Place-holder of Unit

In a numeral expression, if the CL preceding a N-CL compound is *ge*, as in (579a), or a copy of the compound-internal CL, as in (579b), the CL is a place-holder of Unit. It does not express a counting unit. Instead, it is the compound-internal CL that expresses a counting unit. A place-holder CL always c-commands the N-CL compound, regardless of the type of the CL in the compound.

(579) a. *Zhuo-shang you   san   ge xiao shui-di.*
      table-on   have   three CL small   water-CL
      'There are three small drops of water on the table.'
  b. *Zhuo-shang you   san   di xiao shui-di.*
      table-on   have   three CL small water-CL
      'There are three small drops of water on the table.'

Thus the syntactic positions of CLs in Mandarin Chinese vary with the syntactic contexts.

The new understandings of the linguistic notions of countability, number, and nominal-internal functional elements all enrich our knowledge of the syntactic computation system of language.

References

Aboh, Enoch O, Norbert Cover, Marina Dyakonova, and Marjo van Koppen. 2010. DP-internal information structure: Some introductory remarks. *Lingua* 120: 782–801.

Aboh, Enoch, Leston Buell, and Lisa Cheng. 2011. Deriving the word order difference in the nominal domain: Gungbe vs. Mandarin. Paper presented at the Workshop on Analyticity, University of Hong Kong, 20 July.

Acquaviva, Paolo. 2006. Goidelic inherent plurals and the morphosemantics of number. *Lingua* 116: 1860–1887.

Acquaviva, Paolo. 2008. *Lexical plurals: a morphosemantic approach*. Oxford: Oxford University Press.

Acquaviva, Paolo. 2010. Countability and part structure in grammar cognition. Paper presented at the Conference on Empirical, Theoretical and Computational Approaches to Countability in Natural Language, Bochum, 22–24 September.

Acquaviva, Paolo and Phoevos Panagiotidis. 2012. Lexical decomposition meets conceptual atomism. *LingBuzz*/001558.

Agrillo, Christian, Laura Piffer, and Angelo Bisazza. 2011. Number versus continuous quantity in numerosity judgments by fish. *Cognition* 119: 281–287

Ahrens, Kathleen. 1994. Classifier production in normals and aphasics. *Journal of Chinese Linguistics* 22: 203–247.

Aikhenvald, Alexandra Y. 2003. *Classifiers: a typology of noun categorization devices*. Oxford: Oxford University Press.

Akmajian, Adrian and Adrienne Lehrer. 1976. NP-like quantifiers and the problem of determining the head of an NP. *Linguistic Analysis* 2(4): 395–413.

Alexiadou, Artemis. 2011. Plural mass nouns and the morphosyntax of Number. In Mary Byram Washburn et al. (eds.), *Proceedings of the 28th West Coast Conference on Formal Linguistics*, 33–41, Somerville, MA: Cascadilla Proceedings Project.

Alexiadou, Artemis, Liliane Haegeman, and Melita Stavrou. 2007. *Noun Phrase in the generative perspective*. Berlin & New York: Mouton de Gruyter.

Allan, Keith. 1977. Classifiers. *Language* 53(2): 285–311.

Allan, Keith. 1980. Nouns and Countability. *Language* 56: 541–567.

Bach, Emmon. 1986. The algebra of events. *Linguistics and Philosophy* 9: 5–16.

Bale, Alan. 2011. Number, competition and syntactic complexity. To appear in *Proceedings of the 41st annual meeting of the North East Linguistic Society (NELS 41)*.

Bale, Alan and David Barner. 2009. The interpretation of functional heads: Using comparatives to explore the mass/count distinction. *Journal of Semantics* 26: 217–252.

Bale, Alan and David Barner. 2012. Semantic Triggers, Linguistic Variation and the Mass-Count Distinction. In Diane Massam (ed.), *Count and mass across languages,* 238–260. Oxford: Oxford University Press.

Bale, Alan, Michel Gagnon, and Hrayr Khanjian. 2011a. On the relationship between morphological and semantic markedness. *Morphology* 21: 197–221.

Bale, Alan, Michel Gagnon, and Hrayr Khanjian. 2011b. Cross-linguistic representations of numerals and number marking. *Proceedings of SALT 20*: 582–598.

Bale, Alan and Hyrayr Khanjian. 2008. Classifiers and number marking. *Proceedings of SALT 18*: 73–89.

Barbiers, Sjef. 2005. Variation in the morphosyntax of ONE. *The Journal of Comparative Germanic Linguistics* 8: 159–183.

Barbiers, Sjef. 2007. Indefinite numerals one and many and the cause of ordinal suppletion. *Lingua* 117(5): 859–880.

Barner, David and Jesse Snedeker. 2005. Quantity judgments and individuation: evidence that mass nouns count, *Cognition* 97: 41–66.

Barner, David and Jesse Snedeker. 2006. Children's early understanding of mass-count syntax: Individuation, lexical content, and the number asymmetry hypothesis. *Language Learning and Development* 2(3): 163–194.

Barner, David, Shunji Inagaki, and Peggy Li. 2009. Language, thought, and real nouns. *Cognition* 111: 329–344.

Bartos, Huba. 2011. Book review: The Chinese Syntax, C.-T.J. Huang, Y.H.A. Li, Y. Li, Cambridge University Press (2009). *Lingua* 121: 313–319.

Basciano, Bianca and Chiara Melloni. 2013. Verb reduplication in Mandarin Chinese. Paper presented at the 39th Incontro di Grammatica Generativa (IGG 39), Modena and Reggio Emilia, 21–23 Feburary.

Bender, Andrea and Sieghard Beller. 2006. Numeral classifiers and counting systems in Polynesian and Micronesian languages: common roots and cultural adaptations. *Oceanic Linguistics* 45(2): 380–403.

Bisang, Walter. 1993. Classifiers, quantifiers and class nouns in Hmong. *Studies in Language* 17(1): 1–51.

Bisang, Walter. 1999. Classifiers in East and Southeast Asian languages: counting and beyond. In Jadranka Gvozdanović (ed.), *Numeral types and changes worldwide*, 113–185. Berlin & New York: Mouton de Gruyter

Bisang, Walter. 2011. Nominal and verbal classification – why the former is far more widespread than the latter. Paper presented at the Association of Linguistic Typology 9, University of Hong Kong, 21–24 July.

Bisang, Walter. 2012a. Numeral classifiers with plural marking. A challenge to Greenberg. In Dan Xu (ed.), *Plurality and classifiers across languages of China*. Berlin & New York: Mouton de Gruyter.

Bisang, Walter. 2012b. Chinese from a typological perspective. Paper presented at the 4th International Conference on Sinology, Taipei, 20–22 June.

Bloomfield, Leonard. 1933. *Language*. New York: Holt, Rinehart & Winston.

Blühdorn, Hardarik. 2006. Zur Semantik von Numerus und Zählbarkeit im Deutschen. In Grammatische Untersuchungen. Analysen und Ref lexionen, Studien zur deutschen Sprache, vol 36, eds. Eva Breindl, Lutz Gunkel, and Bruno Strecker, 53–77. Tübingen: Gunter Narr.

Bobyleva, Ekaterina. 2011. Variable plural marking in Jamaican Patwa and Tok Pisin: A linguistic perspective. *Canadian Journal of Linguistics* 56(1): 37–60.

Bolinger, Dwight. 1972. *Degree words*. The Hague: Mouton.

Borer, Hagit. 1984. *Parametric syntax: Case studies in semitic and Romance languages*. Dordrecht: Foris.

Borer, Hagit. 1999. Deconstructing the construct. In Kyle Johnson and Ian Roberts (eds.), *Beyond principles and parameters*, 43–89. Dordrecht: Kluwer.

Borer, Hagit. 2005. *In name only*. New York: Oxford University Press.

Borer, Hagit and Sarah Ouwayda. 2010. Playing your Cardinals Right. Paper presented at the Conference on Empirical, Theoretical and Computational Approaches to Countability in Natural Language, Bochum, 22–24 September.

Bošković, Željko. 2012. On the NP/DP parameter, word order, binding relations, and plurality within Chinese NPs. Paper presented at the 13th of the Chinese Languages and Linguistics Symposium, Taipei, 1–3 June.

Bowers, John. 1991. The syntax and semantics of nominals. In *Cornell University Working Papers in Linguistics* 10, 1–30. (Proceedings of the First Semantics and Linguistic Theory Conference.) Department of Modern Languages and Linguistics, Cornell University, Ithaca, NY.

Branigan, Phil. 2011. *Provocative syntax*. Cambridge, MA: MIT Press.

Brattico, Pauli. 2010. One-part and two-part models of nominal case: Evidence from case distribution. *Journal of Linguistics* 46: 47–81.

Bruening, Benjamin. 2010. Language-particular syntactic rules and constraints: English locative inversion and *do*-support. *Language* 86: 43–84.

Bouchard, Denis. 2002. *Adjectives, number and interfaces: Why languages vary*. Oxford: Elsevier Science.

Bunt, Harry C. 1985. *Mass terms and model-theoretic semantics*. Cambridge: Cambridge University Press.

Butler, Lindsay Kay. 2012. Crosslinguistic and experimental evidence for non-number plurals. *Linguistic Variation* 12(1): 27 – 56.

Cable, Seth. 2012. Distance distributivity and plurationality in Tlingit (and beyond). Ms. University of Massachusetts, Amherst.

Cardinaletti, Anna and Giuliana Giusti. 2006. The syntax of quantified phrases and quantitative clitics. In M. Everaert and H. v. Riemsdijk (eds.), *The Blackwell companion to syntax,* V. 5, 23–93. Malden, MA: Blackwell Publishing.

Carstens, Vicki May. 1991. The morphology and syntax of determiner phrases in Kiswahili. University of California, Los Angeles dissertation.

Chao, Wynn. 1988. *On ellipsis*. New York: Garland Publishing, Inc.

Chao, Yuen-Ren. 1948. *Mandarin primer*. Cambridge, MA: Harvard University Press.

Chao, Yuen-Ren. 1968. *A grammar of spoken Chinese*. Berkeley: University of California Press.

Chen, Ping. 2003. Indefinite determiner introducing definite referent: a special use of '*yi* 'one'+classifier' in Chinese. *Lingua* 113: 1169–1184.

Cheng, Chung-Ying. 1973. Comments on Moravcsik's paper. In Jaakko Hintikkia, Julius Moravcsik, and Patrick Suppes (eds.), *Approaches to natural language*, 286–288. Dordrecht: Reidel.

Cheng, Lisa Lai-Shen. 1995. On *dou*-quantification. *Journal of East Asian Linguistics* 4(3): 197–234.

Cheng, Lisa Lai-Shen. 2009. On *every* type of quantificational expression in Chinese. In Monika, Rathert and Anastasia, Giannakidou (eds.), *Quantification, definiteness, and nominalization*, 53–75. Oxford: Oxford University Press.

Cheng, Lisa Lai-Shen. 2012. Counting and classifiers. In Diane Massam (ed.), *Count and mass across languages*, 199–219. Oxford: Oxford University Press.

Cheng, Lisa Lai-Shen and Rint Sybesma. 1998. *Yi-wan tang, yi-ge tang*: Classifiers and massifiers. *Tsing-Hua Journal of Chinese Studies* 28(3): 385–412.

Cheng, Lisa Lai-Shen and Rint Sybesma. 1999. Bare and not so bare nouns and the structure of NP. *Linguistic Inquiry* 30(4): 509–542.

Cheng, Lisa Lai-Shen and Rint Sybesma. 2012. Classifiers and DP. *Linguistic Inquiry* 43(4): 634–650.

Cheng, Lisa Lai-Shen, Jenny Doetjes, and Rint Sybesma. 2008. How universal is the universal grinder? In M. van Koppen and B. Botma (eds.), *Linguistics in the Netherlands* 2008: 50–62. Amsterdam & Philadelphia: John Benjamins.

Cheung, Candice Chi Hang. 2003. An Investigation of the Jingpo Nominal Structure. The Chinese University of Hong Kong MPhil. Thesis.

Cheung, Pierina, Peggy Li, and David Barner. 2010. Individuation and quantification: do bare nouns in Mandarin Chinese individuate? In Clemens, L.E. and C.-M. L. Liu (eds.), *Proceedings of the 22nd North American Conference on Chinese Linguistics (NACCL-22) and the 18th International Conference on Chinese Linguistics (IACL-18)* 2010. Vol 1: 395–412. Cambridge, MA: Harvard University.

Cheung, Pierina, Peggy Li, and David Barner. 2012. *Proceedings of the 34th Annual Cognitive Science Conference*, 210–215. Sapporo: The Cognitive Science Society.

Chien Yu-Chi Barbara Lust, and Chi-Ping Chiang. 2003. Chinese children's comprehension of count-clssifiers and mass-classifiers. *Journal of East Asian Linguistics* 12: 91–120.

Chierchia, Gennaro. 1998. Plurality of mass nouns and the notion of semantic parameter. In Susan Rothstein (ed.), *Events and grammar*, 53–103. Dordrecht: Kluwer.

Chierchia, Gennaro. 2010. Mass nouns, vagueness and semantic variation, *Synthese* 174: 99–149.

Childs, Tucker. 1995. *A grammar of Kisi: a southern Atalantic language*. Berlin & New York: Mouton de Gruyter.

Chomsky, Noam. 1965. *Aspects of the Theory of Syntax*. Cambridge, MA: MIT Press.

Chomsky, Noam. 1970. Remarks on nominalization. In R. A. Jacobs and P. S. Rosenbaum (eds.), *Readings in English Transformational Grammar*: 184–221. Waltham, MA: Ginn-Blaisdell.

Chomsky, Noam. 1994. Bare Phrase Structure. *MIT Occasional Papers in Linguistics 5*. Also in G. Webelhuth (ed.), (1995) *Government and binding theory and the minimalist program*. Oxford: Blackwell.

Chomsky, Noam. 1995. *The Minimalist program*. Cambridge, MA: MIT Press.

Chomsky, Noam. 2000. Minimalist inquiries: The framework. In Roger Martin, David Michaels, and Juan Uriagereka (eds.), *Step by step: Essays on minimalist syntax in honor of Howard Lasnik*, 89–155. Cambridge, MA: MIT Press.

Chomsky, Noam. 2001. Derivation by phase. In Michael Kenstowicz (ed.) *Ken Hale: A life in language*, 1–52. Cambridge, MA: MIT Press.

Cinque, Guglielmo. 1994. On the evidence for partial N-movement in Romance DP. In G. Cinque, J. Koster, J.-Y. Pollock, L. Rizzi and R. Zanuttini (eds.) *Paths towards Universal Grammar*, 85–110. Washington, DC: Georgetown University Press.

Cinque, Guglielmo. 2011. A (partial) map of nominal functinal structure. Paper presented at the Mini-Workshop on Syntax, National Tsing Hua University, Hsinchu, 20 June 20.

Cinque, Guglielmo. 2012. A generalization concerning DP-internal ellipsis. *Iberia: An International Journal of Theoretical Linguistics* 4(1): 174–193.

Cohen, Dana and Anne Zribi-Hertz. 2012. On the lexical OR syntactic sources of *furniture*-types denotations. Paper presented at the colloquim on Mass/Count in Linguistics, Philosophy and Cognitive Science, Paris, 19–21 December.

Colunga, Eliana and Linda B. Smith. 2005. From the lexicon to expectations about kinds: A role for associative learning. *Psychological Review* 112(2): 347–382.

Comrie, Bernard. 1981. *The languages of the Soviet Union*. Cambridge: Cambridge University Press.

Constantinescu, Camelia. 2011. Gradability in the Nominal Domain. Leiden University dissertatioin.

Corbett, Greville G. 2000. *Number*. Cambridge Textbooks in Linguistics. Cambridge: Cambridge University Press.

Cornilescu, Alexandra. 2009. Measure phrases and the syntax of Romanian nouns and adjectives. *Bucharest Working Papers in Linguistics* XI (1): 35–66.

Corver, Norbert. 2009. Getting the (syntactic) measure of Measure Phrases. *The Linguistic Review* 26: 67–134.

Corver, Norbert, Jenny Doetjes, and Joost Zwarts. 2007. Linguistic perspectives on numerical expressions: Introduction. *Lingua* 117(5): 751–757.

Corver, Norbert and Marjo van Koppen. 2011. NP-ellipsis with adjectival remnants: a micro-comparative perspective. *Natural Language and Linguistic Theory* 29(2): 371–421.

Corver, Norbert and Henk van Riemsdijk (eds.). 2001. *Semi-lexical Categories: the Function of Content Words and the Content of Function Words.* Berlin & New York: Mouton de Gruyter.

Corver, Norbert and Joost Zwarts. 2006. Prepositional Numerals. *Lingua* 116(6): 811–835.

Cowper, Elizabeth and Daniel Hall. 2012. Aspects of individuation. In Diane Massam (ed.), *Count and mass across languages, 27–53.* Oxford: Oxford University Press.

Croft, William. 1994. Semantic universals in classifier systems. *Word* 45: 145–171.

Csirmaz, Aniko and Éva Dékány. 2010. Hungarian classifiers. Unpublished manuscript, University of Utah and University of Tromsø.

Dai, Qingxia. 1991. Zangmian yuzu geti-liangci yanjiu. Paper presented at the Fifth International Yi-Burmese Conference, Sichuan, 1–5 August.

Daley, Karen Ann. 1998. *Vietnamese classifiers in narrative texts.* Publication 125. Arlington: Summer Institute of Linguistics and University of Texas.

Dalrymple, Mary and Suriel Mofu. 2012. Plural semantics, reduplication, and numeral modification in Indonesian. *Journal of Semantics* 29(2): 229–260.

Danon, Gabi. 2009. Grammatical number in numeral-noun constructions. Paper presented at the 19th Colloquium on Generative Grammar (CGG-19), Vitoria-Gasteiz, Faculty of Letters (Gradu Aretoa), University of the Basque Country, 1–3 April.

Danon, Gabi. 2011. Agreement and DP-internal feature distribution. *Syntax* 14: 297–317.

Danon, Gabi. 2012. The two structures for numeral-noun constructions. *Lingua* 122: 1282–1307.

Davis, Henry and Lisa Matthewson. 1999. On the Functional Determination of Lexical Categories, *Revue Québécoise de Linguistique* 27: 30–69.

Dayal, Veneeta. 2011. Bangla classifiers: mediating between kinds and objects. Paper presented at the International Workshop on Syntax-Semantics Interface, Academia Sinica, Taipei, 17–18 June.

De Belder, Marijke. 2010. Flavours of n? On the morphosyntax of collective nouns. Paper presented at WCCFL 28, Los Angeles (USC), 12–21 February.

De Belder, Marijke. 2011a. *Roots and affixes: Eliminating lexical categories from syntax.* Utrecht University dissertation.

De Belder, Marijke. 2011b. A morphosyntactic decomposition of countability in Germanic. *The Journal of Comparative Germanic Linguistics* 14(3): 173–202.

Déchaine, Rose-Marie and Meireille Tremblay. 2011. Functional categories: FLN or FLB? Paper presented at GLOW 34, Universität Wien, 28–30 April.

De Clercq, Karen. 2008. Proper names used as Common Nouns in Belgian Dutch and German. In Marjo van Koppen and Bert Botma (eds.), *Linguistics in the Netherlands* 2008, 63–74. Amsterdam & Philadelphia: John Benjamins.

Delsing, Lars-Olof. 1993. The internal structure of noun phrases. University of Lund dissertation.

Denny, J. P. 1986. The semantic roles of classifiers. In C. G. Craig (ed.), *Noun Classes and Categorization: Proceedings of a Symposium on Categorization and Noun Classification, Eugene, October 1983*, 297–308. Amsterdam & Philadelphia: John Benjamins.

Deprez, Viviane. 2005. Morphological number, semantic number, and bare nouns. *Lingua* 115: 857–883.

Deprez, Viviane. 2006. On the Conceptual Role of Number. In Nishida, Chiyo and Jean-Pierre Y. Montreuil (eds.), *New perspectives on Romance linguistics*, 67–83. Amsterdam & Philadelphia: John Benjamins.

Di Sciullo, Anna Maria and Edwin Williams. 1987. *On the definition of word*, Cambridge, MA: MIT Press.

Dimmendaal, G. J. 1983. *The Turkana Language* (Publications in African Languages and Linguistics 2). Dordrecht: Foris.

Dixon, R. M. W. 1982. *Where have all the adjectives gone? and other essays in semantics and syntax*. Berlin: Mouton.

Doetjes, Jenny. 1996. Mass and count: syntax or semantics? In *Proceedings of Meaning on the HIL* (*HIL Occasional Papers in Linguistics* 1), 34–52. HIL/Leiden University.

Doetjes, Jenny. 1997. *Quantifiers and Selection*. Leiden University dissertation.

Doetjes, Jenny. 2010. Count/mass mismatches in the lexicon. Paper presented at the Conference on Empirical, Theoretical and Computational Approaches to Countability in Natural Language, Bochum, 22–24 September.

Doetjes, Jenny. 2012. Count/mass distinctions across languages. In Claudia Maienborn, Klaus von Heusinger and Paul Portner (eds.) *Semantics: an international handbook of natural language meaning*, Vol. 3: 2559–2580. Berlin & New York: Mouton de Gruyter.

Downing, Pamela. 1996. *Numeral classifier systems: The case of Japanese*. Amsterdam & Philadelphia: John Benjamins.

Dowty, David. 1979. *Word meaning and grammar*. Dordrecht: Reidel.

Dowty, David. 1991. Thematic Proto-Roles and Argument Selection, *Language* 67(3): 547–619.

Dryer, Matthew S. 2005. Coding of nominal plurality. In Martin Haspelmath, Matthew S. Dryer, David Gil, and Bernard Comrie (eds.) *The world atlas of language structures*, 138–141. Oxford: Oxford University Press.

Du, Yongdao. 1993. Beijing-hua zhong de 'yi+N' [Yi+N in the Beijing dialect]. *Zhongguo Yuwen* 233: 142.

Ducceschi, Luca. 2012. Bound variable and deictic pronouns in some languages of India. Paper presented at Console 20, Leipzig, 5–7 January.

Duffield, Nigel. 1995. *Particles and projections in Irish syntax*. Dordrecht: Kluwer.

Duffield, Nigel. 1996. On structural invariance and lexical diversity in VSO languages: Arguments from Irish noun phrases. In Ian Roberts and Robert Borsley (eds.), *The syntax of the Celtic languages*, 314–340. Cambridge: Cambridge University Press.

Erbaugh, Mary S. 1986. Taking Stock: The Development of Chinese Noun Classifiers Historically and in Young Children. In Colette Craig (ed.) *Noun classes
and categorization: Proceedings of a symposium on categorization and noun
classification. Eugene, Oregon, October 1983*, 399–436. Amsterdam & Philadelphia: John Benjamins.

Espinal, M. Teresa. 2010. Bare nominls in Catalan and Spanish. Their structure
and meaning. *Lingua* 120: 984–1009.

Espinal, M. Teresa and Louise McNally. 2011. Bare nominals and incorporating
verbs in Sparish and Catalan. *Journal of Linguistics* 47: 87–128.

Fan, Jiyan. 1958. Xing-ming zuhe jian de-zi de yufa zuoyong [the grammatical function of *de* in the adjective-noun combination], *Zhongguo Yuwen* 71: 213–217.

Fang, Fuxi. 1985. 4–6 sui ertong zhangwo Hanyu liangci shuiping de shiyan yanjiu
[an experiment on the use of classifiers by 4-to-6-year-olds], *Acta Psychologica
Sinica* 17: 384–392.

Farkas, Donka and Henriëtte de Swart. 2003. *The semantics of incorporation: From
argument structure to discourse transparency*. Stanford, CA: CSLI Publications.

Fassi Fehri, Abdelkader. 2004. Nominal classes, references, and functional parameters, with particular reference to Arabic. *Linguistic Variation Yearbook* 4: 41–108.

Feigenson, Lisa, Susan Carey, and Marc Hauser. 2002. The representations under-
lying infants' choice of more: Object-files versus analog magnitudes. *Psychological Science* 13: 150–156.

Fodor, Janet and Ivan Sag. 1982. Referential and quantificational indefinites. *Linguistics and Philosophy* 5: 355–298.

Fortin, Antonio. 2011. *The morphology and semantics of expressive affixes*. University of Oxford dissertation.

Gao, Mingkai. 1948. *Hanyu Yufa Lun* [On Chinese grammar], Shanghai: Shangwu
Press.

Gebhardt, Lewis. 2009. *Numeral classifiers and the structure of DP*. Northwestern
University dissertation

Gebhardt, Lewis. 2011. Classifiers are functional. *Linguisti Inquiry* 42(1): 125–130.

Gerner, Matthias. 2003. Demonstratives, articles and topic markers in the Yi group.
Journal of Pragmatics 35(7): 947–998.

Gerner, Matthias. 2006. Noun classifiers in Kam and Chinese Kam-Tai languages:
their morphosyntax, semantics and history. *Journal of Chinese Linguistics*
34(2): 237–305.

Gerner, Matthias. 2010. Compositional and constructional reduplication in Kam-
Tai languages. *Folia Linguistica* 44(2): 267–337.

Gerner, Matthias and Walter Bisang. 2008. Inflectional speaker-role classifiers in
Weining Ahmao. *Journal of Pragmatics* 40: 719–732.

Gerner, Matthias and Walter Bisang. 2010. Classifier declinations in an isolating language: on a rarity in Weining Ahmao. *Language and Linguistics* 11: 579–623.

Geurts, Bart. 1997. Good news about the description theory of names. *Journal of
Semantics* 14: 319–348.

Ghaniabadi, Saeed. 2012. Plural marking beyond count nouns. In Diane Massam (ed.), *Count and Mass Across Languages,* 112–128. Oxford: Oxford University Press.

Ghomeshi, Jila. 2003. Plural marking, indefiniteness, and the noun phrase. *Studia Linguistica* 57(2): 47–74.

Gil, David. 1994. Numeral Classifiers: An E-mail Conversation. In F. Plank (ed.), *Conversations on Noun Phrases, EUROTYP Working Papers*, Series 7, Number 20, 1–30. Berlin: The European Science Foundation, EUROTYP Programme.

Gil, David. 2008. Numeral Classifiers. In Martin Haspelmath, Matthew S. Dryer, David Gil, and Bernard Comrie (eds.), *The World Atlas of Language Structures Online*, Max Planck Digital Library, Munich, Chapter 55.

Gillon, Brendan S. 2012. Mass terms. *Philosophy Compass* 7(10): 712–730.

Goodman, Nelson. 1966. *The structure of appearence* (2nd ed.). Indianapolis: Bobbs-Merrill.

Göksel, Asli and Celia Kerslake. 2005. *Turkish: A comprehensive grammar*. London & New York: Routledge.

Görgülü, Emrah. 2010. Nominals and the count/mass distinction in Turkish. In *the Proceedings of the 26th Northwest Linguistics Conference*, May 8–9 2010, Vancouver, British Columbia: Simon Fraser University.

Graham, Angus Charles. 1989. *Disputers of the Tao*. Open Court, La Salle, Ill.

Greenberg, Joseph, 1974. Numeral classifiers and substantival number: Problems in the genesis of a linguistic type. In *Proceedings of the 11th International Congress of Linguists, Bologna/Florence, August–September 1972*, 17–37.

Greenberg, Joseph. 1990a [1972]. Numeral classifiers and substantival number: problems in the genesis of a linguistic type. In Keith Denning and Suzanne Kemmer (eds.) *On Language: selected writings of Johseph Greenberg*, 166–193, Stanford: Stanford University Press [first published 1972 in *Working Papers on Language Universals* 9: 2–39].

Greenberg, Joseph. 1990b [1975]. Dynamic aspects of word order in the numeral classifier. In K. Denning and S. Kemmer (eds.), *On language: Selected writings of Joseph H. Greenberg*, 227–240. Stanford: Stanford University Press [First published 1975 in *Word order and word order change*, C. Li (ed.), 27–43. Austin: University of Texas Press].

Grimshaw, Jane. 1990. *Argument structure*. Cambridge, MA: MIT Press.

Grimshaw, Jane. 2007. Boxes and Piles and What's in Them: Two Extended Projections or One? In Annie Zaenen, Jane Simpson, Tracy Holloway King, Jane Grlmshaw, Joan Mallng, and Chris Manning (eds.), *Architectures, rules, and preferences: Variations on themes by Joan Bresnan*, 199–206, Center for the Study of Language and Information Publications.

Grinevald, Colette. 2000. A morphosyntactic typology of classifiers. In G. Senft (ed.), *Systems of Nominal Classification*, 50–92. Cambridge: Cambridge University Press.

Grinevald, Colette. 2002. Making sense of nominal classification systems: noun classifiers and grammaticalization variable. In Ilse Wischer and Gabriele Diewald (eds.), *New reflections on grammaticalization*, 259–275. Amsterdam & Philadelphia: John Benjamins.

Guo, Jimao. 1999. Zai tan liangci chongdie xingshi de yufa yiyi [Revisit the grammatical meaning of classifier reduplication], *Hanyu Xuexi* 8(4): 6–9.

Guthrie, Malcolm. 1948. Gender, number and person in Bantu languages. *Bulletin of the School of Oriental and African Studies*, University of London 12: 847–856.

Haas, Mary R. 1942. The use of numeral classifiers in Thai. *Language* 18: 201–205.

Hankamer, Jorge. 1971. *Constraints on deletion in syntax*. New York: Garland Publishing, Inc.

Hankamer, Jorge. 1973. Unacceptable ambiguity. *Linguistic Inquiry* 4: 17–68.

Hansen, Chad. 1972. *Philosophy of language and logic in ancient China*. University of Michigan dissertation.

Harbour, Daniel. 2008. Mass, non-singularity, and augmentation. *MIT Working Papers in Linguistics* 49: 239–266.

Harbour, Daniel. 2011. Valence and atomic number. *Linguistic Inquiry* 42: 561–594.

Hartman, Jeremy. 2011. The semantics uniformity of traces: evidence form ellipsis parallelim. *Linguistic Inquiry* 42: 367–388.

Her, One-Soon. 2012. Structure of classifiers and measure words: a lexical functional account. *Language and Linguistics* 13: 1211–1251.

Her, One-Soon and Chen-Tien Hsieh. 2010. On the semantic distinction between classifiers and measure words in Chinese. *Language and Linguistics* 11(3): 527–551.

Herrity, Peter. 2000. *Slovene: A comprehensive grammar*. New York: Routledge.

Higginbotham, James. 1985. On semantics. *Linguistic Inquiry* 16: 647–593.

Hsieh, Miao-Ling. 2008. *The internal structure of noun phrases in Chinese*. Taipei: Crane Publishing Co.

Hu, Qian. 1993. *The Acquisition of Chinese Classifiers by Young Mandarin-Speaking Children*, Boston University dissertation.

Huang, Aijun. 2009. Count-mass distinction and the acquisition of classifiers in Mandarin-speaking children. Chinese University of Hong Kong MA thesis.

Huang, Aijun and Thomas Hun-tak, Lee. 2009. Quantification and individuation in the acquisition of Chinese classifiers. In Yukio Otsu (ed.), *Proceedings of the Tenth Tokyo Conference on Psycholinguistics*, Tokyo: Hituzi.

Huang, Cheng-Teh James. 1987. Existential sentences in Chinese and (in)definiteness. In Reuland, Eric and Alice ter Meulen (eds.), *The Representation of (In)definiteness*, 226–253. Cambridge, MA: MIT Press.

Huang, Cheng-Teh James. 2009. Lexical decomposition, silent categories, and the localizer phrase, *Yuyanxue Luncong* 39, Beijing: Shangwu Press, 86–122.

Huang, Cheng-Teh James, Yen-hui Audrey Li, and Yafei Li. 2009. *The Chinese syntax*. Cambridge: Cambridge University Press.

Huang, Cheng-Teh James and Masao Ochi. 2012. Remarks on classifiers and nominal structures in East Asian. *Peaches and Plums*, Taipei: Academia Sinica.

Huang, Chu-Ren. 1989. *Mandarin Chinese NP de -A Comparative Study of Current Grammatical Theories*. Nankang, Taipei (Cornell University 1987 dissertation).

Huang, Chu-Ren and Kathleen Ahrens. 2003. Individuals, kinds and events: classifier coercion of nouns. *Language Sciences* 25: 353–373.

Huang, Hansheng. 1981. *Xiandai Hanyu* [Modern Chinese], Shumu Wenxian Press.

Huang, Zaijun. 1964. Cong jiawen jinwen liangci de yingyong kaocha hanyu liangci de qiyuan yu fazhan [A study of the origin and development of classifiers in Chinese from the perspectives of the use of classifiers in oracle bones and bronze inscriptions]. *Zhongguo Yuwen* 1964(6): 432–441.

Huddleston, Rodney and Geoffrey Pullum. 2002. *The Cambridge grammar of the English language*. Cambridge: Cambridge University Press.

Hundius, Harald and Ulrike Kölver. 1983. Syntax and semantics of numeral classifiers in Thai. *Studies in Language* 7(2): 165–214.

Huntley-Fenner, Gavin, Susan Carey, and Andrea Solimando. 2002. Objects are individuals but stuff doesn't count: Perceived rigidity and cohesiveness influence infants' representations of small groups of discrete entities. *Cognition* 85: 203–221.

Hurford, James. 1975. *The linguistic theory of numerals*. Cambridge: Cambridge University Press.

Hurford, James. 1987. *Language and Number*. Oxford: Blackwell.

Iida, Takashi. 1998. Professor Quine on Japanese Classifiers. *The Annals of the Japan Association for Philosophy of Science* 9(3): 111–118.

Ikoro, Suanu M. 1994. Numeral classifiers in Kana. *Journal of African Languages and Linguistics* 15: 7–28.

Ikoro, Suanu M. 1996. *The Kana language*. Leiden: Research School CNWS.

Iljik, Robert. 1994. Quantification in Mandarin Chinese: two markers of plurality. *Linguistics* 32: 91–116.

Iljik, Robert. 2001. The problem of the suffix -men in Chinese grammar. *Journal of Chinese Linguistics* 29(1): 11–68.

Inagaki, Shunji and David Barner. 2009. Countability in absence of count syntax: Evidence from Japanese quantity judgments, in Makiko Hirakawa et al. (eds.), *Studies in Language Sciences (8): Papers from the Eighth Annual Conference of the Japanese Society for Language Sciences*. Tokyo: Kurosio.

Jackendoff, Ray. 1977. *X-bar syntax: a study of phrase structure*. Cambridge, MA: MIT Press.

Jackendoff, Ray. 1991. Parts and boundaries. *Cognition* 41: 9–45.

Jackendoff, Ray. 1997. *The architecture of the language faculty*. Cambridge, MA: MIT Press.

Jackendoff, Ray. 2008. *Construction after construction* and its theoretical challenges. *Language* 84(1): 8–28.

Jespersen, Otto. 1961 [1909]. *A Modern English Grammar on Historical Principles.* John Dickens and Company, Northampton, England. Seven Volumes (originally published in 1909).

Jespersen, Otto. 1924. *The philosophy of grammar*, London: Allen and Unwin.

Jiang, Li Julie and Suhua Hu. 2010. On bare classifier phrases. *Proceedings of the 18th meeting of the International Association of Chinese Linguistics and the 22rd meeting of the North American Conference on Chinese Linguistics*, 230–241.

Jin, Youjing. 1979. Putonghua yi zi shengdiao de dufa [the tone variations of *yi* in Mandarin], *Zhongguo Yuwen* 1979(5): 356–358.

Jing, Song. 1995. Beijing kouyu zhong liangci de tuoluo [the drop of classifiers in Beijing dialect], *Xue Hanyu* 1998(8): 13–14.

Joosten, Frank. 2003. Accounts of the Count-Mass Distinction: A Critical Survey. *Nordlyd* 31(1): 216–229.

Kayne, Richard. 2005a. *Movement and silence*. Oxford: Oxford University Press.

Kayne, Richard. 2005b. Some notes on comparative syntax, with special reference to English and French. In Guglielmo Cinque and Richard S. Kayne (eds.), *The Oxford handbook of comparative syntax*, 3–69, New York: Oxford University Press.

Kayne, Richard. 2012a. A Note on *Grand* and its Silent Entourage. *Stdies in Chinese Linguistics* 33(2): 71–85.

Kayne, Richard. 2012b. Comparative syntax. *Lingua* (to appear).

Kennedy, Chris. 1997. *Projecting the adjective: the syntax and semantics of gradability and comparison*. New York: Garland.

Khachaturyan, Maria. 2012. Plurals in Mano: from nominal number to counter-expectation meaning. The 45th Annual Meeting of the Societas Linguistica Europaea, University of Stockholm, 29 August–1 September.

Kim, Jaeshil. 2005. *Plurality in classifier languages*. University of California, Irvine dissertation.

Kishimoto, Hideki. 2011. Empty verb support as a morphological adjustment rule. *Snippets* 23: 7–8.

Kiss, Tibor. 2010. Introduction to the Conference. Paper presented at the Conference on Empirical, Theoretical and Computational Approaches to Countability in Natural Language, Bochum, 22–24 September.

Kobuchi-Philip, Mana. 2007. Individual-denoting classifiers. *Natural Language Semantics* 15: 95–130.

Kobuchi-Philip, Mana. 2011. The mass hypothesis and Japanese. In Young-Wha Kim (ed.), *Plurality in Classifier Languages: Plurality, Mass/Kind, Classifiers and the DPs*, 283–321. Seoul: Hankukmunhwasa.

Koptjevskaja-Tamm, Maria. 2009. A lot of grammar with a good portion of lexicon: towards a typology of partitive and pseudo-partitive nominal constructions. In Johannes Helmbrecht, Yoko Nishina, Yong-Min Shin, Stavros Skopeteas, and Elizabeth Verhoeven (eds.) *Form and Function in Language Research*, 329–346. Berlin & New York: Mouton de Gruyter.

Kratzer, Angelika. 2008. On the plurality of verbs. In Johannes Dölling, Tatjana Heyde-Zybatow, and Martin Schäfer (eds.), *Language Context and Cognition*, 269–299. Berlin & New York: Mouton de Gruyter.

Krifka, Manfred. 1989. Nominalreferenz und Zeitkonstitution. Zur Semantik von Massentermen, Pluraltermen und Aspektklassen, Wilhelm Fink, München.

Krifka, Manfred. 1995. Common nouns: a contrastive analysis of Chinese and English. In G. N. Carlson and F. J. Pelletier (eds.), *The generic book*, 398–411. Chicago: Chicago University Press.

Krifka, Manfred. 2007. Masses and countables. Paper presented at the workshop on the Syntax and Semantics of Measurement, University of Tromsø, 17–18 September.

Krifka, Manfred. 2008. Different kinds of count nouns and plurals. Handout distributed at Syntax in the World's Languages III, Freie Universität Berlin, Sept. 25–28, 2008.

Kuo, Grace and Kristine Yu. 2012. Taiwan Mandarin quantifiers. In Edward Keenan and Denis Paperno (eds.), *Handbook of quantifiers in natural language*, 647–698. Dordrecht: Springer.

Kuo, Yi-chun and Jiun-Shiung Wu. 2010. Countability in English and Mandarin. In Dingfang Shu and Ken Turner (eds.), *Contrasting Meaning in Language of the East and West*, 493–515. Pieterlen: Peter Lang.

Kung, Susan. 2007. Numeral Classifiers in Lhiimaqalhqama. In Frederick Hoyt, Nikki Seifert, Alexandra Teodorescu, and Jessica White (vol. eds.) and Stephen Wechsler (series ed.), *Texas Linguistics Society 9: Morphosyntax of Underrepresented Languages*, 185–201. CSLI Publications.

Landman, Fred. 2004. *Indefinites and the types of sets*. Malden, MA: Blackwell.

Law, Paul. 2012. Silent nouns in English, Chinese and Naxi. *Stdies in Chinese Linguistics* 33(2): 103–122.

Le Corre, Mathieu and Susan Carey. 2007. One, two, three, four, nothing more: An investigation of the conceptual sources of the verbal counting principles. *Cognition* 105: 395–438.

Lee, Thomas Hun-tak. 2012. Quantificational structures in three-year-old Chinese-speaking children. In Dan Xu (ed.). *Plurality and Classifiers across Languages of China*. Berlin & New York: Mouton de Gruyter.

Lehmann, Christian. 2008. On the function of numeral classifiers. In Floricic, Franck (ed.), *Essais de linguistique générale et de typologie linguistique*, 1–9. Paris: Presses de l'École Normale Supérieure.

Lehrer, Adrienne. 1986. English classifier constructions. *Lingua* 68: 109–148.

Levinson, Lisa. 2010. Arguments for pseudo-resultative predicates. *Natural Language and Linguistic Theory* 28(1): 135–182.

Li, Bingzhen. 2009. Liangzhong biao fei-yuqi-jieguo-yi jiegou de bijiao [Comparison between two constructions referring to unexpected results], *Yuyan Kexue* 8(2): 188–196.

Li, Charles and Sandra Thompson. 1981. *Mandarin Chinese: A functional reference grammar*. Berkeley: University of California Press.

Li, Jinxi. 1924 [1955/1992]. *Xinzhu Guoyu Wenfa* [A new Chinese grammar], Beijing: The Commercial Press.

Li, Jinxi and Shiru Liu. 1978. *Lun xiandai Hanyu zhong de liangci* [On classifiers in Modern Chinese]. Beijing: Commercial Press.

Li, Peggy, David Barner, and Becky Huang. 2008. Classifiers as count syntax: Individuation and measurement in the acquisition of Mandarin Chinese. *Language Learning and Development*, 4(4): 249–290.

Li, Peggy, Yarrow Dunham, and Susan Caray. 2009a. Of substance: the nature of language effects on entity construal. *Cognitive Psychology* 58: 487–524.

Li, Peggy, Tamiko Ogura, David Barner, Shu-Ju Yang, and Susan Carey. 2009b. Does the conceptual distinction between singular and plural sets depend on language? *Developmental Psychology* 45: 1644–1653.

Li, Peggy, Becky Huang, and Yaling Hsiao. 2010. Learning that classifiers count: Mandarin-speaking children's acquisition of sortal and mensural classifiers. *Journal of East Asian Linguistics* 19: 207–230.

Li, XuPing. 2011a. *On the semantics of classifiers in Chinese*. Bar-Ilan University dissertation.

Li, XuPing. 2011b. A phrasal-level diminutive marker /tsiʔ/ in Gan Chinese. Paper presented at the 7th Conference of the European Association of Chinese Linguistics (EACL-7), Venice, 13–15 September.

Li, XuPing and Walter Bisang. 2012. Classifiers in Sinitic languages: From individuation to definiteness marking. *Lingua* 122: 335–355.

Li, XuPing and Susan Rothstein. 2012. Measure readings of Mandarin classifier phrases and the particle *de*. *Language and Linguistics* 13(4): 693–741.

Li, Yen-hui Audrey. 1992. Indefinite wh in mandarin chinese wh words, *Journal of East Asian Linguistics* 1: 125–155.

Li, Yen-hui Audrey. 1998. Argument Determiner Phrases and Number Phrases, *Linguistic Inquiry* 29: 693–702.

Li, Yen-hui Audrey. 1999. Plurality in a classifier language. *Journal of East Asian Linguistics* 8: 75–99.

Li, Yen-hui Audrey. 2012. *de* in Mandarin ↔ *e* in Taiwanese. *Studies in Chinese Linguistics* 33(1): 17–40.

Li, Yu-ming. 2000. Lianchi yu shuci, mingci de nujie [the interactions among classifiers, numerals, and nouns], *Yuyan jiaoxue yu yanjiu* 2000(3): 50–58.

Liao, Wei-wen Roger and Yuyun Iris Wang. 2011. Multiple-Classifiers Construction and Nominal Expressions in Chinese. *Journal of East Asian Linguistics* 20: 145–168.

Lichtenberk, Frantisek. 1983. *A Grammar of Manam* (Oceanic Linguistics Special Publication 18). Honolulu: University of Hawaii Press.

Lima, Suzi. 2010. Bare nouns and plurality in Yudja: mass nouns and the signature property. Paper presented at the Conference on Empirical, Theoretical and Computational Approaches to Countability in Natural Language, Bochum, 22–24 September.

Lima, Suzi. 2012. The count/mass distinction in Yudja (Tupi): quantity judgment studies. Paper presented at the colloquium on Mass/Count in Linguistics, Philosophy and Cognitive Science, Paris, 19–21 December.

Lin, Jo-wang. 1997. Noun phrase structure m Mandarin Chinese: DP or NP? *Chinese Languages and Linguistics* 3: 401–434.

Link, Godehard. 1983. The logical analysis of plural and mass terms: A lattice theoretic approach. In R. Bäuerle, C. Schwarze, and A. von Stechow (eds.), *Meaning, use and interpretation of language*, 302–323. Berlin & New York: Mouton de Gruyter.

Link, Godehard. 1991. Quantity and Number. In D. Zaefferer (ed.), *Semantic Universals and Universal Semantics*, 133–149. Foris.

Liu, Charles. 1980. Measure for verb. *Journal of Chinese Teachers Association* 15(1): 2–40.

Liu, Feng-hsi. 2010. Quantification and the count-mass distinction. Paper presented at IACL-18 & NACCL-22, Harvard University, 20–22 May.

Liu, Hongyong. 2006. The Structure of Complex Nominals: Classifiers, Possessives and Relatives. the Chinese University of Hong Kong dissertation.

Liu, Shiru. 1965. *Wei-Jin Nanbei-chao Liangci Yanjiu* [A Study of Classifiers of the Weijin and Northern and Southern Dynasties], Zhonghua Shuju, Beijing.

Liu, Yue-Hua, Wen-Yu Pan and Hua Gu. 2004. *Shiyong Xiandai Hanyu Yufae* [modern Chinese grammar], Beijing: Shangwu Press.

Lobeck, Anne. 1987. *Syntactic constraints on VP ellipsis*. Seattle: University of Washington dissertation.

Lobeck, Anne. 1995. *Ellipsis: functional heads, licensing, and identification*. Oxford: Oxford University Press.

Loke, Kit-ken. 1994. Is *GE* merely a general classifier? *Journal of Chinese Language Teachers' Association* 29(3): 35–50.

Loke, Kit-ken. 1997. The grammaticalization and regrammaticalization of Chinese numeral classifier morphemes. *Journal of Chinese Linguistics* 25: 1–20.

Long, Tao and Qingzhu Ma. 2008. Duliang-hengliang ci de yuyi gongneng yanjiu [A study of the semantic functions of measure words]. *Zhongguo Yuyanxue Bao* 13: 32–43.

Longobardi, Giuseppe. 1994. Proper names and the theory of N-movement in syntax and logical form, *Linguistic Inquiry* 25: 609–665.

Lu, Jianming. 1987. Shuliangci zhongjian charu xingrongci qingkuang kaocha. [A survey of the insertion of adjectives between numerals and classifiers]. *Yuyan jiaoxue yu yanjiu* 1987(4): 53–72.

Lu, Zhiwei. 1951. *Beijinghua danyinci cihui* [Monosyllabic words in Beijing dialect]. Beijing: Renmin Chubanshe.

Lü, Shuxiang. 1942. *Zhongguo Wenfa Yaolue* [Outling of Chinese Grammar], Shanghai: Shangwu Press.

Lü, Shuxiang. 1983. *Lü Shuxiang Lunwenji* [Lü Shuxiang's works], Shangwu Press.

Lü, Shuxiang. 1990 [1944]. Ge-zi de yingyong fanwei, fulun danweici qian yi-zi de tuoluo [the uses of *ge* and omission of *yi* before classifiers]. In *Lü Shuxiang Wenji* [Collected works of Lü Shuxiang] 2, 144–175. Beijing: Shangwu Press.

Lü, Shuxiang et al. 1999. *Xiandai Hanyu Babai Ci* [800 Words in Chinese]. Beijing: Shangwu Press (1st edition, 1980).

Lü, Shuxiang et al. 2002. *Xiandai Hanyu cidian* [modern Chinese dictionary]. Beijing: Shangwu Press (1st edition, 1978).

Lucy, John. 1992. *Grammatical categories and cognition*. Cambridge: Cambridge University Press.

Luo, Yuanlin. 1988. Guanyu shuliangci zhongjian charu xingrongci qingkuang de buchong kaocha. [A supplement study of the insertion of adjectives before classifiers]. *Hanyu xuexi* 1988(4): 7–12.

Lyons, John. 1977. *Semantics*. Vol. 2. Cambridge: Cambridge University Press.

Massam, Diane. 2001. Pseudo noun incorporation in Niuean. *Natural Language and Linguistic Theory* 19: 153–197.

Massam, Diane. 2009. On the separation and relatedness of classifiers, number, and individuation in Niuean. *Language and Linguistics* 10(4): 669–699.

Mathieu, Eric. 2012a. On the mass/count distinction in Ojibwe. In Diane Massam (ed.), *Count and Mass Across Languages,* 172–198. Oxford: Oxford University Press.

Mathieu, Eric. 2012b. Flavors of Division. *Linguistic Inquiry* 43: 650–679.

Matushansky, Ora. 2006. Head Movement in Linguistic Theory. *Linguistic Inquiry* 37: 69–109.

McCawley, James D. 1979 [1975]. Lexicography and the mass-count distinction, 1975 *Berkeley Linguistics Society*, 1: 314–321; reprinted in McCawley, J. D. 1979. *Adverbs, Vowels, and Other Objects of Wonder*, 165–173. Chicago: The University of Chicago Press.

McKinney-Bock, Katy. 2010. Adjective Ordering Restrictions: Exploring Relevant Semantic Notions for Syntactic Ordering. In *Proceedings of the Arizona Linguistics Circle 3*.

McNally, Louise. To appear. Modification. In M. Aloni and P. Dekker (eds.) *Cambridge Handbook of Semantics*. Cambridge: Cambridge University Press.

Merchant, Jason. 2001. *The syntax of silence: sluicing, islands, and identity in ellipsis*. Oxford: Oxford University Press.

Miao, Xiaochun and Manshu Zhu. 1992. Language development in Chinese children. In H. C. Chen and O. J. L. Tzeng (eds.), *Language Processing in Chinese*, 237–276. Amsterdam and New York: North-Holland.

Mizuguchi, Shinobu. 2004. *Individuation in numeral classifier languages*. Tokyo: Shohakusha.

Moltmann, Friedrike. 2004. Two kinds of universals and two kinds of collections. *Linguistics and Philosophy* 27(6): 739–776.

Moltmann, Friedrike. 2012. Plural reference and reference to a plurality. A reassessment of the linguistic facts, Ms. IHPST (Paris1/CNRS/ENS).

Moltmann, Friedrike. 2013. Proper names, sortals, and the mass-count distinction. http://www.semanticsarchive.net/cgi-bin/browse.pl?search=Moltmann (accessed 13 Feburary 2013).

Morzycki, Marcin. 2009. Degree modification of gradable nouns: size adjectives and adnominal degree morphemes. *Natural Language Semantics* 17(2): 175–203.

Müller, Ana, Luciana Storto, and Thiago Coutinho-Silva. 2006. Number and the mass/count distinction in Karitiana. In Workshop on Structure and Constituency in Languages of the Americas, Vol. 11, 122–135. Vancouver: *UBC Working Papers in Linguistics*.

Munn, Alan and Cristina Schmitt. 2005. Number and indefinites. *Lingua* 115: 821–855.

Muromatsu, Keiko. 2003. Classifiers and the count/mass distinction. In Y.-H. Audrey Li and Andrew Simpson (eds.) *Functional structure(s), form and interpretation*, 65–128. London: Routledge Curzon.

Myers, James. 2000. Rules vs. analogy in Mandarin classifier selection. *Language and Linguistics* 1(2): 187–209.

Myers, James and Jane Tsay. 2000. The Acquisition of the default classifier in Taiwanese, *Proceedings of the International Symposium on Chinese Languages and Linguistics* 7: 87–106.

Ndayiragije, Juvenal and Emmanuel Nikema. 2011. Why classifiers are not determiners: from Chinese to Bantu. Paper presented at the Fifth International Conference on Formal Linguistics, Guangzhou, 10–12 December.

Ojeda, Almerindo E. 2005. The paradox of mass plurals. In Salikok Mufwene and et al. (eds.) *Polymorphous linguistics*, 389–410. Cambridge, MA: MIT Press.

Ōta, Tatsuo. 1958. *Chūgokugo rekishi bunpo* [A historical grammar of modern Chinese, *Tokyo:* Konan shoin], [Chinese translation by S. Jiang and C. Xu, *zhōngguóyǔ lìshǐ wénfǎ*, 2003. Beijing University Press: Beijing].

Ott, Dennis. 2011. Diminutive-formation in German: Spelling out the classifier analysis. *Journal of Comparative Germanic Linguistics* 14: 1–46.

Paris, Marie-Claude. 1981. *Problèmes de syntaxe et de sémantique en linguistique chinose*. Paris: Collège de France.

Partee, Barbara. 1989. Many Quantifiers. In Joyce Powers and Kenneth de Jong (eds.), *Proceedings of the 5th Eastern States Conference on Linguistics*, 383–402. Columbus: Ohio State University.

Partee, Barbara. 1995. Quantificational Structures and Compositionality. In E. Bach, E. Jelinek, A. Kratzer, and B. H. Partee (eds.), *Quantification in Natural Languages*, 541–601. Dordrecht: Kluwer Academic Publishers.

Partee, Barbara and Vladimir Borschev. 2012. Sortal, relational, and functional interpretations of nouns and Russian container constructions. *Journal of Semantics* 29: 445–486.

Paul, Waltraud. 2010. Adjectives in Mandarin Chinese: The rehabilitation of a much ostracized category. In Patricia Cabredo-Hofherr and Ora Matushansky (eds.), *Adjectives. Formal analyses in syntax and semantics*, 115–152. Amsterdam & Philadelphia: John Benjamins.

Pearce, Elizabeth. 2007. Number within the DP: the view from Oceanic. Manuscript. Wellington: Victoria University of Wellington.

Pelletier, Francis. 1975. Non-singular reference: some prelimiaries. *Philosophia* 5(4): 451–465. Reprinted in F. J. Pelletier (ed.), *Mass terms: some philosophical problems*, 1–14. Dordrecht: Reidel, 1979.

Pelletier, Francis. 1979. Non-singular reference. In Francis Pelletier (ed.) *Mass terms: Some philosophical problems*, 1–14. Dordrecht: Kluwer Academic Publishers.

Peyraube, Alain. 1998. On history of classifiers in Archaic and Medieval Chinese. In Benjamin K. T'sou (ed.) *Studia Linguistica Serica*, 39–68. Kowloon Tong: City University of Hong Kong.

Piriyawiboon, Nattaya. 2010. *Classifiers and determiner-less languages: the case of Thai*. University of Toronto dissertation.

Platzack, Christer. 2010. Head Movement as a Phonological Operation, LingBuzz/ 001111.

Polio, Charlene. 1994. Non-native speakers' use of nominal classifiers in Mandarin Chinese. *Journal of the Chinese Language Teachers Association* 29: 51–66.

Pollock, Jean-Yves. 1989. Verb movement, Universal Grammar and the structure of IP. *Linguistic Inquiry* 20: 365–424.

Portner, Paul. 2005. *What is meaning? fundamentals of formal semantics*. Malden, MA: Blackwell Publishing.

Postal, Paul. 2002. The structure of one type of American English vulgar minimizer. In *Skeptical linguistic essays*. New York: Oxford University Press.

Qian, Narong et al. 2002. *Xiandai Hanyu Gailun* [introduction to Modern Chinese], Taipei: Shida Shuyuan Publisher.

Quine, Willard Van Orman. 1960. *Word and Object,* Cambridge, MA: MIT Press.

Quine, Willard Van Orman. 1969. *Ontological relativity and other essays*. New York: Columbia University Press.

Ramchand, Gillian. 2008. Lexical items in complex predications: selection as underassociation, *Tromsø Working Papers on Language and Linguistics: Nordlyd* 35: 115–141.

Ratliff, Martha. 1991. Cov, the underspecified noun, and syntactic flexibility in Hmong. *Journal of the American Oriental Society* 111(4): 694–703.

Rijkhoff, Jan. 1999. When can a language have adjectives? An implicational universal. In Petra M. Vogel and Bernard Comrie (eds.), *Approaches to the typology of word classes*, 217–257. Berlin & New York: Mouton de Gruyter.

Rijkhoff, Jan. 2002. *The Noun Phrase*. New York: Oxford University Press.

Rijkhoff, Jan. 2012. A functional-typological account of NP-clause parallels. Paper presented at the 45th Annual Meeting of the Societas Linguistica Europaea, University of Stockholm, 29 August–1 September.

Ritter, Elizabeth. 1991. Two functional categories in Noun Phrases: evidence from Modern Hebrew. In Susan Rothstein (ed.), *Perspectives on Phrase Structure*, *(Syntax and Semantics* 25), 37–62. New York: Academic Press.

Ritter, Elizabeth. 1995. On the syntactic category of pronouns and agreement. *Natural Language and Linguistic Theory* 13(3): 405–443.

Roberts, Ian. 2010. *Agreement and Head Movement: Clitics, Incorporation, and Defective Goals*, Cambridge, MA: MIT Press.

Roehrs, Dorian. 2009. *Demonstratives and definite articles as nominal auxiliaries.* Amsterdam & Philadelphia: John Benjamins.

Rothstein, Susan. 2009. Individuating and measure readings of classifier constructions: Evidence from Modern Hebrew. *Brill's Annual of Afroasiatic Languages and Linguistics* 1: 106–145.

Rothstein, Susan. 2010a. Counting and the Mass-Count Distinction. *Journal of Semantics* 27(3): 343–397.

Rothstein, Susan. 2010b. The semantics of count nouns. In Maria Aloni and Katrin Schulz (eds.) *Logic Language and Meaning: LNAI 6042*, 395–404. Heidelberg: Springer.

Rouveret, Alain. 1991. Functional categories and agreement, *Linguistic Review* 8: 353–387.

Rullmann, Hotze. 2003. Bound-variable pronouns and the semantics of number. In Brian Agbayani, Paivi Koskinen, and Vida Samiian (eds.) *Proceedings of the Western Conference On Linguistics*, WECOL 2002, Vol. 14, 243–254. Department of Linguistics, California State University, Fresno.

Rullmann, Hotze and Aili You. 2006. General number and the semantics and pragmatics of indefinite bare nouns in Mandarin Chinese. In K. von Heusinger and K. Turner (eds.), *Where Semantics Meets Pragmatics*, 175–196. Amsterdam: Elsevier.

Saalbach, Henrik and Mutsumi Imai. 2007. Scope of linguistic influence: Does a classifier system alter object concepts? *Journal of Experimental Psychology: General* 136(3): 485–501.

Sag, Ivan. 1980. *Deletion and logical form.* New York: Garland Publishing.

Saito, Mamoru, T.-H. Jonah Lin, and Keiko Murasugi. 2008. N'-ellipsis and the structure of noun phrases in Chinese and Japanese. *Journal of East Asian Linguistics* 17: 247–271.

Saka, Paul. 1991. Lexical decomposition in cognitive semantics. The University of Arizona dissertation.

Salvesen, Christine. 2011. Challenging clitics. *Linguist List*, Vol-22-2892.

Sanches, Mary. 1973. Numeral classifiers and plural marking: an implicational universal. *Working Papers on Language Universals* 11: 1–22.

Sandhofer, C., L. Smith, and J. Luo. 2000. Counting nouns and verbs in the input: Differential frequencies, different kinds of learning? *Journal of Child Language* 27: 561–585.

Sandler, Wendy and Diane Lillo-Martin. 2006. *Sign language and linguistic universals.* Cambridge: Cambridge University Press.

Sapir, Edward. 1921. *Language: An Introduction to the Study of Speech.* New York: Harcourt, Brace, and World.

Sapir, Edward. 1944. Grading: A study in semantics. *Philosophy of Science* 11: 93–116.

Sato,Yosuke. 2009. Radical Underspecification, General Number, and Nominal Denotation in Indonesian, LingBuzz/000831.

Schütze, Carson. 2001. Semantically empty lexical heads as last resorts. In Norbert Corver and Henk van Riemsdijk (eds.) *Semi-lexical categories: the function of content words and the content of function words*, 127–187. Berlin & New York: Mouton de Gruyter.

Schwarzschild, Roger. 2006. The role of dimensions in the syntax of noun phrases. *Syntax* 9: 67–110.

Schwarzschild, Roger. 2011. Stubborn distributivity, multiparticipant nouns and the ocunt/mass distinction. In Suzi Lima, Kevin Mullin, and Brian Smith (eds.) *NELS 39: Proceedings of the 39th Annual Meeting of the North East Linguistic Society*, Vol. 2, 661–678. CreateSpace Independent Publishing Platform.

Senft, Gunter. 2000. *Systems of nominal classification*. Cambridge: Cambridge University Press.

Sharvy, Richard 1978. Maybe English has no count nouns: notes on Chinese semantics. *Studies in Language* 2(3): 345–365.

Shi, Rujie and Danqing Liu. 1985. Suzhou fangyan liangci de dingzhi yongfa jiqi biandiao [the definite use of classifiers in the Suzhou dialect and their tone sandhis], *Yuyan Yanjiu* 8: 160–166.

Shu, Chih-hsiang. 2012. Towards a morphosyntactic analysis of Mandarin mood/ aspect marker *ge*. *Language and Linguistics* 13(4): 663–692.

Simpson, Andrew. 2005. Classifiers and DP structure in southeast Asian languages. In R. Kayne and G. Cinque (eds.), *The Oxford Handbook of Comparative Syntax*, 806–838. Oxford University Press: Oxford.

Simpson, Andrew, Hooi Ling Soh, and Hiroki Nomoto. 2011. Bare classifiers and definiteness. *Studies in Language* 35(1): 168–193.

Song, Yuzhu. 1978. Guanyu shuci '*yi*' he liangci xiang-jiehe de chongdie wenti [on the issue of the combination of the numeral *yi* 'one' and reduplicative classifiers]. *Nankai Daxue Xuebao* 1978, Vol. 6.

Song, Yuzhu. 1980. Guanyu liangci chongdie de yufa yiyi [on the grammatical meaning of classifier reduplication]. *Zhejiang Shiyuan Xuebao* 1980, Vol. 1.

Spelke, Elizabeth S. 1985. Perception of unity, persistence and identity: Thoughts on infants' conception of objects, in J. Mehler and R. Fox (eds.) *Neonate cognition: Beyond the blooming and buzzing confusion*, Hilldale, N.J.: Lawrence Earlbaum Associates.

Sproat, Richard and Chinlin Shih. 1988. Prenominal adjective ordering in English and Mandarin. *Proceedings of NELS* 18: 465–489.

Sproat, Richard and Chinlin Shih. 1991. The cross-linguistic distribution of adjective ordering restrictions. In C. Georgopoulos and R. Ishihara (eds.), *Interdisciplinary approaches to languages: essays in honor of S.-Y. Kuroda*, 565–592. Dordrecht: Kluwer.

Stavrou, Melita and Arhonto Terzi. 2008. Types of Numerical Nouns. In Charles B. Chang and Hannah J. Haynie (eds.), *Proceedings of the 26th West Coast Conference on Formal Linguistics,* 429–437. Somerville, MA: Cascadilla Proceedings Project.

Steindl, Ulrike. 2010. *Grammatical issues in the Chinese classifier system: the case of classifier reduplication*. Universität Weien MA thesis.

Stepanov, Arthur. 2012. Voiding island effects via head movement. *Linguistic Inquiry* 43: 680–693.

Stolz, Thomas. 2012. In the no-man's land between lexicon, morphology and syntax: Total reduplication. Plenary lecture given at the conference total reduplication: morphological, pragmatic and typological issues, Brussels, 18–19 November.

Stowell, Tim. 1981. *Origins of Phrase Structure*. MA: MIT Dissertation.

Stvan, Laurel Smith. 2009. Semantic incorporation as an account for some bare singular count uses in English. *Lingua* 119: 314–333.

Svenonius, P. 2008. The position of adjectives and other phrasal modifiers in the decomposition of DP. In Louise McNally and Chris Kennedy (eds.), *Adjectives and adverbs: syntax, semantics, and discourse*, 16–42. Oxford: Oxford University Press.

Swart, Henriette de, Bert Le Bruyn, and Joost Zwarts. 2010. Bare PP – Monolingual, multilingual and comparative explorations in countability, Paper presented at the Conference on Empirical, Theoretical and Computational Approaches to Countability in Natural Language, Bochum, 22–24 September.

Szabolcsi, Anna. 2011. Compositionality in quantifier words. Paper presented at the International Workshop on Syntax-Semantics Interface, Academia Sinica, Taipei, 17–18 June.

Tai, James and Lianqing Wang. 1990. A semantic study of the classifier *tiao*. *Journal of the Chinese Language Teachers Association* 25: 35–56.

Tang, Chih-chen Jane. 1990a. A note on the DP analysis of Chinese noun phrases. *Linguistics* 28: 337–354.

Tang, Chih-chen Jane. 1990b. *Chinese phrase structure and extended X'-theory*. Cornell University dissertation.

Tang, Chih-chen Jane. 2004. Two types of classifier languages: a typological study of classification markers in Paiwan Noun Phrases, *Language and Linguistics* 5: 377–407.

Tang, Chih-chen Jane. 2005. Nouns or classifiers: a non-movement analysis of classifiers in Chinese. *Language and Linguistics* 6: 431–472.

Tang, Chih-chen Jane. 2007. Modifier licensing and Chinese DP: a feature analysis. *Language and Linguistics* 8: 967–1024.

Tenny, Carol. 1987. *Grammaticalizing aspect and affectedness*. MIT disseration, Cambridge, MA.

Thompson, Laurence C. 1965. *A Vietnamese grammar*, Washington: University of Washington Press.

Thoms, Gary. 2010. 'Verb floating' and VP-ellipsis: Towards a movement account of ellipsis licensing. *Linguistic Variation Yearbook* 10: 252–297.

Travis, Lisa. 1999. A syntactician's view of reduplication. In AFLA VI, Carolyn Smallwood and Catherine Kitto (eds.), *Toronto Working Papers in Linguistics* 16(2): 313–331. Toronto: University of Toronto.

References 311

Travis, Lisa. 2001. The syntax of reduplication. *NELS* 31: 455–469.
Tsai, Wei-Tien Dylan. 2003. Three types of existential quantification in Chinese. In Y.-H. Audrey Li and Andrew Simpson (eds.) *Functional structure(s), form and interpretation*, 161–179. London: Routledge Curzon.
Tsai, Wei-Tien Dylan. 2010. On the syntax-semantics correlations of Chinese modals. *Zhongguo Yuwen* 2010(3): 208–221.
Tsao, Feng-Fu. 1977. *A Functional Study of Topic in Chinese: the First Step Towards Discourse Analysis*. Taipei: Student Book Co., Ltd.
Tsoulas, George. 2006. Plurality of mass nouns and the grammar of number. Paper presented at the 29th glow meeting, Barcelona, 5–8 March.
T'sou, Benjamin K. 1976. The structure of nominal classifier systems. In *Austro-asiatic studies II*, edited by Philip N. Jenner, Laurence C. Thompson, and Stanley Starosta, Oceanic Linguistics Special Publication No. 13, 1215–1247. Honolulu: The University Press of Hawaii.
T'ung, Ping-cheng and D. E. Pollard. 1982. *Colloquial Chinese*. Routledge, London.
Tzeng, Ovid, Sylvia Chen, and Daisy L. Hung. 1991. The classifier problem in Chinese aphasia. *Brain and Language* 41: 184–202.
Ueda, Yasuki. 2009. Number in Japanese and Chinese. *Nanzan Linguistics* 5: 105–130.
Van Riemsdijk, Henk. 2005. Silent nouns and the spurious indefinite article in Dutch. In Mila Vulchanova et al. (eds.), *Grammar and beyond, Essays in Honour of Lars Hellan*. Oslo: Novus Press.
Vangsnes, Øystein Alexander. 2008. What kind of Scandinavian? On interrogative noun phrases across North-Germanic. *Nordic Journal of Linguistics* 31: 227–251.
Vázquez Rojas, Violeta. 2012. *The syntax and semantics of Purépecha noun phrases and the mass/count distinction*. New York University dissertation.
Velupillai, Viveka. 2012. *An introduction to linguistic typology*. Amsterdam & Philadelphia: John Benjamins.
Vendler, Zeno. 1968. *Adjectives and nominalizations*. The Hague: Mouton.
Vicente, Luis. 2010. On the syntax of adversative coordination. *Natural Language and Linguistics Theory* 28: 381–415.
Vos, Henerika Margaretha. 1999. *A grammar of partitive constructions*. Tilburg University dissertation, the Netherlands.
Wang, Deguang. 1986. Weining Miaoyu huayu cailiao [Language material in the Weining dialect of the Miao language]. *Minzu Yuwen* 1986(3): 69–80.
Wang, Lianqing. 1994. *Origin and development of classifiers in Chinese*. The Ohio State University dissertation,.
Wang, Shaoxin. 1989. Liangci *ge* zai Tangdai qianhou de fazhan [the development of the classifier *ge* around the Tang Dynasty]. *Yuyan Jiaoxue yu Yanjiu* 2: 98–119.
Wang, Zhirong. 1995. Adjective-Noun Construction in Modern Chinese. In T.-F. Cheng, Y. Li and H. Zhang (eds.), *Proceedings of the 7th North American Conference on Chinese Linguistics/5th International Conference on Chinese Lin-*

guistics. Vol. 1, 303–316. Department of Linguistics, University of Southern California: GSIL Publications.

Watanabe, Akira. 2006. Functional properties of nominals in Japanese: Syntax of classifiers. *Natural Language and Linguistics Theory* 24: 241–306.

Watanabe, Akira. 2010. Notes on nominal ellipsis and the nature of no and classifiers in Japanese. *Journal of East Asian Linguistics* 19: 61–74.

Watanabe, Akira. 2012. Measure words as nouns: a perspective from silent years. *Studia Linguistica* 66(2): 181–205.

Watanabe, Akira. 2013. 1-Deletion: Measure Nouns vs. Classifiers. In Mikio Giriko, Kyoko Kanzaki, Naonori Nagaya, and Akiko Takemura (eds.) *Japanese/Korean Linguistics* 22. Tokyo: CSLI Publications.

Watters, John Roberts. 1981. *A phonology and morphology of Ejagham—with notes on dialect variation*. University of California, Los Angeles dissertation.

Whorf, Benjamin Lee. 1941. The relation of habitual thought and behavior to language. In Leslie Spier (ed.) *Language, Culture, and Personality, Essays in Memory of Edward Sapir*, Menasha, WI: Sapir Memorial Publication Fund. Reprinted in John B. Carroll (ed.). 1956. *Language, thought, and reality: selected writings of Benjamin Lee Whorf*, 134–159. Cambridge: MIT Press.

Wiebusch, Thekla. 1995. Quantification and qualification: two competing functions of numeral classifiers in the light of the radical system of the Chinese script. *Journal of Chinese Linguistics* 23(2): 1–41.

Wierzbicka, Anna. 1985. "Oats" and "wheat": the fallacy of arbitrariness. In John Haiman (ed.), *Iconicity in Syntax*, 311–342. Amsterdam & Philadelphia: John Benjamins.

Wiese, Heike. 2003. *Numbers, language, and the human mind*. Cambridge: Cambridge University Press.

Wiese, Heike. 2012. Collectives in the intersection of mass and count nouns: a cross-linguistic account. In Diane Massam (ed.), *Count and Mass Across Languages*, 54–74. Oxford: Oxford University Press.

Wilder, Chris. 1997. Some properties of ellipsis in coordination. In Artemis Alexiadou and T. Alan Hall (eds.), *Studies on Universal Grammar and Typological Variation*, 59–107, Amsterdam & Philadelphia: John Benjamins.

Wilhelm, Andrea. 2008. Bare nouns and number in Děne Su̱łiné, *Natural Language Semantics* 16: 39–68.

Wiltschko, Martina. 2005. Why should diminutives count? In H. Broekhuis, N. Corver, R. Huybregts, U. Kleinherz, and J. Koster (eds.). *Organizing Grammar: Studies in Honor of Henk van Riemsdijk*, 669–678. Berlin & New York: Mouton de Gruyter.

Wiltschko, Martina. 2009. What's in a determiner and how did it get there? In J. Ghomeshi, I. Paul, and M. Wiltschko (Eds.), *Determiners: Variation and Universals*, 35–66. Amsterdam & Philadelphia: John Benjamins.

Wiltschko, Martina. 2012. Decomposing the mass/count distinction: evidence from languages tha lack it. In Diane Massam (ed.), *Count and Mass Across Languages*, 146–171. Oxford: Oxford University Press.

Wu, Fuxiang. 2006. Wei-Jin-Nanbeichao shiqi hanyu mingliangci fanchou de yufahua chengdu [The degree of grammaticalization of nominal classifiers during the Wei-Jin-Nanbeichao periods]. In *Linguistic Studies in Chinese and Neighboring Languages: Festschrift in Honor of Professor Pang–Hsin Ting on His 70th Birthday*, 553–571. Language and Linguistics Monograph Series 6.

Wu, Fuxiang, Shengli Feng, and Cheng-Teh James Huang. 2006. Hanyu shu + liang + ming geshi de laiyuan [the source of the Chinese construction numeral + classifier + noun], *Zhongguo Yuwen* 314 (2006(5)): 387–400.

Wu, Mary. 2006. Can numerals really block definite readings in Mandarin Chinese? In Raung-fu Chung, Hsien-Chin Liou, Jia-ling Hsu, and Dah-an Ho (eds.) *On and Off Work: Festschrift in Honor of Professor Chin-Chuan Cheng on His 70th Birthday*, 127–142. Taipei: Institute of Linguistics, Academic Sinica.

Wu, Yicheng and Adams Bodomo. 2009. Classifiers ≠ Determiners. *Linguistic Inquiry* 40: 487–503.

Wu, Xiu-Zhi Zoe. 2004. *Grammaticalization and language change in Chinese.* London and New York: RoutledgeCurzon.

Wyngaerd, Guido Vanden. 2009. Semantic Shifts. lingBuzz/001392.

Xing, Fuyi. 1997. *Hanyu Yufaxue* [Chinese Syntax], Dongbei Normal University Press.

Xu, Dan. 2012. Reduplication in languages: A case study of languages of China. In Dan Xu (ed.), *Plurality and Classifiers across Languages of China.* Berlin & New York: Mouton de Gruyter.

Xu, Fei. 2007. Sortal concepts, object individuation, and language. *Trends in Cognitive Sciences* 11: 400–406.

Xu, Liejiong. 1999. A special use of the third person singular pronoun. *Cahiers de Linguistique – Asie Orientale* 28(1): 3–22.

Yang, Defeng. 1996. Liangci-qian shuci yi de yinxian wenti [The issue of the overtness of *yi* before a classifier], In *Selected papers of the fifth conference of the Association of Teaching Chinese as a Foreign Language*, Beijing: Yuyan Xueyuan Press.

Yang, Henrietta Shu-Fen. 2005. Plurality and Modification in Mandarin Nominal Phrases, University of Texas at Austin dissertation.

Yang, Rong. 2001. Common nouns, classifiers, and quantification in Chinese. Newark: The State University of New Jersey dissertation.

Yi, Byeong-uk. 2010. Numeral Classifiers and the Mass/Count Distinction. Ms. University of Toronto, Oct. 6, 2010.

Yi, Byeong-uk. 2012. Numeral classifiers and bare nominals. In Yung-O Biq and Lindsey Chen (eds.), *Proceedings of the 13th International Symposium on Chinese Language and Linguistics (IsCLL-13)*, 138–153. Taipei: National Taiwan Normal University.

Yu, Guangzhong. 1999. *Jiewang yu shifeng* [connecting and the style of poems]. Taipei: Chiuko Press.

Zagona, Karen. 1988. *Verb phrase syntax: a parametric study of English and Spanish*. Dordrecht: Kluwer Academic Publishers.

Zhang, Hong. 2007. Numeral classifiers in Mandarin Chinese. *Journal of East Asian Linguistics* 16: 43–59.

Zhang, Ning. 1997. Syntactic Dependencies in Mandarin Chinese. University of Toronto dissertation.

Zhang, Niina Ning. 2002. Counting and Classifying Eventualities in Chinese. Ms. ZAS-Berlin.

Zhang, Niina Ning. 2006. Representing Specificity by the Internal Order of Indefinites. *Linguistics* 44(1): 1–21.

Zhang, Niina Ning. 2008a. Existential Coda Constructions as Internally Headed Relative Clause Constructions. *The Linguistics Journal* 3(3): 8–54.

Zhang, Niina Ning. 2008b. Encoding Exhaustivity. National Tsing Hua University. *UST Working Papers in Linguistics* 4: 133–143.

Zhang, Niina Ning. 2009. The Syntax of Relational-Nominal Second Constructions in Chinese. *Yuyanxue Luncong* 39: 257–301. Beijing: Peking University Press.

Zhang, Niina Ning. 2010. *Coordination in Syntax*. Cambridge Studies in Linguistics Series 123, Cambridge: Cambridge University Press.

Zhang, Niina Ning. 2012a. Projecting semantic features. *Studia Linguistica* 66(1): 58–74.

Zhang, Niina Ning. 2012b. *De* and the functional expansion of classifiers. *Language and Linguistics* 13(3): 569–582.

Zhang, Qingwen. 2009. The grammatical status of ge in the V+*ge*+XP construction. *Xiandai Waiyu* [Modern Foreign Languages] 32(1): 13–22.

Zhang, Wanqi. 1991. Shi Lun Xiandai Hanyu Fuhe-Liangci [on compound classifiers of modern Chinese], *Zhongguo Yuwen* 1991(4): 262–268.

Zhang, Xiaofei. 2008. Chinese -*men* and associative plurals. *Toronto Working Papers in Linguistics* 28, 407–425. University of Toronto.

Zhu, Dexi. 1982. *Yufa Jiangyi* [Lectures on grammar], Beijing, Shangwu Press.

Zweig, Eytan. 2006. Nouns and adjectives in numeral NPs. In Leah Bateman and Cherlon Ussery (eds.), *Proceedings of NELS* 35, 663–675. Amherst, MA: GLSA Publications.

Subject index

Language index